THE FALKLANDS CO
TWENTY YEARS

In June 2002, exactly twenty years after the cessation of hostilities between Britain and Argentina, many of the participants in the 'Falklands Conflict', as it became known, came together at a major international conference. This conference, held at the Royal Military Academy Sandhurst and organized jointly by RMA Sandhurst and her sister institution Britannia Royal Naval College Dartmouth, aimed to re-examine the events of spring 1982 from the perspective that only twenty intervening years can bring. The result was a fascinating discussion of the origins of the conflict, the political and diplomatic response to the Argentinian action as well as illuminating accounts of the military action to retake the islands, at every level of command. This edited volume brings together the various papers presented at the conference.

THE SANDHURST CONFERENCE SERIES
ISSN 1468–1153
Series Editor: Matthew Midlane

THE FALKLANDS CONFLICT TWENTY YEARS ON

Lessons for the Future

Edited by
Stephen Badsey, Rob Havers and
Mark Grove

FRANK CASS
LONDON • NEW YORK

First published 2005
by Frank Cass
2 Park Square, Milton Park, Abingdon, Oxon OX14 4RN

Simultaneously published in the USA and Canada
by Frank Cass
270 Madison Ave, New York, NY 10016

Frank Cass is an imprint of the Taylor & Francis Group

© 2005 Stephen Badsey, Rob Havers and Mark Grove

Typeset in Sabon by
Newgen Imaging Systems (P) Ltd, Chennai, India
Printed and bound in Great Britain by
MPG Books Ltd, Bodmin

British Library Cataloguing in Publication Data
A catalogue record for this book is available
from the British Library

Library of Congress Cataloging in Publication Data
A catalog record for this book has been requested

ISBN 0–415–35029–8 (hbk)
ISBN 0–415–35030–1 (pbk)

To those who died in the Falklands Conflict.

Contents

Contents

Notes on the Contributors

DR STEPHEN BADSEY is a Senior Lecturer in the Department of War Studies at RMA Sandhurst. He is the editor of *The Media and International Security*, and co-editor with Paul Latawski of *Britain, NATO and the Lessons of the Balkan Conflicts 1991–1999*, both in the Sandhurst Conference Series.

MAJOR GENERAL JONATHAN BAILEY MBE ADC is Director Development and Doctrine. He served as a junior officer with the Royal Artillery in the Falklands Conflict.

VICE ADMIRAL SIR JONATHON BAND KCB RN is Deputy Commander-in-Chief Fleet. He served at Fleet HQ at Northwood during the Falklands Conflict.

COLONEL DAVID BENEST is Director of Defence Studies (Army). He served as a junior officer with the 2nd Battalion, the Parachute Regiment, in the Falklands Conflict.

DR ALASTAIR FINLAN teaches International History and International Relations at the American University in Cairo, and is an honorary Assistant Senior Lecturer at Britannia Royal Naval College Dartmouth.

PROFESSOR LAWRENCE FREEDMAN CBE DPhil is Professor of War Studies at King's College, University of London, and a Fellow of the British Academy. His many publications include *The Official History of the Falklands Conflict* (2003), *Britain and the Falklands War* (1988) and (with Virginia Gamba-Stonehouse) *Signals of War* (1990).

BRIGADIER HORACIO MIR GONZALEZ FAA is Chief of Plans for the Argentine Air Force General Staff. He is a veteran of the South Atlantic conflict.

GROUP CAPTAIN PETER W. GRAY BSc LLB MPhil RAF is Assistant Director of Joint Warfare in the Ministry of Defence, and a former Director of Defence Studies (RAF).

MARK GROVE MA is a Lecturer in the Department of Strategic Studies and International Affairs, Britannia Royal Naval College Dartmouth.

PHILIP D. GROVE is currently a senior lecturer in the Department of Strategic Studies and International Affairs, Britannia Royal Naval College Dartmouth. He has become a regular contributor to the *Naval Review* and is currently completing a book on the Battle of Midway.

DR ROB HAVERS MA is a Senior Lecturer in the Department of War Studies at RMA Sandhurst. His most recent publication is *Re-assessing the Japanese Prisoner of War Experience: The Changi POW Camp, 1942–45*, (2003).

COLONEL (RETD.) I.J. HELLBERG OBE works in the Department of Defence Management and Security Analysis at Cranfield University. He commanded the Commando Logistics Regiment Royal Marines in the Falklands Conflict.

PROFESSOR PETER HENNESSY is Attlee Professor of Contemporary British History at Queen Mary and Westfield College, University of London. His many publications include *The Prime Minister: The Office and its Holder since 1945* (2000), and *The Secret State: Whitehall and the Cold War* (2002).

CAPTAIN (RETD.) PETER HORE RN is Associate Editor of *Warship International Fleet Review*.

SIR ROGER JACKLING KCB CBE is Director of the Defence Academy of the United Kingdom. He was a Head of Division in the Ministry of Defence during the Falklands Conflict.

LIEUTENANT GENERAL J.P. KISZELY MC is Commander Regional Forces at UK Land Command. He commanded a company of 2nd Battalion, the Scots Guards, in the Falklands Conflict.

DR PAUL LATAWSKI is a Senior Lecturer in the Defence and International Affairs Department at RMA Sandhurst.

Notes on the Contributors

ADMIRAL OF THE FLEET SIR HENRY LEACH GCB DL RN was Chief of the Naval Staff and First Sea Lord during the Falklands Conflict. His memoirs were published as *Endure No Makeshifts* (1993).

MATTHEW MIDLANE MA is Director of Studies at RMA Sandhurst.

SIR JOHN NOTT was Secretary of State for Defence during the Falklands Conflict. His political memoirs were published as *Here Today, Gone Tomorrow* (2002).

DR GEOFFREY SLOAN is the Head of the Department of Strategic Studies and International Affairs at BRNC Dartmouth. His publications include *Geopolitics in United States' Strategic Policy 1890–1987* (1988), *The Geopolitics of Anglo-Irish Relations in the Twentieth Century* (1998), and (with Colin Gray) *Geography and Strategy* (1999) and *Geopolitics and Strategic History 1871–2001* (2003).

MAJOR GENERAL JULIAN THOMPSON CB OBE is a Visiting Professor in the War Studies Department at King's College, University of London. He commanded 3 Commando Brigade in the Falklands Conflict. Among his publications are *No Picnic: 3 Commando Brigade in the South Atlantic* (1985), *Ready for Anything: The Parachute Regiment at War 1940–1982* (1989) and *Lifeblood of War: Logistics in Armed Conflict* (1991).

DR FRANCIS TOASE MPhil is Head of the Defence and International Affairs Department at RMA Sandhurst. He is co-editor of *Aspects of Peacekeeping* (2001) in the Sandhurst Conference Series.

ADMIRAL (RETD.) SIR JOHN ('SANDY') WOODWARD KCB RN commanded the Carrier Battle Group during the Falklands Conflict. His memoirs of the conflict were published as *One Hundred Days* in 1992. He retired as Commander-in-Chief Naval Home Command in 1989.

DR EDMUND YORKE is a Senior Lecturer in the Defence and International Affairs Department at RMA Sandhurst. His most recent publications include *The New South Africa* (1998), co-edited with Francis Toase.

Series Editor's Preface

This is the fifth book in the Sandhurst Conference Series charting important themes for the British Army and Armed Forces and, perhaps, for the armed forces of every country in the post-Cold War era and into the twenty-first century. The first volume in the series, *The Media and International Security*, edited by Stephen Badsey, explores the impact of the media on conflict and military operations, and has already been well received by the defence and academic community. The second volume, *Aspects of Peacekeeping*, edited by D.S. Gordon and F.H. Toase, begins to unpack many of the features of contemporary peace support operations. For an institution such as the Royal Military Academy Sandhurst, seeking to understand the often complex relationships present in these operations is of obvious importance. For any academic institution exploring the issues that bind and divide the diplomatic, humanitarian and military communities in peacekeeping, this book provides an exceptionally useful multidisciplinary introduction. The third book, *Negotiation in International Conflict: Understanding Persuasion*, edited by Deborah Goodwin, is a discussion of negotiation at all levels of command from the strategic to the tactical. The fourth book, *Britain, NATO and the Lessons of the Balkan Conflicts 1991–1999*, edited by Stephen Badsey and Paul Latawski, examines the broad impact of the dissolution of the former Republic of Yugoslavia, and in particular the role of British armed forces and of NATO. While it is not intended as a primer on the Balkans, it provides a survey of issues ranging from the historical roots of conflict in the region and the influence of the Second World War through to humanitarian–military relationships in the course of NATO's campaign over Kosovo. A separate section on military relations with the media reflects the continuing importance of this issue, while an analysis of the historical mythology of the region reveals how badly 'lessons' from history may mislead contemporary opinion.

Series Editor's Preface

This fifth book in the series, *The Falklands Conflict Twenty Years On: Lessons for the Future*, is the product of the first of our conferences to be held jointly in association with Britannia Royal Naval College Dartmouth, combining the efforts of our own academic staff with those of their Department of Strategic Studies and International Affairs. In the tradition of the Sandhurst Conference Series, which is now well established, this book represents the bringing together of academic research with the latest doctrinal ideas and concepts from all three of the Armed Services and from within the Ministry of Defence.

The Falklands Conflict, seen at the time as an exception or even an anachronism in British military campaigns, is now being re-evaluated in the light of present and future ideas concerning expeditionary operations and military intervention. It is a notable feature of this volume in the series that it includes memoirs and informed reflections from those who took part in the Falklands Conflict, either as comparatively junior officers who twenty years later have risen to high rank, or from the perspective of the politics of the conflict. The generosity and willingness of contributors to pass on the lessons of their own experience for the future is greatly valued. The manner in which these personal contributions, together with those chapters that discuss the place of the conflict in history, its implications in wider perspective and its lessons for future military operations, all complement each other and make this another valuable contribution to the Sandhurst Conference Series. Further conferences and their associated volumes are presently being planned and we hope you enjoy reading the series.

Mathew Midlane
Director of Studies
Royal Military Academy Sandhurst

Editor's Preface

The Falklands Conflict of 1982, initiated by the Argentinian invasion of the Falkland Islands, came as rather a surprise to all concerned. For the British, the notion of mounting a substantial amphibious operation several thousand miles from friendly bases was an anachronistic one. British defence planning at the time viewed the world in Cold War terms and finite resources were inevitably focused squarely upon NATO, the central front and the threat posed by the Warsaw Pact. By the spring of 1982, in line with these commitments, the last vestiges of a British capability to conduct such operations were in the process of being withdrawn. Notwithstanding the surprise of the international community as well, and the USSR in particular, the war also came as something of a shock to the Argentinians. Despite their pre-emptive use of military force to further their claims to sovereignty over the islands, few if any, Argentinian leaders really believed that the British would respond to the invasion in such a decisive fashion. The ambiguous political and military signals emanating from London in the months leading up to the Argentine action seemed only to indicate Britain's lack of interest in the islands. The 1981 Nott Review, whilst a natural conclusion to the logic of earlier policy decisions, signalled an impending loss of capability and, more immediately, an apparent loss of resolve.

Britain's rejoinder to Argentina's occupation of its South Atlantic possessions, however, was anything but ambiguous. Even before the invasion, with no hope of forestalling the invasion, plans were made to mount an operation to recover the islands although, at that early juncture, few thought such action would ultimately be required. In fact, as history has shown, it did prove necessary to resolve the dispute through force and there followed a British military campaign which was, by any measure, highly impressive.

Military and naval history can often leave the reader, perhaps sub-consciously, with the feeling: 'well, it was bound to be successful, wasn't it?' The reader should be in no doubt that this was not the case with the Falklands Conflict. This was an operation to be conducted some 8,000 miles from the United Kingdom when Britain was supposed to have shrugged off its global pretensions. This was to be the first 'missile-age' naval encounter. It was intended to be directed by a Task Force Commander situated in a bunker in north London. Operation Corporate required a Royal Navy, intended to be used to fight a submarine war in the Eastern Atlantic, to project and support two brigades of troops onto a hostile shore and in a hostile air environment. It was opposed by a modern, numerous airforce when much of the equipment to accomplish such missions – such as conventional aircraft carriers and helicopter carriers – had disappeared in the wake of the numerous Defence Reviews since the mid-1960s. The South Atlantic winter was fast approaching. There was the ever-present wind and the difficult terrain with which to contend but with little of the supporting infrastructure one might have expected in a European conflict. Few vehicles had been taken; there were no roads on which to drive. Helicopters were always in short supply, necessitating the famous 'yomps' and 'tabs' (forced marches in Royal Marine and Parachute Regiment terminology). The Argentine defenders outnumbered the British and were, in many cases, better equipped, and had been dug in for some time.

Those of us privileged to be at the Conference were able to hear, at first hand, a number of accounts from key participants either from the 'stage' or the floor. We were left in no doubt about what was being asked of these men and hence the scale of their achievement.

After an interval of twenty years, now would seem an appropriate interval to re-visit the events of the Falklands War. After two decades the recollections of the participants remain vivid, yet there is sufficient distance for the events of April–June 1982 to be considered within a broader historical context. Much has happened globally since the Argentinian invasion. The shadow of the Cold War, beneath which the events in the South Atlantic developed, has disappeared and a very different world order now pertains. The challenges and commitments that the British armed forces now face have grown exponentially since 1982. The Falklands campaign which, at the time, was seen very much as anomalous action, now in retrospect appears far more relevant to the requirements of today's military than do the many years of rehearsal for war along the inner German border. To attempt to draw too many lessons and too many parallels with then now is, of course, a dangerous pastime. What this volume aims to do, through chapters covering all aspects of the conflict, both political and military, is not to teach new lessons nor to draw any new conclusions but rather to ensure that what was re-learned in 1982 does not need to be re-learned once again.

At a political level, the Falklands Conflict was most certainly a watershed in British twentieth-century history. On a military level this was less clear at the time. More than one contributor to this volume is in broad agreement with Sir Roger Jackling's conclusion that 'Operation Corporate [the plan to re-take the Falklands] did *not* cause a rethink of our policy nor significantly overturn the conclusions and plans which emerged from the Nott Review.' However, post-Cold War and especially post-Britain's Strategic Defence Review (1998) the Falklands Conflict finally has had a significant impact, as the process to procure and design the new generation of carriers (CVF) and amphibious vessels clearly indicates. But its significance goes far wider. For there is no doubt that any country which wishes to exercise global influence must have properly constituted maritime power and, of course, the will and ability to use it.

As the fifth in the Sandhurst Conference Series, this book owes its origins to the international conference of the same title, held at the Royal Military Academy Sandhurst, 12–14 June 2002, to commemorate the ceasefire that ended the Falklands Conflict exactly 20 years before. This was the first occasion, but we hope not the last, on which one of the Sandhurst conferences has been held jointly with the Britannia Royal Naval College Dartmouth.

At the time of publication, a number of contributors to this book were either serving or past members of the British armed forces, or employed by the British Ministry of Defence, or by NATO. The views expressed in this book are those of the authors of individual chapters only and do not necessarily reflect those of NATO, the Ministry of Defence, the Royal Military Academy Sandhurst, Britannia Royal Naval College, Dartmouth or any other institution. Military ranks and appointments, as well as other titles, are those held at the time. Thanks are due to Martin Howard, Director General Corporate Communications in the Ministry of Defence, to Brigadier R.M.M. Sykes, Director of Corporate Communications (Army), to Commodore Richard Leaman OBE, Director of Corporate Communications (Royal Navy) and to Air Commodore P.R. Thomas MBE, Director of Corporate Communications (RAF), as well as their respective staffs.

At the time of the conference and the completion of this book the Commandant of Sandhurst was Major-General P.C.C. Trousdell CBE; without his support this book would not have appeared. The conference organising committee was chaired by Matthew Midlane, with Dr Duncan Anderson, Dr Geoffrey Sloan, Mark Grove, Dr Stephen Hart, Lloyd Clark, Carl Lawson, and Dr Stephen Badsey as its principal members. Invaluable assistance in running the conference was also provided by Tim Bean, Dr Robin Havers, and Dr Klaus Schmider. The three departmental heads of the Sandhurst Academic Faculty – Mr John Allen of the Department of Communications Studies, Dr Francis Toase of the Department of Defence Studies and International Affairs, and Dr Duncan Anderson of the Department of War Studies – and their staffs all provided support. We are grateful to all our speakers and contributors, and wish to express our particular thanks to Brigadier Horacio Mir Gonzalez of the FAA. Additional displays and assistance were provided by Dr Peter Thwaites, Curator of the Sandhurst Collection, by Andrew Orgill, the Sandhurst Librarian, and by members of the Sandhurst staff. Sandhurst public relations and protocol were overseen by Major (Retd.) I.C. Park-Weir.

The editors' thanks are due for help, with both the conference and the production of this book, to Alison Cox, Pat Alner, Yoland Richardson, Christine McLennan and Marian Matthews. Supervision of this book at Frank Cass was in the capable hands of Sarah Clarke, Louise Hulks and Sally Green.

List of Abbreviations and Glossary

AA	Anti-aircraft
AAR	Air-to-air refuelling
ABU	Amphibious Beach Unit (beach exit control)
AEW	Airborne Early Warning/Airborne Electronic Warfare
AIM-9L	In 1982 the most modern version of the ubiquitous Sidewinder ASRAAM
AMRAAM	Advanced Medium Range Air to Air Missile – usually applied to the Aim-120
AOA	Amphibious Operating Area
AOD	Assault Ordnance Detachment
APFC	Air Portable Flexible Container
AQ	Adjutant and Quartermaster staff branches
ASRAAM	Advanced Short Range Air to Air Missile
ASW	Anti-Submarine Warfare
ATCMS	Army Tactical Cruise Missile System
AVCAT	Aviation fuel
AWC	Air Warfare Centre
AWD	Assault Workshop Detachment
B2	Grumman-Northrop B2 *Spirit* 'Stealth Bomber'
BAA	Brigade Administration Area
BAOR	British Army of the Rhine
BBC	British Broadcasting Corporation
BMA	Brigade Maintenance Area
BR	British Rail
BRNC	Britannia Royal Naval College Dartmouth
BSA	Beach Support Area
C2	Command and control
C4I	Command, Control, Communications, Computers, Intelligence

C4ISR	Command, Control, Communications, Computers, Intelligence, Surveillance, and Reconnaissance
CANA	Comando Aviación Naval Argentina (Argentine Naval Air Arm)
CAP	Combat Air Patrol
CDS	Chief of the Defence Staff
CENTCOM	US Central Command
CID	Committee of Imperial Defence
C-in-C	Commander-in-Chief
Civgas	Commercial petrol
CJO	Chief of Joint Operations
Clansman	A type of British secure radio set
CLFFI	Commander Land Forces Falkland Islands
CNN	Cable News Network
CO	Commanding Officer
COMATAG	Commander Amphibious Task Group
COMAW	Commodore Amphibious Warfare
Commando	A title given both to individual soldiers of the Royal Marines, and to the Royal Marine equivalent of a battalion (e.g. 40 Commando, 42 Commando, 45 Commando)
Commodore	Prior to Options for Change in the mid-1990s the rank of Commodore was not a permanent promotion rank. In the Royal Navy the title of Commodore technically referred to an office not a rank. When an officer relinquished his office of Commodore he reverted to the rank of Captain – or Rear Admiral, if advanced to Flag Rank. Therefore during the Falklands campaign Michael Clapp was a Captain who held the *office* of Commodore Amphibious Warfare even though his rank remained Captain. Clapp retired in 1983 as a Captain
CoS	Chief of staff/Chiefs of staff
CTF	Commander Task Force
CTG	Commander Task Group
CVR(T)	Combat Vehicle Reconnaissance Tracked (the Scorpion and Scimitar light tanks used by the British)
CVS	Anti-submarine aircraft carrier

DAER	Daily Ammunition Expenditure Rate (rounds per gun per day)
DCS	Defence Costs Study
DCSR	Daily Combat Supply Rate for the Force (estimated average consumption rate of ammunition, rations and equipment)
DFC	Distinguished Flying Cross
DGCC	Director General of Corporate Communications
DG D&D	Directorate General Development and Doctrine
DGLW	Directorate General of Land Warfare
DJW	Director Joint Warfare
DD	Destroyer
DLG	Destroyer Leader (Guided Missile)
DP	Distribution Point (for supplies of all natures)
Dracone	A towed flexible fuel barge
DS	Dressing Station (sub-unit of Medical Squadron capable of immediate life-saving surgery
Eager Beaver	Eager Beaver Mark 2 Rough Terrain Fork Lift Tractor
EC	European Community
EEC	European Economic Community, the precursor to the EC and later EU
EFHE	Emergency Fuel Handling Equipment (bulk fuel tanks and pumping equipment)
EU	European Union
FAA	Fuerza Aérea Argentina (Argentine Air Force)
FAC	Forward Air Controller
FAS	Fuerza Aérea Sur (Air Force South – Argentina)
FCBA	Future Carrier Based Aircraft
FCO	Foreign and Commonwealth Office (often called just the Foreign Office)
FF	Frigate
FIST	Future Integrated Soldier Technology
FOF	Flag Officer Fleet (e.g. FOF1 was Rear Admiral Woodward)
FRHE	Force Re-enforcement Holding Area
FRO	Field Records Office
G1098	General-purpose stores and equipment

G7	The 'Group of Seven' leading world economic powers
GBAD	Ground Based Air Defence
GPMG	General Purpose Machine Gun
GPS	Global Positioning System
Harrier GR3	RAF version of the Harrier
HCSC	Higher Command and Staff Course
HE	High Explosive
HQ	Headquarters
HLS	Helicopter Landing Site
HVM	High Velocity Missile
ICBM	Intercontinental Ballistic Missile
IGDT	Inspectorate General of Doctrine and Training
ILS	Instrument Landing System
ISTAR	Information, Surveillance, Target Acquisition and Reconnaissance
ITN	Independent Television News
J/Can	Jerry can
JDCC	Joint Doctrine Concepts Centre
JFHQ	Joint Force Headquarters
JIC	Joint Intelligence Committee
JSCSC	Joint Services Command and Staff College
kiloton	1,000 tons of high explosive (or its equivalent)
LAW	Light Anti-tank Weapon
LCM	Landing Craft Mechanical (larger landing craft for landing vehicles etc.)
LCVP	Landing Craft Vehicle Personnel
LMAWS	Light Mobile Artillery Weapon System
LOC	Line of Communications
LPD	Landing Platform Dock (i.e. HMS *Fearless* and HMS *Intrepid*, each with 4 LCMs in their floating docks)
LPH	Landing Platform Helicopter
LRS	Light Rocket System
LSL	Landing Ship Logistic (e.g. RFA *Sir Lancelot*)
LSW	Light Support Weapon
LWC	Land Warfare Centre
LZMT	Landing Zone Marshalling Team (helicopters)
MAOT	Mobile Air Operations Team
MDS	Main Dressing Station (larger surgical capabilities than DS)

Mexeflote	Large motorised pontoons used for moving heavy logistic vehicles and equipment from ship to shore
MLRS	Multiple Launch Rocket System
MoD	Ministry of Defence
MWC	Maritime Warfare Centre
NATO	North Atlantic Treaty Organisation
NBC	Nuclear, Biological and Chemical
NCO	Non-Commissioned Officer
Number 10 (No. 10)	10 Downing Street, the residence of the British Prime Minister
OAS	Organization of American States
OAU	Organization of African Unity
OC	Officer Commanding
OD(SA)	Overseas and Defence (South America) Subcommittee – the British 'War Cabinet'
OOA	Out of area
OPGEN MIKE	Detailed amphibious landing plan
Para	A title given both to individual soldiers of the Parachute Regiment and used as shorthand for individual battalions of the Parachute Regiment, e.g. 2nd Battalion, the Parachute Regiment (2 Para)
PJHQ	Permanent Joint Headquarters
PNG	Passive night goggles
POL	Petrol, oil and lubricants
PODs	2,000-litre rigid fuel tanks carried on 4-tonne trucks (2 × pods per truck)
POW	Prisoners of war
PSO	Peace support operations
Psyop(s)	Psychological operation(s)
RA	Royal Artillery
RAF	Royal Air Force
RAS	Resupply at Sea
RAOC	Royal Army Ordnance Corps
RAOC(V)	TAVR RAOC troops
RCT	Royal Corps of Transport
REME	Royal Electrical and Mechanical Engineers
RFA	Royal Fleet Auxiliary
RHQ	Regimental Headquarters
Rigid Raider	Fast glass-fibre dory propelled by outboard engine

RM	Royal Marines
RMA	Revolution in Military Affairs *or* Royal Military Academy
RN	Royal Navy
Ro-Ro	Roll On-Roll Off
RSRM	Raiding Squadron Royal Marines
SACLANT	Supreme Allied Commander Atlantic (a NATO post)
SAS	Special Air Service
SATCOM	Satellite Communications
SATO	South Atlantic Treaty Organization
SBS	Special Boat Squadron (Royal Marines)
SEAD	Suppression of Enemy Air Defences
SLR	Self-Loading Rifle, the British version of the Belgian FN rifle also used by Argentinian forces in the Falklands
Special Forces	SAS and/or SBS
SSK	Conventional submarine
SSN	Nuclear-powered submarine
SST	Surgical Support Team (part of Medical Squadron)
STOVL	Short Take Off Vertical Landing
STUFT	Ships Taken Up from Trade
TAVR	Territorial Auxiliary and Volunteer Reserve (British Army)
TEZ	Total Exclusion Zone
Trident D5	Nuclear powered submarine carrying Trident ICBMs
TWC	Transition to War Committee
UK	The United Kingdom of Great Britain and Northern Ireland
UKLF	United Kingdom Land Forces
UN	United Nations
UNSC	United Nations Security Council
UNSCR	United Nations Security Council Resolution
Volvo BV 202	Over-snow tracked vehicle
VOR	VHS omni-directional radio
WMR	War Maintenance Reserve (mobilisation stocks of ammunition, rations and equipment

Introduction: A Personal View

ADMIRAL SIR JOHN (SANDY) WOODWARD

I attended the conference on 'The Falklands Conflict 20 Years On – Lessons for the Future' held at the Royal Military Academy Sandhurst in June 2002 less in the hope of learning anything new than to try to ensure that history did not get changed in order to drive 'new' lessons. In late 1982, I called on the then Supreme Allied Commander Atlantic (SACLANT) in Norfolk, Virginia, and he was quick to tell me in so many words that there were 'no new lessons to be learned from your little war'.

This helped to put it all in better perspective for me – he was indeed right. We knew all about fighting that sort of campaign from decades before, but we had moved far away from it in our narrow national concentration on Anti-Submarine Warfare (ASW) in the north-east Atlantic within the North Atlantic Treaty Organisation (NATO) Alliance when the 1974 Defence Review under Denis Healey confined our attentions in that area. The fact that HMS *Ark Royal* went to scrap four years later did not itself signal the change from 'expeditionary capability' – our mindsets had changed years before, beginning perhaps with the decision not to order any replacement for the *Ark* in 1966.

But we hung onto it somehow, though we dressed it up as North East Atlantic ASW with a bit of defence of the Northern Flank, sufficiently well until 1981 when that house of cards came tumbling down.

The strategic lesson I learned from the Falklands War was first encapsulated in my Report of Proceedings of 30 June 1982:

> Finally, and entirely accepting that politics is not my business, I cannot resist a review of the wherefores of this whole affair. Were I Galtieri, I would have observed the Malvinas negotiations of the last few decades and found little hope of early satisfaction. I would have observed that, over the same long period, there had been

1

a progressive withdrawal of and reduction in British overseas military capability. I would have concluded that, at some time in the not so distant future, British policy on the Falklands issue would be all shadow and no substance. When the cuts in the Royal Navy were announced recently, the way ahead must have seemed clear and only awaited a half reasonable excuse. Scrap dealers, and our reaction to them, provided that excuse. Galtieri's reasoning was as impeccable as his timing was previous.

If the Argentinean government, or others similarly minded elsewhere, are not to make the same mistake again, we shall need to provide not only the mark of our resolution on the spot but also the obvious wherewithal to reinforce it. We would not again wish to repair our mistakes the hard way. But after the imperatives of strategic nuclear deterrence and defence of the home base had been met, the last review of Defence decided in favour of the short term, politically expedient, continental-European commitment to the detriment of the long term, long-established maritime world-wide, national interest. So much at least was evident to Galtieri and I doubt he was alone.

Whatever I may have thought before, the Falklands experience has given me a new insight into the immorality and dishonesty of non-democratic governments altogether too common in this turbulent world. I am convinced that such influence as we can bring to bear for our defence money would be better placed where it can affect both European and world affairs than where it can affect, and in a very limited way at that, the policies of our European neighbours only. That such a policy best suits our geographic, economic and political interests is a matter of history; that it also suits our professional military capability, air, sea and land, is now again demonstrated. For consistency's sake alone, we cannot now turn back.

That lesson seemed to have been learned by Governments of both persuasions over the next decade and was re-emphasised by the present government most recently in Distribution Point (DP) 2001. 'Expeditionary force in a turbulent world' is the simplest phrase to describe present policy, as it arguably should have been in 1981.

Today, we have that capability, aimed at keeping any threat as far from our home base as possible. Liddell Hart would be proud of us. At the same time, the single most important tactical (but not new) lesson of 1982 was that the maintenance of an adequate air situation (not 'supremacy', but just-enough-for-the-job) is the fundamental enabler of any expeditionary force venture. This particular question was the cause of most angst in deciding whether or not to despatch the Task Force at all in early April 1982. The Ministry of Defence (MoD) was not prepared to put its money on the Sea Harrier; the First Sea Lord was. In the event, the Sea Harrier, equipped with radar and armed with the Sidewinder Advanced Short Range Air to Air Missile (ASRAAM) did the job rather better than almost everyone had expected (Harriers accounted for the large majority of kills of Argentine Air Force aircraft). But the question was absolutely fundamental to 'Expeditionary Force' – could an adequate air situation be achieved by organic fixed-wing aircraft, the radar and ASRAAM-fitted Sea Harrier? The answer, in the out-turn, was unequivocally, 'yes'.

The Sea Harrier FA2, now in service with improved-performance radar and the vastly improved Advanced Medium Range Air to Air Missile (AMRAAM) – both lessons from 1982, does the job today against a considerably increased threat. AMRAAM, with an effective range out to 40 miles, gives a missile engagement area of some 5,000 square miles as compared with 3 square miles for ASRAAM. It can be used in all weather conditions, whereas ASRAAM is a strictly visual-range weapon largely confined to daylight use only. Finally, AMRAAM can engage sea-skimming missiles – a capability lacking in ASRAAM altogether. The Sea Harrier airframe is capable of further improvement in its extreme-hot-weather performance but that would seem expensive for a service life of some ten or so years before the Joint Strike Fighter arrives and for a single scenario (the Gulf in summer).

Strangely though, the Government decided (in 2001) to throw any possibility of an adequate air situation away by 2006 with the announcement of the early removal from front-line service of the AMRAAM Sea Harrier FA2. They intend to manage without radar-fitted fixed-wing aircraft from 2006 until arrival of the Short Take Off Vertical Landing (STOVL) version of the Joint Strike Fighter some time after 2012. They further intend to manage without AMRAAM, the weapons system which has made the Sea Harrier FA2 the best fighter aircraft in squadron service in Europe. Any British Joint Task Force deployed after 2006 will, therefore, be markedly worse off in straight capability terms than we were even in 1982. This is a very strange development for a Government that advocates 'Expeditionary Force' when the Government in 1982 did not.

I have to conclude that although the tactical lesson on organic fixed-wing air was learned in 1982, it is now being forgotten. As a consequence, so also is the strategic lesson of Expeditionary Force itself. No doubt, the politicians will say that it is only for a few years, but if a week is a long time in politics, six years must be 300 times longer. Plainly, the most obvious lessons are being unlearned even as we considered the matter 20 years on.

18–19 March	Argentine scrap-metal workers land at Leith Harbour, South Georgia, and raise the Argentine flag.
2 April	Operation Rosario. Argentine troops invade Falklands.
3 April	Argentine Marines land at Grytviken, South Georgia. United Nations (UN) Security Council adopts Resolution 502. Margaret Thatcher announces dispatch of task force to recapture the islands.
5 April	Lord Carrington resigns as Foreign Secretary and is replaced by Francis Pym.
7 April	Britain declares a maritime exclusion zone of 200 miles centred on Falklands to come into effect 0400 hours 12 April.
25 April	British forces land on South Georgia (Operation Paraquat). Argentines surrender.
28 April	British government announces further restrictions on transit through 200-nautical mile exclusion zone (amounting to complete blockade), to come into effect 1100 hours 30 April.
30 April	Total exclusion zone comes into effect around Falklands. President Reagan announces support for Britain.
1 May	Pre-dawn raid by single Vulcan bomber on Port Stanley airfield (Operation Black Buck 1).
2 May	Peru offers new peace plan for solving the crisis. UN offers similar services. HMS Conqueror sinks *General Belgrano* approximately 35 miles south-west of exclusion zone.
4 May	HMS *Sheffield* hit by air-launched Exocet missile: 20 crew killed, vessel abandoned. Operation Black Buck 2.
6 May	Britain formally accepts offer of UN mediation.
7 May	Exclusion zone extended to within 12 miles of Argentina's coastline. UN Secretary-General announces peace initiative.
12 May	Decision made to land troops at San Carlos. *QE2* sails from Southampton with 5 Infantry Brigade aboard.
21 May	4,000 troops of 2 Para, 3 Para, 40, 42 and 45 Royal Marine Commandos (with support services) land almost unopposed at San Carlos. Heavy air attacks on naval task force costs Argentines 11 aircraft (five Mirage, five Skyhawk, one Pucará), but latter succeed

	in sinking *Ardent*. Other vessels damaged. British lose one Harrier and two helicopters.
25 May	HMS *Coventry* and container vessel *Atlantic Conveyor* sunk, former by bombs and latter by air-launched Exocet. Three Argentine aircraft destroyed. Air force commander Lami Dozo sends peace envoy to New York.
26 May	UN adopts Resolution 505. Northwood demands that 3 Commando Brigade commence offensive operations. 2 Para advances towards Goose Green.
27 May	45 Commando and 3 Para leave bridgehead for Port Stanley. Vessels carrying 5 Brigade rendezvous near South Georgia.
28 May	2 Para (600 strong) commences attack on Darwin and Goose Green at 0230 hrs. After day-long battle with more numerous Argentine forces, objectives are captured. Approximately 1,300 prisoners are taken. Lieutenant Colonel 'H' Jones killed.
29 May	3 Para reaches Teal Inlet; 45 Commando sets off for Douglas.
30 May	Major General Moore arrives in Falklands to command land forces; 45 Commando and 3 Para secure Douglas and Teal respectively on north side of East Falklands.
31 May	UN Secretary General proposes new peace plan.
1 June	5 Brigade commences disembarkation at San Carlos; 3 Commando Brigade forward base established at Teal Inlet.
2 June	Surrender leaflets dropped on Port Stanley; 2 Para elements airlifted to Bluff Cove.
3 June	Versailles Summit opens. President Reagan presents five-point plan to British.
5 June	Scots Guards embark on *Sir Tristram* for transport to Fitzroy–Bluff Cove area.
6 June	Scots Guards land at Fitzroy, establishing 5 Brigade forward base. Landings at San Carlos completed. British have around 8,000 troops on East Falkland.
7 June	UN Secretary General announces another peace plan.
8 June	*Sir Galahad* and *Sir Tristram* attacked by Argentine aircraft at Bluff Cove. *Sir Galahad* crippled, 46 killed and 150 injured.
11 June	42 Commando attacks Mt Harriet and Goat Ridge; 45 Commando attacks Two Sisters; 3 Para attacks

	Mt Longdon (5 miles west of Port Stanley). All objectives captured by the following morning.
13–14 June	Second phase of attack on Port Stanley; 2 Para attack Wireless Ridge; Scots Guards attack Tumbledown; 1/7 Gurkhas occupy Mt William.
14 June	After negotiations, Brigadier General Mario Menendez surrenders all Argentine forces in East and West Falkland. They are taken prisoner and subsequently repatriated.
12 July	Britain announces that active hostilities over the Falklands are regarded as having ended; the Argentines fail to make any similar statement.
22 July	Total exclusion zone lifted.

PART 1
The Falklands Conflict in History

The Impact of the Falklands Conflict on International Affairs

LAWRENCE FREEDMAN

INTRODUCTION

There is an aspect to contemporary strategy that is impossible to quantify yet is of considerable significance, and is normally summed up by the word 'legitimacy'. This is not quite the same as legality, although a backing in international law certainly helps; nor is it the same as morality, although conformity with traditional 'just war' principles is also an advantage. It needs to be gained abroad as well as at home, so just because a course of action has popular support does not give it legitimacy. Rather it is an amalgam of legality, morality and democracy, and it is the task of a government in a conflict to create a sense of legitimacy around its actions and to cope with the consequences of a failure to do so.

Throughout the Falklands campaign the British Government was very conscious of the legitimacy issue. It barely attempted to make a strong case in terms of strategic or economic interests, avoiding claims to great benefit in terms of Cold War rivalries or future oil wealth. Instead it concentrated on key principles: self-determination for the islanders, the inadmissibility of force as a means of resolving disputes, the inherent right of self-defence under Article 51 of the UN Charter and the importance of not rewarding aggression. In making claims to foreign governments the emphasis was on the precedent set if the Argentinian occupation succeeded rather than the vital interests of the United Kingdom (UK).

The United Nations Security Council Resolution (UNSCR) 502 had played a large part in conferring an aura of legitimacy on Britain's action, while the various declarations of support by other governments and such concrete steps as economic sanctions supported the view that

Britain was acting on behalf of a wider international interest. As the fighting became more serious, however, the issue inevitably moved away from whether Britain's cause was just, to the means adopted by Britain in the name of this cause. The just war tradition argued not only that a war be undertaken to right a wrong, but also that the means employed should be proportionate. This is not straightforward. Any use of armed force has to take into account not only some notional relationship to the ends being employed but also the means available to the opponent. There is an issue of proportion in relation to the threat. Moreover, there was also a question of when the principles at stake could be said to have been honoured: was it enough to get the Argentinians off the islands, if necessary through offering some concessions to their concerns, or must they be denied any face-saving compensation? Abroad, the urge was to get a negotiated settlement as soon as possible: at home, the urge was to see honour satisfied, whatever the damage to Argentinian honour. How should the consequences of actions be included in the calculation? What was the price worth paying for success in terms of lives, military capacity, resources and political goodwill, and how much should it matter if those costs were being imposed on those less directly involved?

BRITAIN'S FOREIGN RELATIONS

The development and implementation of this crisis response, as testing for the diplomatic service as the military campaign was for the armed services, began with the Foreign and Commonwealth Office (FCO) in some disarray. The Argentinian invasion had come at the exact moment when the Head of the Diplomatic Service was changing, although the retiring Sir Michael Palliser was soon asked to continue to advise the government for the duration of the crisis. The two cabinet ministers from the FCO, Lord Carrington and Sir Humphrey Atkins, both resigned, as did Richard Luce, the minister who had been dealing with the Falklands. Senior diplomats who had been handling the issue believed themselves to have been discredited, even though they were not sure what else they might have done, given the approach to the issue taken by the government as a whole. The new Foreign Secretary, Francis Pym, was a figure respected in the Conservative Party and the Commons, but was being thrown in at the deep end and was not notably close to Prime Minister Margaret Thatcher.

Yet this was to be an unusually testing time for British diplomacy. Few other governments, even amongst the most friendly, were quite sure why Britain was putting in such an effort and accepting such high risks to retake an asset with so little real value, and less sure why they should put themselves out to help. Whatever Britain wanted – from access to facilities *en route* to the South Atlantic, to information on arms supplied to Argentina, to adherence to economic sanctions – the case must be compelling and tenaciously argued. Ambassadors and High Commissioners around the world had to become overnight experts on the dispute and its ramifications. At the same time as the FCO became bound up with the many practical demands of the crisis, it had to keep a close eye on the political implications of every military move being planned at the Royal Navy (RN) headquarters at Northwood. It was expected to be at the fore in the search for a negotiated outcome to the crisis, but here the Prime Minister was very much in charge, aware that any apparent concession to Argentina was political dynamite at home.

The critical advice on the diplomatic strategy to be adopted if compromises on the core issues of principle were to be avoided, while entreaties for moderation were respected, was provided largely by the two Ambassadors at the most important posts in Washington and New York. The handling of the United States' government was going to be crucial in arranging any political settlement and as a source of military support. Here the Ambassador was Sir Nicholas Henderson, an unusually experienced and independent-minded diplomat, with a personality admirably suited to making a mark in Washington. The most vital diplomatic battles would be fought in and around the UN in New York, where Britain's Ambassador was Sir Anthony Parsons, a shrewd and popular diplomat, on the rebound from a difficult period as Ambassador to Iran during the time of the Islamic revolution. He understood the culture of the UN and the conflicting pressures that would influence the collective response to the unfolding crisis. Henderson and Parsons together had a clear sense of the amount of flexibility it was appropriate and necessary to show as they faced the unusually demanding audiences of the UN Security Council and the American media.

Sir Anthony helped redeem the FCO in the Prime Minister's eyes by securing a notable victory in the UN Security Council, pushing through UNSCR 502 which put the onus on Argentina to withdraw. Institutionally Britain had an advantage as a permanent member of the Security Council, working from the commanding heights of the organisation and with the capacity to veto any unfavourable resolution. Yet while it had reason to expect solidarity from fellow members of the western alliance and from Commonwealth countries, the UN had been a difficult arena for some time because of the strength of third world opinion with its strong anti-colonial sentiment. The more the Falklands could be presented as a matter of colonialism, which is how it had previously been developed in the UN General Assembly, the more awkward Britain's position could become. It did not help that it so happened that the two European non-permanent members of the Security Council at this time – Spain and Ireland – were the only two with their own territorial disputes with Britain. Moreover, while normally Britain would expect vital support from its closest ally, the United States, Jeanne Kirkpatrick, the United States Ambassador to the UN, was closely associated with the Reagan Administration's Latin America policy and led the pro-Argentina camp in Washington. Argentina's Ambassador, Eduardo Roca, who had arrived only in late March to take up his position in New York, could take Latin American support for granted, and hope for a helpful response from the Soviet bloc by opposing a leading member of NATO, and make the most of the UN's devotion to anti-colonialism, while at the same time relying on a sympathetic hearing from Kirkpatrick.

From the start of April, when few appreciated the potential seriousness of the affair, to the end of May when it was becoming a matter of real concern, international opinion developed in quite distinctive ways. National answers to these fundamental questions of principle varied considerably. Of Britain's traditional allies only the Old Commonwealth gave essentially unconditional backing. Canada, Australia and New Zealand all stood firm, with Prime Minister Robert Muldoon of New Zealand even offering a frigate to enable the RN to release another vessel for Falklands duties. By and large the New Commonwealth was also supportive, with many of the smaller African and Caribbean countries appreciating the need to put regional predators in their place. Although the Indian government adhered to its non-aligned position, Indian public opinion appeared to be with Britain, while publicity about possible South African arms deliveries to Argentina helped reinforce black African support. Kenya and Guyana were particularly helpful in the Security Council.

Elsewhere there was a clear preference for doing as little as possible. Japan, for example, was rarely disposed to disrupting trade on a point of principle. Japan voted for UNSCR 502, although there were reports of some hesitation. Thereafter, although the Japanese government claimed to have spoken firmly to Argentinian representatives and to have warned of the possible economic consequences, they took no clear economic measures for several weeks.

Europe

In Europe, France was in a critical position as being both a leading member of the European Community (EC), a fellow permanent member of the UN Security Council, and from the start, Britain's staunchest ally. President

François Mitterrand had ordered full support for Britain. This led at once to the embargo on arms and trade and support for UNSCR 502. France provided valuable practical help to Britain's armed forces. Mitterrand appears to have been motivated by genuine gratitude at the stance taken by Britain during the Second World War and by the opportunity the crisis provided to demonstrate his socialist government's reliability as a member of the western camp. It did not go down well in the Quai d'Orsay, where there were worries about the impact on relations with Latin America and an extension of Soviet influence. Mitterrand observed on 1 May, 'If there isn't a reflex of solidarity between England and France then between whom could such a reflex exist?' At the same time he made clear that support was for the duration of the crisis and no longer, and certainly did not extend to support for British sovereignty. He was also able to separate this from all other issues, taking the opportunity to move against Britain over EC issues on the budget and agricultural prices. Throughout this period, arguments on budgets and agricultural prices persisted. Britain refused to accept that concessions on these matters were a *quid pro quo* for European solidarity, arguing that the Falklands was a matter of international principle and not just a British national interest.

In West Germany, by contrast, the response was more equivocal. It took until 7 April before Chancellor Helmut Schmidt spoke to Prime Minister Thatcher, although he interrupted his Easter break to preside over an emergency cabinet meeting on the previous day. The West Germans joined enthusiastically in the NATO declaration of support, and despite their strong aversion to embargoes and their reluctance to set precedents which could later be used against them, they applied the arms embargo and agreed to the EC's import embargo with uncharacteristic speed. So far this had been an instinctive gesture of support for an ally, an EC partner and a close friend. At the same time they were cautious about endorsing British policies.

A sense of the trouble which nationalism and a predilection for military solutions could cause led to German unease when observing the surge of patriotic enthusiasm in Britain, fully aware of how unhappy others would be if Germans betrayed the same tendencies. The aversion to armed conflict ran deep, with the supposition always that there must be a better way. For those of this view, it would be best if military action was delayed while the better way was found, even if this meant putting to one side the issues at stake. After the sinking of the *General Belgrano* the position became difficult with West Germany.

The German interest in trade with Argentina was substantial, as they took 28 per cent of all the EC's imports from Argentina in 1980. There was also concern at the diversion of British forces from their NATO tasks. The Berlin parallel was invoked, including by Mayor Richard von Weizsäcker of West Berlin and Federal President Karl Carstens: a country that could respond to aggression against one isolated outpost was likely to respond to a threat to another, although others denied any parallel between the Falklands and one of Europe's great cities.

In some ways the Italian position was the most interesting of all, and while it caused Britain a number of problems this could easily be explained by the political situation within Italy. According to the press the hostilities were 'absurd' and Britain's reaction to the Argentinian invasion disproportionate, but the Italian government was always careful to express sympathy for Britain's position despite the constraints on its own position, and it was known that Italy had condemned Argentina privately and directly. About half of Argentina's population was of Italian extraction. There were over 1 million Italian passport holders in Argentina who were entitled to vote in Italy's national elections and therefore formed an important lobby. Italy also had important commercial interests in Argentina and generally in South America. Against this background many Italians saw sanctions as contributing to the escalation of the conflict, as well as opportunities being created for the Soviet Union, and the adverse effects on long-term relations between Europe and Latin America. Lastly, there was a matter of political culture. British diplomats observed that Italian politicians tended to assume that there was no problem that could not be solved by negotiation. Political life was geared to a search for compromise even if this meant that big issues tend to be sidestepped rather than tackled head on. Sanctions was the difficult issue. There had been a battle over sanctions within the governing coalition, who were desperate for an economic embargo of the shortest possible duration and a negotiated settlement.

Spain was even more difficult. As the conflict broke, delicate negotiations were in progress over Gibraltar. On 20 April, an announcement was due concerning the opening of negotiations between the two Foreign Ministers, 'aimed at overcoming all the differences between them on Gibraltar' on the basis of the Lisbon agreement of 10 April 1980. These were postponed. Yet while the Argentinian Junta represented exactly the sort of outmoded mentality which Spanish democracy was dedicated to opposing – not surprisingly, Francoists were the more enthusiastic supporters of the Argentinians – and Spain was intending to join NATO in 1982 and the EC later, Spain also supported the Argentinian claim to the Falklands, and the Spanish press, while almost unanimously opposing a similar use of force against Gibraltar, was jubilant at the Argentinian invasion. The unavoidable role that Gibraltar was playing in support of the Task Force did not help, however much this was played down.

The extent to which national problems influenced stances on the Falklands can be illustrated further by Greece, where the government had in mind the position of Cyprus. The Greek position on Cyprus was similar to the British view on the Falklands in denying that geographical proximity was in itself the basis for sovereignty, and in opposing the use of force and occupation as a means of asserting sovereignty. Couple this with the Greeks' own unhappy recent experience with a military Junta, and the surprisingly close rapport between Thatcher and Greek Prime Minister Andreas Papandreou, and the basis for Greece's close support for Britain can be found.

Most difficult of all was Ireland, the other European state in a territorial dispute with the UK, and also, like Spain, a temporary member of the UN Security Council. Irish attitudes were consistently exasperating to London, and all too reminiscent of the assertion of neutrality during the Second World War, when London considered itself to be fighting for an international principle while Dublin took the view that 'England's difficulty is Ireland's opportunity'. Initially Dublin had disapproved of Argentina's use of force and supported UNSCR 502. It even went along with EC sanctions, despite claims from the most Anglophobic sections of the community that this stance was inconsistent with Irish neutrality. The Irish were surprised, when claiming that they viewed the issue as a colonial one, how many other ex-colonies, such as Kenya, Uganda and Guyana, supported Britain. There was a 300,000-strong Irish community in Argentina, but perhaps more important was the difficulty in identifying with the Falklanders: an intensely loyal but isolated British community facing a hostile neighbour was too redolent of the Unionist community in Northern Ireland.

The crisis did not come at a good time in Anglo-Irish relations. After the traumas of the hunger strikers, there were serious divergences over Northern Ireland, but also on a range of EC issues. The announcement came that on 18 April a British submarine had accidentally sunk the Irish trawler *Sharelga*. Then came the news of the *General Belgrano*, leading to the Foreign Minister wondering to the British Ambassador whether he should shake his hand in public, while the Defence Minister told a local party meeting that Britain was now very much the aggressor in the South Atlantic. This statement was disowned by Taoiseach Charles Haughey, now in control of Falklands policy, but on 4 May he drafted a statement which marked a decisive shift, calling for the UNSC to get an immediate ceasefire and to seek withdrawal of EC sanctions. He then faced difficulty as clarifications were required to bring this into line with

UNSCR 502 and also with European solidarity. When the British asked for an explanation, the Foreign Minister explained that sanctions had been supported to provide a balanced combination of economic, political and military pressure, but that balance had now been lost with the increase in military activity. The posture adopted was not without costs for Ireland. It encouraged views in Britain of the Irish as unreliable or hostile, and even led to calls for the boycott of Irish goods. At this point the £9.4 million worth of exports to Argentina looked rather puny when compared with £1.5 billion to the UK.

The United States

The Americans came sympathetic to Britain's predicament, and, aware that Washington could not, in the end, condone such blatant aggression against the territory of its closest ally. But a lot of effort had gone recently into cultivating Argentina and those in Washington most committed to this effort, notably Jeane Kirkpatrick and Thomas Enders, Assistant Secretary for Inter-American Affairs, argued vigorously for an 'even-handed' approach. They pointed out that the United States had always been neutral on the substance of the Falklands issue. There seemed to be a strong argument for sustaining this neutrality, given the valuable role that Argentina was now playing in supporting Washington in its anti-communist campaigns in Central America, and the need to correct the hemispheric suspicion that when it came to the crunch the United States would always support Europeans rather than its closest neighbours. The Europeanists, such as the Assistant Secretary for European Affairs, Laurence Eagleburger, were appalled by the very idea of failing to support a NATO ally in these circumstances, especially given the vigorous support which Margaret Thatcher had provided President Ronald Reagan on a number of controversial matters. Anglo-American relations had taken time to recover from Suez in 1956, when the British had been in the wrong. It would be disastrous to desert them now when they were clearly in the right. Secretary of State Alexander Haig's promise to Henderson that there 'cannot be another Suez' was duly underlined.

The political weight was on Britain's side, as a democracy that had been wronged by a dictatorship, and as a country which could call on close ties of affection and interest at all levels of the American political system. Britain received press coverage that remained favourable and 'well ahead of the Administration'. Haig, however, thought the question for American policy to be more complex than a decision on whom to back. Obviously Argentina could not be supported, but that did not mean that a more neutral stance should be ruled out, at least in the first instance. He was fearful that if the United States turned against Argentina the main beneficiary would be Moscow. He tended to view most issues through the framework of the Cold War, and was impressed by the opportunities the crisis presented 'for Soviet mischief-making, either directly, or through their Cuban proxies, in Argentina'. To this concern was added some sense of British responsibility for poor management of this issue in the past, but most of all a belief that the United States was uniquely well placed to facilitate a negotiated settlement. The risk here, including for Haig personally, was that it would fail, and this was understood to be the most likely outcome, given the past difficulties with this dispute and the added factor of military action by Argentina. Any hope here relied on the uncertainty that both sides must face when contemplating further hostilities. Meanwhile, the mediator role would at least allow Washington off the hook when it came to taking sides immediately. All lines of communication would need to be kept open and no unnecessary offence proffered.

Even before Haig's mediation effort ran its course at the end of April (although he did not give up even then) the material support provided by the Pentagon was remarkable. Even diplomatic support was provided when necessary, in keeping allies in line or defending Britain's position in forums as challenging as the Organization of American States (OAS). Yet for London the concern was with persistent appeals to Britain to offer concessions to Argentina to pave the way to some face-saving settlement. These had often been requested not so much to produce a better outcome for the Falklands but to help General Leopoldo Galtieri hold on to power or to deflect Argentinian irritation with Washington.

An assessment of 23 May 1982 in the *New York Times*, after the British landing at San Carlos, was widely assumed to reflect the dominant view in the United States political circles. The gravamen was that Britain could win the war but without necessarily bringing about the complete capitulation of the Argentinians. Any new government in Buenos Aires would be revanchist, and attacks would continue indefinitely from the air, if necessary with borrowed aircraft and crews. This would impose an excessive long-term burden on Britain, provide opportunities for further Soviet and Cuban advances and further damage United States interests. Accordingly, now that Britain had made its point, a settlement of some sort was needed. The Administration saw the whole Hemispheric system unravelling, as a result of Latin American solidarity with a probably Peronist successor, Argentinian regime hell-bent on revenge. Previous reports that Galtieri would never deal with Moscow were now being discounted. There was now real fear that Argentina might turn to the

Cubans and the Soviets as a last hope of averting total humiliation. Galtieri might be swept aside by elements even more opposed to western interests. The expulsion of Argentinian forces would not end the state of war, especially if Buenos Aires had been strengthened by communist support. Against this background of assumptions, the administration was naturally concerned that Britain wanted only a return to the status quo ante without any consideration of the possibility of a long-term negotiated solution. Against this the British stressed how much sacrifice and intransigence had been endured and the unreality of expecting them to get this far, and suddenly pull out before the task was complete.

The wear and tear on relations with the United States and Europe concerned ministers during the war but never became critical. What is also worth noting is the British scepticism with regard to the large geopolitical issues that were raised in these discussions with allies. Without exception all advice from friendly governments pointed in the same direction: compromise and magnanimity in relation to Argentina, to the point of sparing it from a humiliating defeat. While this case was animated by issues of proportionality and the readiness to 'give peace a chance', most governments' concerns were more pragmatic in nature. As already noted, a British victory, it was widely assumed, including by many in Britain, would have three unfortunate consequences. It would radicalise Argentina, alienate Latin America and provide opportunities to the Soviet Union.

The validity of these concerns was rarely challenged directly, although there was good reason during the conflict to believe that they had been exaggerated and based on scanty evidence. The third danger was only true if the first two were real, because what was being postulated was a historic shift in alignments. The Argentinians would be so frustrated at having their territory snatched away from them once again that they would never forgive the British, nor their North American and European accomplices. They would seek every available means of continuing the struggle, however foolish and futile these might be, and become even more extremist politically. The rest of Latin America would follow in sympathy, convinced of the rightness of the Argentinian cause and the inadmissibility of Britain's military response.

Latin America

Even as things stood in late May 1982 there were reasons to be sceptical of these assumptions. At one level they depended on ethnic stereotypes of passionate Latin Americans, ready to give up everything on a point of honour. They supposed that the virulent anti-communism of recent years was extraordinarily superficial and could easily be thrown into reverse. If this adventure went awry and ended in humiliation the right-wing Argentinian Junta would stagger into a communist embrace. They also supposed complete indifference to the economic aspects of the conflict, for western help would certainly be needed if Argentina was to sort out its shattered finances. As for the rest of Latin America, the gloomier analysis assumed a whole-hearted identification with Argentina, when the tensions between Argentina and the other countries of the region were well known. It was quite apparent that support was largely rhetorical, and that no Latin American country had been prepared to incur significant diplomatic, economic or military costs on Argentina's behalf. Moscow, and its local ally Cuba, did try to exploit the conflict but they were not very successful. Contacts were used by Buenos Aires as a means of putting pressure on the west, but they were never going to lead to a move into the Soviet bloc.

Throughout May, Argentina stressed that it was a responsible member of the western community rather than a potential convert to communism. Yet, it was feared, the military, including Galtieri himself, might hope to survive a surrender and retain power if Argentinian forces could hold on. Reports in early June that Argentina had signed a $100 million trade agreement with Cuba, expanding on an already growing commercial and political relationship with Havana, could also on the one hand confirm Washington's worst fears, while on the other appear as a source of discomfort to a generally right-wing political and military elite. A picture of Foreign Secretary Nicanor Costa Mendez (in Cuba to attend a meeting of the Non-Aligned Movement) embracing Fidel Castro had apparently irritated many officers. Even Costa Mendez was said to be unhappy about receiving assistance from communist countries. The more alarmist prognostications related more to the likely next government. It was assumed that the new leaders would be highly nationalistic, reluctant to negotiate with the British and increasingly inclined to blame the United States for Argentina's defeat. Popular support for Argentina's claim would mean that even civilian leaders would have to sustain a nationalistic stance. In arguing against the need to 'save' Galtieri, the British never accepted that the alternatives were likely to be more extreme, or that after the hostilities Argentina would be easier to deal with if it had not been humiliated and had been allowed some return on its original aggression.

In retrospect we can see that not only would something have to be done about the economy and discontent with a repressive regime after the war, which was generally acknowledged, but also defeat would involve an enormous shock to the Argentinian system, and this tended to be understated. Popular anger would be channelled internally, against the regime, rather than against foreign powers. The desire to get rid of military rule was underestimated, as was the need to work closely with western powers if the economy was to recover. Any government would eventually have to cope with the sort of recurrent economic failures prompted by the surge of inflation resulting from the abandonment of fiscal austerity measures. As the conflict wore on, at issue was not whether Argentina was rejecting capitalism but whether capitalism was rejecting Argentina.

Equally, all the economic and commercial arguments in Latin American countries were for strengthening rather than weakening relations with European countries, with which there were close historical and cultural affinities, as well as important markets for their commodities and sources of finance and technology. Britain had played a role in the Latin American independence struggle, and in the region's economic development, while there were still sizeable British communities throughout Latin America. The responses to Argentinian pressures had been slow and reluctant. Only Panama allowed its rhetoric to get out of hand, with chauvinistic comments about Prime Minister Thatcher that were deplored at home. British diplomats found little love for Argentina or for its military government in the region, and in private if not in public there was much condemnation of the Argentinian aggression.

The basic interest in Latin America was to get the whole business over as soon as possible. The governments were aware of western concerns about a realignment, but in using these concerns they took care not to suggest that it was inevitable. They remained the weaker parties in the relationship. Chile was officially neutral although in practice sympathetic to Britain. Brazil also had a recent history of quarrels with Argentina. The Mexicans accepted that Britain was the victim of aggression. When Argentina moved to reconvene the meeting of the Consultative Organ of the Rio Treaty states in late May to consider further action, a harsh resolution was adopted which condemned Britain, called on the United States to cease supporting Britain and invited Rio Treaty signatories to assist Argentina individually or collectively. Four countries, the United States, Trinidad, Chile and Colombia, voted against the resolution. It had no consequences.

The Soviet Union

The other issue was Soviet support. Moscow, already a large importer of Argentinian grain, used the crisis to ingratiate itself with Latin Americans, encouraging the media to denigrate British and United States policies. Its diplomats advocated the exclusion of the United States and Canada from the OAS, and promised to use the UN veto to help

Argentina, although they had failed to do so with UNSCR 502. The Americans saw Moscow seeking to capitalise on a major opportunity to improve its standing in Latin America. The British, however, always doubted that Moscow would make much headway in improving its own position. There were no indications that Soviet equipment had been requested by Buenos Aires: such material would probably present severe technical problems for the Argentinians.

There was a strong Soviet protest to Britain stemming from the disruption of the Soviet–Argentinian grain trade caused by the British blockade. Grain shipments were piling up in Argentinian ports and insurance rates for ships operating out of these ports had been pushed up. Britain – and by extension the United States – would be blamed by Moscow for domestic shortages of grain. The United States was worried that Argentina might seek to obtain new weapons from the Soviet Union after the conflict, on the grounds that they would be offered at bargain prices, western supplies had been restricted, and that this would be a means of helping to pay for grain sales as well as increasing Soviet influence. However, even Moscow was wary of getting too close to Argentina. It had been caught on the hop by the invasion, had avoided vetoing UNSCR 502 and called for an Argentinian withdrawal. Even while condemning British colonial attitudes and describing the invasion as no more than an 'occupation', the Soviet Union was well aware of the Junta's reputation among other leftist groups in Latin America, and had noted that third world support for Argentina was hardly overwhelming, a critical criterion for Soviet foreign policy.

CONCLUSION

The problem then was not that Britain was seriously jeopardising wider western interests in Latin America by pushing so strongly its national interests, but that it was widely assumed by its friends and allies to be doing so. The government therefore had to work hard to prevent a seepage. Continuing military success helped. There were signs that Latin American countries were distancing themselves from Argentina as defeat seemed more likely.

A more substantial help was the Versailles Summit of the 'Group of Seven' leading world economic powers (G7) leading western states between 4 and 6 June. It was used to get the Americans, and the other allies, to understand this while they still appeared to be hankering after a compromise settlement of some sort; solutions which might have been acceptable at an earlier stage of the crisis were no longer realistic in the light of British military exertions and losses. This was coincident with the dramatic vote at the UN at which Britain at last had to use its veto, an event which was overshadowed by the United States delegation's initial veto followed by the later observation that they wished they had abstained. Once Reagan had made a public statement supporting Britain at the Summit, the other countries fell in line. It was assumed that this was the green light for the battle for Port Stanley. After the Summit Mitterrand stated that:

> We wanted to affirm our solidarity with Great Britain, who as it happens, had been the victim of aggression against both its national interests and its national pride, a solidarity which is natural. Great Britain must regain its right (*doit retrouver son droit*), it being understood that we shall do everything, once its right has been regained, so that peace triumphs over war.

At the same time it was already apparent that the other side of the coin was a conviction that, after the hostilities, Britain would be expected to be active in seeking the early lifting of economic sanctions. Slowly the diplomatic focus was shifting to the post-war situation. After the war Britain would – and did – face arguments for magnanimity and pressure to find imaginative solutions to long-term problems, and also to provide its allies with release from economic sanctions and arms embargoes.

As the final battle for Port Stanley began, allied governments had, by and large, been convinced that there was no longer any point in pressing London for some conciliatory gesture. The American media now encouraged Britain to avoid a post-war strategy which could leave Argentina still determined to regain the islands. The *New York Times* was now starting to cast a sceptical eye over the 'calamitous' harm that was being done to the United States relations with Latin America.

Twenty years on we can see that the war helped Argentina back to democracy and not into further dictatorship, that it did the Soviet Union and Cuba no good at all, and that western political relations with Latin America were soon in good repair. I am reluctant to draw lessons from episodes such as this but one does seem relevant. It is often the case that firm action is criticised on the assumption that it will produce an equal and opposite reaction from the opponent and antagonise others. The evidence from this case suggests that governments make their calculations out of their own sense of their interests, which may appear curious, and that the firm action of others can make them uncomfortable, but they rarely act out of pique or unbridled emotion. The fact was that on 2 April 1982 Argentina had lost legitimacy by using armed force without warning to solve a long-standing dispute and this was never regained. Britain's effort had legitimacy and, while this was at times put under strain, it was never lost.

2

The Geopolitics of the Falklands Conflict

GEOFFREY SLOAN

The aim of this chapter is to give an insight into the geopolitics of the Falklands war. To facilitate this I want to do two things. First, to establish the nature of the relationship between geography and international relations. Second, to define briefly what I mean by geopolitics.

The relationship between international relations and geography can be viewed in three ways. First, it can be seen as an objective of policy, a prize in a conflict between two or more states. As a state exercises total control over a territory, any part of that territory can be a source of conflict with another state. It follows from this proposition that one of the primary functions of any state is to defend successfully its delineated borders from external attack. Conversely, a portion of a state's population can, by violent or peaceful means, secede and create a new state, and consequently change the geographic scope of a state's political authority. This is the most common view of geography held by academics in international relations. In essence geography is one of the bedrocks of international politics, like the board of a chess game.

The second view of territory is that of an environment. This perspective is both natural and historical. It includes 'all the features which specialists in fauna, flora, and climate are in a position to discern'.[1] In addition, there is a historical view of the geographical environment, which constitutes a *longue durée* or a long duration. This perspective was developed by French historian Braudel in his now classic work on the Mediterranean.[2] It was a mechanism he developed to deal with the physical geography of the Mediterranean and the restrictions and the opportunities it offered for human development. In essence, time altered little. This view of geography is both an environment and part of a *longue*

23

durée, it means, to paraphrase Braudel, becoming used to a slower tempo, which sometimes almost borders on the motionless. This approach helps to facilitate a study of men and society through territory.

Finally, geography can be interpreted as a theatre of military action. When geography is perceived in this way important changes take place which distinguish this approach from the previous two. First, it becomes more abstract, simplified and schematised. The flora and fauna no longer have some relevance. The military or naval commander will perceive only those geographical features that are relevant to the objectives that he is trying to achieve. The same could be said of a policy-maker attempting to decide priorities.

This perspective of geography as a theatre of military action has a lineage that goes back to antiquity. Sun Tzu writing in the period 400–320 BC developed a typology by which a general could classify geography according to its utility in battle: 'ground may be classified according to its nature as accessible, entrapping, intrusive, constricted, precipitous, and distant'.[3] This typology of Sun Tzu illustrates well the view of geography as a theatre of military action which has become both simplified and schematised as a consequence of being utilised in this manner. Sun Tzu also outlined how geography was pertinent with respect to the battlefield objectives of the commander:

> Conformation [this phrase can be interpreted as meaning topography of the ground] of the ground is of the greatest assistance in battle. Therefore, to estimate the enemy's situation and to calculate distances and the degree of difficulty of the terrain so as to control victory are virtues of the superior general. He who fights with full knowledge of these factors is certain to win; he who does not will surely be defeated.[4]

There is a modern echo of this in FM100-5. This is the US Army's 'How to Fight' manual. The 1982 edition represents an endorsement of Sun Tzu's approach: 'Terrain forms the natural structure of the battlefield. Early in the planning process, commanders must recognize its limitation and possibilities using it to protect friendly operations by putting the enemy at a disadvantage'.[5] Furthermore, it is argued that the ability to analyse terrain is vital at all levels of command: 'every level of command must study the terrain's limitations and opportunities. Platoon leaders concentrate on wood lines, streams and individual hills in preparing their operations. Corp commanders analyze road nets, rail nets, drainage patterns, and hill systems'.[6]

Having defined the nature of the relationship between geography and international relations, I want to spell out briefly what I mean by geopolitics. It can be suggested that geopolitics can be defined as an attempt to draw attention to certain geographical patterns of political history. It is a theory of spatial relationships and historical causation. From this theory explanations have been deduced which suggest the contemporary and future political relevance of various geographical configurations and concepts. This definition raises the question of levels of analysis. Is geopolitics concerned with a sub-state, state or international perspectives and understanding? One answer to this question has been put forward by the geopolitical theorist Geoffrey Parker, who claims that it is concerned with a global perspective, but can also be used in an examination of geopolitical considerations at the state and sub-state level. It is these perspectives that are the prime focus when analysing the Falklands conflict.

It was Henry Kissinger who once cynically summarised the geopolitical importance of the South Atlantic when he stated that: 'Latin America is a dagger pointing at the heart of Antarctica'. What is not revealed by this statement is any understanding of the patterns and structures of the geopolitical challenges that the defence of the Falklands Islands presented to Britain in the period prior to the conflict, and in the struggle to retain sovereignty of the islands. In the years prior to the conflict Britain was able to count upon, in a strategic sense, a layered system of deterrence. It had three elements. The first element was the naval base at Simonstown in South Africa. This base was 4,000 miles from the Falkland Islands. The South Atlantic squadron based there deployed Cat class and Cathedral class frigates to conduct patrols to the Falkland Islands. These ships were anti-aircraft (AA) frigates that had a range of 7,500 miles at 17 knots. The second element was the naval base in Bermuda. This base was 6,000 miles from the Falkland Islands. The West Indian squadron deployed Bay class frigates to conduct patrols to the Falkland Islands. These ships had a range of 10,000 miles at 10 knots. The final element was a dedicated Ice Patrol Ship. The first was HMS *Protector*. The first patrol was in 1955. She was a steam-powered former net layer that had been in service since 1936. In 1968 she was replaced by HMS *Endurance*. She had a range of 12,000 miles at 14 knots. This geopolitical structure had been emasculated by the time of John Nott's fateful decision in 1981 to scrap our 'minimum tripwire'. The Simonstown base had closed in November 1974 and the West Indies Squadron ceased as an independent command in 1976.

This problem of a non-existent basing structure had to be confronted when Britain decided to re-take the islands by force. The solution was Ascension Island. This island had been last garrisoned in 1922. It had naval repair facilities but, by 1982, they had completely decayed. There were two factors that were critical in its fast build-up and pivotal role. First, the climate was an equable one with average temperatures of 60 °F. Consequently, no special storage facilities were needed for the huge quantities of supplies that passed through the island. They were simply laid out on the side of the runway according to their classification codes. Second, the RN utilised the runway to its maximum capacity by running it like the flight deck of an aircraft carrier with limited time slots for fixed-wing and helicopter operations. This approach explains why Ascension was quickly handling more flights than Chicago's O'Hare airport. It is also important to note that the base on Ascension, being 4,225 statute miles from the UK and 3,750 statute miles from the Falklands, was critical for the Royal Air Force's role in the war. Apart from Operation Blackbuck, the vital elements were strategic and tactical air transport. Given that the un-refuelled maximum radius of action of a Vulcan is 1,400 miles, of a Hercules 1,900 miles and a Nimrod 2,200 miles, in-flight re-fuelling was a critical technology to overcome the challenges of geography that the basing structure presented.

In terms of the amphibious assault itself understanding the geopolitical considerations were critical, I would suggest, to the success of the landings. The key element that Commodore Clapp identified was the careful choice of terrain which would help hide RN ships and channel the enemy's aircraft so that the amphibious task group would have to watch in only one or two directions and so could react more quickly. This positioning was achieved during the landings, so that the direction of attacks came mainly north from Fanning Head running south over the Sussex Mountains. *Intrepid* and *Fearless* were positioned at the north and south ends of San Carlos Water to act as citadels and co-ordinate the anti-air battle. The *Canberra* was positioned in San Carlos just at the point where attacking aircraft would have to bank sharply to the right.

In interpreting the geography of San Carlos as a theatre of military action there are a number of salient points that can be made. The approaches with Cape Dolphin and the two headlands, White Rock and Race Point, allowed the minimal use of radar, thus helping 'silent' pilotage. In the inlet there was kelp, but there were several good beaches, space for Helicopter Landing Sites (HLS), a Harrier pad, fuel, farm and a maintenance area for stores and a medical station. All these facilities, once set up, were protected from counter-attack by being on reverse slopes. The utilisation of sheltered, shallow water (not more than between 20 and 30 feet deep) with high ground was the vital combination in the success of this most difficult of operations. Furthermore, it allowed the RN to play a pivotal role in the overall campaign. It was the US naval theorist Bernard Brodie, writing in 1942, who stated that 'naval operations are important primarily because of their influence on land campaigns... the ability to launch operations against the land should be regarded as the general culmination of the naval art'.

I now want to look at a number of key elements of the land campaign. Sun Tzu stated:

> In order to transcend your environment or to reform your relationship to it, you must situate yourself cleverly with the positions where you find yourself. A direct confrontation with your environment should not be mounted until you are beyond its traps.[7]

The positions, or they can be described as generic geographical concepts, according to Sun Tzu, numbered six: 'smooth, entangled, indecisive, narrow, obstructed and distant'.

I would suggest that the geography of the Falkland Islands imposed on the land battle certain challenges and opportunities. The two fingers of high ground that run on a west–east axis meant that Brigadier Thompson decided to make the main route of attack to the north. This had a number of geographical advantages. First, the main advance would keep to low ground, yet even this route had a number of terrain and climatic factors which were salient. For a start, there were no roads that could be used by wheeled vehicles. The only vehicles that could be used were light armoured vehicles. Consequently, a normal logistical supply over land was impossible and 70 helicopter sorties were required for a 'good fight'. This fundamental problem was overcome by using the one geographical advantage that Britain enjoyed, which was freedom of movement at sea. Port Salvador and Teal Inlet were chosen to be the forward maintenance area of 3 Commando Brigade; the stores would be moved forward by helicopter to the front. The other factors of terrain that are worthy of note are the lack of cover for troops, and geographical features such as 'stone runs'. These were dry rivers comprising stones and boulders up to 700 yards wide. These stone-runs were a serious obstacle to movement. Finally, the moorland hills contained spines of rock that were up to 100 feet high. The climatic factors were also critical. The average wind speed in the Falklands is 17 knots, which compares to the UK average of 4 knots. On mountains such as Mount Harriet the temperatures went as low as $-15\,°F$. With troops being continually wet these factors were a real challenge.

I would contend that the amphibious landings and northern route were a classic example in a geopolitical sense of land and sea commanders, to paraphrase Sun Tzu, situating themselves cleverly with the positions that they found themselves in. The same could not be said of the southern route. Initially, Brigadier Thompson had no intention to attack Darwin and Goose Green. At most he was going to raid it. The attack was imposed by the Task Force Commander Admiral Fieldhouse for political reasons. Consequently, I would suggest that commanders were forced to confront their environment before, as Sun Tzu would say, they were beyond its traps. There are two examples of this. First the decision to put 5 Brigade into the southern route was done against a geographical environment that offered few locations for siting of a forward maintenance area for 5 Brigade. The best that was available was Fitzroy, which had only a small beach and was unusable at high tide. Furthermore, it can be suggested that the Argentinian forces were occupying Mount Harriet. In total there was a force of 550 here. They were able to detect the movements of the two ships Royal Fleet Auxiliary (RFA) *Sir Galahad* and RFA *Sir Tristran* as they were moving stores to Fitzroy.

The second example is the 2nd Battalion of the Parachute Regiment at Darwin Hill. In the morning of 29 May, A Company were moving south past Darwin Pond heading for the gorse-filled re-entrant which was to be their route to the top of Darwin Hill. From the British point of view there is one point to be made and one question to be asked. First, if the Argentinians had taken the most basic precautions of siting night sentries and standing to from shortly before to shortly after first light, A Company could not have escaped into the gorse gully so lightly damaged. The Argentinian position was well sited to devastate an enemy force approaching the way A Company came. Second, how did it happen that this discovery of an Argentinian company on Darwin Hill came, according to one A Company officer: 'as a complete and utter surprise to them'? The answer to that question has been given in Spencer Fitz-Gibbon's book and it is a judgement I would agree with: 'Colonel Jones's plan made no attempt to understand the enemy's defensive structure, or even to identify the vital ground'.[8]

What can be said by way of conclusions? There are three things I want to say that pick up a theme of 'lessons of the future'. First, the Falklands Conflict showed that the geography of warfare at sea has a focus on accessibility and mobility. Relative movement dominates the strategy of the sea. Speed of advance and radius of action are the most important factors in naval strategy. The post-1945 addition has been the impact of radar on the range of target identification and the range of fire. The sustainability depends on land support and bases. Second, in terms of the geography of land warfare there are two different kinds of land strategies: single movements by a single force and multiple movements by divided forces. The single movements may be conducted as a direct assault along a front, a penetration or a flank attack. The multiple movements may be in the form of a diversionary action, convergent attack including envelopment or co-ordinated attack along a front. The final point is that a geopolitical analysis has to be integrated with the other elements of strategy. This synthesis has been articulated by Etzel Pearcy in one of the forgotten classics of geopolitical literature – *Military Geography*. In this book he argued:

> the record shows that the outcomes of many battles are decided as much by the loser's errors as the winner's astuteness. In that process geographical factors often have, in one way or another, a multiplying effect on a military operation. The continuing problem is that no one can precisely predict how the environment will influence the progress or outcome of the next battle. All one can be sure of is that in some way they will be formidable. Then, as unknowns appear, and multiply, training, leadership, intelligence and innovation become increasingly important.[9]

What a geopolitical analysis can do is to provide both the commander and policy-maker with both a description and hopefully a prescription of how the geographical environment can shape military and political outcomes. In short, whilst the geographical environment does not define the choices of commanders and policy-makers, it none the less provides an important, if not crucial, conditioning influence. As Sir Halford Mackinder would have put it: 'man and not nature initiates, but nature in large measure controls'.[10]

NOTES

1. R. Aron, *Peace and War: A Theory of International Relations* (London: Weidenfeld, 1966), p. 182.
2. F. Braudel, *The Mediterranean and the Mediterranean World in the Age of Philip II*, rev. edn, trans. S. Reynolds (London: Collins 1972).
3. Sun Tzu, *The Art of War*, trans. S.D. Griffith (Oxford: 1963), ch. 10, verse I, 1971, pp. 127–8.
4. Ibid.
5. *Field Manual 100-5* (Washington, DC: Headquarters Department of the Army, 1982), Chapter 3, p. 2.
6. Ibid.
7. R.L. Wings, *The Art of Strategy, a Translation of Sun Tzu's Art of War* (New York: Doubleday, 1988), p. 126.
8. S. Fitzgibbon, *Not Mentioned in Despatches* (Cambridge: Lutterworth Press, 1995), p. 70.
9. G. Etzel Pearcy and L.C. Peltier, *Military Geography* (New York: Van Nostrand, 1966), p. 53.
10. Sir H. Mackinder, 'The Geographical Pivot of History', *Geographical Journal*, 4/23, (April 1904), p. 437.

3

British High Command during and after the Falklands Campaign

VICE ADMIRAL SIR JONATHON BAND

This chapter is intended to give both a personal perspective of how the British high command worked during the Falklands Campaign – an area on which little has been written since[1] – and an explanation of how joint command has evolved since, informed as it has been by changes in the world order and campaigns such as the Gulf War, to the system we currently have. I also end with some issues Sir John Fieldhouse, the Task Force Commander, thought important and how today's Chief of Joint Operations (CJO) might add to the list.

In 1982, as a junior lieutenant commander, post-warfare appointment and small ship command, I was Admiral Sir John Fieldhouse' s flag lieutenant and naval assistant. By the time the campaign started, I had worked for him for nearly a year. I had his confidence and he used me very much as his operational pincushion. I cannot say he involved me in every single deliberation but I believe I was cognisant of the majority and discussed elements of all the major moves with him. I certainly believe I understood the rationale behind his major decisions and judgements.

THE COMMAND SYSTEM INHERITED BY ADMIRAL FIELDHOUSE

Although both the Second World War and the 1950s and 1960s had seen the employment of joint commanders, and indeed a global system had been put in place by Mountbatten when he was Chief of the Defence Staff (CDS) (1959–64), the 1970s heralded the start of a bleak period for jointery. As Britain was withdrawing its forces from the empire to focus predominately on NATO tasks, the joint commanders became redundant and command and control (C2) became subsumed within NATO. Indeed, by 1982, with the exception of a few small garrisons, Britain's forces were all committed to domestically based single service command structures and combined NATO commands. British forces' focus and force structure were directed towards the priority of combined regional scenarios, something very much reinforced by the 1981 Defence Review. For the RN this saw us concentrating on ASW in the North Atlantic and drawing down on surface capital ships, with HMS *Invincible* to be sold to Australia and the remaining amphibious shipping to payoff. This review also questioned the need for the Joint Services Staff College and Joint Warfare School and announced the closure of both. It was envisaged that non-NATO contingencies would be dealt with by whichever single service Headquarters (HQ) appeared most appropriate, utilising forces that were normally assigned to NATO and with the assumption that such operations would be either combined or small-scale. Who would have envisaged a national-only deployment of 67 warships, 45 merchant ships, a significant number of Royal Air Force (RAF) units and a landing force of 10,000? One recent change in responsibilities was, however, of note. Admiral of the Fleet Lord Lewin, frustrated by being the CDS in name only and limited by his need to act on behalf of the chiefs of staff (CoS), became the government's senior military adviser. He was no longer constrained by his chairmanship of the CoS committee. The CDS, as an individual and not speaking for the CoS collectively, now acted as the primary link between the grand strategic and military strategic level. This change, which came into effect in January 1982, was to be put to good use in the subsequent campaign.

CAMPAIGN COMMAND AND CONTROL

This, therefore, was the higher command background to the situation in which the UK's armed forces found themselves in March and April 1982. Admiral Fieldhouse considered that he had a good basis for a HQ to command the operations envisaged. The sea and air nature of operations required to meet the anti-submarine challenge in the North Atlantic meant that fleet command and that of 18 group of the RAF, under Air Marshal Curtis, was co-located and the relationship between the organisations was working. Flag Officer submarines (Vice Admiral Herbert) was already in the Commander-in-Chief Fleet's HQ at Northwood alongside the CoS to the Commander-in-Chief Fleet, Vice Admiral Halifax. Admiral Fieldhouse asked for the CoS to the commandant-general Royal Marines (RM), Major General Moore to act as his land adviser and

31

commander. He therefore believed that he had the essence of a joint HQ in terms of the components to meet the needs of a predominately maritime campaign. Realising early that logistics was going to have a huge part to play, he set up a tri-service logistics cell and he demanded a special forces cell so that their activities could be co-ordinated. I think it is fair to say that he saw the need for components as driven by the requirement for co-ordination as much as command. He did not see the need for an overall commander in theatre in addition to him back at Northwood, hence the basis for some of the muddle between Rear Admiral Sandy Woodward, Brigadier Julian Thompson and the Commodore of the Amphibious Task Group, Captain Michael Clapp. He saw them as tactical commanders whose roles would be driven naturally by the phases of the campaign. Woodward would get them there and protect them; Clapp would land them and Thompson would fight them to Port Stanley. Woodward as the admiral and most senior would be the *primus inter pares*. Admiral Fieldhouse saw himself as the commander of all the task groups deployed. The issue of the relationship between the tactical commands would have been settled had the task organisation made it clear that Woodward was what we would term now the joint force commander.

It is easy to be an expert after the event and hindsight, we know, is a marvellous tool but I think he created a rather impressive joint HQ. The augmentation around the normal fleet operations/warfare/communications/logistics teams worked well. The plans function was met by the Maritime Tactical School (now the Maritime Warfare Centre (MWC)) and was probably the weakest internal arrangement because they were not on site continuously. As the use of air power and the numbers of aircraft types increased there was pressure for RAF Strike Command to take over all but the embarked air aspects. This would have been quite wrong and was resisted. Strike Command correctly became the 'supporting' and Fleet the 'supported' in current parlance with additional staff joining 18 group and the air deputy.

Likewise, when the size of the landing force was increased to two brigades and it was decided that General Moore would deploy as the land force commander, General Officer Commanding, Southern District, Lieutenant General Trant seamlessly became the land deputy. Again, and as with the air staff, room was tight but co-location and proper staff working was achieved.

Where I think the elements of higher command could have been more robust were the linkages within the MoD, with the campaign occurring as it did before the 1984 organisational reforms of Michael Heseltine, Secretary of State for Defence, the single service staffs dominated activity in the MoD. This led to less than ideal levels of co-ordination between the services but we were spared the micro-management, which became a feature of the Gulf War eight years later.

The aim of the campaign was clear from the very start, namely 'to bring about the withdrawal of Argentinian forces from the Falkland Islands and their dependencies and to re-establish the British administration as quickly as possible'. And the military mission in support was to 'conduct military deployments and order operations in support'. All activity could be related to this aim and mission. Indeed, all specific direction applied by London or the Commander-in-Chief (C-in-C) was covered by this aim and mission, including the instruction to sail early, to retake South Georgia and to move out of the beachhead.

My overall assessment is that the UK C2 worked pretty well, and particularly so, given that the campaign being prosecuted had a scale of operation and logistic complexity not expected. It required improvisation of extant command arrangements and tactical doctrine and working to narrow margins. In this situation the influence of quality, the flexibility of the employment of forces and the responsiveness of C2 were fundamental.

Despite what I said about some of the staff working in the MoD, the grand strategic/military strategic/operational level links were good, with a clear chain of command. The relationships between Mrs Thatcher, Admiral of the Fleet Lewin and Admiral Fieldhouse were well defined, pursued with mutual sympathy and based on professional respect. They had frequent personal contact. One must not forget the role of Admiral Leech, who in a way acted as a supporting commander, galvanising the naval staff in London and acting decisively as CoS. Obviously there were times when the competing demands of diplomacy and military progress led to strong debate and compromise but on all occasions the issues concerned were fairly and squarely put on the table and never once was Admiral Fieldhouse overruled. He was too wise to let himself get into that position. Indeed, his overall concern was always to keep the pressure on, both diplomatically and militarily. His greatest fear was the campaign stalling and our forces being held up in the grip of a full South Atlantic winter.

At Northwood the command system worked well. The Commander-in-Chief generated a marvellous spirit in the staff. He bound the command group together and made them work as a team. This was made easier by their normal peacetime interactions. The personal characteristics of the overall commander in these circumstances were absolutely vital. Fieldhouse was polite, calm, purposeful, innovative and courageous. He always had time for the lesser people (the briefer and the cleaner). He was inclusive in his dealings with staff. There was always room for humour. No one doubted that if he was allowed to do what he thought best and we maintained the initiative the task group would triumph.

33

Out in the front line the C2 arrangements were more at risk. The pressure on the commanders was intense. The distance from the UK, the often foul weather, the narrow margins they were working to, the military challenges they faced and the fragility of communications all added to the high octane of personality and, it has to be said, the underlying fault-lines in the task group organisation. If the tactical level commanders had had the opportunity to meet together more often (only achieved twice, one at Ascension Island when the campaign plan and timings were agreed and once prior to the landing), some of the issues would have been resolved. It is quite clear now that what was needed was an overall joint force commander in theatre to share the load with the joint commander back in the United Kingdom, to provide top cover for the other tactical commanders and also to ensure that the phases of the campaign were executed as planned and that the command relationships were in place to support those phases. But I think one must recognise that, even if there had been one, the communications technology of the day and the characteristics of the campaign would have demanded a close tactical level as well as operational level perspective for Northwood and the C-in-C.

JOINT COMMAND IN THE POST-FALKLANDS PERIOD

What developments were made as a result of the experience of the Falklands campaign? First, the issue of HQ was raised. Should one be permanently designated for such operations? No was the answer but Northwood and RAF High Wycombe were designated as the formal options and given communications enhancements. Wilton, Land Command HQ, had insufficient C2 capabilities to be considered a sensible option. The British armed forces at this stage still wanted flexibility or, put more cynically, were not ready for the fully joint approach. However, to be fairer, and despite the Falklands experience, it was the extant Cold War mind-set and NATO command arrangements that was still largely driving the strategic view. Apart from the required flexibility in HQ, the system also wanted to be able to choose the C-in-C in light of the prevailing circumstances. Indeed, I remember Admiral Fieldhouse as the CDS saying he wanted the flexibility to choose the C-in-C for any future joint campaign/operation. Even today with a CJO and the Permanent Joint Headquarters (PJHQ), it remains possible for the CDS to recommend to the Secretary of State for Defence that one of the three C-in-C is appointed as the joint commander. As I mentioned earlier, the Defence Review of 1981 questioned the need for both the Joint Services Staff College and the Joint Warfare School. The former became the Joint Services Defence College at Greenwich whilst the latter set itself up at Poole, and the UKCICC (O) Committee was tasked to provide a cadre planning focus for future out of area (OOA) contingencies and operations. In addition, all three services made plans to provide away teams and individuals to act as environmental deputies, and the basis of a Joint Force Headquarters (JFHQ) was worked out. The subject of developments of joint doctrine since the Falklands is the subject of another chapter in this book. However, it is clear that the development of what we now recognise as modern joint doctrine started following the Falklands Conflict.

THE GULF WAR

I now move on to discuss aspects of the C2 in the Gulf campaign to see what had been learnt from the Falklands, what was relevant from that experience and what it told us about the future arrangements we would need. As a result of Falklands experience our standing procedures for OOA operations envisaged a controlling four star joint HQ with a two star JFHQ deployed to theatre to exercise tactical control. In peacetime this HQ was maintained in skeleton form at Aldershot under General Officer Commanding, South-Eastern District. These procedures had been regularly practised in a rolling programme of major command post and field exercises. At the beginning of the Gulf crisis, however, it was not clear that a joint UK force would be required. Indeed, the need even for a four star joint HQ was a matter of debate. There were those in the MoD who thought that the joint operations centre in the main building, under the CDS's direction, should run the British contribution and deal direct with the C-in-C of the US Central Command (CENTCOM) on all matters, leaving RAF High Wycombe, which had the initial lead because of the air deployments, to implement deployment and logistic support plans drawn up in the MoD. This would have departed from the well proven chain of command for OOA operations running from the CDS to a four-star C-in-C as the joint commander in the United Kingdom and then to a joint force commander in theatre, simply because it failed to match fully the US command arrangements. Why were some in the MoD thinking like this? Well, of course, the Heseltine changes had taken place in 1984–5. These had created the post of Vice-Chief of the Defence Staff and four departments each with its own staff under a Deputy Chief of the Defence Staff: Personnel, Systems, Commitments and Strategy and Policy. The reforms served to modernise the crisis management organisation and strengthened significantly the power of the centre. Fortunately, during the Gulf crisis the CDS, Marshal of the Air Force Sir David Craig, was persuaded to retain the normal UK command arrangements. If he had not it would have meant divorcing the responsibility for the operational employment of our forces from their deployment and logistic support. Keeping these together is a vital precept of effective command. The MoD's role is to provide the higher political and military direction for the conduct of the war. It is not to command the forces and to fight the battle. The debate over, the joint commander was given operational command of all British forces involved. That decision taken, High Wycombe could and did become a truly purple four star JFHQs with the enhanced facilities provided as a result of the Falklands experience. Land and naval deputies were appointed and the away teams quickly integrated with their light blue colleagues under the Joint Commander's airforce CoS. The JFHQs, although activated, was not deployed initially, although an air force two star was deployed promptly. Once, however, the decision was made to commit UK ground forces, deployment occurred at the same time as General Sir Peter de la Billiere became commander British forces.

This is not the occasion to dwell on the detail of the C2 workings during the Gulf campaign itself or to make objective comparisons with the Falklands. They were after all quite different with the former being a national, go-it-alone operation and the latter a full blown coalition operation with the United States clearly in the lead. However, some broad observations are pertinent. I don't believe the Prime Minister/Secretary of State/CDS/Force Commander relationship during the Gulf War was as strong as it was in the Falklands. The strong centre in the later campaign, whilst allowing the MoD to act collectively in a much more co-ordinated manner, did lead to significant pressure on the joint commander and a level of questioning and back-seat driving which infuriated him. The Falklands campaign was conducted with little joint doctrine to support it. The Gulf campaign, too, had little UK-understood coalition doctrine to underpin it. Both campaigns were conducted at range but the Gulf had a long force generation phase. These operations had the advantage of long passage times to allow teams to settle but presented significant logistic challenges.

POST-GULF

So how was it after the success of these two campaigns that the flexibility provided by two HQ and three commanders-in-chief was judged not to be appropriate for the future? Well, it was the defence cost study in 1994 that provided the catalyst. All ideas that appeared to provide a better support solution for the same or fewer resources were given visibility. Studies of the functions of the MoD and the single service HQ, characteristics of the new world order post the cold war, and the operational lessons from the Gulf crisis all pointed towards the creation of a PJHQ. This was seen by many, particularly in the army and the airforce, to be too radical and a dangerous solution that potentially went to the heart of single service strengths and capabilities. But it had a certain political resonance and so was taken forward. General Wilcocks carried out a feasibility study and General Wallace implemented it. Now six years later and in the time of the third Commander Joint Operations it is hard to imagine why the concept did not gain acceptance more readily. How we thought we would have commanded and managed the range of operations we have embarked upon these last few years under the old structure is hard to imagine. What of course was envisaged was that at some stage the PJHQ and supporting commands would be co-located. This, of course, is yet to happen.

A COMMANDER'S NEEDS

In preparing this paper I have consulted senior officers who served at Northwood, High Wycombe and in the MoD during the Falklands and Gulf campaigns and all three Commanders of Joint Operations we have had. I did this to check my research, knowledge and memory but also to determine what enduring elements there were to operational level command. I knew well what Admiral Fieldhouse thought important at the time of the Falklands and what the Falklands taught him, namely:

- Educate and train your command teams – prepare for the unexpected.
- Insist on clear political intent and translate that into clear command intent.
- Beware of domestic factors.
- Know what the end state is.
- Realise that deployable C2 and lift are key enablers – logistics is often the Achilles heel.
- Put together a red team to think like the enemy – know the theatre, the environment and be known to mean business.

A Commander of Joint Operations twenty years later would probably add:

- Mission command means delegation and trust.
- Plan on multi-nationality – it is the norm and brings useful capabilities.

- Coalition operations will be slower, harder and frustrating.
- Protection of one's own centre of gravity is likely to be seen at times as more important by politicians than attacking the enemy's.
- Information management will be one of the greatest challenges.
- Train for war, prepare for peace support operations (PSO).
- Host nation support will be crucial and hard to come by.
- Targeting requires immense preparation, detailed data, broad bandwidth and advanced agreement on measures of effectiveness.
- And finally once in theatre start planning how to 'draw down' and 'get out'.

CONCLUSION

Providing that the UK's higher command arrangements continue to meet these generic commander's requirements and needs, then our campaigns should continue to be satisfactorily executed. The set-up for Admiral Fieldhouse, which broadly met the needs of that day, was further developed prior to and during the Gulf campaign and provided the basis for the creation of the PJHQ of today in support of an expeditionary strategy which of course was what was asked of Admiral Fieldhouse in the Falklands campaign.

NOTE

1. I am, however, indebted to a paper written by Stephen Prince of the Royal Naval Historical Branch, since published as Stephen Prince, 'British Command and Control in the Falklands Campaign', *Defence and Security Analysis*, 18/4 (December 2002).

4

The Falklands Conflict as a Media War

STEPHEN BADSEY

THE MEDIA, HISTORY AND MEMORY

Any consideration of the Falklands Conflict in history is compelled to start with the perhaps *jejune* observation that history is itself a dynamic activity. All those who experienced the conflict have their own unique memories of the events; and for those who made political or military-strategic decisions outside the immediate theatre of conflict, and especially for those who took part in the fighting, these personal memories are often particularly vivid, shaping both later perspectives and assessments. But even for such partici-pants, the media at the time provided an important part of their experience. More generally, for all those who considered themselves at the time to be in any way involved in the conflict, the media record provided a framework for memory. While the battles of the Falklands Conflict were being fought by sea, air and land, simultaneously (and in many cases perhaps largely unconsciously) a battle for the history of the conflict was being fought out through its media portrayal. After 20 years, that media record still affects the way in which the Falklands Conflict as history is approached.

This process began with the first radio or television announcements on 2 April, and their impact on the political leadership. Margaret Thatcher's own memoirs acknowledge this, stipulating that it was the position of the London newspapers that confirmed Lord Carrington's decision to resign as Foreign Secretary on 6 April, 'having seen Monday's press, in particu-lar the *Times* leader, he decided that he must go'.[1] Throughout the con-flict, the daily business of the interaction between the media, the wider population, and the political leadership never ceased. On 4 April, British newspapers carried photographs of the RM' surrender at Port Stanley, taken by Simon Winchester of the *Sunday Times* and smuggled out by Tony Hunt, son of Governor Rex Hunt. Next day, 5 April, the very public departure of ships of the Task Force began from Portsmouth and Southampton, the media coverage reflecting an important part of British diplomacy in this critical period. There were the MoD press conferences, remembered mostly for the slow, deliberate tones of spokesman Ian McDonald. There was the televised scene of John Nott standing with Margaret Thatcher outside 10 Downing Street on Sunday 25 April to announce the recapture of South Georgia, followed by her exhortation to 'rejoice at that news'. This was an episode that, as Nott has recorded in his memoirs, 'was to dog me on television for the next twenty years', his principal concern being the 'appalling spiv's suit' that he was wearing, made for him by a constituent.[2]

One media moment in particular has entered the history both of warfare and of journalism. On Saturday 1 May, Brian Hanrahan reported by radio for the British Broadcasting Corporation (BBC) from HMS *Hermes*, in partial response to Argentinian claims of British losses. After consultation with Admiral Woodward, Hanrahan reported that 'I'm not allowed to say how many planes joined the raid, but I counted them all out, and I counted them all back'.[3] Alan Protheroe, then Assistant Director General of the BBC, commented that:

> Brian Hanrahan found a memorable phrase to assure anxious listeners of the safe return of the Harriers to HMS *Hermes* after their first attacks on the landing strip of Port Stanley. They were words that echoed around the world, widely quoted as a statement of plain truth. Truth is the only counter to propaganda.[4]

Rival Independent Television News (ITN) reporter Michael Nicholson, who was also on board HMS *Hermes* with Hanrahan and who attributes the origins of the phrase to Lieutenant Commander Rupert Nicol, ruefully records in his own memoirs that 'when I die I expect my epitaph (scratched in cement) to read: 'Here lies the man who did not count them out. Nor even did he bother to count them back.'[5]

An episode that is famous for different reasons came on 4 May, when the sinking of the *General Belgrano* prompted the controversial headline in the *Sun* newspaper – 'GOTCHA!' There was a brief but savage political storm over BBC editorial policy, including a programme from the television current affairs magazine programme *Panorama* on 10 May, claimed to be unpatriotic or, in a choice phrase of the time, 'unacceptably even handed'.[6] There were Robert Fox's remarkable reports for BBC Radio News describing the Battle of Darwin–Goose Green. Finally, there was another front page on 15 June, when the

Evening Standard announced its reporter Max Hastings as the first man from the Task Force to enter Port Stanley at the end of the fighting.

War reporting has been proverbially described as the first draft of history, and like all first drafts it carries the expectation that it will later be corrected and improved. That *Sun* headline appeared only briefly in the newspaper's first edition, reaching northern England, Scotland and Northern Ireland; it was almost unseen in London.[7] Max Hastings has acknowledged that the photograph that accompanied the *Evening Standard* headline was taken not at Port Stanley but three weeks earlier at San Carlos.[8] There is no photograph or film, and no firsthand journalist's report, of the negotiations leading to the Argentinian capitulation. Journalists were excluded on British orders, and according to some sources by Argentinian request since, after a photograph of the surrender at South Georgia had gone round the world, both sides were anxious to avoid a repetition of such a dramatic image. Even so, if reports are accurate, the BBC's broadcast next morning in London of the war's end was heard by Prime Minister Thatcher before she had been notified through official channels.[9] Memory also plays tricks. As in many other wars, even participants in the events refer to media episodes as they have remembered them, rather than as the record shows they took place. Like the legend of Polish cavalry charges against tanks in 1939, the repeated belief that copy from the Falklands took longer to reach London than in the Crimean War appears to have been based on one isolated incident.

An entire mythology has grown around some of the more controversial media episodes; most notably a BBC World Service broadcast on 26 May that British troops were advancing on Goose Green, on which conflicting memories and statements have themselves become part of the historical record. It is particularly notable that Margaret Thatcher's memoirs attribute the leaking of this information to the BBC and other news sources to the MoD, stating that 'Too much talk was giving the Argentinians warning of what we intended, though the fault did not always lie with the media themselves but also with the media management at the MoD.'[10] In contrast, John Nott as Secretary for Defence in 1982 writes in *his* memoirs that:

> Although it was obvious to the world that British forces were about to move forward, we were shocked at the MoD to read in the newspapers that our troops were about to attack Goose Green. It was a classic case of why we had tried to keep the No. 10 briefing machine as much in the dark as possible. The obsession with unattributable background briefing – which today goes by the name of spin – remains the curse of politics.[11]

Investigations into the appearance of this story in British newspapers and on the BBC World Service have emphasised the prevalence of such speculation at the time and generally absolved the media themselves of blame. Members of the British armed forces, however, especially those who served in the Falklands, continue to feel understandable resentment towards the media over this issue.[12]

THE FALKLANDS IN MEDIA WAR HISTORY

Before attempting to answer the question as to how far the Falklands Conflict may be described as a media war, it is clearly important to recognise the meaning of the term itself when applied to such a conflict. Strictly, the use of the term 'media war' in the context of the Falklands is an anachronism. 'Media war' was an expression invented shortly after the 1991 Gulf War to describe the manner in which the news media in all forms, national, international, under direct government control or not, interact with the political and military circumstances of the war.[13] This was at first believed to be describing a new phenomenon caused by changes in media technology, and particularly global real-time television broadcasts; often, if not very accurately, called the 'CNN Effect'. It has also been argued that a twentieth-century 'modern' era of war reporting in which journalists were incorporated into the armed forces was succeeded by a 'late modern' era including the Falklands in which they were notionally independent but subject to manipulation and control, and now by a 'post-modern' era in which having achieved technological independence they are instead 'courted' by the armed forces.[14] In this formulation, the control exercised by armed forces over the media came from their command of communications and transport; and the establishment of global civilian commercial communications has radically changed this relationship.

Given the present military preoccupation with the impact of technology and the Revolution in Military Affairs (RMA) debate, it is important that the Falklands Conflict fell close to the start of the major developments in computer and information technology that have since transformed both military and media communications. In 1975 Microsoft was founded, followed in 1981 by the appearance of IBM's first commercial personal computer or PC, then the launch of the Apple Macintosh and, in 1983, the experimental link between five university supercomputers that became the Internet. The Falklands was in journalists' terms 'the first British war of the photocopier age' and also almost the last war before high-resolution television computer graphics.[15] The Falklands also fell near the start of a process of institutional convergence between the various media that is still continuing, marked in Britain by the purchase by News International of Times Newspapers in 1981 and what became Sky Television in 1983. Cable News Network (CNN), four years old in 1982, was still virtually unknown, and in Britain the fourth terrestrial channel – Channel Four – began broadcasts that year. The BBC still retained its dominance both as a production house and as a national institution; and the changes that, for insiders, would utterly transform it had only just begun. The Falklands played its part in those changes, which is itself an interesting example of war impacting on the media rather than the other way around. Even so, the BBC has remained a unique British institution particularly in times of war, and parallels have been drawn between its confrontations with the government in 1982 over the Falklands, and those with governments over Kosovo in 1999 as well as over Suez in 1956. Veteran BBC news editor John Simpson has argued that 'when British governments have their backs to the wall', to attack the British media is 'a knee-jerk reaction' on their part.[16]

The manner in which print journalism in Britain responded to the Falklands marked an episode in an equally clearly defined historical transition. Daily newspapers had, for more than a decade, faced inevitable defeat in their competition with television to report news as swiftly. By 1982 they were visibly reverting to their much older functions of political communication, editorialising, advertising and entertainment. The editorial policies of the *Sun* in particular during the Falklands Conflict, which at the time evoked some strong responses and may have actually led to a fall in circulation, pointed towards the 'Red Top' tabloid newspaper style that is now prevalent. Both the clash between the government and the BBC, and the clash between the BBC and the *Sun*, examined at the time in immediate cultural and institutional terms, were also symptomatic of these much larger trends.

As with all wars the Falklands had its own rare or unique features regarding the media; but while no one would deny the impact of technology on reporting or warfare, repeated statements that these features will *never* re-occur may be treated with caution. Historical research over the last 20 years has instead confirmed what might have been guessed: that all wars have been media wars, and the interactions proclaimed as post-modern may be clearly seen in the emergence of industrialised communications, mass society and politics, and the mass media in the mid-nineteenth century. Despite rival mythologies, there has never been a golden age of war reporting in which journalists were institutionally free to write what they liked and to bring down governments at war; nor a golden age in which patriotic reporters and newspapers knew their place and obeyed military orders unquestioningly. The most successful military commanders have been those who, whatever their personal preferences, have understood the media at war and their own relationship with it.

In this respect, the Falklands Conflict was a very traditional media war. It featured the same issues and problems – and even the same errors – as the South African War of 1899–1902 and also NATO's media war over Kosovo in 1999. There are several possible explanations for these re-occurrences, of which the most plausible is that (and despite the subtitle of this particular book) these are not 'lessons to be learned' or even problems to be solved, but rather part of the much wider process and context in which warfare takes place, coupled with the extremely short institutional memory that both the media and the armed forces possess. In this as in many other respects, the short duration and self-contained nature of the Falklands Conflict have made it a valuable and frequently used case study, demonstrating several re-occurring issues regarding media war which are seldom addressed in classical military thought.

The Falklands has been described as 'an almost textbook example of a limited war', a term well understood in military circles.[17] In twentieth-century wars of survival, unusual restrictions and demands were imposed on the media in Britain, including a patriotic duty of support; although even in the First World War *The Times* distinguished between its 'task . . . to sustain the morale of the nation' and 'fair criticism of the government of the day'.[18] As originally conceived in the 1950s, limited war theory made almost no mention of such matters, until the Vietnam War demonstrated once again that popular support was an important factor. Since then, the issue has been very much where the boundaries of government and military policy towards the media lie when national survival is not at stake, and how far political or even service interests may equate to national interests. The Falklands was an important early example of the disputes resulting from this issue, particularly in its opening phase when few of those in London or with the Task Force, including journalists, believed that a major war would take place. The debate within the news media themselves concerning independence and impartiality against patriotism and military security was also nothing new.

At present, the term 'media war' is repeatedly confused with the propaganda war, which is quite a different phenomenon. The relationship between political and military deception, government propaganda produced by both sides, and the role of the national and international media is a complex one, and unlike the media war this has been very little studied in the case of the Falklands. The best-known example is Sir Frank Cooper's decision as Permanent Secretary at the MoD to mislead a confidential journalists' briefing on the evening before the San Carlos landings of 21 May; an action which Cooper considered was entirely justified. Admiral Sir Terrence Lewin as CDS also later confirmed that he had sanctioned the use of the media in deception operations.[19] By their nature, deception and what present doctrine calls psychological operations (Psyops) are sensitive and secretive subjects; whereas by definition the media coverage of any war exists from the start in the public domain, although the thinking and institutional structure under-pinning it may not be at first apparent, and often only emerges after considerable historical research.

The Falklands Conflict not only features heavily in the wider litera-ture of the military–media relationship, it is also one of the few modern wars in which media issues are virtually always mentioned, reflecting the degree of controversy raised. In its immediate aftermath it was argued particularly in the United States that there was nothing to learn from the Falklands, in the sense that the experience and conduct of the war reaf-firmed lessons that were already very well known. But this was emphat-ically not the case in respect of the media war, particularly its wider cultural and institutional issues. Several accounts quote the MoD pamphlet given to British reporters with the Task Force as opening, 'The essence of successful warfare is secrecy. The essence of successful journalism is publicity'; a pamphlet reportedly prepared for the 1956 Suez operation. Historical research has now traced this phrase back to what appears to be its point of origin. It was invented by a United States Public Information Officer for the 'Torch' landings of November 1942 in North Africa and was well out of date at the time of the Falklands.[20] In fact, the media lesson of Suez was quite different, and intimately linked to its wider political aspects: as the British commander on Operation Musketeer wrote, 'The one overriding lesson of the Suez operations is that World opinion is now an absolute principle of war and must be treated as such.'[21] Given the rarity of expeditionary operations and the preoccupations of doctrine since 1956 it would be anachronistic to argue that this should have been recognised in 1982. But beyond doubt an awareness of the media and its role by members of the armed forces and within the British defence establishment that was not there during the Falklands Conflict has emerged over the following decades.

WAR REPORTERS IN THE FALKLANDS CONFLICT

The experience of the British media in the Falklands is very well documented, including commentary from a number of journalists (most notably Robert Fox's account *Eyewitness Falklands*) and other participants.[22] Indeed one value of journalists' memoirs is the often colourful pen-portraits they provide of their colleagues. Four British journalists including Simon Winchester of *The Times* were present in Port Stanley for the Argentinian landings. Initial British plans for the Task Force included no provision for the media; but after protests and lobbying 29 British representatives sailed, including one camera team shared between the BBC and ITN, and one radio reporter each. No overseas reporters were permitted with any British units, the foreign press being served by the single Reuters representative. The reporters were accompanied by civilian public relations officers – habitually called 'minders'. Despite the often vitriolic criticism aimed at the minders from all sides, theirs remains one of the largely untold stories of the media side of the Falklands together with those of the uniformed service cameramen and photographers, who took some of the most memorable records, and the unit press officers. Once the Task Force entered the South Atlantic, transmission of newspaper copy depended on the use of a shipboard commercial satellite system known as Marisat. Television film (in fact, ENG video cassette tapes) had to be physically transported back to Ascension Island before being transmitted by satellite. Once the reporters joined the landing forces ashore, newspaper copy also had to be physically taken back to the ships for transmission. Film and radio broadcasts were shared between the BBC and ITN, while written reports were 'pooled' in the sense that they were syndicated rather than exclusive to one newspaper. Once in the war zone reporters came under formal military discipline, although no escort officers accompanied them and throughout they were subject to 'prior security review', widely called censorship. In this case reports were checked in theatre and then again in London before release.

The conventions of British prior security review had their origins in the First World War censorship practice and it was always acknowledged that they required good will and mutual understanding to function properly. But in 1982, as all involved later often ruefully acknowledged, suspicion and antagonism extended from the highest levels of the MoD and the media institutions downwards, and was particularly marked within the Task Force. There was reciprocal willingness to find fault with each other, to suspect each other's motives and integrity, and to regard each other as an unwelcome intrusion into one's own important job. This did not apply to all reporters and all units, but in the climate of suspicion even a good working relationship became suspect. Several accounts contain suggestions or overt claims of favouritism or abuse in order to promote a particular institution or branch of service, or even in self-aggrandisement. To judge from recent memoirs, there is still no meeting of minds on these issues. Particularly, no media aspect of the Falklands caused greater friction than the access of reporters to service communications, and also the failure to provide real-time television transmission facilities. Technical arguments that insecure media communications posed an unacceptable risk, and that at the very best poor quality monochrome pictures might have been achievable, have been met with a conviction that the underlying problem was a lack of political will.

It has been suggested that the long ranges and practical difficulties involved in filming naval and air warfare, the land fighting taking place mostly at night, and the lack of real-time television transmission all combined to make this unusually a print and radio journalist's war.[23] Certainly one unusual feature of the Falklands was that delays involved in getting television film back to Britain meant that the film's arrival itself became a news event. Interviews with survivors of HMS *Sheffield*, hit on 4 May, were aired on British television on 26 May, and BBC cameraman Brian Hesketh's film of the abandoned destroyer, filmed on 7 May, the day before it sank, was aired on 28 May while the Battle of Darwin–Goose Green was being fought. Again, what appeared as specific reporting issues raised by these delays may also be seen as part of a much larger trend. It was the Vietnam War that saw the clear emergence of advocacy journalism, later called the 'journalism of attachment', and in fact itself a revival of nineteenth-century practices whereby journalists recorded their personal emotions and impressions in response to a war, rather than straight factual reporting.[24] In the Falklands the nature of the fighting, the restrictions placed on journalists, and their own uncertainties about what to make public, all contributed to the wider use of this style, of which the military themselves were frequently highly critical. This trend has continued in subsequent wars, paradoxically fuelled by military attempts to restrict and control reporting and by the difficulties reporters face in gaining access. The Falklands throws a valuable perspective on later and more recent controversies about the journalism of attachment, notably those that accompanied the disintegration of the former Yugoslavia in 1991–9.

These difficulties in providing hard news from the war zone in the Falklands also gave much greater prominence to the story from London, including formal press conferences, informal briefings, the use of unattributable sources, and the use of recently retired officers as background 'briefers' or commentators, all of which also raised their own particular problems. According to one thorough analysis, 72 British television interviews with military pundits were shown during the Falklands Conflict, plus 9 with academic scholars, together a larger total than the 74 interviews with Conservative politicians shown.[25] These circumstances also placed considerable strain on the political leadership, the loss of HMS *Coventry* on 25 May placing the MoD in what Sir John Nott has described 'as a very unfortunate but not untypical dilemma' regarding its announcement.[26] The restrictions on hard news also inevitably gave a greater importance to editorialising and commentary, in both television and newspapers, which again fuelled controversy and dispute. One feature of the Falklands that has also occurred in other wars was that reporters with the Task Force were sometimes blamed or held personally responsible for editorialising or reporting from London over which they had no control: a very characteristic military reflex. A further consequence was that the British media were obliged to take news from Argentina. The BBC retained a presence throughout the conflict, bringing ENG cassettes into Uruguay for satellite transmission, and taking Argentinian images. Three British journalists, including Simon Winchester, were arrested for alleged spying in Rio Grande on 13 April and one was kidnapped in Buenos Aires, although rapidly released. It is a traditionally strong argument in Britain against government refusals to release news in wartime that this plays into the hands of a superior enemy propaganda machine, and this claim appeared once more during the Falklands Conflict. At the time, almost any aspect of Argentinian media coverage was dismissed in Britain as government-directed propaganda, although some studies of Argentinian media behaviour have since appeared. One Argentinian journalist, Rafael Wolmann, was present in Port Stanley on 2 April, and at least one Argentinian camera crew was there on 14 June. From recent experience, any country presently contemplating military action against Britain would also have a media strategy, probably including the employment of political lobbyists and public relations firms in various capital cities, possibly including London. The actions of the British embassies in Washington and New York during the Falklands Conflict still make a valuable case study in this respect. The role of non-British media, particularly that of the United States, in covering and presenting the Falklands Conflict still also remains largely under-investigated.

The evidence is overwhelming that the problems of British military–media relations in the Falklands Conflict stemmed from unfamiliarity and improvisation on all sides. Within the MoD suspicion, uncertainty and inconsistency caused confusion, which in turn provoked suspicion and hostility from the media. Unlike the Army and to some extent the RAF, the RN was very unfamiliar with the media, and few reporters with the Task Force had any experience of the armed forces. At the time, the ethos of military professionalism and professional training did not include an understanding of the constitutional position of the media in a democracy: in the title of Robert Fox's book they were the *Eyewitness Falklands* for the British and wider international public. Indeed there was a service view (which has also occurred in other wars) that to suggest that this independent perspective was required was to imply that their own view was inaccurate or inadequate, or even tantamount to an accusation of lying. One of the changes in British service culture that has taken place since the Falklands is that any conception of military professionalism has been extended to include a better awareness of the place of the media.

Some critics, including university-based academics and journalists, see this as an entirely sinister development, known particularly by Professor Noam Chomsky's characterisation as 'manufacturing consent'. At best, they see the institutional confusion and improvisation of British defence media policy in the Falklands as presenting overtly the real attitudes that have since been concealed behind a façade of media courtship in later conflicts. At worst they see a deliberate policy of deceit in which the media institutions have themselves co-operated. Veteran reporter Philip Knightley in his widely read book *The First Casualty* describes the 'brilliant' manipulation of the media by the MoD over the Falklands as 'a model' for the rest of the century, marking the terminal decline of the war reporter as history has known him.[27] Even discounting this conspiracy theory, which is often expressed in the most outspoken terms, the most supportive studies of the armed forces' conduct have acknowledged military–media relations over the Falklands as far from perfect; while most routinely describe British policy as one of deliberate manipulation, censorship and propaganda.[28]

This concern and criticism has cast a shadow over what was, from the British armed forces perspective, a very successful military operation provoking irritation or even stronger emotions. Called before the 1982 House of Commons Defence Committee investigation into the handling of press and public information over the Falklands, Admiral Lewin told them, 'We won, which is what I assume the Government and public and the media all wanted us to do...I am somewhat surprised that there is a need now to have this great post mortem into the media aspects of the campaign.'[29] The change from this position to the twenty-first-century perspective represents a shift in military thinking that is arguably as fundamental as the change from total war to limited war thinking in the 1950s. Although the manner in which the media and the armed forces perceive and relate to each other is not at the centre of these considerable changes, it is one fundamental aspect that lies presently largely unacknowledged in wider military thought. The core of the issue is the tension between, on the one side, the military need to win and, on the other, the military duty to preserve the values of their own society.

It is also noteworthy that, having defended itself robustly before the House of Commons Defence Committee, which itself raised critically many of these issues, the MoD took steps to learn from the experience and to carry out reforms. An internal government enquiry into information policy was launched under General Sir Hugh Beach, reporting in 1983. Two studies were commissioned from universities by the MoD. That undertaken by Valerie Adams for King's College London dealt particularly with the issue of media speculation during the war by retired officers and scholars, and was published in 1986. A second and much wider comparative study of contemporary wars including the Falklands by a team from the University of Wales, Cardiff, led by Derrik Mercer, was published in 1987. All these studies took expert opinion from journalists and media managers as well as from the armed forces.[30]

One consequence of these investigations, which featured criticisms levelled at the civilian 'minders' in the Falklands, was the creation of the uniformed volunteer reserve escorts: the Territorial Army Pool of Information Officers or TAPIOs – since renamed the Media Operations Group (Volunteer) – the Royal Naval Reserve Public Affairs Branch, and 7644 Flight RAF Volunteer Reserve. By the 1991 Gulf War, the practice was to provide regular officers as escorts for front-line journalists. The Falklands also influenced United States military policy towards the media, starting with Grenada in 1983, although there is some dispute as to whether they learned the same lessons as the British.

Other factors may be added to a historical perspective on the Falklands as a media war. In opposition to the 'manufacturing consent' argument, it has been suggested that government and military policies towards the media in wartime since the 1980s have actually been reactions to increasing media power as the state's authority declines.[31] More importantly, the view that prevailed in 1982 that adverse media reporting of a war could turn public opinion rapidly against its prosecution, usually called the 'Vietnam Syndrome', was widely held not just by politicians and armed forces but also by many members of the news media themselves. In a discussion at the Royal United Services Institute in 1970, Robin Day of the BBC gave his opinion that 'one wonders if in future a democracy which has uninhibited television coverage in every home will ever be able to fight a war, however just'.[32] That this belief has now been utterly discredited does not change the extent to which it was held at the time. The MoD's initial reaction in 1982 to exclude all reporters from the Task Force and to keep foreign national reporters from the war zone reflected not just personal or cultural prejudice but also the latest defence thinking of the time. The parallel is exact with Lord Kitchener's ban on reporting in 1914, even including the prior existence of a media plan (in the Falklands case drawn up 1977) that no one at the time remembered.

The belief shared in 1982 by the armed forces and the media in the extreme volatility of British public opinion was also unfounded. As extensive research into the 1991 Gulf War has confirmed, the great majority of people understood that in war secrecy was important and deception took place, and were prepared to tolerate delays in the news. Just as most military intelligence in the last century came from open sources, so in the Falklands it was possible for any informed observer in Britain to build up a reasonably accurate picture of the campaign as it progressed; something that was again even more marked in the 1991 Gulf War. Most people expected that the 'media war' provided to them at the time would be an approximation of the war as it happened. But also, the critical other part of that unwritten constitutional bargain has always been the expectation that the fullest possible account would later be rendered, which is the role of history.

NOTES

1. Margaret Thatcher, *The Downing Street Years* (London: HarperCollins, 1993 – paperback edition 1995), pp. 185–6.
2. John Nott, *Here Today Gone Tomorrow: Recollections of an Errant Politician* (London: Politico's, 2002), pp. 303–4.
3. Brian Hanrahan and Robert Fox, *'I Counted Them All Out and I Counted Them All Back': The Battle for the Falklands* (London: BBC, 1982), p. 21.
4. Ibid., foreword, p. 7.
5. Michael Nicholson, *A Measure of Danger: Memoirs of a British War Correspondent* (London: HarperCollins, 1991), p. 221.
6. Philip M. Taylor, *British Propaganda in the Twentieth Century: Selling Democracy* (Edinburgh: Edinburgh University Press, 1999), p. 252; a lively account of all these episodes is Robert Harris, *Gotcha! The Media, the Government and the Falklands Crisis* (London: Faber and Faber, 1983).
7. Harris, *Gotcha!*, p. 13.
8. Max Hastings, *Going to the Wars* (London: Pan, 2001), p. 307.
9. Michael Clapp and Ewen Southby-Tailyour, *Amphibious Assault Falklands: The Battle of San Carlos Water* (London: Leo Cooper, 1996), p. 265.
10. Thatcher, *The Downing Street Years*, pp. 229–30.
11. Nott, *Here Today Gone Tomorrow*, p. 313.
12. See in particular Valerie Adams, *The Media and the Falklands Campaign* (London: Macmillan, 1986), pp. 119–24.
13. See Stephen Badsey, 'The Media War', in Stephen Badsey and John Pimlott (eds), *The Gulf War Assessed* (London: Arms and Armour, 1992), p. 219.

14. Charles C. Moskos, 'Towards a Postmodern Military: The United States as a Paradigm', in Charles C. Moskos, John Allen Williams and David R. Seagal (eds), *The Postmodern Military* (New York: Oxford University Press, 2000), 14–31.
15. Martin Middlebrook, *Operation Corporate: The Story of the Falklands War, 1982* (London: Viking, 1985), p. 14. See also Asa Briggs and Peter Burke, *A Social History of the Media: From Gutenberg to the Internet* (Cambridge: Polity, 2002), pp. 267–319; David Crowley and Paul Heyer (eds), *Communication in History* (New York: Longman, 1995), pp. 307–48; Brian Winston, *Media Technology and Society – A History: From the Telegraph to the Internet* (London: Routledge, 1998), pp. 321–6; Deborah L. Spar, *Ruling the Waves: Cycles of Discovery, Chaos and Wealth from the Compass to the Internet* (New York: Harcourt, 2001), pp. 287–326.
16. John Simpson, *Strange Places, Questionable People* (London: Pan, 1999), p. 9.
17. David French, *The British Way in Warfare 1688–2000* (London: Unwin Hyman, 1990), p. 223.
18. [Anon.], *The History of The Times, vol. 4: The 150th Anniversary and Beyond 1912–1948*, part I, Chapters 1–12, 1912–1920 (London: Times Printing House, 1952), p. 218.
19. Harris, *Gotcha!*, pp. 94, 110–14; but see also Richard Hill, *Lewin of Greenwich: The Authorised Biography of Admiral of the Fleet Lord Lewin* (London: Cassell, 2000), pp. 364–5, for Lewin's relations with the media.
20. I am grateful to Matthew McPartland for this information, which appears in his PhD thesis, 'The Dynamics of War Reporting: The Media–Military Relationship in the Second World War', Leeds University, 2003.
21. PRO, AIR 8/1940, COS (57) 220, 11 October 1957, 'Part II of General Sir Charles Keightley's Despatch on Operations in the Eastern Mediterranean November–December 1956'; this is also quoted by Professor Peter Hennessy in his chapter of the present book; my own attention was first drawn to it as quoted in Tony Shaw, *Eden, Suez and the Mass Media: Propaganda and Persuasion During the Suez Crisis* (London: I.B. Tauris, 1996), p. 196.
22. See Robert Fox, *Eyewitness Falklands: A Personal Account of the Falklands Campaign* (London: Methuen, 1982). For Fox's own role see also in particular John Frost, *2 Para Falklands: The Battalion at War* (London: Buchan and Enright, 1983), and also Hanrahan and Fox, *'I Counted Them All Out and I Counted Them All Back'*.
23. Nicholson, *A Measure of Danger*, pp. 246–251; Hastings, *Going to the Wars*, pp. 357–8. See also David E. Morrison and Howard Tumber, *Journalists at War: The Dynamics of News Reporting during the Falklands Conflict* (London: Sage, 1988).
24. See Martin Bell, *In Harm's Way: Reflections of a War Zone Thug* (London: Hamish Hamilton, 1995), pp. 127–8; Greg McLaughlin, *The War Correspondents* (London: Pluto Press, 2002), especially pp. 47–82. For 19th-century practices see for example Stephen Badsey, 'War Correspondents in the Boer War', in John Gooch (ed.), *The Boer War: Direction, Experience and Image* (London: Frank Cass, 2000), pp. 187–202; Andrew Lambert and Stephen Badsey, *The War Correspondents: The Crimean War* (Thrupp: Sutton, 1994).
25. Glasgow University Media Group (Lucinda Broadbent *et al.*), *War and Peace News* (Milton Keynes: Open University Press, 1985), pp. 129–30.

26. Nott, *Here Today Gone Tomorrow*, pp. 312–13.
27. Philip Knightley, *The First Casualty: The War Correspondent as Hero and Myth-Maker from the Crimea to Kosovo*, rev. edn (London: Prion, 2000), pp. 478–82; see also Peter Young and Peter Jesser, *The Media and the Military: From the Crimea to Desert Strike* (London: Macmillan, 1997), especially pp. 97–119; Richard Keeble, *Secret State, Silent Press: New Militarism, the Gulf and the Modern Image of Warfare* (Luton: University of Luton Press, 1997).
28. For a highly supportive view of the British military conduct towards the media in the Falklands see Miles Hudson and John Stanier, *War and the Media: A Random Searchlight* (Thrupp: Sutton, 1997), pp. 163–84.
29. Quoted in Harris, *Gotcha!*, p. 149.
30. Adams, *The Media and the Falklands Campaign*; Derrick Mercer, Geoff Mungham and Kevin Williams, *The Fog of War: The Media on the Battlefield* (London: Heinemann, 1987). Both books also make detailed reference to the Beach Report, and to the House of Commons Defence Committee enquiry.
31. See for example A. Trevor Thrall, *War in the Media Age* (Creskill, NY: Hampton Press, 2000).
32. Quoted in Philip M. Taylor, *Munitions of the Mind: War Propaganda from the Ancient World to the Nuclear Age* (London: Patrick Stephens, 1990), p. 228.

PART 2
The Falklands Conflict in Personal Memory

5

A View from the Centre

SIR JOHN NOTT

I very much appreciate the opportunity of speaking at this conference on 'The Falklands Conflict Twenty Years On – Lessons for the Future' at the Royal Military Academy Sandhurst. Two chapters in my own book, *Here Today Gone Tomorrow: Recollections of an Errant Politician* (London: Politico's, 2002) really provide my version of events as Secretary for Defence in the War Cabinet during the Falklands Conflict itself. But as I have come to realise talking to others who were involved 20 years later, it is the context of the times that is important in understanding what was happening elsewhere. In the early 1980s, we were in the middle of the Cold War, the Warsaw Pact hugely outnumbered us in men and tanks on what was then the Central Front dividing East and West Germany, and as Secretary for Defence I was not really thinking about anything else. One of the most shocking things that I discovered on my arrival at the MoD was that we had only about one week's worth of ammunition stocks in West Germany, so we were not able to fight a conventional war on the Central Front for much longer than that. The preoccupation in most of the NATO planning exercises that we held was whether we would have to escalate to nuclear warfare, which was a very frightening prospect. This was also the period in which we were acquiring Trident D-5. The United States, of course, was very supportive, but some of our NATO allies were opposed to Trident, especially the West Germans who thought that the firepower of Trident was far too great, and the House of Commons was divided on the issue. I did not even know if I was going to get the Trident programme through, and in late March 1982 I was preoccupied with that more than any other single thing.

I just about knew where the Falklands were, because the Argentinian scrap merchants had landed on South Georgia on 18 March. I had seen Admiral Sir Henry Leach, the Chief of the Naval Staff and First Sea Lord, and asked if we should send a nuclear submarine down to the South Atlantic, and he explained that he did not think we had one to spare; all those that were available were up in the Barents Sea. Then the whole thing seemed to pass over. I went off to a NATO conference in the United States; I remained in touch with the Ministry about the scrap merchants, but we did not take this matter very seriously. We provisioned one of the RFAs to look after HMS *Endurance*, and we doubled the Royal Marine contingent on the Falklands as a precaution.

Although it is easy to be wise after the event, I really do not see what else we could have done. I do not think that anything other than a trip-wire policy was sensible regarding the Falklands. We could not have kept a nuclear submarine down in the South Atlantic indefinitely. It is something of a great 'What If?' of history, but if we had sent one or two nuclear submarines down there in time, then as the Argentinians were approaching the islands, what would we have done? Having been through the process of agreeing the Rules of Engagement in the War Cabinet throughout the real conflict, I find it very difficult to imagine that we would have given authority to a nuclear submarine to sink approaching Argentinian ships on the high seas. Even if we had given our authority, I do not think that we could have stopped the invasion.

Anyway, nobody was thinking about the Falkland Islands in late March 1982. I was concerned about Belize, on which the Americans were pressing us hard at the time because of their Central American policy, but the Falklands never went through my mind. So I came back from the NATO conference, and on Wednesday 31 March I was off visiting British Aerospace. I came back later to the House of Commons, and Roger Jackling came along to see me with a couple of other people and showed me some intercepted Argentinian signals, and I could see immediately from these that an invasion was almost certain to happen two days later, as indeed it did. I went to see Margaret Thatcher and we spent some time discussing how we could persuade President Reagan to stop this from happening. While we were discussing this, Admiral Leach, who had seen the signals intercepts at the MoD, came to see me, and I suggested to Margaret Thatcher that he should join us. This was extremely fortunate, as Admiral Leach was very positive and said that he could get his aircraft carriers to sea within 48 hours, where they could link up with a large part of the Fleet that was involved in Exercise Spring Train down off Gibraltar. It was a really remarkable achievement getting the ships to sea in so short a time. One of the things that I have always had to say about the RN is that – even more so than the Army and the RAF – it is the RN's *readiness*, a tradition that goes back over 100 years, that is really so admirable.

At the time, my own preoccupation was over what would happen in the House of Commons. We would have had enormous problems if Michael Foot, the leader of the Labour Party, had not originally made his career out of opposing the Fascists and Nazis, and had been enormously staunch in the 1930s against Mussolini and Hitler. What would have happened if the Argentinian Junta had been a socialist government is something that I often wonder. But Michael Foot made an extremely forceful speech in the Commons on Saturday 3 April, and after he had done that we knew the position of the Labour Party, and it became inevitable that we were going to send the Task Force. We had given Admiral Leach authority on the evening of Friday 2 April to make his preparations to put the Task Force to sea, subject to the approval of the Cabinet meeting due to take place the next day. I think that if the Labour Party had been very reluctant then we would have been in an enormously difficult position. In the Commons debate on Saturday morning, at which I am afraid that I spoke very badly and teased the Labour Party, which was a huge debating error, I think that if the Labour Party had not been so aggressively hawkish it could have been a very messy situation indeed.

If I can generalise about the attitudes of over 20 people, few of my Cabinet colleagues really believed that the Task Force was actually going to fight. Certainly the House of Commons, and the majority Conservative Party within the Commons, saw the Task Force as an exercise in power projection related to the diplomatic negotiations. I think that I personally believed that if we sent the Task Force then it would have to fight, but this was not a majority view at the time. Within the Conservative Party itself, around a quarter of our MPs on the left wing of the party also disliked Margaret Thatcher, and to some extent they were quite ambivalent about whether they wanted this particular endeavour to succeed, because they knew that if it was a success then Margaret Thatcher was going to be there for ever.

The most critical meeting that I had throughout the whole period took place in Margaret Thatcher's office in the Commons on Wednesday 7 April. The Americans had just decided that Secretary of State Alexander Haig should come over to try and bring about a negotiated settlement. On the morning of Sunday 4 April, when Admiral Sir Terence Lewin, the CDS, had not yet returned from New Zealand, the CoS Committee brought forward a proposal that we should declare a Maritime Exclusion Zone around the Falklands, and I was due to announce it. But the FCO put enormous pressure on Margaret Thatcher for the announcement to be delayed, their view being that we could not possibly make such an aggressive act while Haig was still in the air on his way to London. Francis Pym had just been appointed as Foreign

Secretary to replace Lord Carrington, and the natural instinct of the Prime Minister was to support her Foreign Secretary. I felt that the announcement had to be made, and that the House of Commons was expecting it from us. So the political members of the War Cabinet gathered in Margaret Thatcher's room at the Commons to discuss it. I thought that I was going to lose the argument, but I pointed out that Parliament would soon be in recess for Easter, and with a second major debate on the Falklands coming up we could not defer the announcement. The argument went on for an hour right up until the time that the debate was due to start, when Francis Pym withdrew his objection, and I was able to make the announcement. It was touch-and-go, and it was the only occasion, right at the start of the conflict, when the military imperatives were almost overridden by the diplomatic requirements.

There was another quite a similar case of the tension between political and military imperatives about the decision to recapture South Georgia. The Parliamentary Conservative Party, the Labour Party and most members of the Cabinet – who did not take part in our War Cabinet meetings – were very much against our firing any shots while the diplomatic negotiations with the Americans were going on. The RN at Northwood were slightly doubtful about whether the operation to recapture South Georgia was desirable, and I was aware of that. But Admiral Lewin and I were intimately involved in both the domestic and international political situation; we felt that as the Task Force sailed further south we just had to have some military action. We were really in a very difficult position, and not just with the Americans, but even with some of our European allies. We never had trouble with the French, who were very helpful, but Spain and Italy had close connections with Argentina, and we were always in difficulty with the West Germans who were never helpful and very neutralist. The recapture of South Georgia was unnecessary from a military point of view, although Rear Admiral Woodward felt that later on it was useful for the Task Force to have use of its harbour; in fact we did it for political reasons.

It turned out to be fortunate that, in the 1981 Defence Review for which I was responsible, Admiral Lewin had felt quite powerless in his position as CDS. As chairman of the CoS Committee he had a very limited briefing team of a few people, was completely dependent on the briefing teams of the three Services and generally he felt that he had very little real power. During the Defence Review, the CoS could not agree among themselves on how we were going to reduce the forward programme. It is nonsense to say – as is often said – that the naval programme was cut back while I was Secretary for Defence. Excluding the Trident nuclear programme, the naval programme by itself grew substantially all the way up to 1985/6. The issue was actually what we were going to do about the latter part of the ten-year costing for the forward programme, which bore no relation at all to the amount of money that was available. That had to be cut back, which is what caused the row that I had with Admiral Leach and the RN.

I tried to get some recommendations from the CoS on what we should do about the forward programme. But the RN, the Army and the RAF just could not agree, and so Admiral Lewin could not really bring me any proper recommendations. He told me that in future the CDS must become the senior military adviser to the government, with his own briefing staff. This was fiercely opposed by the RN, and to some extent opposed by the RAF, but supported by the Army, and it was implemented with Margaret Thatcher's agreement, in the process removing the appointment of separate Service Ministers. So when the Falklands Conflict came along, Admiral Lewin as CDS had real *de jure* authority over the CoS as well as *de facto* authority, and that proved to be crucial.

In a conflict like the Falklands a Defence Secretary does not have very much of a position. I had always been in charge in the MoD, and I still had an important relationship with Parliament, and an important role to play within the War Cabinet. But in times of war the role of Defence Secretary has to be undertaken by the Prime Minister. Margaret Thatcher, taking the advice of Lord Stockton (Harold Macmillan), also decided that Geoffrey Howe, the Chancellor of the Exchequer, should not be part of the War Cabinet. Having had several years' military experience, my preoccupation at the start was to get the shortest possible chain of command, and I consider that to be my main contribution to our success. At that time the CDS was not normally a permanent member of any Cabinet committee, and I insisted that Admiral Lewin should be a permanent member of the War Cabinet. Also, although Margaret Thatcher wanted me to give the military briefings to the War Cabinet, it was also obvious to me that this should be the function of the CDS. Although I was invited to the meetings of the CoS Committee that took place each morning, I did not believe that I should attend, or that I was qualified to participate in discussions of what military actions should be taken. I did attend the early morning Intelligence briefings, which in the early days were almost entirely concerned with what the Soviet Union was doing. We were in fact deeply concerned about Soviet submarines and spy ships. We had no satellite coverage of the South Atlantic, except towards the very end of the conflict when we had problems with the Americans about diverting satellites away from Europe.

Among the members of the War Cabinet, William Whitelaw and I were both obsessed by the traumas of Suez in 1956. I had been astonished at how long it had taken to mount that operation, and that the CoS had not even known about the collusion with Israel. Perhaps I should not have been obsessed by it, but I had seen what a frightful political and military disaster the whole thing had been, and that was my main worry. I also remembered my own great-great-great-grandfather, General Sir William Nott, and his experience in what became the military disaster of the First Afghan War, something that I also mention in my book.

What went most right over the Falklands was that the chain of command was short and simple. Admiral Lewin, because he was participating in all the political discussions, understood the conflict between military necessity and the political imperatives, including the Haig and Peruvian peace plans. He brought the CoS recommendations to me, we discussed them in my office, and then we went jointly to the War Cabinet to argue the military imperatives. In particular, we brought proposals for the Rules of Engagement to the War Cabinet, which spent most of its time considering these. I had only two disagreements with Admiral Lewin throughout the whole of the operation. One was that I did not want the Task Force to sail from Ascension Island before Francis Pym had come back from what turned out to be almost his last round of negotiations in Washington. Of course I knew how vitally important it was to get the Task Force down to the South Atlantic as soon as possible, because of the deteriorating weather. But I held back the sailing for one or two days, because I felt that if it sailed and we then had a negotiated settlement it would appear that we had turned back in defeat. It would look like Suez again, and a national humiliation. The only other disagreement that we had was right at the end of the conflict, when one of our nuclear submarines found the Argentinian aircraft carrier *Veinticinco de Mayo* in Argentinian territorial waters. I was totally against attacking it, as I could not see how we could gain from risking bringing in other South American countries against us by such an act when we had effectively won the war.

Otherwise, Admiral Lewin and I had an excellent relationship throughout the conflict; and the War Cabinet had no difficulty in agreeing to the Rules of Engagement that we brought to it in respect of military actions. The decision to sink the cruiser *General Belgrano* was taken very straightforwardly. Admiral Lewin and I took about two minutes to agree that we should take the request to Margaret Thatcher, and the three of us took about the same amount of time to reach the decision. We then took it to the full War Cabinet about an hour later, and it was really the easiest decision of the war. We did, however, have enormous worries earlier on about what action to take about Argentinian civil aircraft flying over the Task Force on its way down south, reporting its position. The issue was whether we would give authority to the Task Force to shoot down these unarmed aircraft, which we felt unable to do. The other difficult decisions included what to do about the Soviet Union and other political issues, but the military decisions were always very simple.

Whitehall, as such, had very little to do with the running of the Falklands Conflict. The whole system of Whitehall is a well-oiled machine that is there to make sure that nothing goes wrong; it is very good in many ways, but it is not good at crisis management. The Argentinian invasion took Whitehall so much by surprise that there was no time to set up co-ordinating committees, and, other than the War Cabinet, the MoD and Northwood, it was as if Whitehall had ceased to exist. As Secretary of Defence I was not plagued with the dilemma caused by the FCO's negotiations in relation to the military imperatives. In fact, I do not think I ever had such an easy time.

The Falklands Conflict was, of course, a great success for Britain. But the greatest advantage on our side was luck. Napoleon famously asked about a general, 'Est-il heureux?' – Is he lucky? It was an enormously hazardous operation, extremely dangerous. After Admiral Leach left us on the night of Wednesday 31 March, I told Margaret Thatcher that in so far as I had any briefing from the MoD (and really there was very little), there was scepticism about the feasibility of any campaign to recover the islands. My own initial reaction was that this was just not a viable logistic operation. But thanks overwhelmingly to the readiness of the RN, their brilliant logistics, and all the help that they received, it turned out to be a massive success. Undoubtedly, it changed the way in which this country thinks about itself, a confidence that even after 20 years shows no sign of going away.

NOTE

This chapter was prepared from a transcript of the remarks made by Sir John Nott to the conference.

6

Crisis Management and the Assembly of the Task Force

ADMIRAL OF THE FLEET SIR HENRY LEACH

For the first half of the twentieth century it had been the British practice to deploy a South Atlantic Naval Squadron, normally based on Simonstown in South Africa. This was deemed appropriate to support the many British interests in both South Africa and South America and the vital shipping routes through the South Atlantic. But the UK's progressive retrenchment of the 1960s disbanded this Squadron and thereby removed effective deterrence from the area. From then on reliance was placed on a tripwire in the form of a single Ice Patrol Ship (initially HMS *Protector*, later *Endurance*) at sea for only six months in the year; and a small party of 40 RM as the garrison at Port Stanley.

For many years (but especially during the last 16 prior to the invasion in 1982) Argentina had laid claim to the Falkland Islands (Malvinas) in varying degrees of strength and validity. An incident calculated to probe the UK's resolve, if not to provoke her irritation, had been contrived almost annually. Over the years periodic talks between the two countries had been held at junior ministerial level. The pattern had developed of the Argentines demanding and the UK stalling. More recently the issue of sovereignty had featured with increasing prominence. The Argentine demands had become more pressing and the Falkland Islanders' rejection more obdurate if less rational; but because of their British citizenship it was politically difficult not to support their views. Nevertheless, by the end of 1981, there were growing signs in Whitehall that at the next round of Anglo-Argentine talks, due to be held in June the following year, *de facto* sovereignty would be transferred to Argentina under some form of lease-back. The view was held in many

64

quarters that in practical terms the Islanders would not experience any adverse effects from such an arrangement and that adequate safeguards to preserve their rights as British citizens could be written into the agreement. Britain's standing in the eyes of the UN, as well as with one of the most powerful countries of South America, would be enhanced. And the UK would be effectively rid of a distant encumbrance which contributed nothing but difficulty and expense.

Two other factors arose in 1981 which were to have a profound influence on events to come: the UK's Defence Review and the internal situation in the Argentine. The UK's Defence Review was conspicuous neither for its wisdom nor for its statesmanship. So far as the South Atlantic was concerned it was planned to emasculate the Navy and withdraw the Ice Patrol Ship. To the objective observer of the world scene this astonishing performance by an island nation, still dependent on the sea for more than 97 per cent of its imports and exports, could have only one rational interpretation: the UK's growing lack of interest in maritime matters in general and the South Atlantic in particular. And so it was deduced in the Argentine.

Domestically Argentina was in a mess. Public feeling against the 'Dirty War', which had involved the forceful disappearance of thousands and the suspected liquidation of many, had risen to a peak. The economy was in a shambles, as was widely evident. The Administration lacked competence and direction. Public confidence in the Government was at rock bottom. By the spring of 1982, there was rioting on the streets in Buenos Aires. Some immediate panacea was needed to divert attention until a more lasting solution could be devised. In terms of its magnitude and popular appeal, one thing only met this requirement – the Malvinas. That the next round of talks was only two months away and that all the portents were that they would be highly satisfactory for Argentina was just too bad. Two months are too long to wait when the mob is howling at the gate. The fact that the President of the Junta in Buenos Aires was a dipsomaniac and the Head of the Argentine Navy was a rabid Anglophobe did not further the prospect of peace on this occasion.

This, then, was the backdrop to the closing weeks of March 1982. Once more the Falkland Islands situation seemed to be blowing hot. In Whitehall yet again the military options were reviewed – and endorsed – and intelligence updates called for. It was known that the Argentine Fleet was at sea and that it included a sizeable element of amphibious troops; but it was also known that every year at about this time it was usual for the Argentine Navy to conduct a major amphibious exercise with the neighbouring Uruguayan Navy. In January, HMS *Endurance* had paid a routine visit to Ushuaia in the southern part of Argentina and reported that, unusually, her reception had been cold to the point of hostility; but shortly afterwards when she paid a similar visit to Mar del Plata all seemed normal. Understandably, in view of the forthcoming talks, in Whitehall overriding political importance was attached to a policy of non-provocation and this tempered every activity in the early days.

On 19 March, one Davidoff with a party of men landed on South Georgia from an Argentine naval Support Ship. He himself was a scrap merchant who had obtained permission from the British Embassy in Buenos Aires to dismantle and remove the unwanted remains of the whaling station at Leith in South Georgia, abandoned since the mid-1960s. But once ashore the Argentine flag was hoisted and it became clear to the watching British Antarctic Survey scientists that an Argentine toe-hold had been established. This was duly reported to the Governor of the Falkland Islands and in turn to London. *Endurance* was ordered to embark extra RM from the Falkland Islands Garrison and proceed to South Georgia.

In the course of the next few days further incidents occurred in the South Atlantic. The Argentine Naval Support Ship re-embarked most, but not all, of the landed men and sailed from Leith. The Argentine Airline office in Port Stanley was broken into by night and some of its contents defaced. A French yacht in the vicinity of South Georgia was discovered to be in direct contact with the Argentines. There was growing evidence that Davidoff was being directed by the Argentine Navy. The Argentine Foreign Minister began to reveal the pressure he was under from Admiral Anaya, Head of the Argentine Navy; this was confirmed by Intelligence reports. *Endurance* was instructed to wait at Grytviken (a few miles away in South Georgia) and not to proceed to Leith. Meanwhile a second Argentine Naval Support Ship berthed at Leith and was seen to be working cargo.

On 25 March, it became known in London that two Argentine frigates equipped with Exocet anti-ship missiles had been deployed to the sea area between the Falkland Islands and South Georgia. It was also learned that Argentine Forces were being kept informed of the movements of *Endurance* and of the Falkland Islands Garrison. There were indications that the Argentine civilians still in South Georgia would remain there and shortly afterwards this was formally confirmed by the Argentine Foreign Minister. The hawks in Argentina were assuming the ascendancy.

Meanwhile, Whitehall initiated discreet moves against the possibility that on this occasion the Argentinians meant business. The avoidance of provocation continued to dominate all decisions. The withdrawal of *Endurance*, now imminent, was cancelled. To re-supply her and enable her to remain on station a RFA was sailed from the Gibraltar area. The previous Falkland Islands Garrison, due to be relieved by the fresh RM Contingent recently brought from the mainland by *Endurance*, was held, thus effectively doubling the size of the Garrison and bringing its strength up to 80. A nuclear-powered Fleet submarine (SSN) was withdrawn from exercises off Gibraltar, loaded with her war outfit of torpedoes and stores, and despatched to the South Atlantic. Instructions to deploy a second SSN were issued and a third was earmarked but not yet withdrawn from her current operational task. Consideration was given to sailing a force of destroyers/ frigates from the Gibraltar area in the general direction of the South Atlantic but was rejected on the twin grounds of inadequacy and provocation. Whitehall knew the approximate positions of the Argentine naval ships in the vicinity of South Georgia and also of the Naval Task Force including the attack carrier *25th of May* (*Veinticinco de Mayo*), four destroyers and an amphibious landing ship exercising some 800 nautical miles north of the Falkland Islands. It noted that no change in the readiness of the Argentine Air Force had been directed and that the Argentine air service to Port Stanley was operating as usual.

By long-standing arrangement I was due to visit the Admiralty Surface Weapons Establishment on Portsdown Hill on 31 March. Three times in the previous 14 months defence review considerations had caused me to cancel my visit. This time, if I could responsibly do so, I was determined to go through with it. By flying a naval helicopter from Northwood I could be in almost continuous communication with the MoD and within $1\frac{1}{2}$ hours' notice of recall if necessary. I went. It was a useful day and there were no emergency calls from London.

By 1800 hours, I was back in my office. There I found the latest intelligence report and a number of briefs, all relating to the South Atlantic. The former indicated without equivocation that an Argentine invasion of the Falkland Islands seemed likely in the early hours of 2 April. The latter consistently advised that further naval deployments were unnecessary and undesirable. *Endurance* would remain on station and be resupplied; two SSN's were on the way; to deploy further units in circumstances which were potentially no more serious than on many previous occasions – indeed arguably less so in view of the forthcoming talks – would have damaging effects on our other commitments. It was 'the mixture as before' and as before it would all soon blow over.

To me the two, Intelligence Reports and Briefs, were incompatible. There was a clear, imminent threat to a British overseas territory. It could only be reached by sea. What the hell was the point in having a Navy if it was not used for this sort of thing? Even as I decided that the briefs were upside down I learned that my Secretary of State was being briefed from them at that very moment. I strode down the corridor to his office. He was not there.

'The Secretary of State is holding his briefing in his room in the House,' explained his Private Secretary, adding, 'he must be nearly finished by now'. Snatching a House of Commons pass I jumped into my car and was whisked to the main entrance. Being still in ordinary day uniform and moving as quickly as I could among the milling throng waiting to enter the Galleries or see their Members caused a bit of a flurry, but not so with the splendid police officer at his desk in the Central Lobby. Years of handling silly questions from crazy cranks had hardened him to a courteous stone. An impatient First Sea Lord, though in uniform and urgently seeking the Defence Secretary, was chicken feed.

'I'll ring his room, sir,' he said with unruffled calm. 'Hmm. No answer. Would you care to sit on one of the benches over there sir, and I'll try to locate him for you?'

I sat. Various MPs and officials whom I knew passed and exchanged a few words. Then I was collected by one of the junior Whips and taken to the Whips' Room. They were a nice lot, nearly all ex-soldiers and rather intrigued to chat over a much-needed whisky with the Head of the Navy. After ten minutes or so the search for the Defence Secretary was successful. He was with the Prime Minister in her room and I was asked to go up.

'Good evening, Prime Minister,' I said on entering. 'Is there anything I can do to help?'

She was her usual charming, purposeful self. 'Come in Admiral,' she said. 'You are very timely. We are of course discussing the Falklands situation and what we should do about it.' The aura of gloom and uncertainty was almost tangible.

Present also were the Defence Secretary, Humphrey Atkins, Richard Luce from the FCO, the Permanent Secretaries from the MoD and FCO, legal experts from the FCO and the Prime Minister's Private Secretary. Discussion was fairly general, the FCO pressing for the despatch of a third SSN and the Defence Secretary reluctant to initiate any further action. The reality or otherwise of the threat, the importance of not prejudicing the forthcoming talks with Argentina, and the courses of diplomatic action open to us predominated. In due course I had my chance.

'Admiral, what do you think?'

'On the basis of the latest Intelligence,' I replied, 'I think we must assume that the Falkland Islands will be invaded and that this will happen in the next few days. If it does there is no way the Garrison can put up an effective defence against the amphibious force known to be embarked in the Argentine Fleet. Nor, now, is there any effective deterrence that we could apply in time. Therefore the islands will be captured. Whether we take action to recover them or not is not for me to say but I would strongly advise that we did. To do so would require a very considerable Naval Task Force with strong amphibious elements. I believe we should assemble such a force now, without further delay. To be seen to be doing so in sufficient strength might conceivably cause the Argentines to hold off from landing, though I doubt it. Arguably such a move would be too late to provoke them into doing something on which they already seem bent.'

'The Task Force, that would be *Invincible, Fearless* and some frigates?'

'Yes. It would also include *Hermes, Intrepid* (which is currently being put into reserve), a substantial proportion of the operational destroyers/ frigates, very considerable afloat support from the Royal Fleet Auxiliaries and the taking up from trade of a number of merchant ships. The whole of 3 Commando Brigade Royal Marines would be required, supplemented by at least one additional Army Unit.'

'What about the third nuclear submarine?'

'Contrary to the advice I gave my Secretary of State yesterday when I opposed this suggestion, in the light of today's information I think we should sail a third SSN as soon as practicable. For other operational reasons this would not be for a few days but I don't think that would matter.'

'You talk of *Invincible* and *Hermes*; what about *Ark Royal*?'

'The old or the new? The old is in the throes of being scrapped. The new, regrettably, will not complete building for another three years or so.'

'Shall we have enough air cover?'

'We shall be entirely dependent on the Sea Harriers and Harriers embarked in *Invincible* and *Hermes*. No, we have not really got enough. But the Sea Harrier is a highly capable aircraft and I believe it to be more than a match for anything the Argentines could put up. Provided we deploy every single aircraft that can be made operational, including those normally used for training, we should be able to inflict sufficient attrition on arrival in the area to achieve at least local air superiority before the landing. I won't pretend that it will not be an operation involving considerable risk; but in my judgement it is, on balance, an acceptable risk – and anyway there is no better alternative.'

'You keep on about the Sea Harriers. What about the Buccaneers and the Phantoms?'

'They were all transferred to the RAF when the old *Ark Royal* was paid off. They cannot be operated from *Invincible or Hermes* and they cannot get there on their own.'

'How long would it take to assemble such a Task Force?'

'Apart from the Merchant Ships, which would be subject to an Order in Council and then depend on their whereabouts and the time needed to modify or equip them, and *Intrepid* whose precise state I would need to check – 48 hours.'

'And how long would it take to get to the Falkland Islands?'

'About three weeks.'

'Three weeks, you mean three days?'

'No, I mean three weeks. The distance is 8,000 nautical miles.'

'Could the preparations be carried out without it becoming generally known?'

'No. Something on this scale would be bound to get out fairly quickly.'

'Could we really recapture the islands if they were invaded?'

'Yes, we *could* and in my judgement (though it is not my business to say so) we *should*.'

'Why do you say that?' snapped the Prime Minister.

'Because if we do not, or if we pussyfoot in our actions and do not achieve complete success, in another few months we shall be living in a different country whose word counts for little.'

The Prime Minister looked relieved and nodded.

Discussion then turned to other aspects: a telephone call to Al Haig, the American Secretary of State, in Washington; the drafting of a personal message from the Prime Minister to President Reagan; messages to our Ambassadors to the United States and the Argentine and to the Governor of the Falkland Islands. All this lasted well into the night.

When the meeting finally broke up I left with full authority to sail a third nuclear submarine when current tasks permitted and to assemble and prepare the Task Force on the lines proposed, but not to sail it pending further instructions. One thing was certain: faced with a crisis we had a Prime Minister of courage, decision and action to meet it.

I returned to the MoD, issued the necessary instructions and telephoned the Chief of the Air Staff who was Acting CDS to inform him of what had happened. The CDS, Admiral Lewin, was in New Zealand on an official visit but was keeping in close touch.

Next day Whitehall was busy. There were meetings of the Cabinet, the Defence and Overseas Policy Committee and the CoS Committee. Diplomatic activity was further intensified in Buenos Aires, in the United Nations Assembly in New York, and in Washington. Everywhere the Argentine representatives presented an atmosphere of impasse. In this hardening and worsening situation the assessment from Washington was that it seemed likely that the Argentines would now go ahead with a military operation. They could be in Port Stanley in 24 hours. President Reagan would personally telephone General Galtieri.

Invasion of the Falkland Islands now seemed imminent. An advance Task Group of seven destroyers and frigates exercising in the Gibraltar area was sailed towards the South Atlantic under the command of Rear Admiral Woodward, Flag Officer First Flotilla. This was still in the nature of a precautionary move; the Group would later join up with the main Task Force in mid-Atlantic if the latter was deployed.

That evening I had a long-arranged dinner party in my Mall House flat by Admiralty Arch. It included the Permanent Secretaries of the FCO and the MoD. To an extent it was a last desperate attempt to muster sense and curb implementation of the more extravagant absurdities of the 1981 Defence Review – of which the impending sale of *Invincible* was a prime example. Despite the gathering war clouds it was a convivial evening, though not entirely without analogy to a certain game of bowls at Plymouth 400 years previously or to the Duchess of Richmond's Ball on the eve of Waterloo. Our wives had withdrawn and the port had just been circulated a second time when, by prior arrangement, I had to leave my own table to attend another meeting called by the Prime Minister with the Foreign and Commonwealth Secretary and the Secretary of State for Defence.

The discussions in No. 10 Downing Street lasted far into the night. Yet again all possible options were reviewed but no panacea other than continuing high-pressure diplomacy identified. There was considerable debate over what instructions should be sent to the Governor of the Falkland Islands. A message of confidence? Of exhortation to fight to the last? Of restraint on such heroics to reduce bloodshed? After a period of heavy drafting a message in the sense of 'complete confidence in your ability to handle the situation...realize you may be faced with impossible odds...know you will exercise your judgement in avoiding needless loss of life...our thoughts with you at this critical time' was shaped up. To me it seemed at worst back-seat driving and at best a package of platitudes. Evidently I displayed my distaste for the Prime Minister spotted it.

'You're shaking your head, Admiral; you don't agree?'

'Prime Minister, I can only say what I, as an operational commander, would do were I on the receiving end of such a message.'

'What?'

'Put it straight in the wastepaper bin and lose my remaining confidence in Whitehall.'

'What would you say, then?'

'Nothing. At this late stage I should leave it to the man on the spot.' And so it was.

During these long night sessions the Prime Minister was at her very best, exhibiting no sign of the gruelling 16-hour day which normally preceded them. Indeed such were her stamina and resolve in a crisis that I believe she rather enjoyed them. At one stage she rounded on me sharply 'Admiral, supposing we did send the Task Force, what would *you* do if you were C-in-C of the Argentine Navy?'

'I should return to harbour, Prime Minister, and stay there,' I replied.

'Why?'

'Because I should appreciate that although I could take out some of the British ships, they would sink my entire Navy. It would take years to recover, if indeed it were practicable to do so.' As subsequent events were to prove, after the sinking of the *Belgrano* that is precisely what happened.

In the early hours of Friday 2 April I returned to the MoD with authority to sail the Task Force. The Naval Operations Staff were poised awaiting the outcome of the meeting at No. 10.

'Signal C-in-C Fleet to prepare and sail the Task Force,' I instructed. I then telephoned Admiral Fieldhouse personally.

I knew John Fieldhouse very well indeed. Over recent years we had been Flotilla commanders together; he had been an excellent and far-sighted Flag Officer Submarines when I commanded the Fleet, and an outstanding Controller of the Navy during my earlier time as First Sea Lord. I could not have wished for a better C-in-C Fleet in a crisis nor one whose thinking so completely matched my own. We were 'in each other's minds'. Behind his unruffled calm and almost urbane manner lay a keen mind, resolute determination and a fund of good sense.

My greatest anxiety was now to get the Task Force away before political resolve weakened. The operation had yet to be put to Cabinet and Parliament.

'The Carrier Task Force must sail on Monday,' I said.

'Could we not have a little more time, First Sea Lord,' the C-in-C reacted. 'We could then improve the preparation so much.'

'No,' I replied. 'I'm sorry but they must sail on Monday.'

'Understood,' said the C-in-C. And they did.

At dawn on 2 April the Argentine invasion force landed and by 0830 hours the Governor of the Falkland Islands had surrendered. Another chapter in maritime history had been opened.

Other contributors will deal with the course of the war itself. As wars go its scale was less massive and its duration less protracted than most preceding conflicts. It was, in fact, short and sharp. Nevertheless it was the first for many years, in the course of which technological and tactical developments had been significant, and it was fought some

8,000 miles from base. There are some interesting observations to be made and I now consider a few of the more important ones.

If one were to select the single most dominant factor above all others it would be the continuing value and flexibility of sea power and the total relevance of surface ships. Without them the land force could not have been put ashore, there could have been no air cover, no airborne (helicopter) mobility and no naval gunfire support. The same goes for logistics: without adequate surface shipping there could have been no re-supply of food, ammunition and essential stores. Even the main field hospital was afloat. The part played by the Merchant Navy in all this needs special mention; it was crucial. Never before had the Royal Navy/Merchant Navy liaison been surpassed.

Merchant ships were needed for many duties: additional tankers, troop ships, hospital ships, aircraft ferries, solid stores support ships, repair ships, despatch vessels. Some 50 were taken up from trade and, after rapid conversion, fulfilled a key role in the recovery of the islands. Stability standards were a major concern and in some cases it was necessary to limit loads or fit additional watertight sub-divisions. Examples of the necessary modifications were the design and fitting of helicopter pads and flight decks, extra fresh-water-making plants, power generators, weapon and communication fits, replenishment at sea gear, additional fuel tanks, accommodation and workshop facilities.

The majority of the work was carried out in the Royal Dockyards to very short timetables, typically in the order of four days. The greatest credit is due to a host of engineers in the RN, in the Merchant Fleet and in industry: at all levels from managing director to shop floor they worked long hours with commendable skill and enthusiasm; 24-hour working was maintained 7 days a week and a sense of dedication and loyalty shone through, reminiscent of 1939–45. Such was the speed of events that divers were still in the recompression chamber in *Stena Seaspread* when she arrived in port; *Queen Elizabeth 2* was fitted with satellite communications (SATCOM) in five days when normally this would have taken five weeks; *Uganda* was taken off her Mediterranean cruise, disembarked her passengers at Naples, returned to Gibraltar and within two and a half days was converted to a hospital ship, complete with medical stores, helicopter pad, operating theatres, casualty gangways and the extensive lighting and livery required by the Geneva Convention. Trawlers were converted to minesweepers while still with fish in their holds.

Whenever possible small teams of experts flew out to the ship concerned and checked modification design details during the final passage to conversion ports, signalling ahead the main parameters of the work to be done. A sense of urgency, professionalism and determination surmounted obstacles, which might ordinarily have seemed intractable.

As in all wars new lessons were learned and some old ones re-learned. The folly of over-concentration on a particular scenario at the expense of a more general, versatile capability able to cope with the unexpected was brutally exposed. The price to pay for abandoning whole areas of capability to meet the savage cuts of repetitive Defence Reviews (for example Airborne Early Warning (AEW) Radar) was starkly revealed. It was the first UK conflict with SATCOM, and the media resented their denial of free access, made necessary by operational requirements. The fire hazard in ships was re-emphasised, particularly resulting from unused propellant fuel in incoming missiles released at short range and not, as was a popular misconception at the time, from burning aluminium superstructures.

Support from the USA was wholehearted. They accorded us immediate and unrestricted use of their leased facilities on Ascension Island and made available AIM 9L air-to-air missiles which were then only beginning to trickle off the UK production lines. They made other generous offers which, for pragmatic reasons at the time, were not taken up. The French continued to provide technical servicing of the Exocet missiles recently sold to the Argentine and it took a major effort to circumvent further supplies of this weapon.

In terms of world opinion the UK's position had become somewhat equivocal. We had come to be regarded as long on advice but short on muscle to back it. Though we spoke with a loud voice at international gatherings, memories were less clear on when we had last really *done* something – apart from limiting our military capability for intervention by a series of Defence Reviews. There was mounting scepticism over whether we could still act. So far as the Falklands situation was concerned it is probably fair to say that half the world thought we *couldn't* handle it and the other half thought we *wouldn't*. In fact we did.

7

An Argentinian Airman in the South Atlantic

BRIGADIER HORACIO MIR GONZALEZ

I do not want to describe the conflict in the South Atlantic as the Air Force general that I am today, aware of what happened and what mistakes were made on all sides. Rather, I want to remember it as the young officer that I was 20 years ago when I fought in it, to express my goals and my fears at the time. In April 1982, I held the rank of captain in a squadron of Mirage 5s that was part of VI Air Brigade. We were based at Tandil Air Force Base which is about 300 kilometres south of Buenos Aires, not far inland from Mar del Plata. On 6 April, we moved down south to Tierra del Fuego, to the Navy air base at Rio Grande, which was a very important base for us in the conflict. One thing that is very important to understand, and for me to stress, is that the main responsibility of the Argentine Air Force in 1982 was to carry out air-to-air and air-to-ground missions. Our Mirage 5s were intended principally for ground attack. We had never planned to fight against a force at sea, never trained for air-to-sea missions, never even undertaken training exercises against ships of any kind. If, together with this critical point, it is understood that the fact that we were actually going to fight took our operational units completely by surprise, then many of the problems that Argentine Air Force pilots experienced during the conflict become much easier to understand.

Although Argentine Air Force operational units deployed to Rio Grande and other bases, including our main base at Commodoro Rivadavia, our initial role and intention was not to fight against the British Task Force. The first priority of the Air Force was to defend the mainland of Argentina against all the many possible threats that existed at the time. So after the conflict, I had a big problem with my wife: when

I left my house on 6 April she was, of course, very concerned, so I told her 'don't worry!' I never thought that I would have to fly all the way across the ocean in my single-engined Mirage with only our limited amount of fuel. It was just incredible! And after that, of course, my wife has never believed anything I have said to her.

The Air Force regional command, which included our new home at Rio Grande, was designated Air Force South (Fuerza Aérea Sur or FAS), commanded by Brigadier Horacio Ernesto Crespo. And he made what turned out to be a critical decision. On 10 April, he made it very clear to the base commander that he did not know what would happen in the negotiations that were then going on to try and prevent the conflict, but that as military men we would prepare to fight in case we had to do so. That meant that all of us captains and other pilots had about 20 days, from 10 April until the fighting started for us on 1 May, to prepare, to learn, and to train for what would happen. We talked to the Navy and exchanged ideas, trying to predict what would happen, and it became apparent to us that what we were being asked to do was obviously very difficult.

Although the mainland air bases that we were using were those closest to the islands, our Mirage 5s did not have any air-to-air refuelling (AAR) capability, which was our big, big problem. The Mirage 5 could not use the runway at Puerto Argentino (Port Stanley to the British); even to this day there is a debate as to why the Argentinian government did not try to extend the runway. This meant that the biggest problem we had as Mirage pilots was fuel. During the 20 days that we had, we discussed and debated the best configuration for our Mirages, and we decided that the most important issue was not the weapons that they would carry but how to get the maximum possible amount of fuel into each aircraft. The Mirage 5 normally flew with one of two configurations: either three external tanks of 1,300 litres; or the configuration that our squadron used, which was two external tanks of 1,700 litres. This amount of fuel was essential if we were going to reach the islands and get back home. With this, we normally carried one or two standard conventional bombs, which were intended for air-to-ground attack since this was our mission before the war started, rather than for bombing ships.

In our 20-day training and preparation period we studied and tried to learn about all the ships that we would be facing, particularly the Type 42 destroyers and Type 22 frigates and the different weapons that they carried. Really, our main concern, before 1 May, was the Sea Dart anti-aircraft missile system on board these ships. Every night, our dreams and nightmares were about the Sea Dart. We decided that the only real chance that we had, given our fuel problems, was to fly at a very high altitude until we calculated that we had reached the western edge of the islands. Then we would make what is called an 'operational descent', a very steep and fast descent in a few minutes. We would fly over the islands at what were very high speeds for us, about 480–500 knots or even more at very low level, and try to locate the target. We would have only a few seconds over the target itself, still flying very low and at high speed (although we could not use afterburner as that would use up too much fuel). Once we were safely clear of the target we would return to very high altitude and fly back to our base at Rio Grande.

Every mission that we flew, our Mirages landed at Rio Grande with the reserve fuel light on in the cockpit. That meant that the aircraft was down to its reserve of 600 litres of fuel, which for our Mirages was 8–9 minutes of flying time. That was just the beginning of the problem. On our return, one decision that we had to make was which base we were going to use to land. The big problem with the southern part of mainland Argentina for aircraft is the weather in winter. It could be a sunny day when we took off for our missions, and be snowing and with high winds at the same base by the time that we got back. It must be understood that our Mirage 5s at the time had only basic instruments, only a barometric altimeter and a VHS omni-directional radio (VOR) which never worked properly for anybody during the entire conflict, and nothing more. On the way back to base, for the last 20 minutes of flying time we also got information from our ground-based radar, the main value of which was in helping us return safely home, acting like an Instrument Landing System (ILS).

All our flights were exactly like those that we had made when we were trainee pilots learning to fly, way back at the start of the 1960s, or as our fathers had flown in earlier times. When the cloud base was low and clouds covered the islands we flew by time-and-distance to reach our targets. We looked for a gap in the clouds over the islands, descended through the clouds until we could see the ground, and then we tried to spot landmarks, and to check against our charts, thinking '1 minute – 1 minute and 30 seconds – 1 minute and 35 seconds' and so on.

Because the attacks that we mounted typically came in flying at very low level, and the Mirage's speed when we reached the target could be as high as 550 knots or more, we each had only a few seconds over the target. It is again very important to realise that between receiving our mission orders at Rio Grande and taking off we had more or less an hour. Our orders might say that our target was a frigate in the middle of San Carlos Bay, and we took off after one hour's preparation and planning. Our flight time to the islands was about 45 minutes before we made our descent, plus about five minutes low-level flying over the islands to reach our intended target. It meant that we arrived over the target almost two hours after we had received our orders, and during those two hours we received no further information about our mission. After we took off from the mainland we were on our own. For two hours it was entirely our mission and we had to decide what to do. During the flight we kept radio silence of course, that is standard operational procedure. The first time anyone spoke would be when a member of the formation saw the target. We had some intelligence from our forces in Puerto Argentino itself and from reconnaissance flights. When we arrived over our intended target we just had to see what happened! We flew into San Carlos either from the south or from the west; only those two directions were available to us because – once more – of our fuel problem, which meant that we did not have the range to come round from the east or from the north. If we saw our target, or what might be our target, we had only about 20 seconds to decide whether to attack. A question that Argentinian pilots have always been asked after the war is why we attacked the British warships and not their logistics ships. The answer is quite simple: we attacked whatever we could attack, if and when we saw it! We had no forward air controller (FAC) for our Mirage or A-4 Skyhawk aircraft, although some did assist our Pucará aircraft based on the islands in their own air-support missions. Generally, our level of experience in co-operation with our ground forces (what are now called 'joint' operations) was very poor, and we had various problems particularly with different equipment. Sometimes, in truth, we arrived over our intended target area and there was nothing there. It was all due to the two-hour delay between our latest intelligence and our arrival over the islands.

In our conversations with Navy pilots and people who knew about the destroyers and frigates, they explained to us that to attack a Type 42 destroyer (DD) would require at least seven aircraft going in together, and that half of these aircraft would survive the attack – maybe! That made our calculations very easy. Given the number of aircraft that we had, if we used seven aircraft against each ship and lost half of them each time, then after two days we would be wiped out and the conflict would be over for us. Given our circumstances, we decided instead to use no more than three aircraft in formation for each attack. We calculated that this was a very easy formation to manoeuvre in, and also to lead.

We also knew we had a problem with our bombs, meant for ground attack. In the 20-day preparation period that we had before 1 May we tried to get the bombs changed or modified for use against ships. We tried to change the fuses, trying to find the best type to use against the British warships, but this still remained a big problem for us. Since our attack was coming in at a very low level, and we were using formations of three aircraft to attack each target, our problem with the fuse was twofold. We needed enough delay on the fuses so that the first bombs did not explode underneath the last of the three aircraft as it came over, otherwise you would kill your own wingman. But at the same time we needed the delay to be short enough so that the bomb had time to arm and to explode inside the ship's hull when it hit its target. We could see that our bombs were passing straight through the hulls of the ships as they hit them, and exploding outside. In my opinion, this was perhaps our single greatest problem throughout the war, and there was a lot of discussion amongst us on how to solve it. But nothing happened until early June, about two weeks before the end of the war, when our engineers produced a different and better fuse and we changed over to it. This fuse meant that our bombs exploded inside the ship once it penetrated the hull. Because we had never trained for air-to-sea missions, every day we tried to learn, to remember and to understand. One very important lesson that we really learned very quickly was that after the first pass over a target, our pilots could not return to try and attack the target for a second time – never! If you were lucky and escaped being shot down by the frigates on your first pass over the target you never went back for a second pass, because you would not survive. All the pilots flew with this lesson clearly learned.

Another very important lesson that as a young pilot I felt that we learned from the war is this. In our Air Force, although the Mirage 5 that I flew was intended mainly as a ground attack aircraft, our main air-to-air interceptor was the Mirage 3. But these Mirage 3s were kept back on the mainland, chiefly at our main base at Comodoro Rivadavia, and flew only a very few missions during the war. There were two main reasons for this. One was the problem that we had with the Sea Dart; if the Mirage 3s flew as escorts for our missions they would also have had to fly at very high altitude to be safe, and the danger to us was when we attacked at low level. The other problem was protecting our own home; we needed to keep the Mirage 3s back to defend against threats to the mainland. The only occasion on which our Mirage 5s flew air-to-air missions was on 1 May when the Task Force first started its main attacks. We flew a lot of missions over the islands, and for that day only our configuration was two external fuel tanks and two Israeli-made Shafrir air-to-air missiles, which were 'first-generation' missiles. Also on 1 May, we received very clear information from our ground radar at Puerto Argentino about British Combat Air Patrol (CAP). By the end of 1 May, one thing was very clear to us. It was impossible for us to fight against the Harrier – whether the Sea Harrier or the RAF G3 Harrier, especially at low level. The best altitude for the Mirage 5 when fighting is at over 20,000 feet; for the Harrier the best combat altitude is below 20,000 feet. We could not dive to low level in combat because it meant that we would run out of fuel on the way back to the mainland and come down in the ocean. Really, I am a fighter pilot, and I do prefer the ground and not the sea!

So the thing that we learned on 1 May was that in this conflict our main enemy was not going to be the Sea Dart after all. Our main enemy was the Sidewinder; our main enemy was the Harrier. More than 90 per cent of all our aircraft losses were caused by Harriers firing the American-made AIM-9L Sidewinder air-to-air missile. After 1 May, whenever we saw a Harrier in the sky there was only one thing that we could do, which was to dive and fly fast and low, but without using afterburner, because if we put on our afterburners we would not get back home to our base.

When, on 21 May, I flew a mission against a frigate at San Carlos we were flying in a formation of four aircraft. On the approach to the target, flying over the western island we ran into very bad weather, very foggy and rainy, flying down among the low hills, which we saw as our friends protecting us from the Harriers on CAP and the frigates' radar. When we reached our target, one of my wingmen broke radio silence and told me that our number four aircraft had disappeared. When we got back after the mission, I remember that Brigadier Basilio Lami Dozo, the head of our Air Force, was visiting and I explained to him that I had lost a wingman, assuming that he had flown into one of the hills and been killed, which is what I put in my official report. Five days later, my missing wingman, whose name was Lieutenant Luna, called me – he was still alive! 'Did you never see the Harrier?' he asked. He told me that he had experienced trouble with his radio, and was unable to report that behind us were two Harriers, one of which had shot him down with a Sidewinder.

Looking back now as a general 20 years after the conflict and remembering all this and how I felt, there is one more thing that I need to express, and that I think is very important. I would like to pay homage to all the men and women, every one of them, who participated in the conflict, but particularly to all those who lost their lives in it.

8

Force Projection and the Falklands Conflict

MAJOR GENERAL JULIAN THOMPSON

INTRODUCTION

When preparing this contribution I tried to find a definition for Force Projection. The current version of *British Defence Doctrine* (*BDD 01*) does not mention the phrase. In my copy of the 1996 issue of *British Defence Doctrine* (*BDD 96*), I could find Force *Generation*, but not Force *Projection*. Turning to the first edition (1996) of *British Maritime Doctrine*, there was nothing about Force Projection, but against Power Projection it said, 'see Maritime Power Projection'. Here I read, 'The use of sea-borne military forces to influence events on land directly'.

I then turned to the second edition (1999) of *British Maritime Doctrine*. Under Maritime Power Projection I read, 'see Power Projection'. But above it, I spotted 'Maritime Force Projection – The ability to project, sustain and apply effective military force from the sea at global range in order to influence (affect) events on land'. That seemed to me to fit the bill; especially as in my letter to the Commandant of the Royal Military Academy, responding to his invitation to talk at the 2002 Conference, I said, 'My initial thought on specific areas under the title *Force Projection* would be to devote most of my paper to the amphibious and maritime aspects.' Since he did not object, it will come as no surprise that that is what I intend doing. This of course is the *projectile*'s view of projection. Rudyard Kipling, in his historical study *The Irish Guards in the Great War*, recalls a private soldier telling him that they were like fleas in a blanket and could see only the nearest, next wrinkle. Both I and Commodore Michael Clapp (as he was then), could probably 'see' further than that, but on occasions not much, very much, further. In 1982, Michael Clapp was what we now call the Amphibious

Task Group Commander (COMATAG), and I have consulted him in the course of preparing this paper.

Since I have mentioned the word Amphibious, here is how *British Maritime Doctrine* defines an Amphibious Operation; 'An operation launched from the sea by naval and landing forces against a hostile or potentially hostile shore'. At the risk of banging the nail out of sight, I think it is worth further defining an Amphibious Operation by explaining what it is not. It is *not* sea transport. It is *not* the movement of troops from A to B by sea. This is a common misperception, and those who hold this view often ask would it not be easier to take your equipment by sea to a Roll on-Roll off (Ro-Ro) harbour, or by air to an airfield, and your troops likewise. It would indeed if you were confident that a 'red carpet' reception awaited you. The hostile or potentially hostile environment may not have any ports or airfields, or at least ones you can use. Operation 'Desert Shield', the build-up in Saudi Arabia in 1990–1, was a classic Red Carpet operation, that is a build-up in a friendly country, which provided three key assets: airfields, ports, and an enormous bonus, fuel; all without any enemy interference whatsoever – very different from the Falklands in 1982.

On the subject of Amphibious Operations and Power Projection from the sea, it is worth remembering that these also include Raiding and Demonstrations (either in the form of deception, as carried out by the Americans in the Gulf War 1991, as adjuncts to the main landings, to harass the enemy, or as a form of deterrence).

SURPRISE

My wake-up call came in the early hours of Friday, 2 April 1982, when my telephone rang and a voice in my ear said, 'You know those people down south, they are about to be invaded. Bring your brigade to 72 hours notice to load and sail south.' It was Major General Jeremy Moore, my immediate boss. At that time I commanded 3 Commando Brigade, and he commanded Commando Forces.

This call came as a surprise, since my brigade had been stood down only two days before. Furthermore, most of my staff was in Denmark planning a NATO exercise. So I was in the unenviable position of a commander without a staff; there was no question of me saying to them, 'here's what I want done, I will be back in an hour to see how you are doing and take any questions you may have.' It was a case of getting out pens and paper, blank sheets of paper, because there was no contingency plan, and starting from almost square one; almost, because we used the

NATO plan for the amphibious reinforcement of northern Norway during a time of tension as a template. It rapidly became less and less useful as units were added to my brigade demanding more shipping for troops, equipment, and combat supplies.

Fortunately the staff returned by tea-time on that first hectic day. My brigade was spread to the four winds, some on leave or preparing to go on leave, some still returning from Norway, and one company just finishing jungle training in Brunei – hardly an appropriate preparation for fighting in a very cold place where trees are conspicuous by their absence.

THE AMPHIBIOUS SCENE IN 1982

I would like to fill in here with some background to the UK amphibious scene in 1982. Operations in support of NATO was our task. There was no expectation of a British unilateral operation. The amphibious concept was based on the premise that the force would get to Norway, or Denmark, in time to carry out what was called an 'administrative landing'. The plan depended for success on the Soviets not attacking before we had landed – however ridiculous that may sound now.

The status of Great Britain's amphibious art in 1982 is encapsulated by this quote which appeared in *The Times* on 16 July 1981, 'Amphibious: an out of date concept of operations requiring no particular expertise which is temporarily undertaken by the Royal Marines'. This was probably written in the MoD by a cynical staff officer at around the time of the 1981 Defence Review, as part of a satirical A–Z of Defence Terminology. Although penned tongue in cheek, like most caricatures it contained more than a grain of truth; in this case it reflected the low esteem in which amphibious operations were held by the MoD in general and the RN in particular, the major howler in the quote being the implication that amphibious operations are the sole preserve of the RM and a game invented by them for their amusement.

For some years there had been no dedicated amphibious group commander – Commodore Amphibious Warfare (COMAW) as we called him then; now the COMATAG. The post of COMAW was reconstituted only a couple of years before the Falklands Conflict, and less than one year before that war, Commodore Mike Clapp was appointed. He happily moved down to Plymouth alongside my HQ. However, unlike me, he did not have sufficient staff, and any augmentation was at the expense of his boss, the Flag Officer Third Flotilla.

Because of a moratorium on defence spending, Mike Clapp and I had never exercised together in the ten months before the Falklands War. But, as Commodore, he witnessed some minor exercises in Denmark and Norway. He did, however, learn something about the RM, Landing ships Logistics (LSLs), Ro-Ro ferries, and gave much thought to inshore naval operations and the use of Merchant ships. But he had already had three Ship commands, and as an ex-Buccaneer Squadron Commanding Officer (CO) with many hours in all-weather fighters, he knew a lot about air operations; fortunately, as it turned out.

I was in a somewhat better position as far as amphibious practice was concerned, having carried out countless amphibious exercises in every rank from troop commander to brigade commander, as well as having been the CoS of the Commando Brigade. I was also fortunate in having an experienced brigade staff, which I had exercised on several occasions during the previous 15 months in both amphibious operations and conventional land warfare.

APPROACH TO BATTLE

From the first alarm and excursion, seven weeks elapsed until we landed at San Carlos Water. During this time diplomatic negotiations were taking place, and from 1 May onwards, Rear Admiral Woodward, forward with the carriers, was engaged in the battles for sea and air control. In addition he landed Special Forces to carry out reconnaissance, in response to Mike Clapp's and my tasking – in general the Special Boat Squadron (SBS) were tasked by Commodore Clapp, and I tasked the Special Air Service (SAS). The CO of 22 SAS and Officer Commanding (OC) SBS were both in HMS *Fearless*, the Landing Platform Dock (LPD) and amphibious command ship in which both the Commodore and I were embarked. The SAS and SBS troops were forward with the carrier battle group. The Commodore and I sent tasking signals to the carrier battle group, and these could be elaborated over the secure voice SATCOM to Colonel Preston, my liaison officer with Rear Admiral Woodward.

These seven weeks were an invaluable time for us in the Amphibious Task Group. We needed time to get to know each other, organise, do some basic amphibious training especially for those elements of my brigade that had never done any, notably the two parachute battalions, two troops of the Blues and Royals, and others. Most importantly, we needed to develop drills for landing from what one of my staff called the 'British Rail Ferry Amphibious Fleet'. We also had to plan. We spent almost three weeks at Ascension doing just that. Even that was not long enough, and there was a great deal we would have liked to have done, and even more that we certainly should have done. We did, however, achieve a measure of combat loading out of the chaos that ensued as a result of our hurried departure from the UK with combat supplies, and vehicles tipped in any old how.

What was evident was the value of having staffs that knew what was required in an amphibious operation. What do I mean? I referred to the 'British Rail Ferry Amphibious Fleet', Ships Taken Up From Trade (STUFT) for short. Without these we would not have even contemplated an amphibious landing. But, for example, how do you get three battalions or Commandos off a cruise liner into landing craft at night, in a seaway? This was but one of the numerous problems that had to be solved before we reached the Amphibious Operating Area (AOA). Only by applying years of experience in amphibious exercises did the staffs arrive at the answer, and by putting the troops through their paces again and again, by day and night, were able to make it work: first in a hazardous cross-decking operation deep in the South Atlantic, in open waters in marginal weather conditions; later at night in Falkland Sound; and finally in daylight under air attack in San Carlos Water. This is but one example of many where staff experience in amphibious techniques were put to good use in the employment of merchant ships as landing ships, as well as in many other areas.

We had no full-scale rehearsal, or even a turn-away landing (the minimum demanded by the manuals); there were no beaches at Ascension, and no training areas on which we could deploy. Helicopter landings were restricted to the airfield because of the risk of damage to their engines caused by ingesting the volcanic ash that lay everywhere. We needed every helicopter and spare engine for the landings and subsequent operations.

From the time we landed on 21 May, it took six days to complete the amphibious landing. Under NATO plans we were allowed six days to land a two commando group force with combat supplies over Ro-Ro terminals and with a friendly infrastructure. So the Amphibious Group did pretty well to land a brigade of 7 major units and 15 minor ones with guns, ammunition, equipment and combat supplies in much the same time with fewer helicopters, but more landing craft. We were under air attack and there were no Ro-Ro terminals, docksides, or friendly Host Nation Support to speed things up.

It took a further three weeks for the Amphibious Group to land Divisional HQ and 5 Infantry Brigade, and to support the advance on Stanley and the defeat of the Argentinian forces.

In an amphibious operation, the RN provides the sea transports (augmented by Merchant Navy STUFT), as well as escorts, minesweepers, landing craft, support helicopters, the organic air attack and air defence assets (although the latter three may be supplemented and backed-up by the RAF). It may be necessary to fight a maritime and air battle before any landing can take place, and continue to do so while it does. For some time after landing, the landing force is likely to be vulnerable to counter-attack and lack essential equipment. In these circumstances overall command of an amphibious operation falls naturally to a naval officer.

The planning of an amphibious operation cannot however, be a purely naval affair, although it is a naval lead, so it is usual for the landing force commander to be of equal rank to the naval commander and have an equal voice in planning.

An amphibious operation remains a naval responsibility until the landing force commander is satisfied that his force ashore has secured the beachhead and is ashore in sufficient numbers, that he has good communications, sufficient combat supplies and is ready to fight independently. Command is then, in the jargon, 'chopped' ashore.

The Amphibious Group transfers its support helicopters to the landing force commander, and may also transfer other assets such as landing craft. At this stage the Amphibious Group is free to go and collect reinforcements or operate elsewhere. On Operation 'Corporate' the Amphibious Task Group remained in San Carlos Water, landed Divisional HQ and 5 Infantry Brigade, and supported both brigades in the advance to and battles for Stanley. The operational control of support helicopters also remained with the Amphibious Task Group.

Now the command structure for the operation; this is shown in Figure 8.1, and was in force from 2 to 10 April. It subsequently changed, as is discussed later. However, despite these changes, this version seems to have taken root in many minds ever since 2 April 1982, especially in the consciousness of those who viewed the war from Whitehall.

From 10 April, the command chain was changed to the structure shown in Figure 8.2. All three Task Group Commanders reported back to the Task Force Commander at Northwood. Both the Commodore and I would have liked to have seen an in-Theatre overall commander. We were, and are, believers in face-to-face command. We wanted an overall commander who we hoped would spend much of his time visiting his groups, learning their problems and strengths, maintaining a clear operational concept, boosting morale and guiding overall tactical balance in-theatre, and especially keeping the HQ in Northwood off our backs.

The command chain in Figure 8.2 did not make clear how Clapp, as the Amphibious Group Commander, and I, as the Landing Force Commander, should relate to each other. But, we mutually agreed to operate along NATO lines, with the COMATAG taking the lead, until command was 'chopped

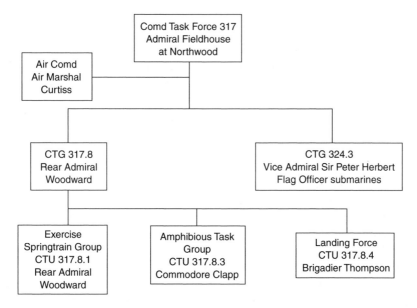

Figure 8.1. Operation Corporate Command Organisation, 2–10 April 1982.

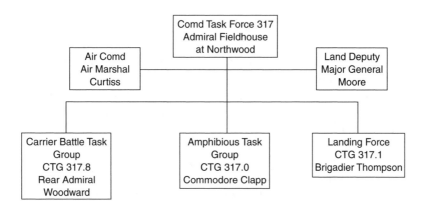

Figure 8.2. Operation Corporate Command Organisation, 10 April–12 May 1982.

Note: South Georgia and Sub-Surface Task Groups not shown.

ashore', as outlined earlier. We lived in the same ship, took all our meals together, shared briefings and spent much of our day together, as did our two staffs, and got on well. However, the command set-up relied on personalities to work. Luckily it did.

The Task Groups rendezvoused at Ascension on 17 April. Admiral Fieldhouse, the Commander Task Force (CTF 317), flew out to visit us with some of his staff and Major General Jeremy Moore. During the course of discussions, Admiral Fieldhouse asked the Commodore to send him plans for three possible landing places in the Falklands so he could submit them to the MoD. We never received an Initiating Directive, from which all amphibious planning should flow.

Even at this early stage, San Carlos Water looked to have possibilities. It offered a relatively secure anchorage and defendable area, but was a long way from Stanley. It was, from a naval point of view, much too close to Argentina for comfort. The other two options we favoured were Cow Bay/Volunteer Bay and Berkeley Sound (the latter only if the enemy looked like 'throwing in the towel', and needed a push to persuade him). Both were less attractive from a naval point of view as they were exposed on one side to submarine and air attack, and the hinterland was not high enough to make it difficult for an air attack from that direction. They were both further from Argentina, but the beaches at Cow Bay/Volunteer Bay in particular were exposed to swell which might make off-loading from landing craft difficult if not impossible. As the name of the game in amphibious operations is fast build-up, anything that jeopardises that, such as using beaches that are exposed to bad weather, should be avoided if at all possible.

Fairly early on, it became clear that we would not be able to use either of the carriers as a Landing Platform Helicopter (LPH), so we dropped the idea of Cow Bay/Volunteer Bay, as we realised the assault would have to be made by landing craft, including using the LCUs as troop landing craft in order to get enough troops ashore in one lift as quickly as possible. For safety this would have to be at night, or at least start at night. Our eyes then lit on Port Salvador. It had obvious landing force advantages over San Carlos, but from a naval point of view it had many of the same limitations as Cow Bay and Volunteer Bay. An LSL could get in through the narrow entrance, but all other ships would have to off-load outside by landing craft or helicopter, and be exposed to weather, swell and air attack. It became our second option.

San Carlos was still the best. It provided a sheltered anchorage without the risk of swell. Ro-Ro ferries and LSLs could be off-loaded without their stern doors pitching wildly and smashing LCUs and large motorised pontoons used for moving heavy logistic vehicles and equipment from ship to shore (Mexeflotes). The holding looked good, and the hills on either side would provide some protection from air attack, or at least channel it and make the enemy easier targets. The submarine and mining threat remained;

we had no minesweepers, but the narrow entrance might be off-putting to a submarine commander.

From my point of view as the Landing Force commander, the benefits of San Carlos were:

- plenty of good beaches
- easily defendable ground
- plenty of elbow room
- an area for our logistic units
- good exits for tracked vehicles
- the enemy would have to lift guns some 30 miles if he wanted to attack us.

The only disadvantage was that it was some 50 miles from Stanley as the crow flies.

Major General Moore visited us at Ascension on 29 April and took our plans back to Northwood. All we now awaited was confirmation from Special Forces and Northwood. We still waited for news on how the 5 Infantry Brigade was to be used.

The first Special Forces insertions were made on 1 May. These were mainly made by helicopter landing patrols at least one night's march away from the objective to avoid compromising the location of the target. Most patrols were extracted for debriefing because, with the exception of a few SATCOM sets taken south by the SAS, the radios available at the time did not have on-line encryption or burst-transmission facilities. Messages could be encoded using a one-time pad, but vital long transmissions giving beach and other information were susceptible to detection by direction-finding equipment and risked compromising the localities in which Clapp and I were interested. So SBS and other patrols were debriefed face-to-face after extraction back to the Carrier Battle Group by helicopter. As pick-up points were similarly distant from the Special Forces objective in question for the same reason, reconnaissance was a time-consuming business – a fact that was not always appreciated in higher HQ.

In early May, Rear Admiral Woodward sent an exclusive highly classified signal to Northwood which he copied to me. He was concerned about the air situation, and his last sentence read; 'a ticket on a train about to leave Ascension will be very expensive'. One did not have to be a genius to work out what he meant. It was not a signal I showed round too widely. By this time the LSLs had been sent ahead of the main body of the Amphibious Group, and it was too late to change loading to take account of the fact that we would not have air superiority over the landing beaches.

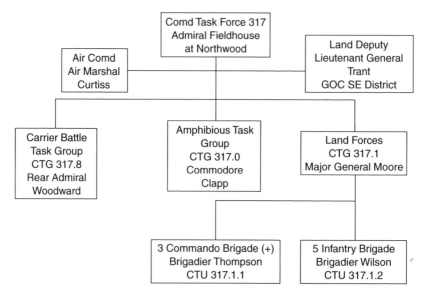

Figure 8.3. Operation Corporate Command Change, 12 May 1982.

We sailed from Ascension on 7 May, and the plans were accepted on 11 May. On 12 May, we received the latest Aim: 'Repossess the Falkland Islands as quickly as possible'. This gave us the go-ahead to plan in detail for the landings. Fortunately we were ready, and we took the 'as quickly as possible' to mean just that.

An interesting situation then arose as Major General Moore flew down to join the liner *Queen Elizabeth 2* on 20 May (D minus one). Lieutenant General Sir Richard Trant, then GOC South East District, took over Moore's job of Land Deputy to the Task Force. Before this a command change as shown in Figure 8.3 was promulgated. Major General Moore had also sent me a directive:

> You are to secure a bridgehead on East Falkland, into which reinforcements can be landed, in which an airstrip can be established and from which operations to repossess the Falkland Islands can be achieved.
>
> You are to push forward from the bridgehead area so far as the maintenance of its security allows, to gain information, to establish moral and physical domination over the enemy, and to forward the ultimate aim of repossession. You will retain operational control of all forces landed in the Falklands until I establish my headquaters in

the area. It is my intention to do this aboard *Fearless*, as early as possible after the landing. I expect this to be approximately on D+7. It is then my intention to land 5 Infantry Brigade into the beachhead and to develop operations for the complete repossession of the Falkland Islands.

Unfortunately the secure communications facilities in the *Queen Elizabeth 2* broke down, and although Major General Moore became the Commodore's opposite number at a critical time in the amphibious operation, neither Northwood, the Commodore, nor I could communicate with him some thousands of miles away. This led to misunderstandings and conflicting instructions.

When we joined up with Rear Admiral Woodward's Group, the Commodore collected his escorts. He then had 19 ships under command, of which 18 would go into San Carlos for the landings:
Task Group 317.0 During the Amphibious Phase

> 2 × LPD (*Fearless* with HQ 3 Commando Brigade embarked, plus 40 Commando cross-decked from *Canberra; Intrepid* with 3 Para from *Canberra*)
> 1 × DLG
> 8 × DD/FF
> 5 × RFA (one with bulk 45 Commando embarked)
> 5 × LSL (one more joins 24 May)
> 4 × STUFT (including *Canberra* with 42 Commando rear elements, 40 Commando and 3 Para embarked, *Norland* with 2 Para embarked)

Later additions/changes:

> 5 × DD/FF
> 5 × RFA
> 4 × STUFT
> 1 × minesweeper support ship
> 5 × minesweeping trawlers
> 2 × offshore patrol vessels

If the *Elk*, stuffed with some 2,000 tons of high explosive (HE; including missiles, gun and mortar ammunition, mines, and explosives) had been hit, the result might have been a 2 kiloton detonation in enclosed waters which could have ruined our day, so the Commodore decided to leave her behind. As the war progressed the size of the amphibious group changed as ships came in and out of the AOA.

On 17 May, we were ordered by Task Force HQ to trans-ship a large number of men from the *Canberra*, deep in the 'filthy fifties latitudes' of the South Atlantic Ocean. How they imagined we were supposed to achieve this I have no idea, but incredibly the weather calmed and the very long swell was just suitable for landing craft. Perhaps the most amazing cross-decking operation in history took place with very little problem. The only catastrophe was the loss of a Sea King helicopter carrying SAS, of whom 17 were killed with two aircrew. I believe they struck an albatross.

Some troops were now in new and unfamiliar surroundings and my landing tables had to be changed. The actual timing of the landing was also changed quite late on, in order to compromise between the Commodore's need to complete the run-in as late as possible, while I, as landing force commander, wanted to arrive as early as possible so that all high ground would be held by dawn.

THE ASSAULT AND BUILD-UP

In general, I think, the landing on 21 May went much better than it might. There had been no chance of a full rehearsal and the delays that occurred were largely through lack of practice, but most of the plans worked out pretty well.

However, the communications in *Fearless* were appalling, as usual. The landing force circuits were totally blanked out by the much more powerful naval ones. This was a familiar problem to me from exercises, and it made command impossible. In my opinion a commander must be able to do three things:

1. find out what is going on;
2. be able to consult with and instruct his staff to sort the problem out;
3. be able to pass his orders to the units who are going to act on his plan changes.

If he cannot do all three, he is in the wrong place. I could do 2, but not 1 or 3. The only solution in these circumstances is to go ashore and see what is going on. My normal routine on exercises was to land my Tactical HQ early on day one, and roam by helicopter, and move my Main HQ ashore to be ready for occupation by first light on D+1 at the latest. This I did and, as on exercises, I stayed ashore, commanding my brigade. In *Fearless* I was unable to achieve anything.

The Commodore, while supporting the idea that I must command in amongst my troops, was not entirely happy with the way it worked out as we lost close contact with each other and the liaison we had arranged was not entirely satisfactory; a casualty of our lack of practice together and lack of realism in peacetime exercises. Mike was under attack even if I was not yet!

The air situation had an adverse effect on my logistics. As shown by Figure 8.4, we had a puny medium and heavy helicopter lift. The maximum numbers of helicopters available were as follows:

Throughout	Sea King Mark 4: 11 aircraft available, but 1 in use for Rapier support and 4 in special use configured night flying with passive night goggles (PNG)
21–26 May	11 (6) Sea King Mark 4; 5 Wessex = 16 (11)
26 May–1 June	as before plus 1 Chinook = 17 (12)
1–9 June	as before but 19 Wessex plus 4 Sea King Mark 2 = 35 (29)
From 9 June	as before but 23 Wessex plus 10 Sea King Mark 2 = 45 (39)

There were no roads, and every bullet and bean had to be carried on men's backs or in helicopters. The helicopter routes forward were very vulnerable to interdiction. Until the enemy air force had taken a hammering, it would have been very foolish to rely on this tenuous heli-borne Line of Communication (LOC). Hence there was no point in rushing off out of the beachhead.

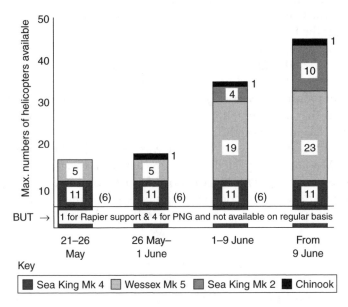

Figure 8.4. Landing force medium/heavy lift helicopter availability.

Despite the air attacks, within a couple of days the Assault and Initial Planned Unloading Phase was complete. It had been well planned and relatively easy to execute. The Amphibious Task Group now entered the General Unloading Phase. Here life became far more worrying and hectic as they tried hard to react to the requests from me, calling ships in for a day and sending others out. It all became piecemeal and chaotic. The Commodore, therefore, settled for emptying ships as fast as he could, day and night. It was not a very satisfactory method but I do not see what else could be achieved. It seemed better to have my Brigade's equipment and combat supplies safely ashore in the mud and rain, rather than possibly pickled in salt and out of depth. Some ships had to be sailed with unit first lines of ammunition, rations and radio batteries still onboard to avoid keeping an otherwise almost empty ship in the anchorage under air threat. Unfortunately it was not always possible to tranship them at sea and bring them back in, so the Landing Force never saw these until the end of the war.

Within six days, the Commodore had landed most of my Brigade's equipment and combat supplies and he sought me out and asked me if I was ready to end the Amphibious Operation. I said 'yes'. I was now preoccupied with plans to take Darwin and Goose Green. The Commodore sailed to collect Major General Moore early and brief him as soon as he could after his long incarceration at sea. They had a lot to discuss. He then brought in the Divisional HQ and 5 Infantry Brigade, and, in some ways, for the Commodore a much less easy, unplanned, period began. He found that the Divisional HQ staff were a breath of fresh air because they had just spent ten days in a luxury liner, largely out of touch with us and Northwood, and had had no part in the confusion and worries of the early planning. They had no hang-ups and were fresh and raring to go. The Commodore's only criticism of them would be that in the low cloud conditions that met them, not all of them, perhaps, took his warnings of air attack seriously enough.

As Landing Force Commander, I was extremely glad to see Major General Moore, having filled his role for ten days. I was now relieved of the chore of dealing with Northwood. At last I could get on with what I found most satisfying, commanding my brigade, and I began to enjoy the Falklands Land Campaign, if enjoy is the right word.

MARITIME POWER PROJECTION

The operation, of course, remained a case of Maritime Power Projection right to the end. Nothing in the land campaign, or indeed the landings, would have been possible without surface, sub-surface and air operations in all their forms. This began with the taking of South Georgia on 25 April, and the enforcement of the Total Exclusion Zone (TEZ) on 1 May. On that same day ships began closing with the coast and bombarding enemy positions by day and night, while air attacks were mounted on Stanley airfield and other targets by the Sea Harriers and, of course, the two Vulcan sorties. It is worth remembering that these operations cost six ships sunk, and considerably more damaged. Some 30 aircraft of all types were also lost. Throughout the war, Maritime Power Projection made possible movements of troops and supplies in craft and ships, of which the transhipment of large numbers of both to Port Salvador and Fitzroy were but two of many.

The air bridge to Ascension was maintained by the RAF from Day 1; and it is still in place today. South of Ascension, RAF Nimrods patrolled, and RAF C-130s dropped urgent supplies into the sea for ships, and also a replacement CO for 2 Para. Victor Tankers refuelled aircraft transiting south of Ascension.

As far as my brigade was concerned, we had always planned to use Port Salvador and Teal Inlet especially as a forward Brigade Maintenance Area (BMA). This would cut down the long turn-round distance for the scarce helicopter force, moving ammunition and other combat supplies forward to my locations in the vicinity of Mount Kent and ultimately Stanley. Instead of having to fly the 100-miles round trip, it would be only some 40 miles.

Another example of Maritime Power Projection was provided by the direct support of units ashore with naval gunfire. This was highly effective and the weight of fire contributed in no small way to our success. While carrying out this task HMS *Glamorgan* was badly hit and survived only by first-class seamanship.

Close air support was provided both by the Sea Harriers and most expertly by the RAF version of the Harrier (Harrier GR3) of Number 1 Squadron RAF. Some GR3s were forward based ashore during daylight hours to provide a quicker reaction time. Of course, the air defence of the AOA and later the positions forward was essential. The distance the carriers were required to maintain from the Argentinian mainland, as well as the needs of the ships for air protection, meant a CAP could not be maintained over the land force all the time.

Logistics were sea-based. This meant that supplies could be held off until required, although sufficient stocks had to be maintained ashore as well. The point is that without Maritime Power Projection assets, there would have been no logistics.

I have only briefly alluded to STUFT. Fifty ships were taken up:

3 Liners
15 Tankers
8 Ro-Ro general cargo
1 Container ship
4 Passenger/general cargo
6 General cargo
4 Offshore support vessels
3 Sea-going tugs
1 Cable ship
5 Motor vessels commissioned as mine-counter vessels.

These ships were all required to steam in convoy, react to naval signals and manoeuvre accordingly, defend themselves, darken ship, and resupply at sea (RAS). One of my most vivid memories of the pre-landing phase was standing on *Fearless*'s bridge wing one night well into the southerly latitudes, watching her taking on fuel from tanker. On the other side was the mighty *Canberra* also refuelling, looking as though she had done it all her life, instead of carrying luxury cruise passengers. One was reminded, if one needed reminding, what fine seamen there are in the Merchant Fleet. Maritime Force Projection operations continued well after the surrender, and of course for months.

LESSONS LEARNED

As far as lessons learned are concerned, I am tempted to say that there were no new lessons learned. Both as a practitioner and a military historian I am inclined to the view that you never learn any *new* lessons in war, only re-learn old ones that have been forgotten or discarded in the exigencies of peacetime budgeting and unrealistic exercises; or perhaps ignoring or misreading the past, especially the old precept, the unexpected always happens. Perhaps I am being cynical.

I offer the following, and I do not include lessons that are peculiar to a particular branch of the armed forces: such as: always have your medics as close up behind you as possible in a land battle; or the importance of damage control at sea. I stick to Force Projection lessons as I see them.

- First a general catch-all: *The Unexpected Always Happens.*
- Next the need for carrier-based air defence independent of shore-based aircraft, equipped with the most sophisticated radar and

missile systems. These may be required to protect ground troops as well as amphibious ships in the AOA and the fleet. Second best will not do. Following from my first premise, the unexpected always happens, it is no good 'situating the appreciation' as we used to call it at the Staff College Camberley – 'situating the estimate' I suppose I should now call it – in other words 'shaping' the threats to fit your capability, and ignoring those to which, inconveniently, you have no response. A good example of 'situating the estimate', is the recent MoD decision to dispense with Sea Harrier Mark II, based on the premise that we need strike aircraft but not air defence fighters at sea, because the enemy we will face will not have a strike capability, or if he does, we will either be operating within the range of land-based air or in alliance with the United States.

- Logistics, and their importance cannot be overemphasized. The critical shortage in the Falklands Conflict was medium- and heavy-lift helicopters, and this had a direct effect on logistics. As part of logistics, the heavy expenditure of ammunition by both ships and shore-based artillery and mortars came as a surprise to some; again not a new lesson. I would like to quote what one of my most battle-experienced company commanders wrote.

> All comments and lessons from the logistics of the campaign should be leavened by the fact that this must be one of the few fought by a regular force since the internal combustion engine became generally available, where the widespread use of wheeled transport was not possible. This, combined with the speed with which it was necessary to put the whole act together, and the enemy's efforts to disrupt the act, makes it arguable that we were fortunate to have any logistics at all.

- One cannot overplay the importance of access to suitable British Flag merchantmen with *British* crews. In order to bring a merchant crew, provided it is British, under Naval discipline, all that is required is to read the Articles of War over them. For the Gulf War it was sufficient to charter ships, of any flag. But, they were not required to Resupply at Sea (RSA), to evade submarines, to steam darkened, to endure air attacks, to transfer troops and equipment by day and night to landing craft in a seaway; sometimes under air attack. Which raises the question, have we got enough British Flag merchant ships?
- There is a need for an overall in-theatre commander who can command forward, and at the same time shield the operational,

component commanders from 'long screw-drivers' being wielded by the superior HQ back in the UK. Although political interference with operational and tactical matters was notable by its absence in the Falklands Conflict, it has certainly been a feature of operations since, and is likely to arise in the future – especially in the case of Governments who are obsessed with media management and image to the exclusion of all else.

- Finally there is a need for staffs trained in all aspects of Maritime Force Projection operations, including Amphibious Operations. It does not take much time and effort to train soldiers to get in and out of helicopters and landing craft. It does take time to train staffs and leaders at all levels to cope with an environment which Admiral Jackie Fisher once described as 'an impenetrable mystery surrounded by sea-sickness'.

9

The Land Campaign: A Company Commander's Perspective

LIEUTENANT GENERAL J.P. KISZELY

It has to be said at the outset that, in the greater scheme of things, a company-level perspective is pretty much a worm's-eye view. To make any assessment of the land campaign as a whole from such a perspective would provide a seriously skewed picture, and this chapter does not attempt such an assessment. What it does try and give is a perspective of the land campaign at company level: what it was like, both at the time, and with '20–20' hindsight. It does not set out to encapsulate a definitive company-level picture, even if such a thing were possible. It is very much 'a' company commander's perspective.

My company in 2nd Battalion of the Scots Guards was called Left Flank because...well, because it always had been, certainly as far as we were concerned. It was one of the Battalion's three rifle companies and consisted of a small HQ plus three rifle platoons, each of which numbered about 30 men, commanded by a subaltern (a second lieutenant or lieutenant). Since there were eight infantry units in the Falklands – either Army battalions or Royal Marine Commandos – mine was one of 24 rifle companies. I had been lucky enough to have been commanding it for about 18 months of a 2-year tour of duty. This 18 months' training experience had given one ample opportunity to make a lot of mistakes where it did not matter. I had also decided at the outset that I would make any personnel changes by the six-month point, and, for better or worse, none thereafter. As a result, we were a very tight-knit team. The British regimental system meant that the battalion as a whole knew each other well, having lived and moved and had its being together over many years. But a company is a special command. As a company commander it is the last one you have which is small enough – about 100 men – for you to get to know them all as individuals really well (and vice versa), and where you are not too senior for them to do so. After that, it is a battalion of about 600 men, where to the ordinary private soldier the CO is, if not God, then certainly closely related to Him.

As a Public Duties (i.e. ceremonial) battalion based at Chelsea Barracks, it might be thought that we could have been surprised, on 5 April 1982, to be nominated to join the Falklands Task Force, but I do not think we were. At that time battalions were not on the extended readiness that many are today, and were expected to be able to deploy at relatively short notice. I guess we were selected because we were available, but we did have some significant advantages: our training had focused on two areas that were critical as far as the Falklands were concerned – shooting and fitness. Indeed we had just completed our annual battalion shooting concentration. And the previous year we had carried out a six-week battalion tactical exercise in Kenya. It was said that we might be used as garrison troops, but I certainly told my company that the more they heard that said, the more certain it was that we were going there to fight. As soon as the battalion was warned, it started a highly intensive training programme which included a fortnight's brigade exercise in the – fortuitously cold and wet – Welsh mountains, and the training continued for the whole of the three-weeks voyage south on the *Queen Elizabeth 2*. So when we landed at San Carlos on 1 June, we had been carrying out specific preparation and training for nearly two months, were self-confident in our ability, and had in large measure what Field Marshal Slim called 'the first essential in the fighting man – the desire to close with the enemy'.

It is difficult now to believe that the whole land campaign, Special Forces operations excepted, lasted less than a month, and for us only a fortnight. And of that fortnight, only the last eight hours were spent in combat. One must, therefore, be careful to avoid over-generalising about lessons to be learnt from such a short campaign in such a special environment, and against a particular enemy. Our first three days were spent in tactical positions around San Carlos Water, getting used to living in the open in the foul South Atlantic winter and operating across the rugged Falklands terrain, before moving in Landing Craft from HMS *Invincible* in a very cold, wet voyage around the coast to Fitzroy where we were deployed into the hills above. But apart from engaging the aircraft which had just attacked Bluff Cove (the battalion fired over 15,000 rounds, and claimed at least two hits) we made no contact with the enemy. It was at Fitzroy that we received our orders for the assault on Mount Tumbledown, and from where we deployed forward by helicopter to an assembly area, just short of the start line for the attack. In our means of deployment we were certainly lucky. Some people, including 45 Commando and 3 Para, had 'tabbed' or 'yomped' all the way from San Carlos, carrying their equipment with them – and, not surprisingly, resented these 'Johnny-come-latelys' who had hitched lifts on passing landing-craft and helicopters.

At this stage of the battle for Port Stanley, the plan was for a series of night assaults on the hills surrounding the capital. On 11 June, Mount Harriet would be taken by 42 Commando, Two Sisters by 45 Commando and Mount Longdon by 3 Para. The next night would see simultaneous attacks on Tumbledown by the Scots Guards and on Wireless Ridge by 2 Para, with the Welsh Guards and the Gurkhas subsequently exploiting to Sapper Hill and Mount William on the outskirts of the town. The original plan envisaged a direct daylight attack on Tumbledown, but happily this was changed. There were two further important amendments. First, the main attack would not take place north up the obvious approach track to Stanley; this would be the direction of a diversionary attack, with the main assault from the western flank. Second, the attacks on Tumbledown and Wireless Ridge would be delayed by 24 hours to allow proper battle procedure to take place and for extra artillery ammunition to be brought forward. Both these amendments were, in my view, the right decisions, and saved casualties.

The delay, although at the expense of momentum at the operational level, allowed the CO to brief the company commanders overlooking the objective; I was able to do the same with my platoon and section commanders. They had, therefore, a firm picture in their minds of the overall plan and their part in it. As I was carrying out my own reconnaissance, I had a serendipitous meeting with a troop commander of 42 Commando who had just carried out their successful assault on Mount Harriet. I sat him down and quizzed him for about an hour, in particular on the enemy, and on what tactics had been successful and what had not. In the absence of any really useful intelligence, this was gold dust, and I was able to pass it all on when I held my own briefings and orders later.

After an uncomfortable day being sporadically shelled, we were keen to get started. Our own battalion attack began at around 2200 hours, and Left Flank's at about midnight. It lasted, if I remember rightly, until about 0700 the next day. The battalion plan was a good one. It was for a diversionary attack – in the event, highly effective – of about platoon strength but with two tracked armoured reconnaissance vehicles, followed by three sequential company attacks, one to gain a foothold on the mountain, one (Left Flank) to take the summit, and one to exploit to the furthest end of the mountain's spine. My own plan was to move with two platoons up in extended line separated by company HQ, with my third platoon behind in reserve.

I do not give a blow-by-blow account but, in outline, very little went according to plan for us and almost everything that could go wrong did. The enemy – the 5th Marine Battalion – were well dug-in and waited until we were about 100 metres away before opening fire with every weapon they had. In the ensuing fire-fight, half my company HQ got separated; both forward platoons were pinned down and, every time they moved forward, took casualties. We continued to be shelled and mortared, and were unable to 'win the fire-fight'. Contrary to expectations, the enemy were standing and fighting. The artillery, key to our ability for fire-and-manoeuvre, had a major problem getting on-target. Without fire, manoeuvre would result in heavy casualties, but that would be the price we would have to pay. Time was ebbing away, and daylight approaching; if we had not succeeded by then, the subsequent attacks would be in broad daylight. And in between the snow flurries, the bitterly cold conditions were resulting in the first signs of exposure in a number of my men.

To cut a long story short, eventually the guns provided fire on target; my left-hand platoon was able to provide some additional fire support from the crags, allowing my right-hand platoon to charge up the hill. A few enemy stayed; most broke and ran. But, largely as a result of casualties, only seven men initially reached the summit, three of whom were immediately shot and wounded. It was about ten minutes before the reserve platoon arrived to secure it, and the following company subsequently passed through to clear the remainder of the mountain. Within about an hour, the enemy in and around Stanley started putting up white flags. The cost to my company was 7 killed and 20 wounded. Among the casualties were a platoon commander, two platoon sergeants, three section commanders, the company sergeant major and my radio operator. All of which was a sobering moment for a company commander in the cold, grey light of dawn.

My abiding memories of the battle itself are of trying to make sense out of incomplete and conflicting information, of trying to get and keep one step ahead of the opposition, to dominate events and not be dominated by them, to try and think clearly despite what Field Marshal Brooke described as 'the thousand and one factors that are hammering away at one's powers of resistance'. Training had prepared us for most of these, but not all. The noise of the battlefield is one. Incoming artillery

The Land Campaign: A Company Perspective

and mortar rounds, grenades exploding near you, have your ears ringing, and at times you become almost completely deaf. You realise this only when you shout at someone to do something, and it is quite clear they cannot hear you. The only way to get your message across is to run over to them, grip them by the arm and shout into their ear. Then there is the effect in the dark of immensely bright flashes of light as the shells and grenades explode. You are blinded, and just as your eyes get accustomed to the dark again, the same thing happens. You also tend to become over-focused on the enemy immediately to your front. The result of all this is disorientation and confusion. At the same time you have a mass of information, much of it contradictory, coming in to you over the radio nets, such as casualty reports. Not just exercise casualties, but real people – your family. And yet there is no time for emotion, that can wait; and hardly time for much fear, you are too busy, and you are responsible for so many people's lives. It is those people, ordinary soldiers, with no such responsibility to keep their minds occupied, for whom it is far, far harder, and who need all their courage and discipline to combat fear. In my company, their courage and discipline was never found wanting, and I found it inspirational.

So, bearing in mind the previous warnings about over-generalising from the particular, what major lessons did I take away then and which remain with me today?

First, the importance of group cohesion. I had no doubts about the cohesion of my company, but I remember saying to the one remaining platoon sergeant later in the morning, 'You know, that was a close-run thing,' and he replied, 'Come on, Sir! No way was Left Flank going to back off that hill!' This goes right to the heart of what makes people fight, and what keeps them going and together in the face of danger. There are, of course, many factors at play here from small-group cohesion and the importance an individual attaches to how he is perceived by his mates, through the tactical entity of the company, to the wider battalion family and its heritage. In this context, two things I have since read have struck a particular chord. The first is from a German training manual, *Truppenführung 1936*: 'Mutual confidence is the secure basis for discipline in times of need and danger.' This seems to me to be at the foundation of group cohesion at the company level, with the implication that mutual confidence is, therefore, a most important goal in peacetime training. It is not something that can be created overnight; it must be built long before the times of need and danger appear. The second is the relevance of tradition on the battlefield, as seen by Field Marshal Slim: 'Regard tradition as a standard of conduct, handed down to you, below which you must never fall. Then tradition, instead of being a pair of handcuffs to fetter you, will become a handrail to steady and guide you in steep places.' It is rather important that we are clear what such cohesion in our Army depends on and preserve it if we are to avoid companies, in future, backing off the hill. And we need to be careful that we do not chip away at its edges, even if so doing will save money, or endear us to one part of society or another. Because at the end of the day, when two companies are facing each other on the hill, cohesion is likely to be the deciding factor as to who backs off.

However, one commonly (though admittedly not universally), found aspect of motivation on the battlefield which was absent in the Falklands – I believe on both sides – was a deep mutual hatred. Certainly as far as we were concerned, our enemy were merely our enemy in a professional sense. We held nothing against them personally, and treated them purely as the opposition that stood between us and accomplishment of our mission. We knew that they were basically conscript forces, who were imbued with a deep love of their country, which included for them what they called the 'Malvinas', about which they felt passionately patriotic. We felt that they were misguided about this; just as I am sure they felt we were misguided in believing that what we called the 'Falklands' were British. As a result, we treated our prisoners properly and professionally, and I think that we believed that we would have been treated no differently had fortunes been reversed. Looking around at conflicts since, I see this as being very out of the ordinary – a deep visceral hatred, more often than not, being an integral part of the *casus belli* elsewhere, and therefore a feature of how participants treat each other on and off the battlefield. In this respect, the Falklands Conflict was different. And undoubtedly this was an important factor in how quickly diplomatic relations were restored, and how quickly both sides were prepared to restrict their mutual rivalry to traditional confines, namely to the football pitch.

Turning now to the nature of conflict more generally, I believe that the Falklands Conflict illustrated graphically the difference in requirement for a company involved in Warfighting from a company involved in PSO. The latter may be just as dangerous for those caught in the crossfire between warring factions, or who need to fire to defend themselves. But a totally different psychology is required for those who find themselves Warfighting, because the object is not to resolve matters peacefully, or to help old ladies across the street (that is noble though), but – to put it bluntly – to kill as many people in as short a time as possible. This requires a very different psychological approach with, for example, a high degree of aggression and ruthlessness, precisely the attributes most unwelcome in peacekeeping. Again, this approach is not an item which can be drawn up from the stores along with the other Warfighting equipment. It is an ethos which must have been inculcated long before.

What were the other deciding factors? Undoubtedly one of the most significant was training. The 5th Marine Battalion's training may have been a cut above many of the other Argentinian units, but I do not believe it was in the same league as ours. Much of the credit for this must be given to our training schools, from the Army Staff College through the battle schools at Brecon and Warminster and Lympstone. The standards at these establishments was (and, for those that remain, is) uncompromisingly high, and universal across the Army and RM. Long may it remain so! The Russian General Suvorov had it right: 'Easy training; hard combat. Hard training; easy combat'. What these schools produced was a common standard, and one that was firmly orientated to Warfighting. It was reflected in all aspects of our training at the tactical level, and I do not believe that was the case with the opposition. I make no such claims, though, for British training at that time above the tactical level. The emphasis on Warfighting is noteworthy today when the vast majority of operations are not Warfighting but Peacekeeping, and when, not unnaturally, much training is devoted to Peacekeeping. With finite amounts of training time and limited resources, training in Warfighting to the necessary standard presents a challenge.

A further key factor was doctrinal, in particular, two aspects. First, was adherence to the 'all-arms' battle – the combination of all the different weapon systems, and those who operate them, in order to produce synergy. In this, we did quite well in the Falklands, although we persistently under-used the little armour we had, in no small measure because senior commanders were reluctant to seek, let alone take, advice from apparently inexperienced, relatively junior officers. The all-arms battle was thankfully not the strong suit of our opponents. For example, had the 5th Marine Battalion mined and wired their position on Tumbledown, I doubt whether we would have taken it. Second, was the ability and willingness to manoeuvre. In the past this has not always been our strong suit. In the Second World War, Field Marshal Rommel was highly critical of the British Army's 'rigid lack of mobility' in defence. On this occasion, it seems to me that it is a valid criticism of our opponents. Had they, for example, been looking for opportunities to counter-attack with just a few people at critical times, such as the period when only a few men held the summit of Tumbledown, the implications could have reached far beyond the tactical battle.

There were undoubtedly lessons that I took away about the effectiveness of weapon systems. The importance of air superiority was certainly one. At company level, its benefit was crucial not only in our ability to manoeuvre, but in its effect on morale – ours and the enemy's. Seeing 1,000-pound bombs crashing into Tumbledown was almost as psychologically significant to us as it was to them, even if these bombs killed no one; the side capable of delivering such a big bang looked to be the bookies' favourite. Indirect fire – artillery, both land-based and Naval Gunfire Support, and mortars – undoubtedly played a critical role, caused many casualties, neutralised the enemy and sapped their morale. The opposition did not appear to mass their indirect fire in the same way. Turning to direct-fire weapons, our heavy Browning machine guns, brought out of retirement, and our anti-tank missiles used against bunkers, provided a highly significant direct-fire punch which would otherwise not have been available. On the other hand, our standard-issue rifle, the Self-Loading Rifle (SLR) without an automatic capability, was outmatched by the enemy's, as were our first-generation night sights against their off-the-shelf buy of something much superior. This latter deficiency cost us dear.

It is worth mentioning here the great difficulty in obtaining the equipment we needed – items such as Bergen rucksacks, radios, heavy machine guns etc. Despite the obvious requirement and the fact that these items were either sitting on the shelves in the stores depots or readily available on the open market, the 'staff answer' was: 'You're not scaled for that, so you can't have it'; fair enough in a full-scale war, but far from fair enough for this small one-off deployment. The matter was eventually resolved in our favour, but in the case of the Bergens, only after questions were asked in the House of Lords. Such inflexibility of mind seemed odd at the time, and seems even odder today.

Perhaps the most enduring lesson for me was that warfare is, just as Clausewitz suggested it was, the province of chaos and uncertainty, at all levels including company level. And one came face-to-face in a very graphic way with friction – 'that which distinguishes war on paper from the real thing'. Then and since, I have seen people of various ranks, from various Services and nations, and in various circumstances, with contrasting approaches to the problem of coping with friction. At one extreme are those who believe that with sufficient force of personality and perseverance the battlefield can be tamed and order imposed upon it, and that to accommodate friction is to surrender to it. At the other extreme are those fatalists who believe that friction is inevitable and that even to try to reduce it or to avoid it is a waste of time. It seems to me that both these extremes are potentially dangerous, and that the Israeli historian Martin van Creveld had it right: 'A good army is one that whether by foresight or experience or in any other way has learned to avoid friction when it can and live with it when it cannot'; and, one might add, not just a good *army*.

A last lesson. After the conflict we were singularly unimpressed when told that we would be among the last to go home. Left Flank was sent to a farm on West Falkland where we lived in barns and haylofts for several weeks. In the event, it was not too bad. We unwound, and most nights we met for a few beers, had a sing-song, talked about those who had not made it, that sort of thing. As a result, by the time we eventually got back to Britain – needless to say, mainly by sea, not air – we had got a lot of the battlefield out of our systems. People who flew straight home after the ceasefire may have thought at the time they were lucky, but they did not have that advantage. And it just did not seem relevant to talk about it to outsiders.

Some of the lessons were more apparent than others immediately after the event. Undoubtedly, there were people in the Army who for some time afterwards did not want to hear anything about the Falklands. And I think that 'We few, we happy few, we band of brothers' should have been more sensitive to the fact that:

> Gentlemen in England, now a-bed
> Shall think themselves accurs'd that were not here
> And hold their manhoods cheap while any speaks
> That fought with us upon Saint Crispin's Day.

But the vast majority were keen to identify and learn relevant lessons. The Post Operational Report gave due consideration to the tactical-level events, but official reports by the winning side in a conflict are always liable to be, as Field Marshal Lord Carver described this one, 'largely an essay in self-congratulation'. I think that the Report did a fair job in capturing most of the significant tactical-level lessons, amplified in the other internal Army reports, that there was an appetite within the Army for the lessons to be learnt and applied, and that they duly were. One area that, in retrospect, clearly deserved more attention than it was given was that of stress-related problems, but our understanding of such things then was very limited compared to the present day.

To what extent was the Falklands ground war at unit level a valuable learning experience? Clearly it was highly valuable to anyone who had been in the fray who wished to learn – but, as alluded to earlier, a fray at a particular place in a very limited arena and against an enemy who, frankly, were not in the premier league. To claim, as some did, that they understood warfare because they had experienced it in the Falklands was, in my view, a dangerous delusion. I have learnt far more from reading and reflection than I ever did from my brief brush with warfare in the South Atlantic. What the Falklands did give me was a sounding board against which to judge some of the things I read about, and an enthusiasm to read more.

Finally, what place does the Falklands have in the evolution of conflict? Twenty years on, the war at company level appears in many ways to have more in common with what was long past than with what followed. A battalion night attack with infantry on their feet, advancing in an extended line with bayonets fixed, was a scene hardly changed from the First – let alone the Second – World War. Even in the Gulf War we did not see quite the same thing. Furthermore, the Falklands as a battlefield was a relatively simple place: no rules of engagement, no difficulty telling the bad guys from the civilian population, no vehicles, no CNN, no allies. So, was the Falklands an archetypal example of combat, the very simplicity of which lends itself as a model that can be transplanted to future times and places? Or does it now appear a throwback to a bygone imperial era, a curious aberration of little relevance to the very different operations of today and tomorrow? There are certainly those who argue the latter; but although history is unlikely to repeat itself, it seems to me that there are certainly aspects of the Falklands Conflict, particularly at the lower tactical level, that have a relevance to the future, and that therefore reward some study.

To end, there is an important context – as it happens, a Regimental one – in which to place the Falklands Conflict. When 1st Battalion Scots Guards went into the line at the start of the First Battle of Ypres in October 1914, it numbered 22 officers and 755 other ranks. When three weeks later it came out, the total number of survivors who formed up in four ranks and marched back down the Menin Road was one combatant officer, the Quartermaster, and 69 men.

10

An Experience with the Commando Logistic Regiment Royal Marines

COLONEL I.J. HELLBERG

MOBILISATION

The situation over the Falkland Islands continued to worsen. By 1 April 1982, strong elements of the Argentinian Fleet and Marine Corps had been reported at sea and it was clear to most people that an invasion of the Falklands was imminent. As CO of the Commando Logistic Regiment Royal Marines (Cdo Log Regt RM, part of 3 Commando Brigade) I assumed that elements of the RN were already at sea and in the vicinity of the Falkland Islands and therefore an invasion would be resisted. Unfortunately, this was not the case and despite a reasonable period of warning no ships (or SSN submarines) had been pre-positioned to prevent an Argentinian landing. At the end of March 1982, elements of the Cdo Log Regt RM were returning by sea from a three-month training exercise in north Norway (as it happened excellent preparation for the forthcoming conflict). Thursday, 1 April, was a day of planning speculation as far as Commando Forces were concerned, but without Government direction contingency planning was unrealistic and we were finally stood down in the evening on the basis that the crisis had been averted through diplomatic agreement. Sadly our respite was short-lived as I was woken at 0400 hours on Friday, 2 April 1982, by my Brigade Commander, Brigadier Julian Thompson, to be told that, following an emergency meeting of the Cabinet, a complete Naval Task Force, including the majority of 3 Commando Brigade, was to be sent with the greatest possible speed to the Falklands.

Fortunately, I had not fully stood the Regiment down the previous evening and had arranged an immediate recall system as I somehow felt we had not yet heard the last of the matter. By 0700 hours the whole Regiment was in camp and the first packet of ten 4-ton vehicles was heading for the ammunition depot. I felt deeply sorry for the men since the whole Regiment was due to go on Easter leave that very same day – leave that was well earned after some hard exercises and, for many, a long three-month deployment in Norway. But I need not have worried as the men accepted the challenge as a real test of their capabilities and set to work with terrific determination and enthusiasm.

The problem of outloading the entire war stocks of a brigade at short notice should never be underestimated. Problems will always arise to defeat even the best-laid plans. First, a weekend was approaching and British Rail (BR) were unable to reposition their rolling stock in time to meet any of the deadlines; it therefore meant that all the War Maintenance Reserve (WMR) stocks from the major depots would have to be outloaded by road rather than the planned rail outload. In consequence, at very short notice, HQ United Kingdom Land Forces (UKLF) had to provide a massive fleet of Royal Corps of Transport (RCT) 16-ton vehicles. Additionally we had to requisition many civilian freight vehicles. Although not planned, these additional vehicles (many driven by Territorial Auxiliary and Volunteer Reserve (TAVR) drivers to augment our own Transport Squadron) provided an excellent service and despite long delays in the depots, probably outloaded more quickly than the rail service could ever have managed! Another serious problem arose from the fact that normally the WMR stocks for at least one complete Commando Group should always remain afloat aboard an RFA supply ship, unfortunately about every four years the vessel comes in for maintenance and the stock is turned over and transferred to another RFA ship. Needless to say, as luck would have it, the crisis occurred right in the middle of this transfer period. Another difficulty (which took a very long time to unravel) arose because the unit first-line stocks were mixed in with the formation second-line stocks within the same depot. However, although the odds seemed against us, the terrific willingness of all the agencies involved both civilian and military, provided the determination to overcome the problems.

In many ways, I was pleasantly surprised that in spite of all these snags the Regiment itself was loaded and ready to go by 1600 hours Saturday 3 April – some 36 hours after the alert had been given. The loading of the initial ten days' WMR stocks on to the assigned LSLs and RFAs took rather longer but the vast majority of stocks had been loaded by 12 noon on Monday 5 April – some 80 hours after the alert had been given. Most of the amphibious task force shipping departed on the evening of the 5 April or on the morning of Tuesday 6 April. Throughout the whole operation I was delighted (and a little surprised) by the tremendous co-operation of the 'notorious' dockyard workers – they were magnificent! Once aboard the ships our fate was to a certain extent sealed by the configuration of our loading plan and also by what equipment and men we had brought and more particularly what we had left behind.

The Commando Logistic Regiment RM is designed to support the Commando Brigade at light scales in almost any environment in the world from the Arctic to the Tropics (see Figure 10.1). The Regiment (which is 80 Royal Marine cap-badged with the balance coming from specialist Naval and Army skills, such as doctors, electronic engineers etc.) had always been under-established for the job it has to do, the Squadrons (HQ, Medical, Transport, Workshops and Ordnance) rely heavily on reinforcements to bring them to war establishment. In peacetime the strength of the Regiment numbered just over 600 men; however, for this particular operation the numbers had been cut right down to 346 officers and men with only 54 prime movers and nine motor cycles. Our only reinforcements were the three Surgical Support Teams (SSTs) which were mobilised to provide the vital surgical capability to medical Squadron. Prior to embarkation, the force was discouraged from taking any vehicles, as there were no roads on the Falkland Islands, the only exception to this rule was the Volvo BV 202 over-snow vehicle, which was about the only vehicle that could cope with the soft peat to be found on the Falklands. It was only after the strongest representation that I was actually allowed to take ten fuel-podded 4-ton lorries, and nine Eager Beaver Mark 2 rough terrain fork lift tractors; at the time I was convinced that fuel would become a major problem and that we would pay a serious price for our shortage of pods and Jerry Cans (J/Cans). I was also concerned that we did not have enough Eager Beavers. At this stage I should mention that the WMR of 3 Commando Brigade consisted of a total of 30 days' stocks of Combat Supplies at Limited War rates with 60 days stocks of technical and general stores. All these stocks (approximately 9,000 tons) were loaded with tremendous speed leaving behind only a small balance of stocks to be loaded onto 'follow-up' ships.

THE JOURNEY TO THE FALKLANDS

The majority of the Regiment including Regimental Headquarters (RHQ), Transport, Workshops and Ordnance Squadron elements left Marchwood early, on 6 April, aboard the LSL *Sir Lancelot*. Medical Squadron with SSTs 2 and 3 were fortunate enough to travel aboard SS

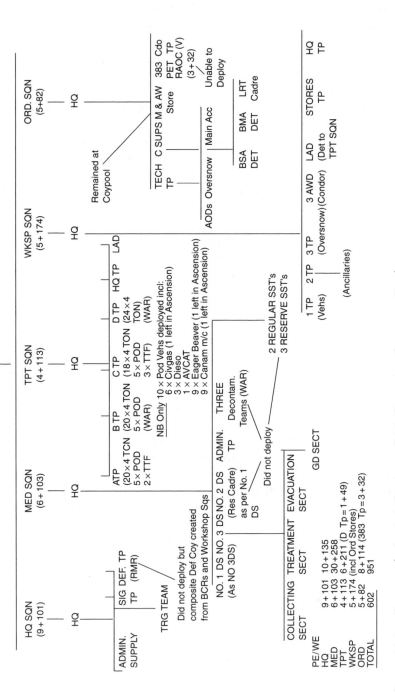

Figure 10.1. Commando Logistic Regiment RM: Operation Corporate Deployment.

Canberra, while SST 1 was embarked upon HMS *Hermes*. With hindsight I suppose one could have been forgiven during those early days in believing that we would be seeing a lot of HMS *Hermes* and it would be comparatively easy to wrest SST 1 back from the RN once they were needed ashore in support of the land battle – how wrong we were!

Our journey down to Ascension Island was spent in accordance with a fairly rigorous training programme covering the following objectives:

- detailed logistic and strategic planning
- physical fitness and circuit training
- terrain briefing (to know the Falklands backwards)
- intelligence briefings (to know the enemy, his strengths, equipment and capabilities)
- first aid
- weapon training and test firings
- minor tactics/field craft
- fire control orders
- voice procedure
- mess deck competitions (all types).

Whilst these basic requirements were being adhered to, I was busy planning how 3 Commando Brigade could best be logistically supported in the Falklands. I was firmly convinced that the most effective method would be to support the Landing Force direct from the ships by helicopter (provided that we had control of the air and seas). My conclusion was that we should have two LSLs each loaded with 2 Daily Combat Supply Rate for the Force (DCSR) of stocks dedicated to Logistic Support, with SS *Canberra* providing the immediate medical support. This concept could thus easily be adjusted to support two possible options, as well as dividing our assets in case one of the LSLs should be sunk. Options were as follows (this extract is taken directly from Cdo Log Regt RM 'Concept of Operations' prior to H Hour):

Option One

Full Brigade option including three Commando Groups with two Parachute Battalions. Option to be supported by two LSLs, the first to be held close inshore to support the land battle and the second to be held in reserve outside the TEZ. Each LSL to carry two DCSR with separate Command and Control Teams together with an AWD and AOD allocated to each ship. Empty LSLs to replenish from the dedicated Stores Ships MV *Elk* and RFA *Stromness*. BSA ashore to be set up as soon as possible after 'H' hour to consist of:

- Command and Control Element (Step up)
- One Dressing Station Complete (DS)
- Defence Rifle Company (Composite)
- Assault Workshop Detachment (AWD)
- Assault Ordnance Detachment (AOD)
- Amphibious Beach Unit (ABU)
- Landing Zone Marshalling Team (LZMT) (Helicopters).

All casualties to be evacuated direct to *SS Canberra* – DS ashore to be used only in emergency (e.g. non flying weather).

Option Two

To support two separate operations in different areas with neither force less than one Commando Group. In this case one LSL to be allocated to support each operation carrying two DCSR stocks each (equivalent to $8 \times DCSR$ for one Commando Group). Both LSLs also to carry DS, AWD and AOD, with separate command and control teams. BSA as above.

The above Logistic concept was put to Brigade HQ aboard HMS *Fearless* on Saturday 10 April and accepted. This led to a complete ship restow in Ascension Island in order to achieve the correct split of stocks, men and machinery between the two LSLs (destined to be LSLs *Sir Galahad* and *Sir Percival*); of course the restow plan had also to cater for the tactical 'Concept of Operations'. At this time the Landing Force, a reinforced 3 Commando Brigade, seemed to be expanding by the hour, whilst the Logistic Regiment was still woefully under-strength to support such a force. I therefore clamoured to get the remainder of the Regiment sent out from the UK aboard HMS *Intrepid* (under my Second in Command) as soon as possible – this I finally justified by stressing the need for extra manpower to form a rifle company to defend the Beach Support Area (BSA).

Before we reached Ascension we began to experience some of the frustrations which bedevil Amphibious Operations. First the Naval Task Force under Rear Admiral Woodward (FOF1) accelerated off at great speed taking with him HMS *Hermes* and our SST 1.

Also HMS *Fearless* (carrying Brigade HQ) kept vanishing into the blue wastes on long periods of radio silence. Our stay in Ascension lasted

11 days (19–30 April), which was spent sweating under the hot sun shifting cargoes from one ship to another. Ascension is not really a romantic tropical island; it is a stark heap of volcanic rubble topped only by one mountain – Green Mountain – of any size, which supports vegetation. Even the seas are uninviting as they attract millions of horrible, piranha-like fish, which voraciously attack and eat anything in sight.

On 30 April, we finally left Ascension Island while diplomatic efforts at finding a settlement were still going on. The Regiment was divided between LSLs *Sir Galahad* and *Sir Percival* with Medical Squadron (less 1 Troop and SST 1) still aboard SS *Canberra*. HMS *Fearless* remained behind at Ascension to await the arrival of her sister ship HMS *Intrepid* with the balance of the Regiment aboard.

Thus began what seemed to be a never-ending journey down to the Falklands. During this time the RN managed to establish complete domination of the seas but seemed to be having considerable problems with the Argentinian Air Force (e.g. the sinking of HMS *Sheffield*). Also the interminable negotiations for a peaceful settlement dragged on, first with the US Secretary of State conducting shuttle diplomacy between London and Buenos Aires and finally with the UN Secretary General involved. At this time the Argentinians were simply gaining time to reinforce their positions – the sinking of the cruiser *General Belgrano* only increased the odds against a settlement. Eventually the Amphibious Landing Force Fleet rendezvoused with the Naval Task Force outside the TEZ on 16 May. I was given my final orders by our Brigade Commander (Brigadier Julian Thompson) aboard HMS *Fearless* on 17 May, which included all the details for the amphibious landings including our choice of Ajax Bay for the BSA. He seemed convinced that Operation 'Sutton' (as the land battle was to be called) was now inevitable. On 18 May, at 1600 hours, I gave my final Regimental Orders with all the details of the plan; it only remained to know when 'D' Day and 'H' Hour would be. We did not have long to wait: at 1100 hours, on 20 May, we crossed the TEZ and 'H' Hour was confirmed to be 210630Z May (0630 GMT 21 May) 1982.

OPERATION SUTTON

The initial landings were brilliantly successful. Complete surprise was achieved and the OPGEN MIKE (detailed plan for landing craft and helicopter timings, etc.) worked like clockwork. All the main objectives had been achieved by first light on 21 May and all the fighting troops were ashore within four-and-a-half hours of 'H' Hour. The SBS and SAS diversionary attacks on Fanning Head and Goose Green together with the Harrier attacks on Port Stanley and Fox Bay seemed to have paid off.

However, the Argentinian Air Force soon made its presence felt. The whole fleet, now tied up in San Carlos Water, was subjected to a great number of air attacks. The Harrier CAP simply could not prevent all the attacks from getting through. HMS *Antrim* and HMS *Argonaut* were hit and HMS *Ardent* sunk; in return the enemy were seen to have lost 9 Mirages, 5 Skyhawks and 3 Pucarás. On land we took only light casualties with 2 Gazelle helicopters shot down and a total of 4 killed and 28 wounded.

The major conclusion of the day was that all non-essential ships would have to be moved outside the TEZ as soon as possible under cover of darkness to avoid risk of air attack. This included the 'prestige' targets of SS *Canberra* and *Norland*. The effect of this short notice decision was devastating to Medical Squadron, as regrettably there simply was not enough time to get everyone off *Canberra*, so one complete DS 2 and SST 3 were left on board and not seen again until 1 June. Also, the LSL support plan was abandoned and LSLs *Sir Percival* and *Sir Galahad* were ordered to run their stocks ashore into the BSA at Red Beach (Ajax Bay) and depart out of danger. MV *Elk*, our other supply ship, was ordered to stay out of the TEZ as the detonation of 2,000 tons of HE might take all the other ships with it.

In consequence all our hard planning had to be changed and our logistic plan was forced to become land-based. Hence terrific pressure was applied to get men, equipment and stocks ashore into Ajax Bay (and the old sheep refrigeration plant) as soon as possible. The main danger was that the ground restricted our ability to disperse stocks adequately – for which we were to pay a high price later on.

From a logistic point of view our main problem was the lack of dedicated movement assets. Normally Commando Logistic Regiment can depend on its own 4-ton trucks to carry supplies forward to the fighting units and therefore helicopters and boats were just a bonus. However, in this operation we were entirely dependent upon the availability of helicopters and landing craft as there were no roads or hardcore tracks that we could use. Regrettably this system did not work; we did not control any single movement asset (not even a rubber boat) and every request had to be submitted through Brigade (now ashore) to COMAW (still aboard HMS *Fearless*) for tasking. Our requests (being of a logistic nature) were usually placed fairly low on the priority table and consequently with the shortage of helicopters almost no resupply was achieved during the first few days.

On 24 May, unexploded bombs hit LSL *Sir Galahad* and *Sir Lancelot* and HMS *Antelope* was sunk. This obviously further confirmed that LSLs (or any other ship) were unsuitable to forward supply without adequate air superiority. It also confirmed that forward resupply would have to be by helicopter – sometimes at considerable range. One important factor did not fully register with me until I got ashore, and that was the size of the Falkland Islands. They are about the size of Wales with long resupply distances involved (e.g. 93 miles direct from Ajax Bay to Port Stanley). The ground was terrible, very wet tussock and bog with huge rock runs and virtually no tracks. Any idea of a quick campaign concluded in about one week was immediately dispelled.

At about this time we managed to lose contact with about 150 of our men who were aboard LSL *Sir Galahad*, including OC Workshops Squadron! Although we knew that *Sir Galahad* had been evacuated because of its unexploded bomb, we simply had no idea which ship they had been taken to and, since we had no means of communicating with the ships, we had no way of finding out. To make matters worse our 'control ship' HMS *Fearless* disappeared again on a mission to pick up, Commander Land Forces Falkland Islands' (CLFFIs') staff somewhere near South Georgia. On 25 May, HMS *Coventry* was hit and sunk and Medical Squadron's Main Dressing Station (MDS) (larger surgical capabilities than DS) was very busy dealing with air-raid casualties. Additionally, the Regiment took on the unplanned role of catering for the many displaced naval personnel ashore – at this stage the crews of *Sir Lancelot* and a number from *Sir Galahad* and *Coventry*. Tentage was in very short supply so these people also had to be herded into our one and only building – the old disused sheep refrigeration plant at Ajax Bay (being also used by Medical Squadron).

There can be no doubt that, even in a limited war of this nature, plans have to be changed by the minute, and success or failure (even with logistics) often rests with the initiative and determination of some of our youngest and most inexperienced NCOs. One of our greatest difficulties revolved around the resupply petrol, oil and lubricants (POL) (commercial petrol (Civgas) in particular). The Regiment's Petrol Troop (383 Troop) was TAVR and therefore had not been mobilised; in consequence, other men from Ordnance and Transport Squadrons had to take their place to become instant 'experts' in fuel of all natures. We found the demand for Civgas extraordinarily high; in particular the Rapier posts on the top of the hills (our first priority) and unit generators seemed never satisfied. Also the Volvo BVs and raiding craft consumed vast quantities of J/Can. The problem was not so much a shortage of bulk fuel, as enough was available on the ships; the real difficulty was getting the fuel ashore (mostly achieved by PODs floated on the Mexeflotes), and then transferring the fuel by hand pumps into a very limited number of J/Can. Whatever the theoretical exponents of bulk refuelling may say, I am now absolutely convinced that in any war situation forwarded units will be screaming for J/Can. The principle of exchanging a full can for an empty one is good in theory, but in a fast-moving battle you cannot expect to guarantee the return of empty J/Can and you certainly cannot deny them a full can simply because they cannot produce an empty! Our experiments with large flexible tanks were not very satisfactory as they were very vulnerable to aircraft strafing and, for many reasons, the only bulk fuel carried ashore were in the PODs and the Air Portable Flexible Containers (APFCs). The only Emergency Fuel Handling Equipment (EFHE) (Dracone system) established was Aviation Fuel (AVCAT) for the Harriers and Helicopters based at Green Beach (Port San Carlos), but even here the problem of setting up such a system without air superiority was both lengthy and dangerous. Just for the record, our Civgas resupply for the entire Brigade at Red Beach was run in the early stages by a private solider and five assistants working around the clock with minimal supervision!

During 26–27 May the Argentinian air attacks continued despite the horrifying losses their aircraft were taking (it was later confirmed even by the Argentinians that one aircraft out of every two never returned to Argentina). In my view their pilots were very brave to press home their attacks at such low level and with such determination. On 26 May, the container ship *Atlantic Conveyor* was hit and sunk by Exocet; tragically she was just about to arrive from the UK carrying our logistic Chinook and other support helicopters. Then on 27 May at 1930 hours the Regiment received its most severe air attack of the war. Skyhawks and Mirages attacked the BSA at Ajax Bay with virtually no warning, twelve 400-kilogram retard bombs were dropped, mercifully only four of which exploded. One of the bombs exploded in the area of the Regimental Galley and the Echelon of 45 Commando killing 6 men and seriously wounding 26 others. Had this happened half an hour earlier the Galley would have been full and there would have been far more casualties. Another bomb exploded amongst the ammunition at the HLS destroying approximately 300 rounds of 105 mm and 200 rounds of 81 mm; this ammunition together with 45 Commando Echelon ammunition went on exploding all night. Three unexploded bombs hit the Medical Squadron MDS in the refrigeration factory, one going straight through and two lodging in the building itself. Had these exploded, half the Regiment would have been killed. Throughout the raid there were operations being performed on the wounded in the DS: and the daily

Adjutant and Quartermaster staff, branches (AQ) logistic conference was just dispersing from the old factory.

Despite the appalling carnage, shock and sorrow, most of the men got straight on with rescuing the wounded away from the exploding ammunition and attempting to put out the fires. To a few, with undue imagination, the horror of the scene and wanton loss of life created a state of numb shock which lasted for quite some time. One of our men was killed by enemy cannon fire whilst engaging a Skyhawk with his General Purpose Machine Gun (GPMG) at point blank range. One thing was quite clear to all of us at Ajax Bay and that was, even with Rapier, we were woefully short of effective air defence weapons. The Regiment had a very large number of GPMGs, which we loaded with 1-in-2 tracer; these guns were very useful in distracting an enemy pilot's aim. However, what was clearly needed was a few 20 mm AA guns (e.g. Rheinmetal systems), preferably with radar control guidance with or even .5 Browning heavy machine guns, both with 3-in-1 tracer. Missiles like Rapier are no substitute for these weapons. Argentinian pilots later related to me that tracer fire was a serious deterrence to their aim and flying. I believe logistic units everywhere should have these weapons and learn to fire them themselves – they would definitely prove more cost effective in the saving of men and stocks in the long run. Rapier is very effective but usually only strikes the attacking aircraft after it has attacked its target. Another matter which saved many lives was the infantry training of all the men in the Logistic Regiment. Not only can they fight as part of a rifle section or troop should the need arise, they also know how to dig in effectively with a good 2 feet of overheard cover – without this our casualty toll would probably have been far higher.

On 28 May, 2 Para unleashed their attack on Goose Green and Darwin. It was a vicious and hard fought battle, which set the tone of things to come, and undoubtedly had a terrifying effect on the Argentinians. The Argentinian forces in the area surrendered on the morning of 29 May. Approximately 1,400 prisoners were taken and over 200 Argentinian dead lay on the battlefield; 2 Para lost 18 dead with 53 wounded. From a logistic point of view the ammunition rates of fire were incredibly high, for example 105 mm HE actually ran out at one point. Generally speaking, approximately 4 Daily Ammunition Expenditure Rate (DAER) was expended in 24 hours at limited user rates – 5 DAER in the case of 105 mm HE and 81 mm mortar rounds. Clearly we would have had great resupply problems had battle been sustained at this intensity for any further length of time.

At this point I feel that a word or two about the press would not go amiss. As is now common knowledge, our designs on Goose Green were made known to the world by the media 24 hours before the attack went in. It is understood that as a result of this knowledge the Argentinians reinforced Darwin–Goose Green with troops from 12 Infantry Regiment. It is also known that the media told the world (and of course the Argentinians) that their aircraft bombs were not detonating and they consequently made great efforts to overcome this failing. When *Sir Galahad* was hit the world was told of this fact long before anyone had a chance of notifying families or next of kin of the casualties, thus causing great alarm amongst all families who thought their men might be on board (in this particular case the whole of Commando Logistic Regiment RM). What saddens me is that some members of the press and the BBC were very responsible and were equally horrified by these blatant breaches of security and lack of consideration or understanding. The media enjoyed privileged information but this must be bounded by responsibility; equally I believe that the MoD (Press Office) must be held responsible for some major indiscretions. The media may consider that the public have an unrestricted 'right to know', but this cannot be allowed at the expense of men's lives.

During the next few days the Brigade started to move forward and take the outlying settlements; 45 Commando and 3 Para took out Douglas and Teal settlements without opposition. At the end of all these actions the Regiment found itself with another sometimes forgotten responsibility – that of burials. Most of our own dead were brought back to Ajax Bay for burial and we prepared the graves and very often arranged a service and provided the bearer parties. We held a particularly special service for our own dead on 27 May taken by our own Chaplain. It was a sad, yet moving, occasion; however, it is my perception that it caused many people to think more deeply about a personal Christian faith.

As the Brigade moved forward into the area of Mount Kent, we followed up by creating a forward BMA at Teal settlement (commanded by OC Transport Squadron) with a DP forward near Estancia House. The plan was once again to move large quantities of supplies (particularly 105 mm and 81 mm) forward to Teal by LSL supported by helicopters for immediate requirements. Supplies from Teal could then be moved forward to Estancia either by boat (Landing Craft Vehicle Personnel (LCVP) or Rigid Raider), by Volvo BV 202 or by helicopter. Unit Echelons could then pick up direct from the DP or the forward BMA, as they would be co-located at either one of these locations. The system worked well, although once again the helicopter availability caused shortages of some items – particularly packed Civgas. Our logistic communications worked extraordinarily well throughout the operation even over these extended distances and the Clansman VRC321/PRC320 sets proved their worth as well as the expertise and determination of our Signals Troop.

THE ARRIVAL OF 5 INFANTRY BRIGADE

The period 1–2 June saw the arrival of HQ LFFI (with Major General Jeremy Moore as Commander Land Forces Falkland Islands (CLFFI) and his staff aboard HMS *Fearless*) together with 5 Infantry Brigade (2 Scots Guards, 1 Welsh Guards and 1/7 Gurkha Rifles). Regrettably, 5 Infantry Brigade brought very little logistic support with them and Commando Logistic Regiment was directed to become 'Divisional Troops' and take on logistic resupply for the whole division including 5 Infantry Brigade. To help us we were given elements of 81 and 91 Ordnance Companies under operational command; unfortunately, although they came with enough stock, they brought with them virtually no extra movement assets (e.g. podded 4-ton vehicles, Eager Beavers, Landing Craft or logistic support helicopters).

In order to support 5 Infantry Brigade (who were ordered to move forward to Fitzroy) we established a forward BMA at Fitzroy with a DP at Bluff Cove to support their Echelons. The support of this Brigade did not go as well as we had hoped as their logistic communications and procedures were not as well tested as 3 Commando Brigade. Nevertheless, we simply made the logistics work even if it meant 'commandeering' helicopters or landing craft. Just as we were setting up the Brigade Administration Area (BAA) at Fitzroy, on 8 June the two LSLs (*Sir Galahad* and *Sir Tristan*) were attacked by Skyhawks and set on fire; both vessels were abandoned and resulted in tragic loss of life on *Sir Galahad* (43 killed and over 200 injured – mostly from the Welsh Guards). Also most of the surgical equipment of 16 Field Ambulance was destroyed on the *Sir Galahad*. Once again a terrible price was paid for our lack of air defence equipment – in this case even the Rapier Posts had not had enough time to be properly established. Our Medical Squadron MDS at Ajax Bay was inundated with all the injured (mostly with terrible burns and in great pain) since the MDS of 16 Field Ambulance had effectively been destroyed. Fortunately by this time the hospital ship SS *Uganda* was permitted to come in daily to Grantham Sound and was soon able to absorb the overcrowding. Virtually all the men in the Regiment were involved with the wounded at this time – often simply by sitting beside the stretchers and comforting those in fearful pain. The men were magnificent!

At this point I must make mention of Medical Squadron (MDS), which was based in the old refrigeration plant at Ajax Bay. The teamwork achieved by the 'Red and Green Life Machine' was fantastic and a great many friends and foes alike owe their lives to the dedication of the skilled surgeons and lowly Medical Assistants. It was also a confident opinion of the doctors and surgeons that without the very high standards of first aid practised by the men at the time of wounding in the front line (the buddy-buddy system) then once again many more would never have reached the MDS alive. Once the men reached the MDS alive their chances of survival were exceptionally high, as virtually all the wounded were both very fit and determined to survive. Out of just over 1,000 casualties received in the MDS and the two FDSs (Teal and Fitzroy) only three subsequently died. In all 202 major operations were performed at Ajax Bay (MDS) and altogether 108 such operations were performed at Teal, Fitzroy and on SS *Uganda*. Of these figures approximately 30 per cent of the casualties treated were Argentinian (see below).

OPERATION CORPORATE LOGISTIC STATISTICS

Strength

Regimental strengh on initial deployment on LSL Sir Lancelot

RHQ/HQ Sqn	34
Medical Squadron (1 Troop on LSL *Sir Lancelot*; 3 Troop on SS *Canberra*)	92
Transport Squadron	42
Ordnance Squadron	23
Workshop Squadron	65
Total	**256**

Regimental reinforcements

HMS *Intrepid*	132
BCRs	30
SST 1 (HMS *Hermes*)	23
SST 2 (SS *Canberra*)	22
SST 3 (SS *Canberra*)	17
Band	37
Total	**261**

Regimental strength (Ajax Bay)

Regimental Strength	517
ABU	28

SATCOM	30
Postal	3
FRHU/FRO	16
PW Control (BCRs)	43
Inteligence Cell	2
Bomb Disposal (RN/RAF)	14
81/91 Ordnance Company	20
Total (Ajax Bay)	**673**

81 Ordnance Company Royal Army Ordnance Corps (RAOC) (attached at Fitzroy and San Carlos)	130

Tonnages

Total stocks outloaded from UK	17,000
Total Ammo stocks outloaded from UK	8,600
Stocks movements on Falklands	9,080

Ammunition

Ajax Bay off-loaded from shipping	3,500
To Teal from Ajax Bay	1,200
To Fitzroy from Ajax Bay	1,000
To DP (Estancia House) from Teal	36

Rations

Total rations moved	1,200
Hexemine	300
Biscuits	90

POL

APFC/J/Can	1,414
Defence Stores	280
Technical General Stores	60
Grand Total Tonnage	**9,080**

Casualties (Medical Squadron figures)

Casualties treated at Ajax Bay	700+
Casualties treated at Fitzroy/Teal	300+
Total	**1,000+**
Major Surgical Operations at Ajax Bay	202
Major Surgical Operations: Teal/Fitzroy/SS *Uganda*	108
Total	**310**
Died of wounds after care (on SS *Uganda*)	3
Casualties in Ajax Bay:	
killed	6
seriously wounded	26
minor wounds	10

Another group of people who were working for the Regiment (although not always under command!) were the Mexeflotes and landing craft. There is no doubt that the vast capacity of the Mexeflote was of enormous value for off-loading supplies. The RCT operators are to be congratulated on their standard of seamanship and their cheerfulness in the face of appalling weather on exposed decks. Also the Landing Craft Mechanical (larger landing craft for landing vehicles etc.) (LCMs) of Landing Craft Squadron RM were tremendously useful and could carry a really worthwhile load. These craft, together with LCVPs, Rigid Raiders and Geminis (Raiding Squadron) were absolutely invaluable. Nevertheless at least a proportion of these craft should have been placed under the operational command of the Cdo Log Regt RM.

THE FINAL VICTORY AND RECOVERY

The final plan for the capture of Port Stanley involved a three-phase assault: 3 Commando Brigade was to take Mount Longdon, Harriet and Two Sisters early in the morning of Saturday, 11 June, followed by a 5 Infantry Brigade attack on Mount William and Tumbledown. Wireless Ridge was then to be taken by 2 Para as a preliminary to the final assault on Sapper Hill and Port Stanley by 3 Commando Brigade RM. From a logistic point of view it meant that at first line every man would have to carry two days' supply of ammunition and food and all vehicle fuel tanks had to be full. Guns and mortars were to have 500 rounds per gun actually on the gun lines prior to each phase, with the ability to resupply a further 500 rounds straight from the BMAs at Teal and Fitzroy. The plan was completely successful and only two phases were necessary before the Argentinians decided to surrender. Although 500 rounds per gun per day sounds a lot of ammunition, it should be noted that some guns and mortars did actually run out (as also happened at Goose Green). Other ammunition items, which were used far in excess of their theoretical scales, were 7.62 mm link and tracer, L2 grenades, 66 mm HEAT, 84 mm HEAT and Milan. Other items constantly asked for but not held were 2-inch mortar HE and .5 Browning heavy machine gun ammunition. Maybe this should be looked at again for future operations.

The final surrender of the Argentinians took place during the evening of Monday 14 June (this also included their surrender of West Falkland). The Regiment had to move round from Ajax Bay to Port Stanley as soon as possible to support the force now concentrated in that area. We took up residence in the offices of the Falkland Islands Company. We left behind a DP at Ajax Bay to look after 40 Commando and other units in the area; also we had to leave behind a large guarding party and administrative facilities to look after the 500 'special category' POWs (mostly officers). Although we attempted to look after these prisoners as best we could (and certainly they were more comfortable than my own men since they were inside out of the cold), I received a most remarkable 'document of redress' made out to me as 'Commanding Officer of the Concentration Camp'. The document was drawn up by one of their very senior officers, citing many trivial complaints under the terms of the Geneva Convention. It was clear to me that the Argentinian officers were not used to any discomfort and certainly they avoided mixing with their men. Another interesting observation was the fact that Argentinian officers enjoyed great privilege with better clothing and equipment. They also had a special high calorie ration pack with a small whisky bottle (naturally very popular with my men!). What particularly interested me from various informal discussions I had with some of their most senior commanders was their deep regret that this invasion of the Falklands had ever taken place. They believed that they had now totally alienated the inhabitants of the Falklands for at least the next generation (certainly true!). They also believed that they would not repeat the adventure again for a long time. To a man they blamed the Americans for not discouraging the invasion; they maintained that the Americans knew about their intentions well in advance and did nothing positive to stop them – this they took as a sign of encouragement.

Once in Port Stanley the Regiment spent a lot of time helping to clear up the most appalling mess left by the Argentinian troops. Their troops (all 11,000 of them) were confined to the airfield area until ships became available to take them back to Argentina. One of the greatest horrors of holding Argentinian prisoners was their appalling lack of 'house training', no amount of encouragement would persuade them to use the toilets provided – they just lowered their trousers where they stood in front of everyone. In reality most of their conscripts were very young and often illiterate peasants who did not understand what the dispute was all about – they simply became disillusioned.

On 28 June, the Regiment finally departed from Port Stanley aboard LSL *Sir Percival*. The logistic support responsibility for the garrison force had been handed over to 81/91 Ordnance Companies RAOC, 10 Field Workshops Royal Electrical and Mechanical Engineers (REME) and one RCT Transport Troop. Sadly we had to leave behind much of our equipment to allow them to fulfil their function properly (e.g. podded fuel vehicles and Eager Beavers). Our return journey was very well arranged: LSL *Sir Percival* made us most welcome as far as Ascension Island (apart from a devastating Force 12 storm just after leaving the Falklands!) then most of the Regiment took a VC10 flight from Ascension to Brize Norton via Dakar (Senegal). Medical Squadron once again managed to squeeze a voyage back on the SS *Canberra*! Our reception back into England on 9 July was overwhelming and most exciting, and the subsequent receptions and memorial services concluded what had been a remarkable operational experience.

Rather than finish this account by drawing 'conclusions and recommendations' from what had been in effect our first full-scale amphibious operation and limited war for at least 30 years, I have listed the 'logistic problems and recommendations' as a summary of the logistic problems and recommendations that were made to the MoD after the operation.

LOGISTIC RECOMMENDATIONS FROM OPERATION CORPORATE – COMMANDO LOGISTIC REGIMENT RM

Outloading

- Outloading by rail impractical – BR unable to pre-position rolling stock in sufficient time.
- Excessive vehicle delays at Depots and poor administration for drivers.
- 383 Commando Petrol Troop TAVR ROAC troops (RAOC(V)) could not be mobilized; consequently the Regt deployed without any fuel analysts and POL expertise and testing equipment.

Operation Sutton

- Some of the logistic helicopters and landing craft must be firmly placed under operational command of the Cdo Log Regt RM from the outset – this is essential where no roads exist, otherwise supplies cannot be guaranteed.

- Supply and support shipping unload/loading to be controlled by Cdo Log Regt RM in accordance with priorities given by the staff.
- J/Can holdings and POD equipment insufficient. Flexible tank policy to be reviewed.
- Eager Beavers performed magnificently but there were not enough! Suggest Eager Beavers be replaced simply by more Eager Beavers.
- 1 Raiding Squadron Royal Marines (RSRM) ABU and LC FOB should come under operational command of the Log Regt. It is further recommended that 1 RSRM should also return to administrative command of Log Regt.
- LSLs played a vital role – those lost must be replaced.
- Ammo scaling to be reviewed particularly 7.62 link and tracer, L2 grenades, 66 mm HEAT, 84 mm HEAT, Milan and 2-inch mortar HE.
- Limited war scaling of ammo for 3 Cdo Bde is unrealistically low.
- Logistics units/installations must have better air defence weapons. Rapiers must be complemented with good AA Gun and .5 Browning HMG.
- Re-emphasis required on Infantry skills for logistic troops. Particularly camouflage, field craft, defence, patrolling and use of ground to disperse stocks (also avoiding obvious buildings!).
- Mobile Air Operations Team (MAOT) to be established permanently with Regt.
- General–purpose stores and equipment (G1098)/Establishment to be revised to cater for large number of POWs.

It is equally clear that without adequate shipping, helicopters and air power the operation could not have been mounted or sustained. It was a close run thing and even a year later we might not have been able to contemplate the operation from a logistic point of view. The LSLs that were lost were critical to the logistic success of the operation. Finally I must pay tribute to the men, who were fantastic, and without their tenacity and enthusiasm nothing would have been possible; I am deeply indebted to their support, as well as all those who supported us back home – in particular I would remember our long-suffering families.

PART 3
The Falklands Conflict in Wider Perspective

11

'War Cabinetry': The Political Direction of the Falklands Conflict

PETER HENNESSY

We had all sorts of War Books for running a government in World War III, but no guidance at all on how to run a limited war in the South Atlantic while at the same time maintaining a normal peacetime administration at home.

> (Lord (Robert) Armstrong of Ilminster, 2002, recalling the spring of 1982 when he was Secretary of the Cabinet[1])

I know that Whitelaw, Lewin and I, in the early stages [of the Falklands Conflict], thought 'Suez, Suez, Suez'.

> (Sir John Nott, 2002, recalling March/early April 1982 when he was Secretary of State for Defence[2])

[Y]ou mustn't get to the stage where people were losing confidence in the whole way things were being organised and happening. In that sense, yes, one inevitably harked back to Suez.

> (Sir Frank Cooper, 1998, recalling his 'how to run a war' briefing of Mrs Thatcher on 4 April 1982[3])

She was scrupulous throughout. Everybody had their say, the chance to ask questions and she was a much better listener than she was on many other occasions. And I think you're right; the public persona was very different from the working persona.

> (Sir Frank Cooper, 1998, recalling Mrs Thatcher's conduct of the Falklands Conflict[4])

On 26 June 1981, the day after the publication of the Nott Defence Review, I had lunch with an old Whitehall friend much concerned with the fate of the surface fleet, who said to me, 'The only thing that can save us now is a small colonial war a long way away requiring a lot of ships.' During the first week of April 1982, I rang my friend (now, sadly, dead) and said, 'Do you remember our lunch in the Garrick last June and what you said about the Defence Review?' 'I do', he replied. 'X', I said, 'this time you've gone too far.'[5] Neither of us laughed as it was not a laughing matter. Like the JIC, Mrs Thatcher and her Cabinet committee on Overseas and Defence Policy, my much-respected chum had not foreseen the invasion of the Falkland Islands. Like everyone else in those first post-invasion days he was putting everything into getting the Task Force to the South Atlantic and as equipped as possible for recapturing the islands in the absence of a detailed, long-standing contingency plan for doing so.

Should there, however, have been a planning gap of the kind Robert Armstrong described? Since the formation of the Committee of Imperial Defence (CID) with its own secretariat in 1904, Britain had been a War Book nation *par excellence* with a style of administration which believed in funding one generation with its predecessors' experiences. That tradition had certainly been sustained in the planning for a transition to a Third World War should it occur. We can now see this at the Public Record Office by examining, for example, the Ministry of Defence's detailed and comprehensive 1963 War Book[6] (though the Cabinet Office's central Government War Book is still deemed too sensitive for the eyes of myself and my students[7]).

That grand War Book planning tradition, however, had by the inter-war years been developed by Sir Maurice Hankey, the quite extraordinary Royal Marine who was both Secretary of the CID and later, from December 1916, the very first Cabinet Secretary, into a *smorgasbord* approach to war cabinetry of varying intensity. The paper Hankey prepared for the CID in 1928 should, I think, have been the first section of a limited-war War Book as late as the early 1980s (had such a thing existed) so brimming is it with both experience and clarity of mind. Here is its essence:

> Each case must be considered on its merits by the Prime Minister of the day. It must be remembered that the appointment of a War Cabinet involves a very considerable dislocation of the ordinary machine of Government. Moreover, the exclusion of Ministers who in normal times are members of the Cabinet from the conduct of the vital affairs of the nation could never be popular among the excluded Ministers, and would only be tolerated in case of a national emergency of the very gravest kind.[8]

Hankey described four models for the supreme control of war (for the inter-war CID read, in today's circumstances, the Cabinet Committee on Overseas and Defence Policy which, like the CID of old, the Prime Minister chairs):

(A) The normal peace system, the Cabinet, advised by the Committee of Imperial Defence.

(B) The Cabinet, assisted by a Special Cabinet Committee, with powers of decision on questions within the order of ministerial competence [i.e. those ministers actually sitting on the Special Cabinet Committee], but not necessarily designated 'The War Committee'.

(C) The Cabinet, assisted by a 'War Committee' with fuller executive powers than the Cabinet Committee referred to in (B) above.

(D) A War Cabinet, which absorbs the functions of both the Cabinet and the Committee of Imperial Defence.[9]

'Whichever of the above systems is adopted', Hankey continued, 'the Supreme Control must be provided with: (a) co-ordination advice on questions of detail; and (b) adequate secretarial staff.'[10]

In the early 1980s, had I been so commissioned, my 'structure of a limited war cabinet' brief would have been based upon Hankey's wisdom supplemented by John Nott's 'Suez, Suez, Suez' factor. And my starting point here would have been the remarkably candid inquest on that disastrous affair prepared for the CoS by the operation's commander, General Sir Charles Keightley. 'The one overriding lesson of the Suez operations', he wrote in 1957,

is that world opinion is now an absolute principle of war and must be treated as such. However successful the pure military operations may be they will fail in their object unless national, Commonwealth and Western world opinion is sufficiently on our side.[11]

Keightley emphasised the degree to which 'this factor' had been 'categorically stated in appreciations to Her Majesty's Government', throughout the 'planning period' prior to the invasion of Egypt, 'and the intervention of the United Nations and the ultimate result of the whole operation confirmed its truth'.[12]

Keightley was even more brutally damning in his assessment of the American factor. 'But it was the action of the UNITED STATES which really defeated us in attaining our object', Keightley declared, recalling the anxiety caused by the moments of the US Sixth Fleet in the Mediterranean as the Anglo-French Task Force steamed towards Port Said:

> Her action in the United Nations is well known, but her move of
> the 6th Fleet, which is not so generally known, was a move which
> endangered the whole of our relations with that country. It is not
> difficult to appreciate the effect of the shooting down of a United
> States aircraft or the sinking of a United States submarine, but both
> these might easily have happened if EGYPT had obtained certain
> practical support from outside which she tried to get [presumably
> a reference to possible Soviet assistance] or our Commanders had
> not shown patience and care of the highest order.[13]

Keightley concluded the 'World Opinion' section of his report with a
piece of pure political judgement which, in effect, became the *leitmotif*
of British foreign policy for the remainder of the twentieth century and
into the first years of the twenty-first century. 'This situation with the
UNITED STATES', said Keightley baldly, 'must at all costs be prevented
from arising again'. Returning to the management of the Suez crisis he
wrote, 'Conversely a united Anglo-American position would have
assured a complete success of all our political objects with the minimum
military effort. The achievement of this is a political matter but the
effects on military operations are vital.'[14]

Keightley also had some very relevant things to say about domestic, as
well as world political opinion before and during a politico-military crisis
that is turning into warfare. As he put it acidly and succinctly about the
autumn of 1956: 'Her Majesty's Opposition "rocked the landing craft".'[15]

As a historian I am very careful to avoid falling into the trap of using
the past excessively as a guide to the future. At most, in certain carefully
delimited circumstances, one can draw up a list of do's and don'ts. This
is what my early 1980s stab at the principles of war cabinetry would have
looked like, sharpened very much by Sir Anthony Eden's conduct of the
Suez Crisis. I think the essential requirements can be reduced to six:

1. The 'War Cabinet' should have as close and constant a relationship
   with the full Cabinet as possible. As Hankey put it when designing
   the breed,

   > All decisions of a 'War Committee' should be communicated as soon
   > as possible to the full Cabinet, those of a more secret character, on
   > which the success of operations or the lives of men may depend,
   > being communicated verbally. The experience of the [Great] War
   > showed that for the smooth working of Cabinet Government it was

essential that the general results of the War Committee's deliberations should be known to the Cabinet. Otherwise suspicion and friction are apt to be engendered.[16]

2. The War Cabinet should consist of no more than six constant ministerial attendees. For the efficient conduct of affairs, diplomatic or military, it needs to meet regularly and have a bias towards the taking of decisions rather than deferring them. The War Cabinet needs to have adequate military, Civil Service and Diplomatic Service back-up, an efficient advice system and a constant flow of high-quality intelligence assessments from the Joint Intelligence Committee (JIC).

3. The War Cabinet should take pains to avoid the 'tunnel vision and technical overload' that can afflict small groups directed towards a single overriding purpose under conditions of great stress. Here, in requirement 3, I am drawing especially upon Colin Seymour-Ure's work on 'War Cabinets' which he wrote in the aftermath of the Falklands Conflict.[17]

4. There needs to be a constant awareness of the needs, priorities and attitudes of allies (or potential allies) and the politics of those international organizations in which, to whatever extent, the conflict is being monitored or played out politically.

5. As full, accurate and timely disclosures as possible on matters affecting the conflict or near-conflict should be made to Parliament, the media and the public, given the requirements of operational security.

6. Ministers in the War Cabinet should remember at all times, as a thoughtful airman put it over a quarter of a century ago, that the essential nature of armed conflict is 'to destroy things and kill people',[18] and that the highest duty on politicians in authority is, therefore, to ensure that all steps that can be taken to avoid war – whether through early preventive action, quality diplomacy or high-grade intelligence – are taken.

Over that fraught first weekend of the Falklands Crisis, Mrs Thatcher did not, as far as I know, receive a Hankey-style written brief; she sent for a human equivalent instead – a man not known for his love of Whitehall's paper culture, Sir Frank Cooper, the veteran Permanent Secretary at the MoD, by this stage a mere eight months away from retirement. It became well known fairly swiftly after the Falklands Conflict that Mrs Thatcher had had a 'how to run a war' session with Harold Macmillan in the early days of the crisis – on Tuesday 6 April

135

in fact – and I shall return to this. Her session with Frank Cooper over the Sunday lunchtime of 4 April did not reach the public domain until the mid-1990s.[19]

Sir Frank had had direct personal experience of all the 'War Cabinets' since 1945. Our first conversation about it in 1996 was conducted in a very Cooperesque style. 'What nobody knows', he said 'is what I told her at a private lunch on the Sunday. I was ushered up to her little flat on the top floor. Carol [Thatcher] took lunch out of the fridge – a bit of ham and salad. We had a gin and she [Mrs Thatcher] asked me "How do you actually run a war?," I asked if he came with anything written down. 'No, I didn't write it down. I knew it and I said, "First, you need a small War Cabinet; second, it's got to have regular meetings come hell or high water; thirdly you don't want a lot of bureaucrats hanging around." Then we talked about its composition.'[20] I wondered in what sense did Sir Frank 'know it' ?'One had seen it so often in a funny sort of way,' he replied. 'I knew about Berlin, Korea, Malaya. We'd had Suez which was a monumental cock-up. Cuba was different – very much a Number 10–Kennedy thing. And we'd have this Transition to War Committee (TWC) [in 1956 it was called the Defence (Transition) Committee; it became the TWC in 1961],[21] which actually met at the time of Suez and was the biggest shambles of all time. The one thing I was quite clear about was that you couldn't have this bloody thing where people weren't going to take decisions.'[22]

In a later interview, Cooper elaborated still further upon his conversation with Mrs Thatcher on 'Falklands Sunday'. He stressed to her that 'the chain of command should be kept as simple as possible'.[23] In return Mrs Thatcher 'raised some ideas of her own...she didn't, for example, want to have too many ministers on the core group and she didn't want the Chancellor [of the Exchequer]...She thought that the money could be too much of a distraction.'[24] Sir Frank's evidence is significant here as the idea of keeping the Treasury out of the 'Falklands War Cabinet' is usually attributed to Harold Macmillan who, as is well known, called on Mrs Thatcher just after Prime Minister's Questions the following Tuesday (6 April 1982) to be asked the same question she had asked Cooper: 'Harold, how do you run a war?'[25]

It is interesting to compare the versions of the two participants in the Macmillan–Thatcher exchange. First the seasoned old Prime Minister in conversation with Ludovic Kennedy in 1983:

MACMILLAN: I did try to help her about how to run a war because it's such a long time since anybody's run a war – I mean the technical methods of running a war – which she did very well.

KENNEDY: What were you able to draw on there in your own experience?

MACMILLAN: Well, I mean, that you have to have a War Cabinet, you have to have a Committee of Chief of Staff, that the Secretary of the Committee of Chiefs mustn't be Secretary of the War Cabinet. It must be the nearest thing you could get to Lord Ismay [Military Secretary to the War Cabinet 1939–45 and, in effect, Churchill's personal chief of staff]...it was just the tip of how to run it...All of which I'd learnt from Churchill of course.[26]

Now Mrs Thatcher's account in her memoirs of the formation of her Overseas and Defence (South Atlantic) Committee, commonly known as the Falklands 'War Cabinet':

> Its exact membership and procedure were influenced by a meeting I had with Harold Macmillan who came to see me...to offer his support and advice as the country's and the Conservative Party's senior ex-prime minister [reliable inside knowledge suggests that Macmillan asked to see her rather than the other way around].[27] His main recommendation was to keep the Treasury – that is Geoffrey Howe – off the main committee in charge of the campaign, the diplomacy and the aftermath. This was a wise course, but understandably Geoffrey was upset. Even so I never regretted following Harold Macmillan's advice. We were never tempted to compromise the security of our forces for financial reasons.[28]

There was, as always with Uncle Harold, slightly more to the occasion than met the eye. Macmillan did not care for Mrs Thatcher or her style of government. Seven years earlier, shortly after she had become Leader of the Opposition, he had told me, 'You couldn't imagine a woman as Prime Minister if we were a first-class power.'[29]

On that April day in 1982 he shuffled in 'doing his old act',[30] and gazed around the room he had come to know so well between 1957 and 1963. It was unusually empty. Mrs Thatcher was due to see a group of her backbenchers that evening and space had been made ready. 'Where's all the furniture?' said the old anti-privatisation statesman to the new, 'You've sold it all off I suppose.'[31] Not the subtlest or easiest of starts!

The first question he asked her was 'Have they got the Bomb?'[32] On being told the Argentinians had not, he imparted his wisdom about keeping the Treasury out and bringing in a 'Pug' [Lord Ismay's nickname]. In fact, Whitehall could not produce an Ismay. Some figures with real fighting experience were considered, such as the former CDS, Lord Carver. But he was not a sympathetic colleague for Mrs Thatcher, being in her view 'unsound' on Trident and other defence matters.[33] So Sir Michael Palliser, the outgoing Head of the Diplomatic Service, was kept on to do the job.[34]

After consulting Frank Cooper and Harold Macmillan, Mrs Thatcher set up a Falklands war machine which held good throughout. A small 'War Cabinet', technically an offshoot of the standing Cabinet committee on Overseas and Defence Policy and known as OD(SA), was created to bring together an inner group of war-waging ministers with their technical advisers from the politico-military, diplomatic and intelligence worlds.

She followed Macmillan's advice and kept the Chancellor, Geoffrey Howe, off it. He was understanding enough about this in his memoirs ('It was no part of the Chancellor's duty at such a time to argue against the use of defence forces for the very purposes for which they had been provided.'[35]) OD(SA) consisted of Francis Pym, Lord Carrington's replacement as Foreign Secretary, John Nott, the Defence Secretary, Willie Whitelaw 'as my deputy and trusted adviser', as Mrs Thatcher later put it,[36] and Cecil Parkinson 'who not only shared my political instincts but was brilliantly effective in dealing with public relations'[37] (not a view universally shared; he was seen as a safe vote for her should the 'War Cabinet' encounter serious disagreement,[38] though it turns out that John Nott had asked for Parkinson to join OD(SA) since, as Parkinson put it, 'he felt that he needed a contemporary to be a member of the Committee to counter balance the influence of the two ex-Chief Whips, Willie [Whitelaw] and Francis [Pym]'[39].) The CDS, Sir Terence Lewin, was a constant attendee, as was the Attorney General, Sir Michael Havers,[40] described by one participant as 'a very good hand-holder – he'd been in the Navy as well and was really rather good at it',[41] who also gave advice on the legality of the operations in terms of UN resolutions and the Royal prerogative (which is of central importance if war is not formally declared, as it was not).[42]

The 'War Cabinet' met at least once, sometimes twice a day throughout the war, usually in Number 10 Downing Street but occasionally at Northwood and often over weekend sessions at Chequers. It is quite plain that Suez served as a 'how not to' guide for Mrs Thatcher. Frank Cooper recalled that during the their 'Falklands Sunday' conversation:

> She said something like 'I'll have to tell the Cabinet from time to time what's going on down there and if it comes to something, obviously they'll have to be involved.' I don't think she ever envisaged evading

or had any fundamental stand against going back to the full Cabinet. I think I certainly used Suez to stress the need to keep everybody in line – and you mustn't let the whole thing get out of control at any place, because once it's started it would have been a domino effect.[43]

Mrs Thatcher did keep 'control' but not – and it is a significant 'not' in terms of the 'she who must be obeyed' (as a senior official once called her[44]) image that has come down to posterity in a stark and caveat-free fashion – at the expense of Cabinet Government.

In her conduct of OD(SA) meetings she was markedly non-strident, though as one attendee put it the role of the FCO and their 'attitude of mind' continued to irritate her; 'It took some time for her to under-stand... that they were doing their duty and that the Foreign Office task was to see if you could achieve an honourable peace.'[45]

Apart from animus towards a department she later claimed always took the view 'that a little bit of appeasement is no bad thing'[46] ('When I'm out of politics, I'm going to run a business called "Rent-A-Spine,"' she contemptuously remarked in the context of her views on the FCO during the television version of her memoirs,[47]) 'War Cabinet' meetings were, as one insider recalled, 'pretty relaxed on the whole'.[48]

It is plain from insiders that, although determined to win, Mrs Thatcher was far from sanguine about the loss of life likely to be involved, and the memoirs are an almost tangible account of her sense of the precariousness of the operation from start to finish. The Second World War veterans amongst her ministerial colleagues, and her military and Civil Service advisers were very sensitive to this side of her. As one of them expressed it:

> People very much wanted to help her. People were aware this was something new to her. They probably had some sexist things [in mind] – here is a woman who doesn't know anything... about war anyway. And there's no doubt in my mind that people went out of their way to try and say this could be very difficult, this might be very nasty... she was terribly grateful to people like Willie and Michael Havers... He [Whitelaw] would say 'Are you *sure* that's all right?' in response to something one of the Chiefs had said... People went out of their way to tell her that people would get shot, aircraft downed or ships sunk.[49]

The Prime Minister reserved all serious and detailed operational decisions to OD(SA). It was in this forum, for example, on the Wednesday before Easter, that the decision was made to cast a 200-mile Maritime Exclusion

Zone around the Falkland Islands before Alexander Haig, the US Secretary of State, set out on his shuttle mediation between London and Buenos Aires.[50] It was a 'War Cabinet' meeting at Chequers too, on 2 May, which took the decision that the Argentine cruiser *General Belgrano* should be sunk by its shadowing submarine HMS *Conqueror*.[51]

In keeping such operational matters to her inner war group, Mrs Thatcher was firmly in accord with the prescription laid down by Sir Maurice Hankey in his classic paper for the CID some fifty-four years earlier. She did, however, take the need to keep the full Cabinet abreast of the wider picture sufficiently seriously to establish a second weekly meeting of the full Cabinet solely for this purpose.

Shortly after the war, one of Mrs Thatcher's braver Cabinet critics (though he was never critical of her on the Falklands issue) told me he had no complaints about her style in this instance. She had consulted the full Cabinet before the Task Force was despatched and again before the landing was made at San Carlos.[52] Nigel Lawson, as Energy Secretary, was not closely involved in the war, but his memoirs provide a good account of the special Falklands full Cabinets, as one might call them:

> Margaret introduced the practice of holding a second weekly Cabinet... Throughout the critical weeks of May and June, there was a full Cabinet meeting every Tuesday after the daily War Cabinet.
> The Chiefs of Staff were present and, although sensitive military matters were not discussed, it was possible always to gauge the balance of the conflict.[53]

Lawson hints at less than total unanimity in the Cabinet about victory at all costs, which throughout was the essence of the Thatcher line. 'What was the alternative?' she inquired in her memoirs. 'That a common or garden dictator should rule over the Queen's subjects, prevail by fraud and violence? Not while I was Prime Minister.'[54]

Lawson was a recapturer, too, 'I was convinced from a very early stage in the conflict that the various diplomatic manoeuvrings would amount to nothing and that it would be necessary to retake the islands by force, and said as much. This view may not have been universally shared.' Lawson reckons that if the Argentinian Junta had been persuaded:

> to place the islands under the indefinite jurisdiction of the United Nations, it is possible that the recall of the Task Force would have commanded a majority in Cabinet. Very foolishly it did not do so. As a result, there was no dissension within Cabinet throughout the war, even if one or two members may have nursed private doubts.[55]

John Nott, to his credit, has praised John Biffen, the Trade Secretary, for his courage in expressing his doubts about the sending of the Task Force at the Cabinet meeting on the evening of Friday 2 April.[56]

But it was within the confines of OD(SA) rather than the full Cabinet that Mrs Thatcher faced the most precarious moment in her pursuit of complete victory over the invaders. For the Prime Minister 'Saturday 24 April was to be one of the most crucial days in the Falklands story and a critical one for me personally'.[57] Pym wanted the Haig plan, based on a UN-supervised condominium over the islands, accepted as the basis for a settlement. She thought its contents 'were totally unacceptable', as she told her Foreign Secretary early that morning. Havers, the Attorney General, confirmed her view that acceptance would make impossible a return to the *status quo ante* and be an abandonment of 'our commitment to the principle that the islanders' wishes were paramount'.[58]

OD(SA) was to meet that evening. Her fury at Pym's advocacy (which was entirely consonant with his beliefs and prerogatives as Foreign Secretary) seared the pages of her memoirs a good ten years after the event:

> Despite my clear views expressed that morning, Francis put it in a paper to the War Cabinet recommending acceptance of these terms. Shortly before 6 o'clock that evening ministers and civil servants began assembling outside the Cabinet Room. Francis was there, busy lobbying for their support. I asked Willie Whitelaw to come upstairs to my study. I told him that I could not accept these terms and gave him my reasons. As always on crucial occasions he backed my judgement.[59]

A majority of OD(SA) backed her too, but it was John Nott who suggested a way out. Haig should be asked to put his plan to the Argentinians first. If they accepted, the Thatcher position would be very difficult. If Galtieri and the Junta rejected it, the Prime Minister would ask President Reagan to bring the United States firmly down on Britain's side (which is exactly what happened). 'And so,' she wrote 'a great crisis passed. I could not have stayed as Prime Minister had the War Cabinet accepted Francis Pym's proposals.'[60] On 29 April, the full Cabinet was briefed on the outcome after the deadline had passed for a reply from Buenos Aires.[61] The following day,[62] Reagan came out in support of the UK's determination to recapture what he quaintly, if erroneously, called 'that little ice-cold bunch of land down there'.[63]

After what one insider called 'the one time' she had an argument with Francis Pym, 'on grounds that he was trying too hard to find a negotiated settlement', Mrs Thatcher's relationships were essentially harmonious.[64]

On Tuesday 18 May, OD(SA) took the decision to authorise an assault on the islands subject to the Cabinet's final approval two days later, which was forthcoming. 'They were proper Cabinets with proper decisions,' a collectively-minded Whitehall figure attested:

> She was aware that the nearer she got, the surer she had to be that people were with her...She was seen as an able and acceptable leader of a team of people...she spent much more time asking questions and weighing up the answers than she is reputed to have done in all other areas. With hindsight, the fact that she was a woman, that she did not have military experience and that she had a clear and penetrating mind were all pluses.[65]

How far, then, did Mrs Thatcher's war cabinetry match the six requirements that an early 1980s updating of the Hankey criteria might have supplied? Pluses abound here, too; so much so that I suspect the War Book for limited war, which *has* been kept in good repair for the last 20 years,[66] and has been used a good deal since 1997,[67] still rests quite firmly on the 1982 experience.

1. There was a good, genuine and regular relationship between the 'War Cabinet' and the full Cabinet.
2. The 'War Cabinet' was kept small, it met regularly, it had a bias towards decision and the civil, diplomatic, intelligence and military inputs were blended effectively.
3. It did avoid 'tunnel' vision thanks to criteria 1 and 2 being met.
4. The imperatives of handling and influencing world and allied opinion were recognised throughout. The garnering of support for what became United Nations Resolution 502 is one of the greatest triumphs of post-1945 British diplomacy and the embassies of Sir Anthony Parsons at the UN in New York and Sir Nicholas Henderson in Washington have – justifiably – acquired a gold standard status.
5. Parliament, the media and the public were pretty well served, given the needs for operational security and some of the technical difficulty involved in getting reports and pictures back to London from the press attached to the Task Force.
6. War avoidance. This is problematic as the most cursory reading of the Franks Report on the origins of the conflict attests.[68]

This is not the contribution in which to review the Franks Committee's review of the events leading up to the Argentinean invasion of the

Islands. But can I finish by quoting from a fascinating, unpublished paper that Lord Franks delivered to the Alastair Buchan Society in Oxford in 1989? He reminded his audience that his inquiry's autopsy was critical of the JIC's Assessments Staff for being:

[T]oo passive in operation to respond effectively to rapidly chang-ing situations. It was because they looked too much at their own special product, intelligence reports from the intelligence agencies, and not, or not enough, at public decisions like that to withdraw HMS *Endurance* with the encouragement it gave the Argentines to feel that the British Government was no longer interested in the protection of the Falkland Islands through the Royal Navy and that it might therefore be safe to have a go.

Franks itemised other evaluative shortcomings on the part of the JIC's Latin America Current Intelligence Group, concluding that 'the assess-ments staff suffered from a degree of personal deformation. They looked for what they were accustomed to look at; habit and tradition were too strong; they missed the point.' What remedies might there be, Franks wondered before his Oxford audience? The recruitment of outsiders?

A fresh mind, it could be argued, would be more likely to pick up a change of gear. But this had its difficulties. Open minds can be empty minds. If one has not followed the evolution of Argentine politics and policies about the Falkland Islands, surely a necessary expertise is lacking.[69]

Franks's chief recommendation in his 1983 report was that the JIC chair-man should henceforth be given a more independent and full-time role, and that the committee and its supporting organisation should stand more apart from the agencies and departments that fed into its all-source analysis.[70] But plainly, six years after he delivered his inquest to Mrs Thatcher, he was still bothered by this aspect of pre-Falklands statecraft. 'I can't help remembering,' he told the Buchan society:

an occasion, many years ago, when as a Trustee of the Rockefeller Foundation I was asked to visit the International Rice Institute ... in the Philippines. I met there its Director, a Texan who for more than twenty years had spent his time breeding new and improved vari-eties of rice. He was supported by a considerable scientific staff, agronomists, soil scientists, chemists, pathologists, botanists. I walked with him in his rice gardens ... I asked him how he decided

143

what crosses to make to reach his objectives. He said, I walk out in
the rice gardens as we are doing now, and I look around me, muse,
and suddenly think, if I put these two together, it might work.

So all the years of experience, the expertise of the scientists
became concentrated in a leap of the imagination, the jump from
analysis to creation. He had acquired a seeing eye, or nose, a flair,
it could be.

Lord Franks concluded:

> that the interpretation of intelligence, to succeed, needs, supervening
> on skill and experience, a flair which goes beyond the immediate facts
> and, almost with an artist's eye, describes a pattern.[71]

In a letter to me, Lord Franks dismissed his 1983 Buchan Society paper
'as of no real worth'.[72] That was not my evaluation of it. I suspect that
it would have more than a little resonance today for John Scarlett, the
Chairman of the JIC and those of his people who are charged with fash-
ioning the intelligence feed to the latest marque of British 'War Cabinet',
Tony Blair's Cabinet committee on international terrorism DOP(IT).[73]

Perhaps the current JIC process *has* already built in the possibility of
meeting that mercurial, intangible Franks criterion. Over the past two
years, the format of its more important assessments has changed.
Though rightly proud of its tradition of *not* telling its ministerial cus-
tomers what to do on the basis of its analyses, the JIC nonetheless has
added a short 'implications' section to its reports and, on occasion, a
further 'what-if-we-are-wrong' supplement.[74] Whether that amounts to
the committee collectively acquiring 'a seeing eye, or nose' or a special
'flair' as wished upon them by Oliver Franks, it is impossible, certainly
for an outsider, to tell.

NOTES

1. Letter from Lord Armstrong of Ilminster (Sir Robert Armstrong) to Peter
   Hennessy, 7 March 2002.
2. John Nott, *Here Today Gone Tomorrow: Recollections of an Errant
   Politician* (London: Politico's, 2002), p. 247.
3. Sir Frank Cooper in conversation with Tom Dibble and Peter Hennessy,
   11 June 1998.
4. Sir Frank Cooper in conversation with Tom Dibble and Peter Hennessy,
   4 August 1998.
5. Private information.

6. Public Record Office [PRO], DEFE 2/225, 'Ministry of Defence War Book, August 1963'.
7. Letter from Mrs Tessa Stirling, Cabinet Office, to Peter Hennessy, 26 January 2001.
8. PRO, CAB 104/124, CID, 'Supreme Control in War'. I am very grateful to Dr Chris Brady for originally bringing this document to my attention.
9. Ibid.
10. Ibid.
11. PRO, AIR 8/1940, COS (57) 220, 11 October 1957, 'Part II of General Sir Charles Keightley's Despatch on Operations in the Eastern Mediterranean November–December 1956'.
12. Ibid.
13. Ibid.
14. Ibid.
15. Ibid.
16. PRO, CAB 104/124. 'Supreme Control in War'.
17. Colin Seymour-Ure, 'British "War Cabinets" in Limited Wars: Korea, Suez and the Falklands', *Public Administration*, 62 (summer 1984), pp. 181–200.
18. Private information.
19. I published the details (but without identifying Sir Frank by name) in Peter Hennessy, *A Question of Control: UK 'War Cabinets' and Limited Conflicts since 1945* (Bristol: CESER, University of the West of England, 1996). I named him (with his permission) in Peter Hennessy, *The Prime Minister: The Office and its Holders since 1945* (London: Penguin, 2000), pp. 103–5.
20. Conversation with Sir Frank Cooper, 17 May 1996.
21. PRO, CAB 161/13, 'Cabinet Office: Committee Organisation Book, 1963'.
22. Conversation with Sir Frank Cooper, 17 May 1996.
23. Sir Frank Cooper in conversation with Tom Dibble and Peter Hennessy, 11 June 1998.
24. Ibid.
25. Private information.
26. The television programme *Reflections*, transmitted BBC1, 20 October 1983.
27. Private information.
28. Margaret Thatcher, *The Downing Street Years* (London: HarperCollins, 1993), p. 188.
29. Conversation with Harold Macmillan, 27 August 1975.
30. Private information.
31. Ibid.
32. Ibid.
33. Ibid.
34. Ibid.
35. Geoffrey Howe, *Conflict of Loyalty* (London: Macmillan, 1994), p. 246.
36. Thatcher, *The Downing Street Years*, p. 188.
37. Ibid., pp. 188–9
38. Hennessy, *Cabinet* (Oxford: Blackwell, 1986), pp. 118–19.
39. Cecil Parkinson, *Right at the Centre: An Autobiography* (London: Weidenfeld and Nicolson, 1992), p. 192.
40. Thatcher, *The Downing Street Years*, p. 189.
41. Private information.

42. Hennessy, *The Prime Minister*, pp. 138–40.
43. Sir Frank Cooper in conversation with Tom Dibble and Peter Hennessy, 11 June 1998.
44. Private information.
45. Ibid.
46. The television programme *The Thatcher Years – Part 1*, transmitted BBC1, 6 October 1993.
47. The television programme *The Thatcher Years – Part 2*, transmitted BBC1, 13 October 1993.
48. Private information.
49. Ibid.
50. Nott, *Here Today Gone Tomorrow*, pp. 287–90.
51. Ibid., pp. 308–9.
52. Private information.
53. Nigel Lawson, *The View from No. 11: Memoirs of a Tory Radical* (London: Bantam, 1992), p. 126.
54. Thatcher, *The Downing Street Years*, p. 181.
55. Lawson, *The View from No. 11*, pp. 126–7.
56. Nott, *Here Today Gone Tomorrow*, p. 264.
57. Thatcher, *The Downing Street Years*, p. 205.
58. Ibid., p. 207.
59. Ibid.
60. Ibid., p. 208.
61. Ibid., p. 211.
62. Ibid., p. 212.
63. Michael Charlton, *The Little Platoon: Diplomacy and the Falklands Dispute* (Oxford: Blackwell, 1989), p. 158.
64. Private information.
65. Ibid.
66. Ibid.
67. Peter Hennessy, '"Tony Wants": The First Blair Premiership in Historical Perspective', Royal Historical Society/Gresham College, Colin Matthew Lecture 2001, 7 November 2001.
68. *Falkland Islands Review. Report of a Committee of Privy Councillors*, Cmnd 8787 (London: HMSO, 1983).
69. Lord Franks's paper, which was untitled, was delivered to the Alastair Buchan Society on 2 February 1989.
70. *Falkland Islands Review*, Cmnd 8787, pp. 85–6.
71. Lord Franks to the Alastair Buchan Society, 2 February 1989.
72. Letter from Lord Franks to Peter Hennessy, 14 February 1989.
73. Hennessy, 'Tony Wants'.
74. Private information.

12

The United Nations Security Resolution 502

FRANCIS TOASE

INTRODUCTION

Argentina's use of force to take over the Falkland Islands, or as Buenos Aires put it, to take back the Islas Malvinas, led to the convening of the most powerful organ of the world's premier international organisation, the Security Council of the United Nations Organisation (UN). Indeed this use of force brought about a marked change in the UN's handling of the long-running dispute between Britain and Argentina over the islands. Up until this time the UN had treated the dispute as a decolonisation issue rather than as an international peace and security issue *per se*; the dispute had been considered by the General Assembly and associated committees, not by the Security Council, and only sporadically by the Assembly at that. The crisis precipitated by Argentina's use of force on 2 April 1982, however, gave rise to consideration of the dispute as an international peace and security issue and at the highest level, resulting in a Security Council resolution that was to have profound implications for both parties to the dispute and for third parties too. The purpose of this chapter is to examine this resolution together with the deliberations which led up to it.[1]

GENERAL ASSEMBLY RESOLUTIONS 2065 (XX), 3160 (XXVIII) AND 31/49

The question of the Falkland Islands (Islas Malvinas)[2] was placed formally on the agenda of the UN in August 1964 when Britain, in line with its continuing policy of decolonisation and in accordance with its obligations

147

under the UN Charter's (Chapter XI) provisions on non-self-governing territories, put the Falkland Islands on the UN's decolonisation list.[3] This initiative indicated that Britain was willing to release the islands from colonial control, but it was a move that raised more questions than it answered. Decolonisation usually meant granting a territory independence – a task which Britain had performed many times already – but in the case of the Falkland Islands things were not usual. The inhabitants, some 2,000 people of British descent, did not want independence from Britain and would have had difficulty sustaining independence even if they had wanted it. Their opposition to independence was shared by the nearest state, Argentina, but for entirely different reasons. Argentina had long regarded the islands as part of its national territory. It insisted that decolonisation in this instance must not mean independence or continued association with Britain, but that sovereignty over the islands be transferred to Buenos Aires. Argentina even contended that the inhabitants of the islands were not an interested party in the dispute, on the grounds that the Argentinian inhabitants of the islands had been removed by force by the British in 1833 and replaced by British settlers, and that therefore the dispute should be settled by bilateral means between the colonial power, Britain, and the 'rightful' owner, Argentina. With this in mind, Argentina responded to Britain's initiative by launching a diplomatic offensive at the UN designed to attract support for their position.[4]

The provisions of the UN Charter did not necessarily favour this position. Chapter XI referred to the need to promote the self-government of the people of non-self-governing territories, and to this end 'to take due account of the political aspirations' of such people, thus implying free choice for these peoples.[5] Moreover the UN's Declaration on the Granting of Independence to Colonial Countries and Peoples, General Assembly Resolution 1514 (XV) of 14 December 1960, while proclaiming the necessity of bringing to a speedy and unconditional end 'colonialism in all its forms and manifestations', rejected the subjection of peoples to alien domination and stressed the right of peoples to self-determination, that is, to their right to be allowed to determine freely their own political status.[6] On the other hand, the political climate at the time was such that any non-aligned state making a case against a Western colonial power at the UN was likely to get a sympathetic hearing. The UN had become dominated numerically by non-aligned states. These states, whatever their political differences, would usually vote as a bloc on matters to do with decolonisation. Their voting strength, coupled with the reluctance of either Eastern or Western countries to be seen to be defending colonialism, usually ensured massive majorities for any non-aligned state on a decolonisation matter. Thus when the Falklands question came before the General Assembly, the latter on 16 December 1965 adopted by 94–0–14 a resolution, 2065 (XX), which specified the dispute as a colonial problem, reminded the Assembly that under Resolution 1514 (XV) the UN was pledged to bring to an end everywhere colonialism in all forms, and invited Britain and Argentina

> to proceed without delay with negotiations...with a view to find-ing a peaceful solution to the problem, bearing in mind the provi-sions and objectives of the Charter of the United Nations and of General Assembly resolution 1514 (XV) and the interests of the population of the Falkland Islands (Malvinas).[7]

In other words, the Assembly asked Britain to negotiate the termination of the colonial presence while offering a safeguard, albeit limited, for any misgivings the islanders might have about the question by stating that their interests, though not their wishes, needed to be taken into account. Britain, which did not put up much resistance to the Argentinian claim and abstained on the vote, agreed to negotiate on these terms.

The negotiations the Assembly had recommended duly took place, though whether they can be described as quick and peaceful, given that they were held intermittently over seventeen years and were accompa-nied at times by bellicosity and eventually by the use of armed force on Argentina's part, is debatable. Argentina saw the purpose of the talks as being that of 'recovering' the islands and continued to make this goal a matter of high priority in its foreign policy. Successive British govern-ments were willing to negotiate with Argentina, perhaps judging that they could divest themselves of a distant defence commitment and enhance diplomatic and economic relations with Argentina in particular and Latin America in general by pushing the islanders into closer links with their neighbour. But the future of the islands was never really a pri-ority for Britain and anyway British governments had difficulty in rec-onciling their willingness to accommodate Argentina's views with their commitment to take into account the views of the islanders, who vehe-mently objected to becoming part of Argentina and were backed in this by a small but powerful lobby in Parliament and the Press. Thus when the British government (after secret talks with Argentina) announced in December 1968 that it had reached an agreement with Buenos Aires on transferring sovereignty, the government ran into stiff opposition in Parliament and even in Cabinet and had to reconsider its policy. Further bilateral talks in 1970–1 resulted in a series of agreements called the

Communications Agreements, themselves regarded with suspicion by the islanders and their supporters. But subsequent attempts to accommodate Argentinian demands while respecting the wishes of the islanders were problematical, whether for Labour (1974–9) or for the new Conservative government under Margaret Thatcher (1979–90), as Foreign Office Minister of State Nicholas Ridley found when he tried to justify a 'lease-back' scheme to the House of Commons in December 1980. Talks continued in February 1981 and February 1982 but the latter were soon to be overtaken by events. As tension mounted over the affair of the Argentinian scrap-metal merchants on South Georgia in March 1982, the Argentinian Junta decided to activate a plan to use force to 'recover' the islands before the 150th anniversary of their capture by Britain.

By this time, the UN had given more support to Argentina on the Falklands question. On 14 December 1973, the General Assembly adopted by 116–0–14 (with five absences) a resolution which expressly praised Argentina for its efforts to bring about the decolonisation of the territory and pressed the parties to make progress in negotiating an end to the colonial situation. This became Resolution 3160 (XXVIII).[8] On 1 December 1976, the Assembly passed by 102–1–32 a similar resolution, 31/49, which also invoked the authority of declarations emanating from conferences of non-aligned countries at Lima in August 1975 and Colombo in August 1976. On this occasion, unlike the previous one, Britain voted against the resolution.[9] Moreover, Argentina could derive some encouragement from the UN's earlier response to India's use of armed force to invade the Portuguese colonial enclave of Goa on 17 December 1961. The Security Council rejected a draft resolution calling on the UN to support India, but it also rejected a draft calling on India to withdraw. The result therefore was that the UN acquiesced in India's use of force to 'recover' a territory it claimed had been taken from it in an act of aggression in 1510. Argentina could take heart too from the UN's response to Indonesia's takeover of West Irian in 1963 and East Timor in 1975 and Morocco's takeover of the former Spanish (Western) Sahara in 1976. The Junta therefore had reasons for assuming that their use of force to 'recover' Las Malvinas would be condoned rather than condemned by the UN. They seem to have given less emphasis, however, to the UN's various declarations on the inadmissibility of the use of force to resolve disputes. In particular, they seem to have overlooked the General Assembly's landmark Declaration on Principles of International Law Concerning Friendly Relations and Cooperation Among States of October 1970. This specifically proclaimed the need to refrain from using force to alter boundaries or resolve disputes and stated that the people of each colony had the right freely to choose independence, integration with another state or free association with the mother country.[10]

THE UN CALLS FOR RESTRAINT

Notwithstanding the General Assembly's resolutions of 1965, 1973 and 1976 on the Falklands question, Argentina's use of force to settle the dispute caused shock and surprise at the UN, hitting the Security Council, to use the words of Britain's Permanent Representative there, Sir Anthony Parsons, 'like a bolt from the blue'.[11] True, the Falklands question had already been given consideration by the General Assembly. Yet it had never been a mainstream issue there, had never been given more than sporadic consideration by the Assembly and had never been before the Security Council at all. Few delegations were aware of the dispute, or even of the exact location of the islands, at the time. Moreover, few delegations were aware of the talks that had been held in New York in February 1982, still less of the subsequent diplomatic exchanges between the two governments. The tension that had built up over South Georgia had not reached the Security Council, which was preoccupied with events in the Middle East. Unexpected or not, however, the Falklands question was to become, temporarily at least, a prominent item on the UN's agenda, leading to extensive deliberation by the Security Council. This being the case, it might be appropriate before looking at the Council's meetings to remind ourselves of Security Council membership and voting procedures. The Council had 15 members, of which 5 were permanent (the 'P5'), these being the UK, the USA, France, the USSR and China and 10 were non-permanent, elected for 2-year terms, these being at the time Uganda, Zaïre, Togo, Panama, Jordan, Guyana, Japan, Ireland, Spain and Poland. Nine votes were needed to adopt a resolution, which meant that a sponsor needed the votes on at least some of the six non-aligned states on the Council to get a draft adopted. Even then, a vote against a draft by any of the P5 would veto it. It is also worth remembering that non-members could request the right to participate without vote, under Article 31 of the UN Charter.[12]

First to attempt to raise the issue at the Security Council was Argentina, which sought to argue that Britain's response to the South Georgia affair justified Argentina's use of force in the South Atlantic. On Wednesday, 31 March 1982, the newly arrived Argentinian Permanent Representative, Mr Eduardo Roca, called on the President of the Security Council for the month of March, Mrs Jeane Kirkpatrick of the USA, to tell her that his government was contemplating bringing the question of South Georgia to the attention of the Council. Kirkpatrick's preference was to prevent the question from going to the international arena. She was inclined therefore to arrange a private discussion between Roca and the British representative without recourse to the Council. This was to be overtaken by events, though on 1 April Roca circulated a letter to the Council in which he stated that the British were embarking on aggression over South Georgia.[13]

On the following morning (Thursday 1 April 1982), the recently appointed Secretary-General Javier Perez de Cuéllar, on hearing news of the crisis, summoned the British and Argentinian ambassadors separately and asked them to appeal to their governments for maximum restraint. Parsons responded positively to this appeal. The Secretary-General then made this appeal publicly at a midday press conference and reiterated it that afternoon at New York airport before leaving for a pre-arranged visit to Europe.[14]

That day too the newly appointed President of the Security Council for the month of April, Ambassador Kamanda of Zaïre, was to make a similar appeal. This was precipitated by the British Ambassador. Parsons had been informed by lunchtime by his government that an Argentinian invasion was imminent and had been instructed to call an emergency meeting of the Security Council so as to take pre-emptive action. Consequently, he asked Kamanda early in the afternoon for a meeting of the Council. There followed soon afterwards an informal meeting at which Parsons explained what he saw as the seriousness and urgency of the situation and pressed for a public meeting of the Council as soon as possible. This was granted and the Council met later that day.[15] At the meeting,[16] Parsons explained that his government had reason to believe Argentina was preparing to invade the Falkland Islands. He also outlined the increasing tensions arising in his view from Argentina's actions in South Georgia. Emphasising that Argentina had abandoned peaceful negotiations and was preparing to use force, he asked the Council to call upon Argentina 'to exercise the utmost restraint and to refrain from the use or threat of force in the South Atlantic'.[17] Roca, who had asked to participate in the discussion and was granted this in accordance with Article 31 of the Charter (i.e. without the right to vote), gave a lengthy account of what he called Britain's use of force to take the islands from Argentina in January 1833 and Britain's refusal to implement Resolution 2065 (XX) by peaceful negotiations. He also asserted that in South Georgia, Argentina was once again being subjected to British aggression.[18] Roca's case, however, failed to convince the Council. The

President, after consulting the members of the Council, made a statement which echoed Parsons's call. On behalf of the whole Council, Kamanda expressed concern about the tension in the region of the Falkland Islands (Islas Malvinas); called upon the governments of Argentina and the UK to exercise the utmost restraint and in particular to refrain from the threat or use of force in the region; and urged the parties to continue to search for a diplomatic solution.[19] Parsons assured the President that he would abide by the appeal. He challenged Roca, who seemed taken aback by the Council's actions, to do likewise. Roca remained silent, giving rise to a realisation among Council members that conflict was imminent.[20]

That evening Parsons and his team, anticipating the use of armed force by Argentina, decided that they needed to ready themselves to take immediate action in the Security Council. They agreed that they should base their case not upon Britain's claim to sovereignty over the islands but upon the argument that Argentina had acted illegitimately in using force to settle a dispute and had committed an unprovoked act of aggression. Their reasoning was that Argentina could cite previous UN resolutions on the sovereignty issue favourable to its position, whereas it was vulnerable on the charge of violating Charter provisions that Member States should use peaceful means to resolve disputes (Article 2, paragraph 3) and should refrain from the use or threat of force (Article 2, paragraph 4) except in self-defence (Article 51) as well as on the charge of aggression – a charge which many countries on the Council, having been or fearing they could become victims of aggression, might agree with. The British team also agreed that they must try to get a resolution through quickly – within the 48 hours minimum if possible – so as to get a decision before extraneous considerations such as 'vote-swapping' or 'horse-trading' came into play. In Parsons's words, they decided that they must 'act quickly and avoid becoming mired in the long negotiations which normally precede the adoption of a resolution by the Council'. To this end they prepared a draft resolution to table at the Security Council. This was drawn up by the mission's lawyer David Anderson and was approved by his government with very few changes. The draft was couched in Chapter VII language (i.e. that chapter of the Charter entitled Action with Respect to Threats to the Peace, Breaches of the Peace, and Acts of Aggression): it stated that there existed a breach of the peace; demanded an immediate cessation of hostilities; and demanded an immediate withdrawal of all Argentine forces from the Falkland Islands. These preparations were to prove timely, because the following morning, 2 April 1982, Argentinian forces were invading the Falkland Islands.[21]

The next morning (Friday 2 April 1982), after 'hurried consultation with London', Parsons informed the President of the Council that Argentine armed forces were invading the Falkland Islands and requested an immediate meeting of the full Council.[22] This was granted and the Council soon began the first of two sessions to be held on the Falklands crisis that day.[23]

Speaking first, Parsons said that his government's worst apprehensions, those which led to his calling of the Council into session, had now been realised. Argentina, he said, had ignored two appeals of the Secretary-General and the appeal of the President of the Council for restraint and for the avoidance of the threat or use of force and was launching a massive invasion of the Falkland Islands. This invasion, he asserted, constituted 'a blatant violation of the Charter of the United Nations and of international law...an attempt to impose by force a foreign and unwanted control over 1,900 peaceful agricultural people who have chosen in free and fair elections to maintain their links with Britain and the British way of life'. He proposed that the Council should act at once and to that end read out his delegation's draft resolution which he urged the council to adopt at once so as to heal 'this undoubted breach of the peace'.[24]

Roca, who was allowed to participate without vote as at the previous meeting, said that he could not accept either the description or the interpretation of events given by the British representative at the previous day's meeting or at that day's. He stated that he wished

> to inform the Council that today the Government of Argentina has proclaimed the recovery of its national sovereignty over the territories of the Malvinas, South Georgia and South Sandwich Islands, in an act which responds to a just Argentine claim and is also an act of legitimate defence in response to the acts of aggression by the United Kingdom.

He added that his government was ready to negotiate but not about sovereignty. He also asked that the Council defer discussion of the draft until he had received further instructions from his government.[25] Exercising his right of reply, Parsons stated that if Argentina stood ready to negotiate, then 'what they have done today is a curious way of expressing such readiness'.[26]

When the debate resumed at a second session later that day, Parsons received trenchant support from Australia, New Zealand, Canada,

France and, to a lesser extent, from Ireland.[27] The representatives of the three Commonwealth countries mentioned, who were speaking under Article 31, all expressed full support for the UK draft.[28] France's representative was if anything even more outspoken in defence of the British stance, condemning Argentina's actions as 'a glaring violation of the provisions of Article 2, paragraph 4 of the Charter... a totally unjustified armed attack... and a breach of international peace' which deliberately disregarded the appeals for restraint made by the Secretary-General and the President of the Council.[29] Ireland's representative suggested that regardless of the rights and wrongs of the dispute – on which he reserved his position – he favoured a firm response because Argentina had flouted the Council's unanimous call for restraint and challenged its authority.[30] Roca declined to comment on these statements. He said that his country's Foreign Minister was on his way to inform the Council of Argentina's position and therefore asked for a postponement of any decision on the matter before the Council until the Foreign Minister had been heard.[31] Parsons, who had originally intended to press for a vote that day, 'readily acceded to pressure from members of the Council to wait until 3 April'.[32]

When the Council resumed its deliberations the next day (Saturday 3 April 1982), Argentina's Foreign Minister Dr Nicanor Costa Mendez spoke first and at great length.[33] He played the anti-colonial card, saying that Argentina was an ex-colonial and anti-colonial state, a victim of imperialism like Latin America in general and Africa and Asia, which was completing the decolonisation of Latin America by righting a wrong perpetrated by a colonial power in 1833. He dismissed accusations that Argentina had violated Article 2, paragraphs 3 and 4 of the UN Charter, suggesting in a somewhat complicated and novel piece of legalese that the UN Charter's reference to the non-use of force only applied to disputes which began after 1945, when the Charter came into effect. He also dismissed the UK's draft, saying that this was essentially the same as that presented by Portugal on 18 December 1961 when India 'recovered' Goa, one that was rejected by the Council at that time. He asked how his country could have 'invaded' a territory which was part of Argentina and said he wondered why, if the UK wanted the withdrawal of forces by Argentina, it had not withdrawn its own forces 149 years after it had used force to seize the islands. He added that the UK's despatch of warships to the region justified Argentina's actions in defence of its rights.[34]

It soon became apparent, however, that Costa Mendez's use of the anti-colonial gambit was not as effective as he had hoped. Jordan's representative stated that the Council was not meeting to discuss claims and counter-claims to the islands, but to consider the issue of the use of force to settle a dispute; for this reason, he said, he supported the UK draft.[35] Japan's representative asserted that Argentina had violated one of the most important norms of international law, the non-use of force to settle international disputes.[36] The USA's representative made a short and measured statement but he too expressed support for the British draft.[37] Several Latin American states did offer support, to a greater or lesser extent, to the Argentine position, these being Brazil,[38] Bolivia,[39] Peru[40] and Paraguay[41] (all of which countries participated without vote), and Panama,[42] a Council member at the time. Even so, with only one exception these Latin American states reaffirmed their preference for the peaceful settlement of the disputes. The exception was Panama, whose representative in a lengthy speech gave strong support to Argentina, arguing that the latter could not have invaded the Malvinas because a state could not invade its own territory. Panama's representative concluded by proposing a draft resolution supporting Argentina: it proposed that the UK refrain from the threat or the use of force and join Argentina in discussions based on respect for the latter's sovereignty over the Malvinas, South Georgia and South Sandwich Islands. He asked for a suspension of the debate so that the Secretariat could translate the document into all the working languages of the Council and circulate it. This proposal, described by Parsons as a 'delaying tactic',[43] failed to attract sufficient support, however, gaining only seven votes in favour (China, Ireland, Japan, Panama, Poland, Spain and the USSR), not the affirmative nine votes needed, to three against (France, the UK, the USA), with four abstentions (Guyana, Jordan, Togo and Zaïre) in a procedural vote.[44]

Exercising his right of reply, Parsons sought to refute the main points made by Costa Mendez and his supporters. He began by reminding the assembled delegations why he had called for meetings of the Council: not to discuss the rights and wrongs of the dispute but because of the imminence and then the actuality of an armed invasion of the Falkland Islands. He emphasised that, contrary to what Costa Mendez had implied, the current crisis had arisen not from the relatively trivial incident of the illegal presence of a few Argentinians on South Georgia, but from Argentina's invasion of the Falklands. He rejected what he called Costa Mendez's proposition that the principles of the Charter relating to the peaceful settlement of disputes (Article 2, paragraphs 3–4) were not necessarily applicable to situations that arose before the Charter was adopted, as a very dangerous one, which if accepted could lead to numerous conflicts around the globe. He maintained that the people of the Falkland Islands, whether they numbered 1,800 or 18,000 or 18 million, were entitled to the protection of international law and to have their freely expressed wishes respected. Finally, dealing with the argument that no invasion had taken place because the islands were part of Argentina, he pointed out that the UK had been accepted by the UN as the Administering Authority. Concluding, Parsons said that he had asked the Secretariat to prepare a revised draft with 'Islas Malvinas' in parentheses following the words Falkland Islands wherever they occurred, to accord with standard UN practice. But he wanted, he said, to have a vote on the draft (as revised) that day. In view of the urgency of the situation, he explained, his government had originally wanted a vote on the previous day, when he introduced the draft. He had willingly acceded to the opinion of the President to postpone the vote until 3 April, he continued, since he had not given Council delegations the conventional 24 hours' grace before being asked to vote on the draft and also because he was willing to allow the Argentine Foreign Minister to put his case. But he wanted a vote on his revised draft now, he said, after which the Council could consider Panama's draft.[45]

Panama, in fact, again tried to come to Argentina's rescue. The Panamanian representative contended that the Council must await the British draft in its final form before voting and therefore proposed a suspension for this purpose.[46] This proposal was accepted by Parsons and a suspension for just over an hour followed.[47] The President then asked the Council to prepare to vote on the revised draft.[48] Panama's representative now intervened to question whether the UK was entitled to vote. He opined that if the draft was submitted under Chapter VI of the Charter, as operative paragraph 3 of the draft seemed to suggest, then Article 27(3) of the Charter came into play (i.e. a party to a dispute should abstain from voting on the matter[49]). Parsons, who subsequently described this procedural intervention as an attempt 'to rob me of my vote', replied that the draft had been proposed not with reference to clauses of the Charter dealing with dispute settlement but with those dealing with breaches of the peace, therefore the provisions of Article 27(3) did not apply.[50] His view was endorsed by the Spanish representative, an acknowledged expert on UN procedures, whereupon Panama decided not to press for a procedural vote.[51]

Several representatives now exercised their right to explain their votes before casting them. Spain's representative said that he could not support the UK draft, because it failed to mention the need to settle disputes in conformity with UN resolutions, but neither could he support Panama's because this neglected the use of force by Argentina.[52] Uganda's representative said his government's position was consistent with that of the non-aligned countries: it supported Argentina's claim but not its use of force, which was contrary to the Charter and would set a dangerous precedent if accepted as a method of setting disputes. It would therefore vote for the UK draft.[53] Togo's representative reserved his position on the substance of the case but supported the British draft on the basis that governments should not use force to settle disputes.[54] The USSR's representative made a short statement identifying his government with anti-colonialism. He said the British had not complied with UN requests to decolonise the islands and that as the draft disregarded this aspect of the problem, his government would not support the draft.[55] Ireland's representative repeated what he had said at an earlier session. The real issue was not the merits of the case but the use of force in the face of a call for restraint by the Council: his country would vote for the British draft as this called for a cessation of hostilities, an immediate withdrawal by Argentina and a diplomatic solution.[56] Zaïre's Kamanda, too, expressed support for the British draft. He said he would vote for the draft because, regardless of the merits of Argentina's claim, he felt it would set a dangerous precedent to accept the use of force as a way of settling disputes.[57] He then reverted to his role as President and called for the vote.[58]

The result of the debate was that ten voted in favour (France, Guyana, Ireland, Japan, Jordan, Togo, Uganda, the UK, the USA and Zaïre), one voted against (Panama) and four abstained (China, the USSR, Poland and Spain).[59] Several representatives who had not yet contributed to the debate made statements after the voting. Guyana's representative said he had supported the draft because of Argentina's use of force, which he described as a clear violation of the Charter.[60] Poland's representative took a similar line to that of the USSR.[61] China's representative, in a short statement, said he would not support the draft but wanted a peaceful resolution of the problem.[62] Panama's representative asserted that the adopted draft would aggravate rather than solve the problem. He stated that he was withholding his own draft but reserved the right to resurrect this, or strengthen it, at a later meeting.[63] Argentina's Costa Mendez representative expressed deep regret at the Council's actions.[64] Parsons welcomed those actions.[65] Thus was born Resolution 502, which differed from the UK's original draft only in so far as after each mention of the words Falkland Islands a parenthetical reference to the Islas Malvinas was included.[66]

Why did the Council accept the British draft resolution?

The result of the debate, at first sight, was highly surprising. After all, the British were seeking the endorsement of the Security Council – and this necessarily meant they required support from the non-aligned countries – to deny a non-aligned country possession of a colonial territory in a non-aligned continent. To approach the Council in these circumstances, let alone to secure enough votes, seemed a forlorn hope. Costa Mendez, for his part, seems to have assumed that as the representative of a non-aligned state he was bound to have the advantage over a colonial power, especially as the non-aligned group in the General Assembly had endorsed Argentina's view on the sovereignty issue. He seems also to have assumed that Britain would have difficulty in convening a meeting of the Council, that if it did succeed in convening a meeting it would have difficulty in securing enough support for a favourable resolution, and if it did attract enough support Russia could be persuaded to adhere to the anti-colonial cause and veto such a proposal.[67] Parsons too saw his team's chances as being slim. He recounted that they would proba-bly get seven or eight votes, but would need luck to get nine and unbe-lievable luck to get ten. He described the result as 'better than we had dared to hope for'.[68]

That Costa Mendez's expectation of a *fait accompli* was confounded was due to a combination of factors. One was what Clausewitz in a mili-tary setting has referred to as 'friction' or chance. The invasion was badly timed in terms of Argentina's diplomacy at the UN.[69] The Presidency of the Council – and the president can have a strong influence on both the tim-ing and procedure of meetings – was changing to Argentina's disadvantage. The outgoing president for March, America's Ambassador to the UN Jeane Kirkpatrick, was in US State Department parlance a 'Latinist' rather than an 'Atlanticist'. She had for some time been a leading advocate of the line that the United States should be positive towards the Argentinian regime, which had given its support to US anti-communism in Latin America. She felt that the United States might prejudice its influence in Latin America by siding with the British over the Falklands question. Consequently, she had not been sympathetic to Parsons's attempt to convene an emergency meeting of the Security Council as the crisis loomed, reportedly trying to block such an attempt, and might have been less than helpful to Parsons had she remained in post (she in fact distanced herself from what became Resolution 502 by sending her deputy to participate in the debate).[70] She was replaced on 1 April by someone who turned out to be more sympa-thetic to Parsons, someone who not only held the emergency meeting but by issuing a call for restraint rendered Argentina's post-invasion stance dif-ficult to support even among non-aligned Council members. The timing of the invasion was also unfortunate for Argentina in terms of the availabil-ity or otherwise of diplomats with UN experience. One such diplomat, the Argentinian Ambassador to the UN, had just left. His successor Eduardo

Roca, distinguished lawyer though he was, had arrived only on 24 March and had barely had time to familiarise himself with UN procedures, personalities and politics, let alone to lobby for support by the time the crisis broke. Costa Mendez arrived only in time for the debate on 3 April. The invasion found the UK, by contrast, with a diplomat with over two years' experience at the UN available – just (he was about to retire in June) – and he was not only persuasive but popular with it.

A second factor, which follows naturally from the first, is that the British proved more adept at the lobbying which preceded and accompanied the Council debate than their Argentinian counterparts.[71] Costa Mendez was not available to do any pre-invasion lobbying, but when he did try his hand, on 3 April, his efforts proved to be at best ineffectual and at worst counter-productive. Costa Mendez spoke to the non-aligned delegates before he addressed the Security Council, but he appears to have done literally that: he spoke to them rather than consulted them. Apparently he took their votes for granted, brushing aside their questions about the use of force and told them, rather than asked them, to vote for Argentina. His lobbying of the Soviet delegation was not successful either, though this may have been beyond any Argentinian's powers: he urged Russia to remember such issues as non-alignment, anti-colonialism and Argentinian grain exports to Russia, but Moscow seems to have told the Soviet delegation to keep to their policy of not using the veto except on drafts that directly affected their vital interests and, perhaps, not to get out of step with the non-aligned countries on the Council. Panama's foreign minister Jorge Illueca's efforts to lobby on Argentina's behalf were not particularly successful either, in part perhaps, because he had an irritating manner. Parsons, by contrast, lobbied with great success. He is reported to have displayed what one UN admirer called 'good old fashioned diplomatic legwork' to gain the nine votes he needed to get the Council summoned on 1 April.[72] He then displayed similar skills in attempting to attract support for his draft on 2–3 April, his personal intervention being instrumental, for example, in facilitating the affirmative votes of both Uganda and Jordan, and perhaps Togo: the French were asked to secure Togo's vote, and obliged. What diplomatic bargains, if any, were struck, remain unidentified, but one pair of journalists offered an apposite comment on what was probably involved when they wrote that: 'At times like this a diplomat must draw on every resource at his disposal – an old favour done, a personal contact kept in good repair, a trade deal or cultural exchange in the offing, perhaps simple friendship'.[73]

This merges into a third factor, that of presentational skill in the debates themselves. Unlike most Council debates, this one involved, to an extent, an opportunity for speakers to influence voting behaviour. As Parsons has commented:

> It was an open contest and I felt, as never before in my UN experience, that the listeners were hanging on the words of the speakers, and that a significant number of delegations were ready to decide their votes in the light of the debate, not in the light of previously entrenched positions as [had] for years been the case over, for example, the Middle East and Southern Africa.[74]

The open nature of the debate resulted perhaps from several factors: the speed with which the crisis broke; a lack of knowledge on the part of many delegations about the Falklands question; the lack of an established stance on it; and the dilemma it posed for the non-aligned countries, who had committed themselves almost ritualistically at successive summits to the Argentine position on the question of sovereignty, but also to the non-use of force to settle political disputes. Whatever the reasons, the debate was relatively open and the British seem to have put forward a more convincing case in the debate than did the Argentinians.[75] The British argument that Argentina had violated the provisions of the Charter on the non-use of force to settle disputes and had thereby set a dangerous precedent for other territorial disputes had resonance for many of the non-aligned countries at the Council. Uganda, for one, was persuaded that Argentina's action constituted aggression. Guyana, with a neighbour (Venezuela) that claimed much of its territory, was persuaded that the use of force to settle territorial disputes should be discouraged. Costa Mendez's assertion that his country was justified in using force to right a colonial wrong attracted hardly any support, notwithstanding previous voting patterns in the General Assembly on the sovereignty issue. The Argentinians failed to match Britain's case that international law and international security were at stake. Arguably Costa Mendez inadvertently helped the British case when he claimed that Articles 2(3) and 2(4) of the Charter applied only to disputes that had arisen after 1945. Just about every delegation at the Council came from a country which was involved in disputes that went back long before the Charter came into effect. As Parsons has commented, 'I could see votes changing in my direction pretty well as he said that.'[76]

Resolution 502 assessed

Security Council Resolution 502 did not formally condemn Argentina and accuse it of aggression. Nor did Resolution 502 formally empower or authorise Britain to use force to remove the Argentinians from the Falklands. But to infer from this, as one reputable Argentinian scholar has done, that the resolution therefore represented a partial success for her country seems to be highly debatable to say the least.[77] The resolution may not have formally condemned Argentina as an aggressor or formally authorised Britain to use force, but it provided little if any succour for Argentina. Costa Mendez did not get the sympathetic response at the UN he saw as central to his diplomatic offensive. Instead, he was presented with a resolution which by UN standards was unusually robust: it characterised his government's action as a breach of the peace; demanded he remove his armed forces from the islands immediately; and instructed him to resume peaceful talks with the British so as to seek a diplomatic solution and to respect fully the purposes and principles of the UN Charter. His country's seizure of the Falklands was in effect declared null and void, while its subsequent non-compliance with the resolution lent legal and moral weight to the British case that their use of force to eject the Argentinians from the islands was legitimate. The British government, on its part, saw the resolution as a triumph. After its adoption the British were able to respond to any antipathy to their dispatch of the task force by saying that if Argentina wanted peace all it had to do was to withdraw its forces from the Falklands in accordance with UN Security Council Resolution 502. As Margaret Thatcher commented in her memoirs, the resolution provided 'almost perfect backing for our [Britain's] position'.[78]

CONCLUSIONS

Before 1 April 1982, the UN, in the shape of the General Assembly, had sought to promote a settlement of the dispute over the Falkland Islands by recommending that the two disputants negotiate a settlement. The Assembly had in effect endorsed 'Argentina's contention that the removal of British rule from the Falklands was in keeping with the sacred mission of decolonisation'.[79] This being the case, one might criticise the UN for neglecting the islanders' right to self-determination, to determine for themselves which government they wished to live under: after all, respect for the aspirations of the inhabitants of non-self-governing territories is enshrined in the UN Charter and has underlain decades of decolonisation. Furthermore, one might criticise the UN for creating conditions in which Argentina felt emboldened to use force to settle the dispute. Against this, however, it could be argued that the Assembly was doing one of the things it was there to do, that is, to reflect world opinion (more precisely it reflects the opinions that the governments wish to be seen to be holding), and that the Assembly had asked for a *peaceful* settlement of the dispute: if Argentina chose to interpret UN resolutions as justifying the use of force, then this was Argentina's miscalculation and not the UN's fault.

When news arrived at the UN (on 1 April 1982) that Argentina was about to launch an armed attack to settle the dispute, the UN, this time in the shape of the Secretary-General and the President of the Security Council, appealed to both sides to refrain from the use or threat of force. This raises another criticism: that the UN failed to avert war. Clearly it did, but this argument revolves around the wider issue of whether the theory of collective security actually works in practice, an issue which lies outside the scope of this chapter.[80] Suffice it to say here that as the UN had no warning of an imminent attack and no armed forces to deter such an attack, an appeal for restraint, the use of moral suasion, was about as much as it could do in the circumstances to preserve peace: the UN could not (arguably cannot) prevent a crisis of this sort but it did act swiftly once it was warned that a crisis was imminent.

This brings us on to the UN's response once Argentina had disregarded its appeals not to use force. At this juncture the UN, this time in the shape of the Security Council, became judge and jury. Somewhat surprisingly, in the light of the UN's previous resolutions on the dispute, it now decided that Argentina was in the wrong, that Argentina had breached the peace and should withdraw its forces from the islands immediately. The Council might be criticised in this respect for not going further, for not authorising 'collective measures' under Chapter VII, in common parlance for not imposing 'sanctions' of some sort on Argentina. But given the UN's track record on enforcement this was perhaps unrealistic. Even the UK felt inclined to avoid the use of the word aggression – a very strong word indeed in UN-speak – believing that this would have placed Council members in a quandary about collective measures. The British preferred instead to use language designed to maximise support for their draft. The upshot was that, if the UN Security Council can be said to be a dispenser of international legitimacy, the Council denied such legitimacy to Argentina but conferred the same on Britain. The Security Council was to qualify this decision at subsequent meetings during the Falklands Crisis, but it did not rescind the decision.[81]

NOTES

1. This examination was facilitated by the librarian of the London School of Economics and Political Science (LSE), who kindly allowed the author to

consult relevant official records and documents of the UN held there. It was also facilitated by the librarian of the Royal Military Academy Sandhurst, Mr Andrew Orgill, who drew the author's attention to an article by Sir Anthony Parsons, Britain's permanent representative at the UN at the time of the Falklands conflict, entitled 'The Falklands Crisis in the United Nations, 31 March–14 June 1982', *International Affairs*, 59/2 (spring 1983), pp. 169–78; to a chapter by J.E. Spence, 'The UN and the Falklands Crisis', in G.R. Berridge and A. Jennings (eds), *Diplomacy at the UN* (London : Macmillan, 1985), Chapter 5, pp. 59–72; and to several books of relevance, notably Michael Charlton, *The Little Platoon: Diplomacy and the Falklands Dispute* (Oxford : Basil Blackwell, 1989); Alberto R. Coll and Anthony C. Arend (eds), *The Falklands War: Lessons for Strategy, Diplomacy and International Law* (London : Allen and Unwin, 1985); and Alex Danchev (ed.), *International Perspectives on the Falklands Conflict: A Matter of Life and Death* (Basingstoke: Macmillan, 1992). The author also found parts of the following works of value: Michael Bilton and Peter Kosminsky, *Speaking Out: Untold Stories from the Falklands War* (London : André Deutsch, 1989); Lawrence Freedman and Virginia Gamba-Stonehouse, *Signals of War: The Falklands Conflict of 1982* (London: Faber and Faber, 1990); Virginia Gamba, *The Falklands/Malvinas War: A Model for North–South Crisis Prevention* (London: Allen and Unwin, 1987); Max Hastings and Simon Jenkins, *The Battle for the Falklands* (London: Book Club Associates, 1983); Martin Middlebrook, *Operation Corporate: The Falklands War, 1982* (London: Viking, 1985); and The Sunday Times Insight Team, *The Falklands War: The Full Story* (London : Sphere, 1982).

2. Whereas the British used the name Falkland Islands to refer to the territory in question Argentina used the name Islas Malvinas. Standard practice at the UN from 1964 on was to use the British designation followed by the Argentinian one in parentheses. In the interests of brevity the author has used the British designation only unless the context requires otherwise.

3. Gamba, *The Falklands/Malvinas War*, p. 88.

4. For an Argentine perspective on Britain's 'listing' of the territory, ibid., pp. 88–90.

5. See UN Charter, Chapter XI, Declaration Regarding Non-Self Governing Territories, Article 73.

6. For the text of the resolution, see *Yearbook of the United Nations 1960* (New York: United Nations, Office of Public Information, 1961), pp. 49–50.

7. For the text of the resolution, see *Yearbook of the United Nations 1965* (New York: United Nations, Office of Public Information, 1967), pp. 578–9.

8. For the text of the resolution see *Yearbook of the United Nations 1973*, Vol. 27 (New York: United Nations, Office of Public Information, 1976), pp. 713–14.

9. For the text of the resolution, see *Yearbook of the United Nations 1976*, Vol. 30 (New York: United Nations, Office of Public Information, 1979), p. 747.

10. For a summary of the UN's handling of the Goa episode, see *Yearbook of the United Nations 1961* (New York: United Nations, Office of Public Information, 1963), pp. 129–31. For an authoritative comment on the

precedent set by Goa, see Claude, 'UN Efforts at Settlement of the Falkland Islands Crisis', in Coll and Arend, Lessons. pp. 122–3. For further details of the Declaration on Principles of International Law Concerning Friendly Relations and Cooperation Among States, see *Yearbook of the United Nations 1970* (New York: United Nations, Office of Public Information, 1972), pp. 784–92. For authoritative comment, see Thomas M. Franck, 'The Strategic Role of Legal Principles', in Coll and Arend, Lessons, pp. 24–5.

11. Parsons, 'Falklands Crisis', p. 169.
12. This article states that any Member of the UN which is not a member of the Council may participate, without vote, in the discussion of any question brought before the Council whenever the latter considers that the interests of that Member are specially affected. See UN Charter, Chapter V, The Security Council, Article 31.
13. Parsons, 'Falklands Crisis', pp. 169–70. For Roca's letter, see UN document S/14940 dated 1 April 1982.
14. Parsons, 'Falklands Crisis', p. 170.
15. Ibid. The Council met in response to a letter dated 1 April 1982 from the Permanent Representative of the UK to the President of the Council. See UN document S/14942 dated 1 April 1982 for the letter.
16. For details of the public meeting, see the *United Nations Security Council Official Records (UNSCOR), Thirty Seventh Year, 2345th Meeting, 1 April 1982*, pp. 1–9, paragraphs 1–85.
17. For Parsons's speech, ibid., pp. 1–3, paragraphs 3–24, quotation at p. 3, paragraph 24.
18. For Roca's speech, ibid., pp. 3–8, paragraphs 26–73.
19. For Kamanda's statement, ibid, p. 8, paragraph 74. His statement is reproduced as appendix 1 of UN document S/14944 and as Appendix 1 of this chapter.
20. See *UNSCOR Thirty Seventh Year, 2345th Meeting, 1 April 1982*, pp. 8–9, paragraphs 82–5 for Parsons's right of reply; see Parsons, 'Falklands Crisis', p. 170 and Parsons in Charlton, *Little Platoon*, pp. 198–9 for Roca's silence and the conclusions drawn from this.
21. This assessment of the British team's preparations is based on Parsons, 'Falklands Crisis', p. 170; Parsons in Bilton and Kosminsky, *Speaking Out*, p. 32; and Parsons in Charlton, *Little Platoon*, p. 199.The quotation is from Parsons, 'Falklands Crisis', p. 170. See also The Sunday Times Insight Team, *Falklands War*, p. 110 and Hastings and Jenkins, *Battle*, pp. 99–100 for these preparations. For the UN Charter provisions mentioned see UN Charter Chapter 1, Purposes and Principles, Articles 2(3) and 2(4) and Chapter VII, Action with Respect to Threats to the Peace, Breaches of the Peace, and Acts of Aggression, Article 51. See also Chapter VI, Pacific Settlement of Disputes, Articles 33 and 37.
22. Parsons, 'Falklands Crisis', p. 170; for the British letter, see UN document. S/14946 dated 2 April 1982
23. For the first of these sessions on 2 April 1982, see *UNSCOR, Thirty Seventh Year, 2346th Meeting, 2 April 1982*, pp. 1–2, paragraphs 1–19.
24. For Parsons's speech, ibid., pp. 1–2, paragraphs 4–8, first quotation at p.1, paragraph 5, second at p. 1, paragraph 7. For the draft resolution, see UN document S/14947 dated 2 April 1982. This is reproduced as Appendix 2

of this chapter. Parsons took what he described as 'the almost unprecedented step of bypassing the customary stages of circulating a "working paper" leading to a preliminary draft resolution, a "blue draft," in order to put the Council on notice that (a) we would not accept amendment to our draft, and (b) we would, according to the conventions, insist on a vote within 24 hours of tabling'. Parsons, 'Falklands Crisis', p. 170.

25. For Roca's statement, see *UNSCOR, Thirty Seventh Year, 2346th Meeting, 2 April 1982*, p. 2, paragraphs 10–17, quotation at p.2, paragraph 12.
26. Ibid., p. 2. paragraph 18.
27. For the second meeting that day, see *UNSCOR, Thirty Seventh Year, 2349th Meeting, 2 April 1982*, pp. 1–4, paragraphs 1–40.
28. Ibid pp. 2–3 paragraphs 20–4 for Australia's statement; p. 3 paragraphs 26–30, for Canada's; and pp. 3–4, paragraphs 32–6, for New Zealand's.
29. Ibid., p. 1, paragraphs 5–9, paragraphs 7, 8 and 9 respectively for quotations.
30. Ibid., pp. 1–2, paragraphs 10–18.
31. Ibid., p. 4, paragraphs 38–40.
32. Parsons, 'Falklands Crisis', p. 170.
33. For this session, see *UNSCOR, Thirty Seventh Year, 2350th Meeting, 3 April 1982*, pp. 1–24, paragraphs 1–289.
34. Ibid., pp. 1–5, paragraphs 5–45.
35. Ibid., pp. 5–6, paragraphs 56–65.
36. Ibid., p. 6, paragraphs 66–70.
37. Ibid., pp. 6–7, paragraphs 71–4.
38. Ibid., p. 5, paragraphs 47–55.
39. Ibid., p. 7, paragraphs 77–83.
40. Ibid., pp. 7–8, paragraphs 85–92.
41. Ibid., p. 14, paragraphs 148–54.
42. Ibid., pp. 8–13, paragraphs 93–134. See UN document S/14950 for the Panamanian draft resolution.
43. Parsons, 'Falklands Crisis', p. 171.
44. *UNSCOR, Thirty Seventh Year, 2350th Meeting, 3 April 1982*, pp. 13, paragraph 145. The motion was put to the vote in accordance with rule 33 of the provisional rules of procedure.
45. Ibid., pp. 14–16, paragraphs 156–80. For the revised UK draft, see UN document S/14947/Rev 1, dated 3 April 1982.
46. Ibid., p. 16, paragraph 184.
47. Ibid., p. 17, paragraphs 185–6. Parsons's proposal to retype the draft may have been an attempt to play for time. Jordan, having declared in favour of the UK, was then instructed from Amman not to vote with any colonialist cause. Parsons's delegation telephoned London and Mrs Thatcher then spoke personally to King Hussein of Jordan and asked him to support the UK. He did so. Hastings and Jenkins, *Battle*, p. 100.
48. *UNSCOR, Thirty Seventh Year, 2350th Meeting, 3 April 1982*, p. 17, paragraphs 187–8.
49. Ibid., p. 17, paragraphs 189–91. Under Article 27(3) in decisions under Chapter V1 (Pacific Settlement of Disputes) a party to a dispute – in this case the UK – shall abstain from voting.
50. Ibid., pp. 17–18, paragraphs 193–7. For quotation see Parsons, 'Falklands Crisis', p. 171.

51. UNSCOR, *Thirty Seventh Year, 2350th Meeting, 3 April 1982*, p. 18, paragraphs 200–1; Parsons, 'Falklands Crisis', p. 171.
52. Ibid., pp. 18–19, paragraphs 203–7.
53. Ibid., p. 19, paragraphs 210–16.
54. Ibid., pp. 19–20, paragraphs 217–24.
55. Ibid., p. 20, paragraphs 225–31.
56. Ibid., pp. 20–1, paragraphs 232–44.
57. Ibid., pp. 21–2, paragraphs 245–53.
58. Ibid., p. 20, paragraphs 254–5.
59. Ibid., p. 20, paragraph 255.
60. Ibid., p. 22, paragraphs 257–62.
61. Ibid., pp. 22–3, paragraphs 263–7.
62. Ibid., p. 23, paragraphs 268–72.
63. Ibid., p. 23, paragraphs 273–8.
64. Ibid., p. 24, paragraphs 280–4.
65. Ibid., p. 24, paragraphs 285–6.
66. For the text of Resolution 502 see UN document S/14947/Rev. 1, *Yearbook of the United Nations 1982* (New York: United Nations, Department of Public Information, 1986), p. 1347. It is reproduced as Appendix 3 of this chapter.
67. Parsons, in Charlton, *Little Platoon*, p. 201 and in Bilton and Kosminsky, *Speaking Out*, p. 32; Spence, in Berridge and Jennings, *Diplomacy*, p. 63; Hastings and Jenkins, *Battle*, p. 49 and 99.
68. Parsons, 'Falklands Crisis', pp. 171–2.
69. See Hastings and Jenkins, *Battle*, pp. 98–101; The Sunday Times Insight Team, *Falklands War*, pp. 108–13; Freedman and Gamba-Stonehouse, *Signals of War*, pp. 134–41; and Parsons, in Bilton and Kosminsky, *Speaking Out*, p. 32.
70. For a discussion of Kirkpatrick's stance, see Jeane J. Kirkpatrick, 'My Falklands War and Theirs', *The National Interest*, (winter 1989/90), pp. 11–20. For Parsons's view, see Parsons, in Charlton, *Little Platoon*, pp. 199–201. See also, for the view of the British Ambassador to the US at the time, Nicholas Henderson, *Channels and Tunnels: Reflections on Britain and Abroad* (London: Weidenfeld and Nicolson, 1987), pp. 87–8.
71. See Hastings and Jenkins, *Battle*, pp. 98–101; The Sunday Times Insight Team, *Falklands War*, pp. 108–13; Freedman and Gamba-Stonehouse, *Signals of War*, pp. 134–41; Parsons, in Bilton and Kosminsky, *Speaking Out*, pp. 32–3; Parsons, in Charlton, *Little Platoon*, pp. 201–2; and Spence, in Berridge and Jennings, *Diplomacy*, p. 63.
72. Hastings and Jenkins, *Battle*, p. 99.
73. Ibid., p.100.
74. Parsons, 'Falklands Crisis', p. 171.
75. For a discussion of the case presented by the British, see Thomas M. Franck, 'The Strategic Role of Legal Principles', in Coll and Arend, *Lessons*, Chapter 3, pp. 22–33.
76. Parsons, in Bilton and Kosminsky, *Speaking Out*, p. 33. Parsons also comments on Costa Mendez's 'own goal' in Charlton, *Little Platoon*, pp. 201–2.
77. See Gamba, *Flaklands/Malvinas War*, pp. 148–9.
78. Margaret Thatcher, *The Downing Street Years* (London: HarperCollins, 1993), p. 203.
79. Claude, in Coll and Arend, *Lessons*, p. 123.

80. For a discussion of this point see Anthony C. Arend, 'The Falklands War and the Failure of the International Legal Order', in Coll and Arend, *Lessons*, Chapter 5, pp. 52–63.
81. For Parsons's assessment of these further meetings, see his 'Falklands Crisis', pp. 172–7. See also Spence in Berridge and Jennings, *Diplomacy*, pp. 66–7.

APPENDICES

1. Statement by the President of the Security Council, 1 April 1982

The Security Council has heard statements from the representatives of the UK and Argentina about the tension which has recently arisen between the two Governments.

The Security Council has taken note of the statement issued by the Secretary-General, which reads as follows:

> The Secretary-General, who has already seen the representatives of the United Kingdom and Argentina earlier today, renews his appeal for maximum restraint on both sides. He will, of course, return to Headquarters at any time, if the situation demands it.

The Security Council, mindful of its primary responsibility under the Charter of the United Nations for the maintenance of international peace and security, expresses its concern about the tension in the region of the Falkland Islands (Islas Malvinas). The Council accordingly calls on the Governments of Argentina and the UK to exercise the utmost restraint at this time and, in particular, to refrain from the use or threat of force in the region and to continue the search for a diplomatic solution. The Security Council will remain seized of the question.

2. Security Council Resolution 502 (1982) 2 April 1982; Meeting 2,346

Draft by United Kingdom (S/14947):

The Security Council,

Recalling the statement made by the President of the Security Council at the 2,345th meeting of the Council on 1 April 1982 calling on the Governments of Argentina and of the UK to refrain from the use or threat of force in the region of the Falkland Islands,

Deeply disturbed at reports of an invasion on 2 April 1982 by armed forces of Argentina,

Determining that there exists a breach of the peace in the region of the Falkland Islands,

1. *Demands* an immediate cessation of hostilities;
2. *Demands* an immediate withdrawal of all Argentine forces from the Falkland Islands;
3. *Calls* on the Governments of Argentina and of the UK to seek a diplomatic solution to their differences and to respect fully the purposes and principles of the Charter of the United Nations.

3. Security Council Resolution 502 (1982) 3 April 1982; Meeting 2,350

Draft by United Kingdom (S/14947/Rev.1)

The Security Council,

Recalling the statement made by the President of the Security Council at the 2,345th meeting of the Council on 1 April 1982 calling on the Governments of Argentina and the UK to refrain from the use or threat of force in the region of the Falkland Islands (Islas Malvinas),

Deeply disturbed at reports of an invasion on 2 April 1982 by armed forces of Argentina,

Determining that there exists a breach of the peace in the region of the Falkland Islands (Islas Malvinas),

1. *Demands* an immediate cessation of hostilities;
2. *Demands* an immediate withdrawal of all Argentine forces from the Falkland Islands (Islas Malvinas);
3. *Calls* on the Governments of Argentina and the UK to seek a diplomatic solution to their differences and to respect fully the purposes and principles of the Charter of the United Nations.

Vote in Council as follows:

In favour: France, Guyana, Ireland, Japan, Jordan, Togo, Uganda, United Kingdom, United States, Zaïre.
Against: Panama
Abstaining: China, Poland, Spain, USSR.

13

'The Empire Strikes Back'?
The Commonwealth Response to
the Falklands Conflict

EDMUND YORKE

> As I speak to you this morning the news was coming in of the success of British forces in the Falklands. I know you will share a sense of great rejoicing and of deep relief – sentiments that will be echoed around the Commonwealth...what is on any assessment a day of great victory, not merely for Britain...but for the cause for which she stood steadfast – a cause let us remember above all else which was not Britain's alone.
>
> (Sir Shridath Ramphal, Secretary-General of the Commonwealth, address to the Commonwealth Press Union, Marlborough House, London, 15 June 1982)

This speech delivered, as Port Stanley fell, by no less a figure than Sir Shridath ('Sonny') Ramphal, represented a remarkable gesture of Commonwealth solidarity with Britain. And yet, this exuberant, steadfast response belied the earlier deep anxieties felt both by Britain, and indeed the Commonwealth as a whole, as to the potential extent and nature of Commonwealth support for the Falklands Conflict, a conflict which, from the start, had exhibited distinct colonial overtones. This contribution will seek to both explore and analyse the responses of the 42-member Commonwealth to the Falklands Crisis and the implications for the future of the Commonwealth as an integrated arm of British foreign policy. It will also incorporate what the distinguished Commonwealth commentator, Nicholas Mansergh,[1] has termed constitutional, moral and strategic factors which determined such responses and which,

170

in turn, reflected their marked disparities in geography, demography, culture and historical experience. Some reference will also be made to the important role of selected ex-Imperial and Commonwealth members who still sustained close links with Britain, notably South Africa, Eire and Pakistan. Finally, the strength of the Commonwealth response, both individually and collectively, will be gauged by close and continuous comparison to pre-Falklands crises.

COMMONWEALTH RESPONSES TO PRE-FALKLANDS CRISES

The quarter century preceding the Falklands Conflict had not been an auspicious period for Commonwealth unity. The British Commonwealth was rocked by a succession of crises ranging from the Suez crisis of 1956 (which arguably nearly destroyed the Commonwealth), to the heartrending disputes over policies towards the avowedly apartheid regimes of South Africa and Rhodesia. Commonwealth unity was further strained by the shocks caused to Commonwealth trade relations by Britain's belated 1973 entry into the preferential trading bloc, the European Economic Community (EEC).

Nevertheless, hopes for an emerging powerful Commonwealth bloc forming a potential political, economic and even military giant which would dominate world affairs had persisted for the five decades prior to Suez. On the outbreak of both the Anglo-Boer War in 1899 and the First World War in 1914 the Empire had stood (albeit with little constitutional choice in some cases) shoulder to shoulder for 'King and Country'. In both, thousands of Australian, New Zealand, Canadian, Indian and African soldiers were sacrificed to the Imperial cause in costly campaigns ranging from Gallipoli to Vimy Ridge. During the late First World War period, however, as constitutional changes rapidly occurred, epitomised in the 1917 Imperial War Conference and the 1926 Imperial Conference chaired by Lord Balfour, and catalysed by the rising nationalist challenges to British rule in for instance India, such unequivocal Commonwealth solidarity had become less assured. The first substantial, if selective, concessions to foreign policy autonomy within the Empire, reflecting recognition of the war contributions of both India and the 'white' Dominions, appeared in the 1917 Imperial War Conference. This asserted that, 'the constitutional relationships of the component parts of Empire...should be based upon a full recognition of the Dominions as autonomous nations of an Imperial Commonwealth'. Accordingly, the Dominions (Australia, New Zealand, Canada and South Africa) and India signed the 1919 Versailles Peace Treaty *individually* and had their own representatives in the League of Nations. Under the 'Balfour formula' the 1926 Inter-Imperial Relations Committee formalised the status and mutual relationship of these members, declaring that:

> They are autonomous communities within the British Empire, equal in status, in no way subordinate one to another in any aspect of their domestic or external affairs, though united by a common allegiance to the Crown as Members of the British Commonwealth of Nations.[2]

This principle was legally formulated in the Statute of Westminster of 1931 which gave effect to this fully independent status of the Dominions in relation to Great Britain and by implication in relation to each other.

These new constitutional arrangements played an important role in determining the nature of the Empire and Commonwealth response to subsequent crises and, in particular, to the outbreak of the Second World War in 1939. There was no longer to be unanimous, across the board support for Britain, and historical experiences of relations with Britain as well as demographic factors largely determined the different responses. The issue of war with Nazi Germany provoked serious debates in both the Irish Free State and South Africa, each nation encompassing political groups which expressed some historical animosity towards Britain. In South Africa it was only a crisis debate in the South African Parliament on 4 September 1939 in which leading Afrikaner politicians made speeches opposing war on Britain's side which, fortuitously, led to a dissolution of Parliament and the coming to power of the pro-British Prime Minster Jan Smuts. He, later, narrowly carried a vote in favour of war alongside Britain. The fiercely republican-dominated government of the Irish Free State, led by Eamon De Valera, veteran of the 1916 Easter Rising against the British, firmly opted for neutrality. De Valera, in a February 1939 speech to the Irish Parliament or Dail, had already defiantly declared, 'there is no Commonwealth constitution...no Commonwealth foreign policy...we have declared our right to be neutral.' In Canada, Prime Minister William Mackenzie King, whilst exhibiting strong support for Britain, showed awareness of a vociferous isolationist minority and of Canada's already close relationship with the United States, by insisting that only the Canadian Parliament and no other authority could decide the question of peace and war. Nevertheless, whilst stressing Canada's role primarily as a mediator, he accepted that, 'if England is at war, we are at war and liable to attack'. Both Australia and, in particular, New Zealand, nations of predominantly British stock and clearly threatened by Japanese aggression in the Pacific, almost duplicated their 1914 stand. Neither in Wellington nor Canberra was there any disposition to conform to Mackenzie King's formula that

Parliament should decide. Thus, on 3 September 1939, the Australian Prime Minister, Robert Menzies, declared without consulting the Australian Parliament, 'Britain is at war, therefore Australia is also at war.' An even more extreme, uncompromising declaration of loyalty came from New Zealand, already a long-term critic of Britain's appeasement policies. Prime Minster Michael Savage dramatically declared 'where she goes, we go: where she stands, we stand'.[3]

The Second World War, however, revealed ominous signs that the Commonwealth could never be a completely reliable military surrogate for British foreign policy. Differing security concerns, often reflecting the markedly diverse geopolitical positions of the Commonwealth created friction, even explosive rows with the 'mother country'. In 1942, for instance, the Australian Prime Minster, John Curtin, clashed with Churchill over the redeployment of Australian troops from the Middle East theatre to Australia in order to defend the homeland from Japanese attacks. Similarly, Canadian public opinion was dismayed by the appalling Canadian losses incurred during the failed 1942 Dieppe raid, widely blamed on British incompetence. The defence of India against Japanese invasion was secured in 1942 only by means of a hastily brokered deal with Mahatma Gandhi, leader of the Indian National Congress Party, which allowed for Indian independence after the war in return for assistance with civil defence and recruitment.

The immediate post-war period confirmed the growing divergence in security perspectives between Britain and her former dependencies. In 1952, for instance, the ANZUS Pact, negotiated between Australia, New Zealand and the USA, effectively confirmed the realities of power under the USA-dominated 'new world order' with a decisively weakened, near bankrupt Britain now too overstretched to protect her closest Commonwealth allies in the Pacific region.

Nevertheless, the hopes for the Commonwealth as a British-led political giant on the world's stage persisted well into the post-war period, and was embodied in the 1948 Churchillian concept of three concentric circles of post-war political relations, with the Commonwealth positioned alongside the USA and Europe.

It was the 1956 Suez debacle which dealt a near mortal blow to what was fast becoming a somewhat unrealistic, flawed, even naive vision of sustained Commonwealth unity. From the outset President Nasser's nationalisation of the Suez Canal enjoyed the support of the three newest members of the Commonwealth, India (1947), Pakistan (1947) and Ceylon (1948). To these three nations Nasser's actions appeared 'unambiguously as an act of retributive justice, as militant nationalism commendably asserted itself against the remnants of imperialism in Asia'.[4] These postures were powerfully reinforced by the Soviet Union and her Eastern Bloc allies. As during the European crisis of 1939, and by stark contrast to the Asian 'new Commonwealth' members, Britain received the whole-hearted support of Australia and New Zealand, both countries significantly controlled by Governments dominated by Second World War ex-Servicemen. The Australian Prime Minister Robert Menzies even went so far as to appear on British radio to back Prime Minister Eden's position, while the New Zealand Prime Minister Sidney Holland announced that Britain could count on New Zealand standing by her through thick or thin, 'the Suez Canal is vital to Britain and vital to New Zealand...when she's in difficulty we are in difficulty'. The Canadian Government, however, reflecting Canada's close bonds with the USA, maintained a more restrained position, urging caution and settlement by conference or through the UN. South Africa, already seriously embarrassed by international criticism of apartheid policies, maintained a discreet silence and in the words of Foreign Minister Johannes Strijdom kept her 'head out of the beehive'.[5]

The failure of negotiations over Suez, notably the attempts at mediation through the Suez Canal Users Association London Conference, and the resultant Anglo-French resort to force, tested even the most loyal members of the Commonwealth. The invasion of Egypt and the distinct lack of prior consultation with both the USA and the Commonwealth were greeted by shock and incredulity by most Commonwealth countries. Their reaction was described by one leading observer as 'the strongest and most variable aroused by an international issue since the "new Commonwealth" had come into being in 1947'.[6] Some Commonwealth governments only first heard the news of the invasion from the radio, and Canada and South Africa, accustomed to the formal practice of consultation through the Dominion Office, were especially incensed. The British 'lion' had roared but it was clear that, for the first time, some of her 'cubs' were no longer prepared to play. The outrage was most keenly felt by the new Asian members, who reacted with a mixture of disbelief and indignation. In a speech to the Indian Parliament, the Lok Sabha, on 16 November 1956, Indian Prime Minister Nehru described the invasion as, 'a flagrant case of aggression by two strong powers against a weaker country...I find it difficult to deal with this record of unabashed aggression and deception,' confirming that, 'I am convinced that colonialism, whatever new look it may put on, can revert to its old brutal self'. Similar comments came from Ceylon and Pakistan and there were strong pressures to secede from the Commonwealth. One Indian MP, Shri A. K. Gopalan, asserted,

> India...the biggest country in the Commonwealth was not consulted or informed...we consider it absolutely necessary that

India...should immediately sever its connection with the British Commonwealth. Our membership...gives the British the prestige which enables it to deceive world opinion.[7]

By contrast, the right-wing governments of Australia and New Zealand, with their own oil interests in the region, comprised two of only five nations who supported Britain in her opposition to the UN resolution demanding withdrawal (the others, of course, being Israel and France). New Zealand's loyalty through 'thick and thin' was expressed in Prime Minister Leslie Munroe's assertion, 'our ties [with the UK] are never closer than in times of stress and danger'. Canada, however, whilst already angry over the lack of consultation, ruled firmly against the use of force and opted for a mediating role, strongly upholding international law on this issue. 'Our policy...was to get the UN into the matter at once; to seek through the UN a solution which would be satisfactory to all sides.'[8] This she achieved creditably.

In the event it was not UN but American action (the United States Government being particularly incensed at the lack of consultation and damage to its Middle East position), which, by overwhelming financial pressure, forced an ignominious withdrawal by the British and subsequently the French and Israelis. The vitriolic split within the Commonwealth, however, had engendered a particularly traumatic impact on British policy-makers, and their growing disillusionment with the Commonwealth links had serious implications for the handling of subsequent crises such as the Falklands.

The Commonwealth had only narrowly survived the impact of the Suez crisis. Over the next two decades the nature and extent of the Commonwealth radically changed as independence was granted to nearly all the remaining Imperial territories. The membership of the Commonwealth vastly expanded and increased from a mere seven members in 1956 to 42 by 1982. Similarly, waves of migration in the 1960s and 1970s diluted the 'Britishness' of the 'old dominions', notably Australia, Canada and to a lesser extent New Zealand. Most striking was the change resulting from African membership, as between 1957 and 1964, virtually all the major African colonies were granted independence.

With new African and Caribbean membership came a renewed crisis with racial overtones which at times threatened to reach Suez proportions. The Rhodesian crisis of 1965–80 created bitter divisions between Britain and many African states which were incensed by the failure of successive British governments to topple the illegal Smith regime which had firmly ruled against holding free elections and African majority rule. While apartheid South Africa had been successfully pressurised to leave the Commonwealth in 1962, Rhodesia remained a thorn in Commonwealth relations with African governments deeply suspicious of Britain's alleged 'kith and kin' sympathies. The advent of Margaret Thatcher's Conservative government in 1979 confirmed the suspicions of the Front Line African states as she instantly ruled out any negotiations with the 'terrorist' nationalist ZAPU and ZANU parties led respectively by Joshua Nkomo and Robert Mugabe. The crisis was only finally resolved at the Commonwealth Heads of Government Meeting at Lusaka in 1979, where the combined pressure of both black and white Commonwealth members 'converted' Thatcher to British support for all parties, and paved the way for successful resolution of the crisis at the Lancaster House Agreement of December 1979.[9]

THE ARGENTINIAN INVASION: INITIAL COMMONWEALTH RESPONSES

Suez and Rhodesia had been 'a close run thing' for the credibility, indeed the survival, of the Commonwealth. The arrival of the Falklands Crisis in April 1982 engendered very real fears for British policy-makers as the crisis initially displayed distinct colonial overtones. There was a real prospect of a 'Suez' effect on Commonwealth thinking, particularly if Britain resorted to the use of force. As Sir Nicholas Henderson, British Ambassador to the United States, recalled: 'we were very frightened as it had colonial overtones which had provoked suspicions over Suez'.[10] How would the Commonwealth perceive this dispute over a clear remnant of Empire? Would, for instance, General Galtieri be perceived as another Nasser merely rectifying old colonial injustices? More ominously, there was also the recent precedent of Goa where many Third World and Commonwealth nations had accepted, if not applauded, the Indian use of force to recover this territory from Portugal in 1961.

In the hours and days after the invasion of 2 April, the Argentine Government made strenuous efforts to play the 'colonial card', perceived as a veritable chink in the British armour, and thereby win over both Commonwealth and Third World support in general. Britain was branded by Argentinian spokesmen as the 'aggressor', citing her earlier ultimatum to the South Georgia scrap merchants and stressing how Britain's long illegal occupation of the Falklands represented a gross violation of Argentinian sovereignty. On 3 April, the day after the invasion, the Argentinian Foreign Minister Nicanor Costa Mendez made his first formal statement, launching a tirade against Britain at the UN. After a lengthy historical survey of the dispute, Costa Mendez claimed that

Argentina had done nothing more than recover national sovereignty which had been violated by an illegitimate act of force in 1833. It was a position strongly supported by the Soviet Union and her Eastern Bloc allies, who repeatedly drew colonial parallels with Britain's actions.

During these first few critical days of the crisis the British Government worked furiously to both dispel and thwart these and other Argentinian attempts to draw parallels with Suez. The British launched a massive diplomatic offensive to win over international support not only from their key allies, the USA and the EEC but also from the Commonwealth. As Foreign Minister Richard Luce recalled of the weekend before his dramatic resignation; 'my role at the ministerial level was to generate world-wide support for a vote in support of our position at the UN and in the Security Council'.[11]

The support of the Commonwealth was, indeed, considered vital. Politically, with 42 members, the Commonwealth comprised over 30 per cent of the membership of the UN and played a key role in other important world bodies such as the Non-Aligned Movement and crucial regional organisations, notably the OAS and the Organization of African Unity (OAU). For other reasons the Commonwealth still occupied a pivotal role in British foreign policy. Economically, by 1982 and despite the 1973 EEC entry, the Commonwealth still took nearly 13 per cent of British exports. Encompassing up to a quarter of the world's population, Commonwealth countries represented a rapidly expanding market for British goods. In 1981, Nigeria alone bought over £1 billion of British exports, as one of the three largest British markets outside the industrial world. Commonwealth countries accounted for some 35 per cent of British income from non-oil investment overseas. The Commonwealth therefore remained a key focus of British diplomacy throughout the crisis. During the first Parliamentary debates on the Falklands Crisis held on 3 April and 7 April, ministers such as the recently resigned Richard Luce again publicly stressed that 'all diplomatic means must be used including working closely ... with all our allies and friends'. In her autobiography, Margaret Thatcher more precisely defined Britain's friends. One 'long term goal' was to 'ensure maximum support from our allies, principally the US but also the members of EEC, the Commonwealth and other important Nations'.[12]

Any parallels with Suez were brusquely and decisively dismissed. During the 7 April Commons debate Opposition MP Denis Healey asserted,

> The argument in Suez was about property rights – that in the Falklands is about human rights. At Suez the British Government

violated the UN Charter. In the Falklands crisis the Argentine Government have violated the UN Charter...Suez offers no precedent here.

At the same time, with an obvious eye to the attitudes of the Commonwealth and other allies, he warned against any repeat of the Suez debacle: 'The other danger is that of a large scale military effort with Argentina in circumstances that cost us the support of the UN and world opinion.'[13] The British Foreign Office took pains to make it clear that the Falkland Islanders were of British nationality and that Argentina had been the first to use force. This direct contrast to Suez was made abundantly clear, and Britain's allies agreed. As Alexander Haig, the United States Secretary of State, later asserted at a meeting of the OAS, 'It is impossible to speak of colonialism when a people is not subjugated to another, and, as we all know, there is no such subjugation on the islands.'[14]

The Commonwealth was not slow to respond to the crisis, the vast majority accepting the British case and refuting attempts by the Argentinian Government to play the 'colonial card'. Over a decade earlier the Commonwealth as a whole had signed up to the principles of self-determination and democracy in the 'Commonwealth Declaration' of January 1971. Argentina was clearly no democracy, with an appalling human rights record, and the obviously ethnically British Falkland Islanders had clearly demonstrated their desire to remain with Britain through free and fair elections. In this context the use of force was widely seen as unacceptable. As the Commonwealth Secretary-General Sir Shridath Ramphal later so aptly put it:

> In the case of the Falklands, Argentina has attempted to blur that distinction between claims to sovereignty and the attempt to enforce them by arms – by two arguments. In the first place it raised the spectre of colonialism. This in a bid to secure Latin American solidarity and win wider Third World support, for decolonization is a worthy banner to which many will rally. It was a facile ploy. Argentina did not invade the Falklands to liberate the people of the Islands from British rule, but to impose Argentine rule over them against their will.[15]

The countries of the 'Old Commonwealth' emphatically shared this view over Argentina's use of force, although initially few had any knowledge of the reasons for the crisis, or indeed, the background of the dispute over what President Reagan endearingly termed that far away 'ice-cold bunch of land'. By 6 April, New Zealand, traditionally the most loyal of the old dominions, had broken off diplomatic relations with Argentina and ordered its Ambassador to leave within seven days. The Argentinian airline's monthly flight schedule to New Zealand was also cancelled. Virtually duplicating the New Zealand response in the 1939 European crisis and 1956 Suez crises, New Zealand Premier Robert Muldoon announced that it had been 'made clear to Mrs Thatcher' that 'we stand ready to help'. The Australian response was equally fulsome but significantly less inclined to offer practical aid. The Australian Federal Government, like New Zealand, decided to recall its Ambassador for 'urgent talks' and Anthony Street, the Australian Foreign Minister, expressed 'deep concern and condemnation of the Falklands invasion'. While the Federal Government 'considered' the imposition of trade sanctions against Argentina, Prime Minister Malcolm Fraser ruled out sending Australian troops to the area. 'He did not see Australia going to war in the Falkland Islands' but 'he had written to Mrs Thatcher' and 'indicated that Australia strongly supported Britain'. Canada, as in the 1956 Suez crisis, while strongly protesting over the Argentinian invasion and occupation, took a more restrained attitude ruling out any break in diplomatic relations. Echoing the initial stance of Canada's close neighbour the United States, the Canadian Government strongly emphasised the importance of negotiations. Thus Mark MacGuigan, the External Affairs Minister, whilst describing the invasion as 'deeply shocking', asserted that Canada would not break diplomatic relations with Argentina, 'while there was a chance of talks which could result in withdrawal'. Nevertheless, the Canadian Government imposed some trade restrictions, banning military shipments to Argentina, and cancelled a planned visit there by officers of the Canada's National Defence College. However, there was deep internal criticism of Canada's overly neutral or passive stance and of its alleged self-interest. The refusal, for instance, to close down work by Canadian scientists on an Argentinian nuclear reactor elicited strong protests from leading newspapers. The Canadian self-styled national newspaper, the *Toronto Globe & Mail*, expressed doubts about 'the wisdom of continuing nuclear technical sales to Argentina' which 'has amply demonstrated its contempt for international opinion and for its obligations under the UN Charter'. The Opposition New Democratic Party went further, calling for a breaking of diplomatic ties with Argentina.[16]

The British Government was particularly grateful for the highly supportive responses from the Caribbean Commonwealth nations. At a working lunch with no less than President Reagan on 9 April 1982, the Prime Ministers of Barbados, Dominica, St Vincent, the Grenadine

Islands, St Kitts and Nevis, Antigua and Barbuda urged Reagan to put immediate pressure on Argentina to withdraw its forces from the Falklands. A spokesman reported that, 'they left no doubt in Mr Reagan's mind about where they stood and that they were talking not about mediation but about pressure'.[17]

The African members of the 'New Commonwealth', despite the general lack of press coverage of the Falkland Islands crisis, also afforded massive support in these opening weeks of the crisis. The Kenyan Government led the way expressing 'deep concern at the invasion' and calling upon Argentina, 'to withdraw its forces and seek a peaceful settlement of the dispute'. As Chairman of the OAU, Kenya was widely interpreted as 'giving a lead to other African states'. In West Africa, Sierra Leone, Ghana and Nigeria strongly empathised with Britain's position; Sierra Leone, for instance, called on Argentina to withdraw its troops and hoped that, in the meantime, 'nothing will be done to aggravate the situation'. In a grimly worded statement the Sierra Leone Government echoed the words of the Secretary-General of the Commonwealth, asserting that the invasion had 'posed an immediate threat to international peace and security' and 'denied the people of the islands the right of self-determination and infringed the territorial integrity of the islands'. Gambia, Sierra Leone, and even non-Commonwealth Senegal, accordingly provided port and airfield facilities for British forces. *The Times* of London presented a succinct explanation for the warm and positive response of the African Commonwealth nations:

> It is not altogether surprising...that black African countries such as Sierra Leone, Kenya and Zambia should have decided to back Britain in the dispute rather than show their accustomed solidarity with their fellow non-aligned states and its claim that the conflict is purely a colonial issue. First, there is in Africa a widespread recognition that 'imperialist Britain' in dismantling its empire has always, if sometimes belatedly for some African states, taken the wishes of the inhabitants of its colonial territories into account when deciding on their future. Second, the Argentine appeal to fellow African states is weakened not so much because of its repressive internal record but because of its close links with the South African Government.[18]

Indeed, Pretoria's neutral stance in the Falklands dispute, strikingly reminiscent of its role in the Suez crisis, reflected not merely its resentment over its position as a pariah state within the international community, its rejection from the Commonwealth in 1961 as an apartheid state, and its historically divided loyalty to Britain, but also its alleged more sinister links with Argentina. Foreign Minister R.F. Botha's outwardly non-committal statement, *not* condemning Argentina but expressing hopes for United States mediation and other efforts for a peaceful solution, concealed the existence of a secret decade-old military pact with Argentina, a shadowy informal body called the South Atlantic Treaty Organization (SATO). This was reportedly set up in 1967 and its membership was said to include South Africa, Argentina, Uruguay and Paraguay. SATO's main function was to 'provide mutual protection against arms boycotts through an exchange of information and informal arrangements in certain contingencies'. Not surprisingly, South Africa was reputed to be one of the few countries to receive early warning of Argentina's plans to invade the Falklands, during a visit in 1981 by General Mario Benjamin Menendez, the Argentinian CoS. An irritated Whitehall soon confirmed the existence of the Treaty, widely interpreted as a consequence of the British abandonment of her naval base at Simonstown, now paying host to Argentinian warships![19]

The response of the Commonwealth Asian bloc proved disappointing, and to some extent mirrored that of ex-Commonwealth South Africa. The Indian Foreign Minister P.V. Narasimha Rao merely 'regretted' the resort to force by Argentina and offered no practical help for the British position.[20] Similarly, President Zia's Pakistan, although not a member of the Commonwealth since 1972 when she angrily resigned over the India–Pakistan War of the previous year, maintained a discreet silence. Geopolitically far remote from the crisis, Malaysia and Singapore, the key nations of the South-East Asian Commonwealth, maintained a subdued but not unsupportive attitude towards the British position.

Even after the virtually bloodless recapture of South Georgia by British forces, staunch support from the vast majority of Commonwealth countries was sustained. The Australian Premier Malcolm Fraser, for instance, described the British attack on South Georgia as 'inevitable...we must hope that even at this last minute, Argentina will see sense and end her aggression'. On 28 April, three days after the Argentinian surrender on South Georgia, President Kaunda of Zambia continued unequivocally to support Britain because 'Argentina was in the wrong'. Again New Zealand demonstrated exceptional loyalty, her government 'applauding' Britain's repossession of South Georgia. Premier Robert Muldoon further described Argentina's invasion as 'naked aggression' to which the only response was to say 'Get out or we'll throw you out'.[21]

This initial, predominantly positive response from the Commonwealth was expressed in deeds as well as in words, and its role was not merely limited to declarations of support for Britain. At the UN, the crucial agency through which Britain need to secure international legitimacy for her actions, the Commonwealth had played an important, some observers argue crucial, role. To decisively out-manoeuvre the Argentinian Government it was essential for Britain to succeed in passing a resolution condemning the Argentinian invasion and calling for withdrawal. However, as Thatcher was deeply aware:

> With the Cold War still underway and given the anti-colonialist attitudes of many nations at the UN, there was a real danger that the Security Council might attempt to force unsatisfactory terms upon us. If necessary we could veto such a resolution but to do so would diminish international support for our position.[22]

The veteran British Ambassador at the UN, Sir Anthony Parsons, reconfirmed the potential fragility of Britain's position. 'The non-aligned had committed themselves at successive summits to the Argentine position on sovereignty yet all non-aligned states in the UN have a healthy antipathy to the use of force to solve political problems.' With no fewer than three fellow Commonwealth countries currently sitting on the 15-member Security Council, their support was vital to securing the key Resolution 502 calling for Argentinian withdrawal. In the event, all three Commonwealth countries, Guyana, Togo and Uganda, loyally supported the Resolution, with ten to one in favour and four abstentions. Nine votes were needed to secure a passing of the Resolution and, in short, alongside Britain, nearly half of the Security Council votes in favour of the Resolution had come from the British Commonwealth bloc. Such strong Commonwealth support at the UN had wider implications for the perceptions of the superpowers – not only for the already secretly pro-British USA, but for China and in particular the Soviet Union, both acutely sensitive to their relations with Third World countries. Significantly, both the Soviet Union and China abstained and, writing two years later, the British Foreign Secretary Sir Geoffrey Howe remained 'convinced that Commonwealth support for Britain among non-aligned countries was a significant fact in deterring the Soviet Union from vetoing Security Council Resolution 502'. With the Resolution safely passed, the way was open for Britain to use force to reoccupy the Falklands under Article 51 of the UN Charter. In the words of Sir Anthony Parsons:

> We had secured a firm base of international support amongst a wide spectrum of member states, without which, in my view, it would

have been difficult to persuade our partners, friends and allies to join us in the economic and political measures which, coupled with military action under Article 51 of the Charter (the inherent right of individual or collective self defence), formed the three planks of the British Government's policy, accepted by all parties in Parliament, in reacting to the Argentine aggression.[23]

By the end of April, Margaret Thatcher herself was to praise the almost unanimous, unequivocal support of the Commonwealth:

> The response of the Commonwealth, with the partial exception of India, had been very supportive. In particular, Malcolm Fraser in Australia banned all imports from Argentina, except those under existing contracts. Bob Muldoon and New Zealand were, if anything, even stronger in their support.[24]

A 'WOBBLY' COMMONWEALTH?

By early May, as the intensity of the conflict rapidly escalated and the United States government recognised the failure of the Haig Mission, effectively declaring against Argentina, Britain's international position became less secure. The bloody days of May were indeed a watershed. The news of the sinking of the Argentinian cruiser *General Belgrano* with 323 dead, and the subsequent attack on HMS *Sheffield* with 20 dead 'marked the end of the diplomatic war over the Falklands and the start of the shooting war'.[25] The British Government became extremely fearful about the effects of Argentinian propaganda on Third World and Commonwealth countries in particular, many of which were deeply shocked by the loss of life incurred by the sinking of the *Belgrano*. Argentinian allegations backed by Cuban, Soviet and East European propaganda which claimed, for instance, that the British had machine-gunned survivors from the *Belgrano* in the water, had already had a very adverse effect on South American opinion, particularly in Brazil. *The Economist* confirmed the damage to the British diplomatic position. On 8 May the journal reported:

> A large part of the world seemed to be turning against Britain this week as the casualty lists in the Falklands conflict mounted. Much has changed since the UN Security Council voted 10–1 on 3 April for the British resolution that demanded the immediate withdrawal of the invading Argentine forces.[26]

Canada and India showed particular concern over this more violent swing in British policy towards the Falklands. On 4 May, after news of the *Belgrano* and *Sheffield* attacks, Mark MacGuigan the Canadian External Affairs Minister asserted that, while the government had so far given 'strong moral support to Britain besides banning military exports to Argentina and allowing Britain the use of communications facilities on Canada's west coast', he was, nevertheless, 'concerned about the increasing loss of life...and had ordered Canadian diplomats at the UN to increase their efforts in support of a negotiated solution'. In Parliament, a prominent Canadian MP Robert Wenman, while morally supporting Britain's cause, observed critically that 'several hundred people had now died protecting the rights of 1,800 Falklanders'. He appealed to his Government, 'Don't you have an obligation to draw them back from the fight?' Again, however, there was some internal resistance to this posture. Canadian Opposition MPs again accused the Government of hypocritically supporting Argentina by continuing supplies of nuclear fuel, although the Government defended its contract on the basis that if it was broken Argentina might use the facilities 'in ways in which we would not approve'.[27] On 21 May, Canada further stepped back from unequivocal support for the British position by joining calls for a ceasefire.

There were other small but ominous signs of a wavering of support amongst certain Commonwealth members. India, while condemning the use of force by Argentina in April, suddenly adopted a far more ambivalent position in mid-May. The Indian Foreign Minister P. V. Narasimha Rao, while still condemning Argentina's initial use of force, amazingly expressed open support for Argentina's *claim* to the Falkland Islands.[28] The reasons for this somewhat unsupportive attitude by the Indian Government was perhaps understandable. India had been the sternest critic of Britain during the Suez crisis and general relations with Britain since independence had been volatile. In the 1960s and 1970s, India enjoyed equally close political and defence links with the Soviet Union, a keen supporter of the Argentinian position over the Falklands. Above all, the Indian Government's lukewarm, if not unhelpful, response had been almost certainly conditioned by India's earlier seizure, by force, of Goa. Nevertheless, by contrast, Indian public opinion, as expressed through the main Indian newspapers, remained generally sympathetic to the British cause.

Worse was to come from two former Commonwealth countries, both of which shared a close association with Britain from the days of the Empire. On 25 May, as British forces commenced landings at San Carlos Bay, fresh allegations against South Africa, accusing her of supplying arms to Argentina, provoked a significant political row in both Britain and South Africa. The *Johannesburg Star* claimed that such supplies included surface-to-surface Gabriel missiles for Argentinian frigates and spares for her Mirage aircraft. The South African government significantly refused to comment on these allegations, declaring that it was a South African principle not to disclose details of delivery of arms, and only conceding that Exocet missiles or parts would not be delivered. The issue was raised on 25 May during a House of Commons debate by an angry John Silkin, Shadow Defence Secretary, and the London *Financial Times* cryptically noted that 'firm evidence of supplies to Argentina would cause great bitterness within South African society in view of the close links between Britain and part of the local white population'. The *New African* speculated further on the covert relations existing between the two pariah states of Argentina and South Africa, reflecting, it asserted, not only South African anger over her international isolation, but deeper historical tensions:

> Observers believe that if it came to the crunch Pretoria would choose Argentina because there is no love lost between the Afrikaner and the British. The Afrikaner still resents British subjugation of the Boers – the first white settlers in South Africa – for more than a century.[29]

But it was the role of Eire, a country enjoying intimate if ambivalent links with Britain, which provoked the most anger and disappointment in London. As at Suez, the Irish Government sustained a generally negative attitude to the British position on the Falklands. In mid-May Premier Charles Haughey's government refused to renew the EC ban on exports to Argentina. Eire had firmly supported the earlier Peruvian peace proposals, and on Friday 21 May the Irish Government went further, convening an emergency meeting of the UNSC to press for a ceasefire. This put Britain on the diplomatic defensive at a critical time for her military forces, which were still desperately trying to establish a beachhead on the Falklands. After fierce attacks from the British press, Haughey fell back on the traditional argument of Irish neutrality. He dismissed such criticism and allegations of a 'stab in the back' as the 'price we have to pay for trying to discharge our honourable role'. But there were clearly deeper political reasons. The bitterness felt in Eire over the 1981–2 republican hunger strikes in Northern Ireland and dislike of British devolution plans for this province undoubtedly conditioned the generally negative Irish government response. Prime Minister Thatcher was less forgiving, confirming that 'the Irish caused us some concern'. Enraged Conservative right-wing MPs went further, and even tried to remove the rights of Irish citizens to vote in British elections.[30]

The vast majority of the Commonwealth, however, loyally maintained their support as British forces became immersed in bloody fighting on the Falklands mainland. Again at the UN, during the debates of late May culminating in a call for a ceasefire, 'strong statements in support of Britain were issued by Commonwealth allies notably New Zealand, Canada, Australia, Kenya, Guyana and other Caribbean representatives'.[31] Two Commonwealth leaders, Robert Muldoon and Sir Shridath Ramphal, originating significantly from both the 'Old' and 'New' Commonwealth, played a key role in rallying and sustaining Commonwealth support for Britain's cause on the Falklands during this critical period for British arms. As Britain experienced her first heavy casualties in early May, New Zealand Prime Minister Robert Muldoon took extraordinary action in support of Britain's cause. On 6 May, as the British Government reeled from the news of the *Sheffield* disaster Muldoon secretly sanctioned the deployment of the Royal New Zealand Navy Leander class frigate HMNZS *Canterbury* to South Atlantic waters in support of Britain. Unfortunately for Muldoon this enormously generous 'loan' was not publicly announced until as late as 25 May after a private dinner in London between himself and Prime Minister Thatcher. Robert Muldoon, like President Reagan, was an ardent admirer of Thatcher, and his action in his words was 'a gesture of solidarity...it is a way in which we think we can best express our positive support for Britain if the necessity arises, and at the moment it looks somewhat as though it will'. Although he denied that the ship would be used 'in a combat role in the Falklands area', he returned home to a major constitutional row. The Labour Party Opposition accused him of misleading Parliament, referring to an earlier denial on 6 May of the loan of the ship. In a ferocious attack, Labour Party leader Bill Rowland accused Muldoon of 'grandstanding in London' – 'the Prime Minister', he alleged, 'was more concerned with getting headlines overseas than having an informed public at home'. More tellingly, he argued that by committing the frigate to the RN 'New Zealand was, by implication, entering the war'. Despite his knife-edge majority Prime Minister Muldoon's dominant blustering style ('where Muldoon goes New Zealand goes', the London *Observer* wryly commented) won the day, helped by the lukewarm support for the Opposition from New Zealand public opinion. Nevertheless, there was some indication that sections of the New Zealand public did consider that Prime Minister Muldoon had grossly exceeded his constitutional brief. The loyalty of some New Zealand groups, particularly farmers, had been severely tested by Britain's entry into the EEC and the subsequent quotas placed on New Zealand lamb and dairy exports to Britain. At least one group of New Zealanders angrily disassociated themselves from Muldoon's 'war spirit'. Writing to *The Times*, they claimed that their Prime Minister's jingoistic 'unconditional support' for the 'motherland' did 'not reflect the deep worry and concern felt by a large number of New Zealanders'. Deprecating his 'carte blanche' offer to Mrs Thatcher, they complained:

> While we hope that the Falklands crisis is solved with the minimum loss of life we believe that New Zealand should not become involved in military action in the South Atlantic on the basis of 'where Britain goes we go'. All New Zealand has to offer Britain is lives. In our opinion the apron strings of Mother England are not strong enough to justify our lives in this particular dispute.[32]

Despite these minor rumblings of discontent at ground level, the New Zealand Government position represented an outstanding show of official support, duplicating the blind loyalty of the New Zealand governments in 1939 and again during the 1956 Suez crisis.

Australia, at government level, was less attached to 'the apron strings of Mother England'. She never afforded such a direct level of practical support, beyond offering to relinquish her contract for HMS *Invincible*, due to be sold in August 1982 under the 1981 Nott Defence Review. As has been pointed out, 'there was a certain wariness in the Anglo-Australian relationship' at this time. Prime Minister Malcolm Fraser was a 'strident Australian Nationalist' and had upset the Thatcher Government by his earlier precocious defence of Third World interests at previous Commonwealth summits. The same author has confirmed that:

> Australian attitudes to the Falklands war were ambivalent. On the one hand the Government rigorously supported the British position...on the other hand it limited its sanctions against the Argentine to imports from that country which were almost non-existent while continuing to export to the Argentine at a handy profit.[33]

Both Australia and New Zealand shared one self-interest, however, in maintaining stability in the South Atlantic region. As co-supporters and members of the 1959 Antarctic Treaty they had a deep vested interest in forestalling Argentinian aggression or ambitions in the area.[34]

Prime Minister Muldoon's inspired support for Britain was paralleled by no less than the Secretary-General of the Commonwealth himself, Sir Shridath Ramphal. In a series of speeches delivered in May and early June

1982, he rallied the bulk of the Commonwealth to Britain's side. His justification for supporting Britain in her hour of need rested not merely on sentimental ties but on the principle of self-determination and freedom from aggression. It was a principle or argument that weighed heavily with the smaller Commonwealth countries which proportionally gave much more direct support to Britain than their larger 'brothers'. As *The Economist* succinctly observed, 'in Africa, South East Asia, and the Caribbean there is a lively awareness of the need to discourage sudden pounces on small and vulnerable places by over mighty neighbours'. Hence Guyana, which gave Britain virtually lone support in the OAS and at the UN, was keenly aware that the Argentinian example could 'encourage its own big neighbour, Venezuela, to jump on it in pursuance of a similar historical claim'. As Ramphal stressed in a speech delivered at Madrid on 12 May:

> As the current conflict in the South Atlantic underlines, international legal order is itself under grave threat. That aggression should even have been attempted to advance territorial ambitions...is an indication of how fragile is the rule of law world-wide. Graver still is a fact that the principal victims of its breakdown would be the most vulnerable members of the international community – the smallest, the weakest, the poorest. They know that the quality of their own security is also at stake in the Falklands.[35]

In a speech in Boston on 23 May he continued his theme, warning against a return to 'law of the jungle' and stressing: 'there are many "Falklands Islands" scattered across the globe and with some forty border disputes in Asia, Africa and Latin America, there is no shortage of irredentist neighbours ready to prey upon them.'[36] These were principles which strongly appealed to the many smaller Commonwealth nations ranging from Botswana, Zambia, Zimbabwe and Tanzania, bordering an aggressive apartheid South Africa, to Gibraltar, adjoining a powerful if democratic Spain.

As British forces finally re-entered Port Stanley on 14 June, it was left to Commonwealth Secretary-General Ramphal to summarise the main principles which had ensured continued Commonwealth unity and support for Britain aside from any existing sentimental ties:

> Britain's stand in the Falklands, with all the sacrifice and heart searching and danger inevitably involved, could yet secure an even wider cause if it helps to ensure for the future that the burden of making the world safe for all is shared by all – aggression in any part of the world is a crime against the whole world.[37]

CONCLUSION

The Falklands Crisis had proved a testing time for both Britain and her Commonwealth 'family of nations'. At the outset there had been a prospect of a real division of opinion within the Commonwealth, confronting a crisis with potential colonial if not specifically Suez overtones. For one or two members there was clearly some empathy for Argentinian claims that they were merely redressing colonial injustices. The Argentinian use of force, however, and the blatant violation of the sacred principle of self-determination, had ensured that the vast majority of the Commonwealth stood firmly by Britain. Suez had ultimately proved irrelevant and, indeed, in the Commonwealth context, the crisis helped to further exorcise the 'ghost of Suez' which had haunted British policy makers for over two decades. It was a unity not solely based on sentimentality for the mother country – all Commonwealth nations to a greater or lesser degree were clearly responding from a basis of national self-interest. The smaller Commonwealth states primarily feared a breakdown in international order, the Argentinian invasion being seen as a precedent for future threats to their own security. The responses of the larger Commonwealth states such as Australia often reflected their own economic and political interests in the region. Recent bitter historical experiences had shaped some responses – ex-members Pakistan and South Africa resented a Britain which had helped make them international pariahs. India's response struck a discordant note which probably reflected not only her own memories of Suez and the bittersweet legacy of the Raj, but her own seizure of Goa and friendships with pro-Argentinian states such as the Soviet Union. Eire's often negative role as a former Commonwealth state but close neighbour of Britain clearly reflected the deep divisions in the previous decade over the current and future status of Northern Ireland. Nevertheless, despite all these widely differing historic, economic, political and strategic influences the vast majority of the Commonwealth, with the possible exception of the Indian Government, had consistently stood by Britain in what was a singularly *British* war. It was a heartening experience for a British Government which, prior to the Falklands Conflict, had expressed some disillusionment with the role and future of the Commonwealth. Later, British Foreign Secretary Sir Geoffrey Howe, in a glowing tribute, summed up deep British gratitude for the support of her Commonwealth:

> The Commonwealth saw it as their duty ... to help us discharge a British commitment ... Many of you will remember Mr Ramphal's speech at the height of the Falklands conflict. Its title was 'Not

Britain's Cause Alone'...another clear example of a situation in which the Commonwealth came to the aid of Britain in dealing with what was technically a national responsibility. The great majority of Commonwealth states gave us strong support after the Argentine invasion.[38]

It was a sentiment quoted and warmly endorsed by Francis Pym, British Foreign Secretary throughout the Falklands Crisis, who confirmed the Commonwealth's rehabilitation as an integral third arm of British Foreign policy: 'The Commonwealth embodies our international approach...it is a grouping of great value to us and to international cooperation more widely...as the support we were given over the Falklands showed.'[39]

NOTES

1. Nicholas Mansergh, *The Commonwealth Experience* (London: Weidenfield and Nicolson, 1969), *passim*.
2. I. Cumpston, *The Growth of the British Commonwealth 1880–1932* (London: Edward Arnold, 1973), p. 35. See also, W.D. McIntyre, *Colonies into Commonwealth* (London: Blandford Press, 1966), pp. 131–43 for extended discussions of imperial devolution; and the *Commonwealth Year Book 1982*, p. 3.
3. All quotations are from Nicholas Mansergh (ed.), *Documents and Speeches on British Commonwealth Affairs 1931–1952* (Oxford: OUP, 1952), vol. 1, pp. 440, 479 and 491.
4. J. Eayrs, *The Commonwealth and Suez* (Oxford: OUP, 1964), p. 18.
5. Ibid., pp. 15 and 62.
6. J.D.B. Miller, *Survey of Commonwealth Affairs: Problems of Expansion and Attrition, 1953–69* (Oxford: OUP, 1974), p. 34.
7. Quotations from Mansergh, *Documents and Speeches*, vol. 1, p. 522.
8. Eayrs, *Commonwealth and Suez*, p. 168, and Mansergh, *Documents and Speeches*, vol. 1, pp. 482–3 and 514.
9. For an extended discussion of the Commonwealth's 'Rhodesian Crisis' and its role at the 1979 Lancaster House Agreement, see especially E.J Yorke, ' "A Family Affair": The Lancaster House Agreement', in D.H. Dunn (ed.), *Diplomacy at the Highest Level* (London: Macmillan, 1996), pp. 200–19.
10. Interview with Sir Nicholas Henderson, in the BBC television documentary series *Oceans Apart – Episode 4*, transmitted 1985. Such colonial overtones were readily and rapidly exploited by the Soviet Union and her East European allies, who, as the Thatcher Government ominously recognised, enjoyed close links with some Commonwealth nations. For a detailed discussion of the Soviet perspective, see, especially H.M. Hensel, 'The Soviet Perspective on the Falklands War', *Round Table* (1983), pp. 288, 395–432.
11. Lord Luce in a letter to the present author, 15 September 2002.

12. *The Falklands Campaign: A Digest of Debates in the House of Commons, 2 April to 15 June, 1982* (London: HMSO, 1982), and Margaret Thatcher, *The Downing Street Years* (London, HarperCollins, 1993), p. 182.
13. *The Falklands Campaign: A Digest of Debates*, p. 30.
14. Alexander Haig, 'Address to Rio Treaty Foreign Ministers, Washington, 27 May, 1982', International Communications Agency, US Embassy, London, 28 May 1982.
15. Shridath Ramphal, 'Not Britain's Cause Alone: Address to the Commonwealth Press Union, 15 June, 1982' (London: Commonwealth Secretariat Library, Marlborough House, 1982).
16. All quotations are from *The Times*, 6, 7 and 8 April 1982.
17. Ibid., 10 April 1982.
18. 'Freetown Condemns Non-aligned Partner', *The Times*, 8 April 1982. In the event, only the Zimbabwe Government (belatedly) showed any dissent. Whilst condemning the Argentinian seizure of the Falklands, President Mugabe, never a close friend of the Thatcher Government, opposed Britain's military campaign to retrieve them. When asked at a Press Conference if Zimbabwe sided with Britain because of its Commonwealth ties or with Argentina as another Third World country, he ambiguously replied, 'we are an ally of peace and we support peace. We don't support the war at all.' Quoted in *The Times*, 26 May 1982.
19. 'Falklands: the South Africa Connection', *Foreign Report*, 22 April 1982, and 'Pretoria: Military Pact with Argentina Denied', *The Times*, 13 April 1982. See also John Nott's oblique reference to South Africa's perfidious role, J. Nott, *Here Today Gone Tomorrow: Recollections of an Errant Politician* (London, Politico's, 2002), p. 305.
20. *The Times*, 13 April 1982.
21. *The Times*, 13 and 27 April 1982, and 'Falkland Islands: The World View', *The Economist*, 8 May 1982.
22. Thatcher, *The Downing Street Years*, p. 182.
23. Sir Anthony Parsons, 'The Falklands Crisis in the United Nations, 31 March–14 June 1982', *International Affairs*, 59/2 (1983), pp. 171–2, and Geoffrey Howe, 'Britain and the Commonwealth Today', *Round Table*, 289 (1984), 289, p. 9.
24. Thatcher, *The Downing Street Years*, p. 182.
25. Martin Middlebrook, *Operation Corporate: The Story of the Falklands War, 1982*, (London: Viking, 1982), p. 12. For other specialist works concerning the international politics of the Falklands Conflict, see especially Lawrence Freedman and Virginia Gamba-Stonehouse, *Signals of War: The Falklands Conflict of 1982* (London: Faber and Faber, 1990) and Alex Danchev (ed.), *International Perspectives on the Falklands Conflict* (London: Macmillan, 1992).
26. 'Falkland Islands,' *The Economist*, 8 May 1982.
27. 'Ottawa is Accused of Hypocrisy', *The Times*, 5 May 1982.
28. *The Times*, 13 May 1982.
29. 'Special Report: Why South Africa is Rooting for Argentina in Falklands Crisis', *New African* (June 1982), p. 34; and 'Pretoria Said to be Supplying Argentina', *Financial Times*, 5 May 1982.
30. *The Times*, 24 and 26 May 1982; and Thatcher, *The Downing Street Years*, p. 191. *The Economist* further speculated that Irish 'emotions may also

have been affected by the discovery that it was a British submarine...that had accidentally got tangled in the nets of an Irish trawler...sinking it some 20 miles from Dublin on April 18th', *The Economist*, 8 May 1982.

31. Parsons, 'Falklands Crisis', p. 175.

32. Letter published in *The Times*, 25 May 1982; see also 'Muldoon offers a Frigate', *The Times*, 21 May 1982, 'Muldoon in Row over Loan of Frigate', *Observer*, 23 May 1982. A recent biography of P.M. Muldoon, however, suggests that, as well as the genuine loyalty felt towards Britain, even he had ulterior motives as New Zealand support could be useful in future negotiations with the EC over continued access for New Zealand primary exports. B. Gustafson, *His Way* (Auckland: Auckland University Press, 2000), p. 324.

33. T.B. Millar, 'Australia and the United Kingdom', in P.J. Boyce and J.R. Angel, *Diplomacy in the Market Place* (Melbourne: Longmans, 1992), p. 200. New Zealand's outstandingly generous offer revives memories of the cruiser loaned to Britain as an integral part of the Royal Navy in 1913, see McIntyre, *Colonies into Commonwealth*, p. 133.

34. For a detailed discussion of the Australian and New Zealand Antarctic 'agenda' see especially Klaus Dodds, 'The end of a Polar Empire? The Falkland Islands Dependencies and Commonwealth Reactions to British Polar Policy 1945–61', *Journal of Imperial and Commonwealth History*, 24/3 (September 1996), pp. 391–421. In mid-May 1982, the New Zealand Foreign Minister Warren Cooper even threatened to call off an international conference on Antarctica because of the Falklands conflict, as reported in *The Times*, 13 May 1982.

35. Shridath Ramphal, 'North and South: Reaching People World-wide. Address to the International Press Institute, Madrid', 12 May 1982 (London: Commonwealth Secretariat Library, Marlborough House, 1982); and see also 'The Falkland Islands', *The Economist*, 8 May 1982.

36. Shridath Ramphal, 'Global Consensus for Survival: Address to the Commencement Ceremony, Boston, 23 May, 1982' (London: Commonwealth Secretariat Library, Marlborough House, 1982).

37. Shridath Ramphal, 'Not Britain's Cause Alone'.

38. Geoffrey Howe, 'Britain and the Commonwealth Today,' pp. 8–9.

39. Francis Pym, 'British Foreign Policy: Constraints and Opportunities,' *International Affairs* (1983), pp. 4–5.

14

War Culture: The Royal Navy and the Falklands Conflict

ALASTAIR FINLAN

The Falklands Conflict of 1982 was a seminal event in international relations. Britain's triumph over Argentina revitalised an island nation that had endured a steady (occasionally catastrophic in the case of Suez in 1956) decline in prestige and influence in global society with the retreat from empire after the Second World War. The nation characterised by industrial disputes and immensely unpopular political leadership emerged blinking from the gun smoke in the South Atlantic with new-found self-respect and standing in the wider world. What is often forgotten in the triumphalism and jingoism of the post-Falkland euphoria is that much of the credit for the success of the campaign lies with one of the quieter members of Britain's armed forces, the RN. It was this service, through the conduit of the First Sea Lord Sir Henry Leach, that pressed the case for the force option and persuaded the Prime Minister, Margaret Thatcher, of its viability at the critical crisis meeting of her key advisers on 31 March 1982. Other voices like the Secretary of State for Defence, John Nott,[1] and indeed the United States,[2] had not unreasonable doubts about Britain's ability to execute such an operation but the RN carried the day and the rest is history.

This study suggests that a cultural interpretation of the Royal Navy's actions during Operation Corporate can shed new light on the performance of the service as a whole. It argues that the predominance of a 'war culture' in the officer corps can account for the initial drive for the mission but at the same time the significant amounts of friction that occurred during the campaign. As such it will examine not only how culture is generated in the RN but take specific examples such as the First Sea Lord's intervention, the sub-cultural dimension and strategy as well as operations in San Carlos to demonstrate how this factor manifested itself at critical moments.

HOW DOES A MILITARY ORGANISATION
REGENERATE ITS CULTURE?

Military culture and strategic culture have become quite vogue topics in international relations. Recent studies by Theo Farrell, Colin Gray, Alastair Iain Johnston, Elizabeth Kier and Jeffrey Legro,[3] to name a few have illustrated a field of inquiry that is likely to grow considerably in the future. At the heart of the various debates resides the questions of what role culture plays and how it can be measured. Johnston's definition of culture is useful:

> Culture consists of shared decision rules, recipes, standard operating procedures, and decision routines that impose a degree of order on individual and group conceptions of their relationship to their environment, be it social, organisational, or political. Cultural patterns and behavioural patterns are not the same thing. Insofar as culture affects behaviour, it does so by presenting limited options and by affecting how members of these cultures learn from interaction with the environment. Culture is therefore learned, evolutionary, and dynamic, though the speed of change is affected by culturally influenced learning rates, or by the weight of history. Multiple cultures can exist within one social entity (i.e. community, organisation, state, etc.) but there is a dominant one that is interested in preserving the status quo. Hence culture can be an instrument of control, consciously cultivated and manipulated.[4]

In this specific case, the focus is on institutional culture within a military organisation as opposed to the much broader and distinctly different dimension of strategic culture.[5] Furthermore, the culture of each service will be unique, according to the prevalence of particular beliefs and doctrines in that organisation. This raises very awkward questions about how far the notion of 'jointery' can be developed in view of the existence of these powerful internal influences. In addition, it is important to separate institutions from the average organization. Institutions are the bedrock on which the state is constructed and the military have a very explicit purpose: to protect the state in times of crisis and war or more succinctly, as Bernard Brodie has suggested, 'to win wars'.[6] With regard to the RN, it is a very old institution and has a history of great success in ensuring the survival of British political administrations against external attack, be it the Spanish Armada, Napoleon, Kaiser Wilhelm II, Hitler or General Galtieri.

Military organisations are highly codified, self-regulatory bodies that must possess a robust and reliable method of cultural regeneration, given that personnel losses are likely in warfare. How do such organisations maintain a consistent identity over periods that are measured in hundreds of years? The answer is simple: people and above all else their leaders or officers. The officer corps makes the key decisions within a military organisation and the process by which officers are exposed to their service culture is through intense indoctrination. Military academies like Britannia Royal Naval College (BRNC) and the Royal Military Academy Sandhurst (known colloquially as Dartmouth and Sandhurst) are in essence enormous disk drives into which officer cadets are inserted. The formatting procedure is comprehensive in scope to alter norms, values, beliefs and appearances radically. Norms in this case represent, as Katzenstein suggests:

> collective expectations for the proper behaviour of actors with a given identity. In some situations norms operate like rules that define the identity of an actor, thus having 'constitutive effects' that specify what actions will cause relevant others to recognise a particular identity. In other situations norms operate as standards that specify the proper enactment of an already defined identity. In such instances norms have 'regulative' effects that specify standards of proper behaviour. Norms thus either define (or constitute) identities or prescribe (or regulate) behaviour, or they do both.[7]

Norms represent some of the most important 'invisible' aspects of the RN's institutional culture that are perpetually in motion. The high level of consistency between officers in terms of behaviour at the most general level can be accounted for only by the universal adoption of norms. To varying degrees, every organisation utilises norms but as Kier points out these 'total' institutions have the ability to isolate their members from society and to generate a greater format than that of most other employers.[8] Rosen takes this theme of isolation further by suggesting that certain armed services can do this to a greater degree than others:

> Organisations such as the military have some freedom to isolate their members from society and to develop internal structures that govern their members, and that may differ from those found in the society as a whole. Second, military organisations will be less likely to reflect the structures of the larger society, the more the military organisations are small relative to society, and are isolated from their society – physically, by deployments or by war; temporally, by long service of soldiers and officers in the military away from society;

and psychologically, as the result of inculcated professional habits. Military organisations such as navies and air forces, the structures of which are strongly affected by the nature of their tasks by, for example, technological requirements, will also be less affected by the general norms and social structures.[9]

From a purely British naval perspective, the boundaries with society are rigorously controlled during this very important process of converting a civilian to a military officer. All officer cadets stay 'on board' for at least the first seven weeks of training, work intensively for 16 hours a day and gradually through instruction, osmosis as well as environment, the recruit becomes navalized. Dropouts and those considered unfit for the RN are quickly excluded from the primary group. Competition with other officer is encouraged from day one and creates a highly charged promotional ambition that will remain with the officer's throughout their career in the service. Should a naval officer leave the service, then the bonds are broken forever and that individual counts for very little within this explicitly service-orientated community. As such, it is an inwardly looking format that generates a high degree of dependency on an institution that caters for every need whether it be physical or social.

The barriers thrown up by military organisations to the outside world does create difficulties in identifying the implicit belief system of a service; however, it is possible to see through the carefully orchestrated veneers of pomp and ceremony. Schien's model of cultural analysis (see Figure 14.1) offers a particularly useful method of understanding the visible and invisible aspects of military culture that looks at the culture layer by layer. At the surface lie artefacts and creations like technology. Just below the surface can be found the inherent values or the sense of what 'ought' to be within the organisation. At the heart of the institution reside the basic assumptions and beliefs, which are taken for granted.[10] This model can be applied quite effectively to the RN but it requires modification in terms of language and meaning in order to be more appropriate to its character. In the case of artefacts, the RN places a high degree of importance on what is better described as trophies and commemorations that include victorious paintings of successful military leaders. Such artefacts are most apparent at Dartmouth and represent visual manifestations of the 'way of the warrior' but specifically that of a naval officer who is distinct almost in a tribal sense from army or air force equivalents. For the most part these trophies, that include some very expensive ornaments like candlesticks, are absorbed through a process of osmosis rather than any specific periods of instruction but they along with the

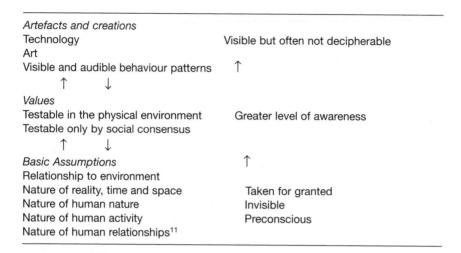

Figure 14.1. Levels of culture and their interaction.

paintings (the most impressive collection of which reside in the Senior Gun Room – the mess for junior officers) provide a forum for the most important annual ritual of the service, Trafalgar night.

It is no accident that the RN should select Nelson out of a host of famous commanders to represent the essential identity of the RN. Trafalgar encompasses the ideal image of naval warfare and an image that the institution wishes to inculcate into future generations. First and foremost, the ambience of the Senior Gun Room with its row upon row of paintings conveys a 'win' culture spanning hundreds of years. The psychological corollary is that these highly successful and aggressive commanders are what the young officers should aspire to be. Second, the image includes an 'offensive spirit' even in the face of an enemy fleet superior in terms of size and the importance of the decisive battle. Andrew Gordon in his excellent study of Jutland provides a masterful account of the desire of the Grand Fleet for such a decisive action a century after Trafalgar,[12] and Roskill records the offensive nature of operations in the Second World War that the Admiralty stressed that naval officers should try and engage the enemy as much as possible.[13] Finally, the most important technology is the surface ship or more accurately the capital ship. It is no surprise that even today surface ships comprise the bulk of the fleet and the planned future aircraft carriers exemplify the aspirations for capital ships. This is the essence of the RN's war culture that it promotes within its officer corps.

The selection of Admiral Nelson to represent the 'ideal' image of the complete naval officer has generated powerful yet contradictory beliefs within the institution. Nelson spent most of his life at sea, which is still today where the front line exists. War provided the environment in which his promotions and career flourished. Indeed, the Nelsonian image is constructed on the foundation that warfare is the most desirable vehicle towards success in the RN. In personal terms, Nelson is also famous for his married mistress that symbolises hyper-sexuality as an acceptable if not desirable characteristic of the successful officer. The contradictions within this imagery are numerous. On the one hand, Nelson had a great deal of combat experience that a contemporary naval officer simply will not accrue if the last 50 years of history are anything to go by. He was also the master of essentially static technology that had not changed much over hundreds of years, in stark contrast with the rapid pace of development in modern weaponry. In social terms, the institution promotes his image on an annual basis yet court-martials officers who copy his active personal life.

The origin and perpetuation of institutional memory within military forces is a significant area of study that has received little attention. How do armed services sift through the hundreds of years of collective experience and select the appropriate imagery to be passed on to the new generation of officers? Institutional memory is a vital element for inculcating beliefs and assumptions within personnel inside an organisation. Memory is an important factor in human relationships for learning and making choices when faced by dilemmas or crisis. It provides an essential database for achieving the simplest of tasks and organisations must retain some form of corporate memory in order to perpetuate beliefs about specific issues. But how far back does it go? Observers like Alvesson have raised the pertinent question of to what extent a founder's influence is retained within organisational cultures,[14] and Legro too has touched lightly upon this issue of 'cultural birth'.[15] In the case of the RN (an institution that some historians suggest traces its roots back to Alfred the Great[16]), the memory of the founders has been forgotten largely owing to the huge distance in time from point of origin to present day. However, what does exist in the form of the memory of Nelson and the preservation of his flagship, HMS *Victory* (still a commissioned ship!) are cultural touchstones or, in modern jargon, instantly accessible reference points. These cultural touchstones remind the RN about its past and help shape the aspirations of the future. It was no accident that after the announcement of the new strike carriers in the Strategic Defence Review that the Second Sea Lord should hold a dinner for all his senior officers on board HMS *Victory*, dining and drinking in the very cabins where Nelson had planned his greatest victory.[17] The symbolism is self-evident and testimony to the enormous cultural impact of Nelson in the contemporary officer corps. Interestingly, Britain's memorial to Nelson (his column in London) is representative of the historical heights – political and social – that the RN had attained within the British state in previous centuries. The key difference is that to the nation in the twenty-first century Nelson is just a figure of history rather than a revered symbol of identity whose actions nearly 200 years ago still reverberate loudly within the institution.

Institutional memory is maintained in different ways within the RN and, aside from cultural touchstones, tradition is a significant vehicle for the perpetuation of certain beliefs, but often at a very crude level. All naval officers will know of the battle of Trafalgar because it is celebrated each year but very few will know how the battle was fought in detail. Memory in this case is didactically learnt through a social evening but not explored any further and falls into a category of general assumption rather than detailed knowledge. Assumptions, however, are assimilated more quickly and fit well within the naval pattern of shortening language into abbreviation (VMT means very many thanks) which when applied to knowledge in the same way facilitates the speed of transmission. Tradition is the highest form of legitimacy for behaviour within a military institution. It represents the official creed and acts as a covenant that binds people in a social sense. Pierre Nora suggests that 'tradition is memory that has become historically aware of itself'.[18] Traditions are memory chips that transmit beliefs through serving personnel. Yet, these memory chips are not perfect and are liable to data corruption over time due to the symbiotic relationship with people. People act as information highways for the transmission of beliefs but, owing to the nature of humans, with no two individuals being the same, data will alter over time through the subjective interpretative processes involved. It is inevitable that traditions will change incrementally over the years but those most likely to survive in the long term intact will stem from the least complex information. Time itself is a degrading process for information transmission within military institutions. After hundreds of years – a period that clearly extends beyond the lifespan of individuals – the original reason behind a particular tradition will have been forgotten but it remains unquestioned. The continuation of sword drill at BRNC is a good example. A sword was primarily a weapon in Nelson's day and second a status symbol with which a young officer was required to be proficient (or immersed in battle culture). Today, the Navy has forgotten the primary purpose of the sword and in fact a young officer can spend years in the service without touching personal weapons despite the fact that it is an age of expeditionary warfare in which such personnel increasingly find themselves deployed ashore. However, it has remembered that the sword is a status symbol and officer cadets spend days of training with an implement that retains absolutely no value whatsoever in modern warfare.

THE FALKLANDS CONFLICT: THE FIRST SEA LORD'S INTERVENTION

Britain's decision to use force to resolve the issue of the Argentine invasion was extraordinary. First, it represented a distinct break with Margaret Thatcher's previous emphasis on a negotiation process. The Conservative government did not, unlike the Labour administration under Callaghan, use the threat of force to reinforce diplomacy.[19] In fact, its defence policy with the 1981 Defence Review, 'The Way Forward' (Cmnd 8288) and the emphasis on severely reducing the strength of the RN's conventional fleet provoked the opposite effect.[20] The most immediate effect, apart from nullifying Britain's ability to regain the Falklands in the short term with the reduction of surface forces and specialised amphibious shipping, was the removal of the symbol of the nation's presence in the region, the patrol ship HMS *Endurance*. With hindsight, Sir John Nott regrets refusing pleas from the FCO under Lord Carrington to reprieve the ship for diplomatic purposes,[21] but its publicly announced withdrawal was a powerful signal to Argentina, that reportedly considered it as a political gesture concerning the protection of the islands.[22] The critical crisis meeting of 31 March in Margaret Thatcher's private chambers in the House of Commons radically altered the course of British diplomacy to the now anticipated (from intelligence sources) Argentine invasion of the Falklands Islands on 2 April. The intervention of the First Sea Lord, Sir Henry Leach, was quite by accident – he was looking for John Nott to discuss the last intelligence reports of Argentina's intentions. Nott's recently published memoirs offer a rare insight of the psychological impression of Sir Henry's contribution to the meeting on the Prime Minister:

> At this juncture, a secretary took me aside and said that Henry Leach was outside the Prime Minister's room and had asked to see me. After I had suggested to Margaret Thatcher that he should join us, Henry did so in full naval uniform. The sight of a man in uniform always pleases the ladies and Margaret, very much an impressionable lady, was always impressed by men in uniform. She asked for Henry's

views. With great assurance, he said that it was possible to prepare a large task force. This would include *Hermes* and *Invincible*, together with the greater part of our destroyer and frigate forces, which were exercising off Gibraltar. He declared that the task force could be ready to sail early the following week, so long as he had authority to prepare it, with instructions to sail to follow later. This assertion greatly boosted the confidence of Margaret Thatcher; it was met by some scepticism among the rest of us.[23]

The Defence Secretary's account of this meeting adds a unique gender equation into the debate about why Margaret Thatcher took the decision to use force and though the decision to sail the fleet was not given until two days later, the weight of evidence suggests that the Royal Navy's intervention at this particular moment fundamentally altered the course of British policy. Much speculation exists within the literature as to why the First Sea Lord took this course of action. Inevitably, a great deal implies that Sir Henry Leach seized his opportunity to save the Navy from the axe of the 1981 Defence Review.[24] This argument is undermined by several factors, the most notable of which was that victory was not a foregone conclusion. The single biggest impediment to the British forces was distance. According to the Franks Report, the Falkland Islands are 6,761 nautical miles from the UK,[25] but in the bulk of the literature 8,000 (statute) miles is more commonly used and in one recent account by a former SAS soldier 9,000 miles – though this may have something to do with the fact that members of his unit were in Argentina![26] In addition, Argentine forces possessed the bulk of the strategic advantages not only from being closer to the islands (around 400 miles distance at a given point[27]) but they could also devote their entire military assets to this venture. As the official British report into the lessons of the Falklands campaign notes, the Argentine Air Force outnumbered the British aircraft by 'more than six to one'.[28] The fleet was quite aged,[29] but losing it against a developing country located in South America would have done far more damage than any Defence Secretary looking to save money from his budget by cutting back on ships.

Perhaps the source of the First Sea Lord's reasoning was not so much the desire for political gain (though it would be part of the prize for winning) but rather a more powerful motivating force, that of institutional culture. To get to the position of First Sea Lord, the institution selects the officer who reflects the cultural values of the service to a greater degree than his/her contemporaries. In addition, Sir Henry was no stranger to warfare, having served with distinction in the RN during the Second World War, most notably on board HMS *Duke of York*, the vessel that sank the *Scharnhorst* on 26 December 1943. Furthermore, attacking an enemy that possesses superior qualities either numerically or qualitatively and still winning was not unusual for the RN. Nelson did it at Trafalgar and Cunningham as well as Vian did it on a regular basis during the battles in the Mediterranean Sea in the Second World War.[30] Sir Henry Leach's intervention at the meeting of 31 March was entirely consistent with the institutional culture of the RN and suggests that it is likely that any naval officer in his position would have (and will in the future) proffer the same advice.

THE SUB-CULTURAL DIMENSION AND STRATEGY

Officers of the RN all undergo the same formatting process during basic training but afterwards go on to specialise within certain branches of the service. These specialisations range from the fighting arms such as naval aviation (pilots and observers), the submarine service, the surface warfare branch and the often forgotten engineers of various types through to the support services like supply, administrative and education officers. In essence, these branches represent the sub-cultural dimension within the officer corps and competition, as it is inculcated from the start of their careers, is a highly evident characteristic in the relationship between the specialisations of the Navy. It can be directly compared to the rivalry of the combat arms of the British Army, the infantry, the cavalry, the artillery and the engineers, to name a few. Inevitably, each sub-culture will approach operational strategy (not grand strategy) in different ways related to the merits of their technology. The RN is a techno-environment: in other words the relationship between personnel and equipment is radically different to that of armies and air forces since the ship or submarine is not just a fighting platform but a home as well. The artificial environment of a sea-going vessel dominates the social behaviour and language of the Navy. Shore establishments are run like concrete ships: toilets become 'heads', rooms are 'cabins', and floors are 'decks'. Officers who are made aware of something are 'pinged' just as sonar makes a ship or a submarine aware of an object in the distance. It provides not only the physical parameters but also the social parameters. The ship or submarine is the common denominator between the crew; its dimensions and technology fix the social and strategic reference points. Stated simply, officers who specialise in submarine warfare, surface warfare or aviation will consider naval strategy from that perspective, through the filter of the capabilities of a specific technology, particularly if they have spent years on operational duties.

An assessment of the naval command structure during the Falklands, from a sub-cultural perspective, is revealing. Submariners dominated the chain of command and held the highest ranks. The overall commander of Operation Corporate, Admiral Sir John Fieldhouse (CINCFLEET) was a specialist in SSN and his command HQ was located in Northwood. Below him was Admiral Peter Herbert (also Northwood) who as Flag Officer, Submarines (FOSM) was in charge of the SSN sent south to the Falklands. At the operational level the senior commander in terms of rank (not status) was Admiral Sir John (Sandy) Woodward, another submariner (who had worked for Fieldhouse in the past) and now found himself in charge of the carrier battle group. Of equal status but of junior rank were Captain Michael Clapp (an observer by training), Commodore of the amphibious task group, and Brigadier Julian Thompson RM of the land forces, who would be replaced in theatre by Major General Jeremy Moore RM after the initial landings. It is questionable whether there existed a degree of asymmetry between the nature of the command structure (predominantly submariners) and the nature of the operation – a long-distance amphibious assault that would rely heavily on aircraft carrier and surface ship operations. Even Woodward remarks in his memoirs about how astonished he was that the natural choice for his command, Admiral Sir Derek Reffell (Flag Officer Third Flotilla in charge of the aircraft carriers, with significant amphibious experience) was not given the job.[31] Clapp recollects his surprise at this set of circumstances as well but also mentions that Reffell had been refused access to Northwood and so his highly valuable experience was never utilised.[32] Unsurprisingly, bearing in mind the enhanced position of the submariner sub-culture, the most memorable and controversial feature of the naval strategy was the sinking of the *General Belgrano* by the nuclear-powered submarine HMS *Conqueror* on 2 May.

Navigating the narratives of the Falklands Conflict reveals significant amounts of friction between the various sub-cultures of the RN on how to prosecute the 'other' operations (not involving submarines). The air strategy concerning the remarkable Sea Harrier aircraft is a good example of how conflicts between sub-cultures can have a detrimental effect on the deployment and even opinions about air assets. In the Falklands Conflict, the Sea Harrier was highly successful. The highest praise comes from the official lessons of the Falklands:

> There was a 95% availability at the beginning of each day and 99% of all planned missions were flown. Sea Harrier demonstrated itself to be more than a match for Argentine conventional fixed wing aircraft with 20 confirmed and 3 probable kills, of which

16 and 1 respectively are attributable to Sidewinder AIM 9L missiles. Six Sea Harriers were destroyed, of which two were lost to enemy fire – one to small-arms fire and one to a Roland surface-to-air missile. Three GR3s were also lost to enemy fire, all to ground gunfire.[33]

Several points can be derived from this: first, despite the remarkable reliability of the aircraft, it was the Fleet Air Arm pilots that made the difference. Flying a single-seat aircraft up to hundreds of miles from a ship in the South Atlantic (in which ditching was likely to be fatal through exposure) requires a special breed of aviator – one that the RN has been producing for decades. Second, a chronic problem facing them was not enemy fire but flying schedules that generated dangerous levels of fatigue sanctioned at the highest levels by non-aviators that inevitably led to accidents.[34] Third, the main cause of aircraft losses was ground-fire. The Harrier, whether GR3, Sea Harrier or US Marine AV-8 in the Gulf War,[35] is particularly susceptible to ground-fire over land but in its role as an air defence fighter it is superior to most aircraft. Had Britain possessed the FRS2 (the Sea Harrier upgrade currently in service) with the AMRAAM,[36] then the air battle for the Falklands could have been very different. As it was, the air defence of the beach-head was by no means perfect mainly because the planners lacked confidence in the Sea Harrier[37] and lacked the confidence to allow the people with the most knowledge of the aircraft (relatively junior officers because it was only recently introduced to the Navy) to construct the air defence strategy. The performance of the Sea Harrier was good in the Falklands but it could have been much better if sub-cultural factors had not been so evident in the planning process.

OPERATIONS IN SAN CARLOS

Military technology, as Schien would suggest, is an artefact of an institution's culture and the RN's ships in the Falklands Conflict were designed for a very different type of war than the high-intensity combat (or battle conditions) in the South Atlantic. All of the warships had been constructed to fight the Cold War against the Soviet Union and so possessed weapons and systems that were attuned to that sort of warfare. The Task Force that fought in and around the Falkland Islands was geared towards nuclear warfare with excellent Nuclear, Biological and Chemical (NBC) facilities and an explicit focus on ASW but rather limited means to knock down Argentine aircraft attacking at low level. Gordon suggests that the Navy of 1982 knew 'a good deal more about warfare than did their forebears of 1914',[38] but the parallels with the Grand Fleet are striking. The RN in the First World War was geared towards fleet actions but, come the moment of truth, the Battle of Jutland in 1916, it did not execute this primary task particularly well. Likewise, the Task Force of 1982 had specialised in ASW for years but under the operational conditions in the South Atlantic did not perform well either. New research suggests that the warships fired over 200 anti-submarine torpedoes,[39] without hitting anything of military significance (though the whale population of that region probably declined in relative numbers).

The emphasis on the Cold War environment had significant ramifications on the operational performance of the RN while defending the amphibious area of operations around San Carlos. The most notable shortcoming on the bulk of the vessels was the lack of dedicated AA guns. Perhaps it was too much to expect the Task Force to possess the devastating Phalanx multi-barrelled 20 mm gun (a Gatling gun powered by an electric motor) as it had arrived in service with the US Navy just two years earlier,[40] but the shortage of effective weapons suggests that the Navy had forgotten the gun. The reasons for this remarkable oversight appear to stem from an orientation towards a nuclear (war) environment in which AA guns littering a deck of a ship would allow 'hot spots' or concentrations of radioactive material to accumulate so uncluttered decks were desirable. In addition, and equally significant, the Navy from the 1950s onwards was increasingly seduced by missile technology that appealed to its 'win' culture. The advantage of missile technology as opposed to guns is the ability to strike targets at longer ranges. Ostensibly, a single missile (in theory) equated to a downed air-craft. Since the Second World War, the balance of advantage between aircraft and surface ships had swung heavily in favour of aircraft, requiring the latter to have a significant amount of friendly air cover in order to operate successfully,[41] and missiles appeared to offset this trend. To a service inculcated with the notion of the ship being the most desirable technology this argument was highly persuasive. The problem for the RN in 1982 (and to this day) is that missile technology prom-ises more than it can deliver. To take an example, most of the escorts in the waters around San Carlos possessed the Sea Cat missile system that was claimed to have achieved eight hits during the Falklands Conflict. British official sources judge this system as having had 'some success' in the campaign,[42] but omit the critical statistic of how many missiles were fired per downed aircraft. Other sources reveal just that one out of ten Sea Cat missiles hit their target and that, by any stan-dard, is a poor record.[43] The incorporation of the Sea Cat missile also reduced the ability of ships to engage more than just two targets at any time whereas the proliferation of AA guns would have allowed each individual vessel significantly better defensive firepower. Finally, had the primary defensive missile systems been knocked out, ships like the Type 21 frigate had just a 4.5-inch gun and two 20 mm guns to put up a defence,[44] apart from volunteers on deck with small arms.[45] Put simply, missile technology from ships was not as effective as missile technology from aircraft, and the Sidewinder missile fired by Sea Harriers was without doubt the most successful example of this technology in the campaign.

CONCLUSION

For Britain, the Falklands Conflict could only have been fought through the RN – the other two services were quite impotent without the ships of the Task Force fighting their way through to the islands and putting the land forces ashore. It is quite unsurprising, given the cultural construction of the RN, that it should press for the force option in 1982. Undertaking a risky operation in the face of an enemy with the bulk of the strategic advantage was entirely consistent with experiences that the institution celebrates on a regular basis. A war culture dominates the officer corps of the RN. It manifests itself in a preference for offensive operations against usually superior opponents; a desire for a decisive encounter (why else did the RN want to draw the Argentine fleet to sea?) and an innate predilection towards surface ships and within this category those of the highest order, the capital ship which in contemporary times is the strike aircraft carrier.[46] Through the officer corps, the RN regenerates these cultural values in its new recruits that go through the often-underestimated process of initial training at Dartmouth. In recent years, owing to financial constraints, the service has tried to cut down on the amount of time that officer cadets spend in this intense indoctrination phase but all it does is reduce the depth of the formatting process. It raises the question, how important is the inculcation of naval values in the new officer with regard to the 'will to fight' in operational combat? If significant, then less intense indoctrination will have an adverse effect on fighting effectiveness but the litmus test will be revealed only in the next major campaign. As a total institution, the RN manages to keep alive its memory through important cultural touchstones like Nelson (with all its contradictory beliefs) and tradition that symbolises wars gone by rather than the battles of the future. In short, naval officers are masters of twenty-first century technology but slaves to a culture whose origins are rooted firmly in the nineteenth century but one that has produced extraordinary success in the twentieth century.

The First Sea Lord's intervention decisively altered the course of British policy towards the issue of the predicted Argentine invasion of the Falklands Islands on 31 March 1982. The basis of his advice was entirely congruent with the institutional culture that had selected him above all other officers to represent the service at the highest levels. That said, it could be extrapolated that any naval officer in his position would offer (and perhaps will in the future) the same advice in view of the strength of the cultural format. In addition, given the rarity of modern naval combat, how many officers would refuse an opportunity to be able to practise their profession? Kier and Johnston both suggest culture limits means and choices,[47] but perhaps the term 'limit' suggests more latitude than is present. Decisions within military institutions often boil down to simply 'yes' or ' no'. Officers are trained to make decisions with these 'solution orientated cultures' and the emphasis from the initial training establishment upwards is to be positive. 'Yes' has a (strong) connotation whereas 'no' conveys a negative (weak) impression. A variety of factors may have influenced the First Sea Lord's decision but institutional culture offers perhaps the most accurate explanation. Sir John Nott's description of him is apt:

> I cannot give him greater praise than to say that he was a fighting admiral, in the Nelsonian tradition, and I would have been happy to have served under him as a junior officer. But, alas, that was not to be the nature of our relationship or of our respective roles. Henry Leach was a naval traditionalist; the Royal Navy, and good for him, was his life.[48]

The existence of sub-cultures through specialized branches in the RN adds another dimension to existing interpretations of the naval campaign in the Falklands Conflict. Each sub-culture will be inclined towards a specific operational perspective based on the merits of their technology whether it is an aircraft, a ship or a submarine. In the context of the South Atlantic campaign, it was surprising, given the nature of the operation, that submariners dominated the command structure and unsurprising that those submarines should play such a prominent role. Undoubtedly, this predominance had a significant effect on other types of operations and that was particularly evident (from recent narratives)

207

in relation to the air strategy. The lack of confidence in the ability of the Sea Harrier hindered a more effective use of this highly versatile aircraft that, despite doubts, still managed to account for more Argentine aircraft than any other type of platform. Ward puts forward his alternative strategy for the use of the fixed-winged assets (very Nelsonian) in his memoirs:

> We would therefore suggest to the Command that a maximum possible number of CAP [combat air patrol] aircraft should be employed on day one over the area of immediate interest, Port Stanley, to ensure engagement with enemy fighters. Once combat superiority had been established (and we were confident we could achieve this), the presence of CAP aircraft would act as a real deterrent to any air raids by enemy fighter and ground-attack air-craft; and such deterrence was half the battle in establishing air superiority.[49]

This strategy, if implemented, would have concentrated the British air assets so that their effect would have been much greater (physically and psychologically) than their subsequent use in an aerial form of 'penny packets'[50] that characterised much of the air combat.

The military technology used in the operations around San Carlos or the warships (as cultural artefacts) were designed for a very different war environment than the battle conditions that they faced in the South Atlantic. Nevertheless, even in the role that the RN had specialised in for decades – ASW – its application proved highly problematic. The Falklands Conflict revealed that ideas about enhancing the power of ships (the institution's preferred technology) over the more dangerous air threat with guided missiles did not live up to its vaunted potential. Sea Cat's performance as the most numerous missile system in the Task Force was disappointing but understated whereas other more modern missiles did better but developed poor reputations by being associated with sunk ships.[51] Sea Wolf was the most effective AA missile (actually designed to hit missiles) in the fleet but suffered the twin problems of being on just three ships and being thrown into battle while relatively new.[52] The RN while planning for a nuclear conflict had forgotten the AA gun and this memory loss continues in a form today with the absence of close-in weapons systems (radar-guided guns like Phalanx or Goalkeeper) on the most numerous ships in the fleet, the Type 23 frigate. The most potent missile platform in the conflict was the underestimated Sea Harrier and Sidewinder AIM 9L combination that together severely degraded the Argentine Air Force's ability to gain air superiority over the amphibious area of operations.

Institutional culture explains a great deal about the actions and motivations of the RN. For the most part, the social separation of the institution from wider society means that much of what is done within the service is hidden from view. A virtual wall of silence surrounds the inner workings of this notoriously reticent service. The Falklands Conflict was a noteworthy event in international relations because it acted as a fissure in this wall and for a brief moment a great deal of information was revealed, wittingly and unwittingly, about the RN and how it prefers to fight. The basic conclusion of this study suggests that the RN is significantly influenced by a war culture that generated not only the impetus to respond forcefully to the Argentine invasion of the Falkland Islands but also substantial levels of friction at the operational level between subcultures and aspects of battle technology. Nevertheless, the Senior Service supplied the bulk of the strategic resources like aircraft, ships, submarines and assault soldiers (in the form of the RM) for a campaign whose successful culmination can be described as the most important British military victory since the Second World War.

NOTES

1. John Nott, *Here Today Gone Tomorrow: Recollections of an Errant Politician* (London: Politico's, 2002) p. 258.
2. Sandy Woodward and Patrick Robinson, *One Hundred Days* (London: Fontana, 1992), p. xvii.
3. Theo Farrell, 'Culture and Military Power', *Review of International Studies*, 24 (1998), pp. 407–16; idem, 'Professionalism and Suicidal Defence Planning by the Irish Army, 1921–1941', *Journal of Strategic Studies*, 21/3 (September 1998), pp. 67–85; Colin Gray, *Modern Strategy* (Oxford: OUP, 1999); Alastair Iain Johnston, *Cultural Realism: Strategic Culture and Grand Strategy in Chinese History* (Princeton: Princeton University Press, 1995); Elizabeth Kier, *Imagining War: French and British Military Doctrine between the Wars* (Princeton: Princeton University Press, 1999); and Jeffrey W. Legro, *Cooperation under Fire: Anglo-German Restraint during World War II* (Ithaca, NY: Cornell University Press, 1995).
4. Johnston, *Cultural Realism*, p. 35.
5. Kier, *Imaging War*, p. 30.
6. Bernard Brodie articulated this explicit purpose of military institutions to win wars when he first wrote about the significance of the atomic bomb in military strategy. See Bernard Brodie, *The Absolute Weapon* (New York: Harcourt Brace, 1946), p. 76; idem, *War and Politics* (London: Cassell, 1973), p. 377.
7. Peter J. Katzenstein (ed.), *The Culture of National Security: Norms and Identity in World Politics* (New York: Columbia University Press, 1996), p. 5.
8. Kier, *Imaging War*, p. 29.

9. Stephen Peter Rosen, 'Military Effectiveness: Why Society Matters', *International Security,* 19/4 (spring 1995), p. 29.
10. Edgar H. Schien, *Organizational Culture and Leadership* (Oxford: Jossey-Bass Publishers, 1991), p. 14.
11. Ibid., p. 14.
12. Andrew Gordon, *The Rules of the Game: Jutland and British Naval Command* (London: John Murray, 2000).
13. Captain S.W. Roskill, *The Navy at War 1939–1945* (London: Collins, 1960) p. 36.
14. Mats Alvesson, *Cultural Perspectives on Organisations* (New York: Cambridge University Press, 1993) p. 86.
15. Legro, *Cooperation*, p. 24. See also Farrell, 'Culture and Military Power', p. 411.
16. Susan Rose, 'The Wall of England to 1500', in J.R. Hill (ed.), *The Oxford Illustrated History of the Royal Navy* (London: BCA, 1995), p. 2.
17. The Commodore of BRNC attended this dinner.
18. Pierre Nora, *Realms of Memory, vol. 3* (New York: Columbia University Press, 1997), p. ix.
19. Britain's Prime Minister, James Callaghan, sent two frigates and a nuclear-powered submarine to the South Atlantic in late 1977 to support British negotiations with Argentina over the Falkland Islands if necessary [my emphasis]. Despite doubts in the Franks Report as to whether the Opposition knew about the deployment, Argentina decided not to use force over the Falklands Islands that year. See extract from the Franks Report in Tim Coates (ed.), *War in the Falklands 1982* (London: HMSO, 2001), pp. 52, 100 respectively.
20. Under the auspices of the 1981 defence review (in view of its focus on the surface fleet), the Royal Navy would retain just two instead of three aircraft carriers (with the rather old HMS *Hermes* to be phased out and the brand-new HMS *Invincible* to be sold to Australia) and reduce its forces of frigates and destroyers from 59 to around 50. The ageing amphibious ships, HMS *Fearless* and HMS *Intrepid*, would also be withdrawn from service early in the period 1982–4. See *The United Kingdom Defence Programme: The Way Forward*, Cmnd 8288 (London: HMSO, 1981), p. 10.
21. Nott, *Here Today Gone Tomorrow*, p. 255.
22. Lawrence Freedman and Virginia Gamba-Stonehouse, *Signals of War: The Falklands Conflict of 1982* (Princeton: Princeton University Press 1991), p. 20.
23. Nott, *Here Today Gone Tomorrow*, pp. 257–8.
24. See Michael Charlton, *The Little Platoon: Diplomacy and the Falklands Dispute* (Oxford: Basil Blackwell, 1989), who puts this question directly to Sir Henry Leach in an interview, pp. 189–90; and Hew Strachan, *The Politics of the British Army* (Oxford: Clarendon Press, 1997), pp. 254–5.
25. *The Franks Report*, Cmnd 8787 (London: Pimlico, 1992), p. 106.
26. Ken Connor, *Ghost Force: The Secret History of the SAS* (London: Orion, 2000), p. 397.
27. *The Falklands Campaign: The Lessons*, Cmnd 8758 (London: HMSO, 1982), p. 6.

28. Ibid., p. 6.
29. The Flagship of the Task Force, HMS *Hermes*, was 23 years old in 1982; 13 RN ships were 14 years old and above, not to mention all of the six RFA LSLs, which fall into the same age bracket. See David Brown, *The Royal Navy and the Falklands War* (London: Leo Cooper, 1987), pp. 358–65. Only three of the ships possessed the latest Sea Wolf missile system and just two of these were Type 22 Batch I (the most advanced frigate in the RN).
30. The Battle of Matapan (28 March 1941) and the Battles of Sirte (17 December 1941 and 22 March 1942) are good examples of aggressive yet inferior RN units defeating more powerful Italian forces. Correlli Barnett in his excellent study *Engage the Enemy More Closely* (London: Penguin, 2000) suggests that the failure of the often superior Italian fleet to defeat the much smaller RN can be attributed in part to the absence of a battle history (and the accompanying tradition within its institution).
31. Woodward and Robinson, *One Hundred Days*, p. 343.
32. Michael Clapp and Ewen Southby-Tailyour, *Amphibious Assault Falklands: The Battle of San Carlos Water* (London: Orion, 1996), p. 83.
33. *The Falklands Campaign: The Lessons* (note 27), p. 19.
34. See Commander Sharkey Ward, *Sea Harrier over the Falklands* (London: Cassell, 2001), p. 283, for a very different and controversial version of the air war over the Falklands.
35. Edward J. Marolda and Robert J. Schneller Jr, *Shield and Sword: The United States Navy and the Persian Gulf War* (Washington, DC: Government Reprints Press, 2001), p. 195.
36. See *The Eleventh Report from the Defence Committee, Sea Harrier Mid-Life Update, HC 445* (London: HMSO, 1990) for an insight of how the lessons of the Falklands were incorporated into the updated aircraft.
37. Ward, *Sea Harrier*, p. 356.
38. Gordon, *Rules of the Game*, p. 598.
39. Lt Cdr Clark V. Brigger USN, 'A Hostile Sub is a Joint Problem', *Proceedings*, 126/7 (July 2000), p. 52.
40. Marolda and Schneller, *Shield and Sword*, p. 28.
41. See Richard Overy, 'Total War II: The Second World War', in Charles Townshend (ed.), *The Oxford Illustrated History of Modern War* (Oxford: OUP, 1997), pp. 123–4.
42. *The Fourth Report from the Defence Committee, Implementing the Lessons of the Falklands Campaign, HC 345 – I* (London: HMSO, 1987), p. xxxvi.
43. Department of the Navy, *Lessons of the Falklands, Summary Report* (Official US Navy Report), February 1983, p. 31 [my emphasis].
44. Brown, *Royal Navy and the Falklands War*, pp. 359–60.
45. On the Type 21 frigate HMS *Ardent* even the NAAFI manager, Mr J.S. Leake (a civilian in charge of the ship's shop) was firing a machine gun on deck! Ibid., p. 195.
46. See Woodward and Robinson, *One Hundred Days*, p. 133, n.2.
47. Johnston, *Cultural Realism*, p. 35; and Kier, *Imagining War*, p. 31.
48. Nott, *Here Today Gone Tomorrow*, p. 214.
49. Ward, *Sea Harrier*, p. 98.

50. This was the term used to describe the disastrous dispersed use of British tanks against the concentrated German tank formations in the early stages of the Second World War.
51. Sea Dart had a good war in the South Atlantic but two of its platforms; HMS *Sheffield* and HMS *Coventry* were sunk in combat. It was also credited with eight kills and a major deterrent effect on attacking aircraft. See *The Falklands Campaign: The Lessons*, p. 21.
52. Sea Wolf shot down five aircraft. Ibid., p. 21.

15

The 'Logistics Miracle' of Ascension Island

CAPTAIN PETER HORE

In the spring of 1982, I had been selected for promotion to Commander and was employed in London on a study into the complement of a new class of warships (the Type 23), and visiting frequently the Old Admiralty Building. There I often drank a glass or two of sherry in the office of an officer who shared my interest in South America. He had visited the Falklands Islands in a frigate and later married an Argentine girl; I had visited the Argentine twice and had taken an expedition, by Landrover, across the Andes from Puerto Montt to Buenos Aires. We both spoke Spanish and I, who had once been madly in love with a beautiful Anglo-Argentine girl, had many friends in that beautiful country.

Quite improperly we had put ourselves on the Ministry of Defence's internal distribution list for all signals about the growing crisis in the South Atlantic, and no one thought it strange to deliver highly classified messages, for example, from Captain Nick Barker in the Antarctic patrol ship *Endurance*, to the dim attics of the Admiralty. There, after work, we read and analysed the signals avidly: it was clear to us that that something quite extraordinary was happening, initially in South Georgia and then in the region as a whole, and the invasion of the Falklands seemed to be obvious and inevitable.

After the war I read the Franks Report. Lord Franks had been commissioned by the government of the day to enquire into the what prior notice there had been of the war, and he had concluded that the British government had no warning of the decision by the Junta in Buenos Aires to invade the islands and that 'the invasion of the Falkland Islands on 2 April could not have been foreseen'. I was fairly flabbergasted.

I had also read the Rattenbach report. Lieutenant General Benjamin Rattenbach had chaired a commission which looked into the failings of the war from an Argentine perspective and he was considerably more critical than Franks. I had had some difficulty getting hold of the Rattenbach report since Argentine publications were, in the mid-1980s, still banned from import into the UK and I had to ask a friend in an intentional humanitarian agency to help me. Quite apart from the charges which Rattenbach proposed should be drawn against the Junta and individuals in the Argentine armed forces (he had been politically opposed to the Junta and had spent the war in exile), the timetable for the war which he gave seemed more probable than any set out by Franks. It was clear that the Argentines not only had the capability but also every intention of invading the Falklands, and it was not that they lacked a plan of invasion but that they had too many! The principal plans were called Alfa (the reinforcement of South Georgia), Rosario, and Azul.

Anglo-Argentine talks over the future of the Falklands had stuttered to a halt in September 1981. Consequently, in December 1981, President Galtieri had discussed invasion plans with his chief of navy, Admiral Anaya, with a view to impelling the British into 'serious and definitive negotiations', though it was not until February that the chief of the air force, General Lami Dozo, the third of the three-man Junta, was brought into their confidence. The renewal of talks which the foreign minister, Costa Mendez, proposed on 27 February 1982, were intended to proceed in parallel with military planning. However, when Costa Mendez issued a veiled threat to that purpose on 2 March, stating that the Argentine would close 'the proceedings by means which best suited its interests', he was forced by his own military to retract it the following day lest he gave away any plans.

Nevertheless, the naval attaché in London reported that Costa Mendez's speech had thoroughly alerted London to the probability of an invasion. As we now know from the Franks Report, the attaché was wrong and the only officers who realised what was up were two middle-ranking officers who had no input into the assessments submitted to the JIC.

In brief, Plan Rosario was for an operation against the Falklands by the Argentine navy (ARA) and Plan Azul (or Blue) was for a joint operation by the Argentine armed forces. Plan Azul was formally named, and Rosario was subsumed into it, on 23 March 1982, and, after a few days more work on the plan, D-Day was set as 1 April 1982 with 2 or 3 April as alternative dates. There was, however, no plan for what to do after the Falkland Islands had been conquered.

Be that as it may, on the morning of Friday 1 April, I was warned off to join the Naval Emergency Advisory Group the following Monday. In the afternoon, now at home in Devon, I was told, obliquely, that I would instead be flying in a Hercules transport aircraft to Ascension Island for a task which was not revealed to me. I just had time to visit the local library and glean what I could about my destination: there were about three lines in very large gazetteer and I duly packed all my tropical white uniform.

Had political and diplomatic events turned out otherwise in the early months of 1982, Task Force 317 would have been just another group of distant ships at sea, and the operational and logistic achievements of British forces on Ascension Island might have been the only British operations in the South Atlantic that year. As it was, heroic and historic events further south have eclipsed the happenings on Ascension Island, and after focusing on the island for three weeks, world attention switched further south.

Like the Argentine plans, the British operation, named Corporate, commenced as an essentially naval operation and, as far as Ascension was initially concerned, in a very small way. The original signalled requirement stated that the probability existed of passing small quantities of urgently needed air-portable freight through a temporary airhead on Ascension. The response to this statement was the 5 officers and 20 men who arrived on the island during the first weekend of the Falklands War. They found Ascension, in the words of Admiral Fieldhouse's official despatch, to be largely devoid of all resources and possessing 'totally inadequate technical and domestic back-up'.

From this unpromising beginning the story of how Ascension grew to be the Forward Operating Base, assessed as critical and vital to the war in the South Atlantic, deserves a minor place after the many other greater achievements during that war. Ascension, a rugged, remote island, doubled its population in a few weeks, and became briefly the busiest airfield in the world, and a crowded training ground for brigade strength forces. Yet, despite its newly found prominence, little was – and is yet – widely known of Ascension and many misconceptions persist. No adequate or correct description existed in any of the standard reference works, though the best is probably given in *The Pilot*.

Ascension Island is 38 square miles of the most hostile environment one can imagine. The nightmare landscape consists of volcanic ash and dust, clinker, broken rock, lava flows, frowning mounds of slag and extinct volcanoes. Newcomers to the island are struck by the jaggedness and sharpness of the rock apparently newly blasted from a quarry, though in fact Ascension is geologically speaking young (a few million years) and the rock has had little time to weather or be eroded. Situated 8° South and 14° West in the trade winds, Ascension Island enjoys a stable climate; the temperature is about 65–70 °F year-round and a prevailing south-easterly breeze at about 18 knots on 364 days of the year carries an all-pervading dust. On the coast there is some 6 inches of annual rainfall; according to *The Pilot* this falls in form of light showers or drizzle but, in early 1982, much of it fell in heavy tropical downpours which caused flash floods and large pools of standing water, though these quickly evaporated. In contrast, Green Mountain on the windward side of the island and at nearly 3,000 feet has some 20 inches of rain. Formerly, water was stored in catchments but by 1982 these were disused. On the upper slopes of Green Mountain is a derelict farm, once successfully run by Cable and Wireless as the island's primary source of fresh meat and vegetables. Records suggested that plant colonisation of Ascension is still taking place, and may in turn bring more rain, as the early farm managers hoped. The island would be an ideal subject of botanical and agricultural study.

The verdant appearance of Green Mountain contrasts starkly with the barrenness of the lower slopes. Some bays have beaches of marvellous soft white sand but are enclosed by sharp rocks, and all round the island the unexpected swell, strong undertow and offshore set, to say nothing of the voracious sea life (blackfish, moray eels, sharks) are a discouragement to bathing. In short, Ascension would be an ideal holiday for hay fever-suffering non-swimmers!

Not unexpectedly Ascension went unclaimed by any nation from its discovery in 1501 until 1815. In the year of Napoleon's exile the RM garrisoned Ascension to forestall any French rescue attempts. Thus Ascension became the second most remote inhabited island in the world. From 1815 to 1922 the Admiralty administered the island, but in the latter year control passed to the Eastern Telegraph Company. During the Second World War and again from 1964 the Colonial Office appointed a career diplomat as Administrator, though subordinate to the Governor of St Helena. During the Second World War the USA obtained a lease of parts of the island and over 4,000 men were employed building and manning an airstrip. From March to July 1942 they underwent prodigies of endurance, living on two pints of water a day and without re-supply for three and a half months. On 15 June 1942, the first landing on Ascension by aircraft was by a Swordfish on anti-submarine reconnaissance flown from HMS *Archer*. Nearly inaccessible by sea, Ascension was joining the twentieth century.

As a consequence of its history and its lack of water or any other natural resource, Ascension has no indigenous population and there are no irredentist claims on its territory. The British Crown owns all land, and only the Governor of St Helena may grant 'certificates to occupy'. In 1982, the residents were all employees or contractors of British companies and American agencies working on the island, such as GCHQ, Cable and Wireless (C&W), the BBC, PanAm, South Africa Cable (SAC), NASA, NSA, etc. The European and St Helenian workforce lived in quarters built by their employers, and the American workforce lived in quarters provided by various agencies, but administered by PanAm. Although some of this accommodation was used by British forces, its availability could not be guaranteed. The residents lived pleasant, sociable, if precarious lives: most worked shifts, and they enjoyed two of the world's worst golf courses. The soil if irrigated is fertile and keen gardeners bought treated effluent from the sewage works to grow flowers around their temporary homes.

In April 1982, the population of Ascension Island consisted of about 1,000 people, including 58 European families and 600 St Helenians, amongst whom there were some 200 schoolchildren, and about 200 American unaccompanied civilians. No one else was allowed to land on the island without permission nor to reside there unless employed by one of the companies or member of HM Forces on active service. Children on reaching 18 years of age are obliged to leave unless, exceptionally, they find employment. Pensioners must return home.

In 1982, the attitude of the St Helenians and the expatriates on Ascension was vital to the success of the British operations, and they were, to a man, totally loyal, enthusiastic and co-operative. Although invidious to mention any individual or group of islanders, special mention must be made of two of them as examples of the rest. First, the airfield staff, such as the fire and security men, who worked 12-hour shifts, and, second, the ever versatile C&W maintenance men. The latter, in addition to their normal duties of public works, took on the initial renovation of derelict buildings and the operation of the pier head. Much is made of increased air activity on Ascension (of which a little more later) but the success of the harbour operations deserves at least as much acclaim. Until Operation Corporate, the pier head had been used just once or twice every two months or so, and use by night was considered impracticable. However, despite the ugly sea conditions and antiquated machinery men and material were soon pouring over the pier head. For instance, the timely and cheerful response of the St Helenians and their British managers expedited the despatch of a company of RM on their way to retake South Georgia. Without this help the despatch of the first troops from Ascension would certainly have been delayed by at least 24 hours. Other work included, for example, the manufacture of

217

spigots for mounting machine guns in southbound ships and helicopters. All this and much other work required individual effort far above the normal course of duty yet all went sadly unrewarded when it came to the distribution of honours after the Falklands War.

In 1982, the 1,000 residents lived in three centres, Georgetown on the west coast, Two Boats in the centre and the American camp near Wideawake Airfield. The Americans had a commissary and a small shop plentifully supplied from the continental USA by regular Military Airlift Command (MAC) flights. The British had two shops managed by NAAFI under contract to the London Users Committee (LUC), a consortium of British firms. The shops and the majority of islanders were supplied by steamer at about two-monthly intervals. The appearance of being an NAAFI shop would cause trouble later.

There being no airfield on St Helena, sea passage is the only link with the outside world and ship, using a small freighter, RMS *St Helena*, the only transport home of the St Helenians working on Ascension Island. British civilians could fly to UK about once a quarter using an air charter, and this was very much a feature on the residents' calendar since it brought in rare fresh produce and milk. When the air charter was stopped from taking up fuel at Ascension the consequent absence of spare space for freight was grievously missed. Also, at the beginning of Operation Corporate the small freighter RMS *St Helena* was due and the air charter had only recently left. In the early days of operations the fortuitously high stocks on the island were essential to the welfare of the newly arrived British forces, and the residents allowed generous access to these stocks until shortages began to appear.

There is no port on Ascension and only a landing at a stone pier in Clarence Bay, on the western side of the island. An unpredictable swell in the bay ranging from 4 to 40 feet governs the use of boats in the bay and landing at the pier. The height of the swell is attested by the sand, which over the years has been thrown into Fort Thornton 200 feet above the pier. The unpredictability of the swell is rather like the Loch Ness monster – only believed by those who have seen it. While the author was showing the view of the anchorage from Cross Hill to some VIPs, out of a flat calm sea came three rollers which swept across the bay and broke over the pier head. Minutes later the sea was flat again – and the only evidence of this phenomenon a loaded lighter that had been turned through 90 degrees.

The so-called American Base was much misunderstood. The very words conjure up visions of acres of runway, several choices of clubs, a large PX and unlimited resources. Little could be further from actuality. The USAAF Auxiliary Airfield, Wideawake, just to give its full name, had a uniformed complement of one: the Base Commander, a Lieutenant Colonel, who was probably not destined to be a future chief of the USAAF. There were no other American servicemen. There was one run-way and normal activity was two or three aircraft per fortnight. There was certainly no base in any operational sense.

The legal situation regarding the use of the United States auxiliary airfield at Wideawake on Ascension Island is interesting. Ascension was one of a series of British islands which the Americans had acquired the use of in the Second World War under lend-lease. There have been a number of reviews of the treaty arrangements, the latest an agreement between the governments of Britain and the USA dated 1956. This agreement lasted until 20 July 1975 and 'there afterwards until one year from the day of which either Contracting Government shall give notice to the other of its intention to terminate'. By 1982, the treaty had expired with neither side having given notice, and the Americans regarded the treaty to be fully effective while the British considered the Americans to lease parts of Ascension Island on 12 months' notice: perhaps no more than a negotiating point, but also a perspective which affected the view of each Government's appropriate representative on the island. Nevertheless, both parties regarded the 1956 agreement to be fully enforceable while neither had given notice. However, an exchange of notes in 1962 obliged the Americans to grant such 'logistic, administrative or operating facilities at the Airfield [as] are considered by the Government of the United Kingdom to be necessary in connection with its use by ... United Kingdom military aircraft'. Credit must be given to the draftsman of the exchange of notes who had added the essential clause, even though the wide interpretation it would receive during 1982 could not have been foreseen. In summary, the British disposed of their own island as a sovereign nation, there was no American operations base on Ascension, and such American facilities as the British did use were obligated by treaty.

The build-up of the forward operating base on Ascension from 25 officers and men during the first weekend to 800 personnel after three weeks, and then to a peak of 1,400 including transitees, happened in three overlapping phases: the initial phase and crises which developed internally on Ascension, a phase of intense operations, and a final phase of widening horizons before the organisation was handed over in mid-July to the RAF, after victory in the Falklands. The remarkable thing is that the organisation developed and functioned without written orders for several weeks, yet succeeded so well in melding together diverse units, many of whose personnel had no experience of tri-service operations. Though differences in attitude and manning were revealed, force

219

of personality, clear objectives and daily and regular briefing united the team. The rest of this chapter concentrates on the first two phase of three weeks and more.

The first to arrive on Ascension on the weekend of 2 April 1982 were not, as the *Sunday Times* Insight Team reported, 'technicians and engineers equipped with radar and traffic-control apparatus', but two officers from the RAF's 38 Group, an officer and six men to form the RN Forward Logistics Unit, a Commander and eight ratings to support naval helicopters, and a number of RN aircrew and maintainers. All others Forces came later. The senior officer was an air engineer around whom the team coalesced until the arrival of a naval Captain who took the title of Commander British Forces Support Unit (BFSU).

An early discovery was that although the reinforcement plan for Ascension Island had been recently revised, it had not been reviewed by the island authorities, and the contents were inaccurate and largely irrelevant. A large volume of signals, received via GCHQ, had to be read through, but at first there was no means of replying except by ordinary landline. Initially, surplus accommodation was available from C&W and PanAm to feed and roof up to about 200 personnel, and the pressing problems were to unload and sort pallets of stores and ammunition, and to reassemble some naval helicopters which had been brought in over the first weekend of the war. The early arrivals changed in the sunshine and set to work, and, after an 18-hour flight in a Hercules, most men then worked non-stop for 36 hours. Similar work rates continued for a long time, with men working in the open quickly acquiring enviable suntans.

The organisation that developed under the command of CBFSU had three elements: first, naval operations including all rotary-wing aircraft; second, RAF operations which in particular encompassed the tremendous achievements of transport command; and logistics. This third function covered the internal support and administration of Ascension Island as a forward operating base, as well as, more importantly, support from Ascension to the front.

By noon on 6 April 1982, the British base had been operating for many hours continuously. Three Lynx helicopters were flying, and two Wessex helicopters were being prepared for ground running. In Clarence Bay the fleet auxiliary *Fort Austin* was being loaded by lighter. Hercules were arriving on regular schedule, about six or eight per day. There had been little control over the flow of men and cargo: men arriving at Lyneham simply wrote their names on an open passenger list. Units and individuals brought with them whatever equipment they or their commanders believed necessary. Stores depots diverted everything in the pipeline including ammunition to Lyneham. At Ascension this caused immediate difficulties. Some men had responded to telephone calls telling them to go south and had no orders beyond Ascension. Others arrived days or weeks in advance of their proper ships. All had to be fed and accommodated and most were taken under command and given work. For example, the task of renovating and making ready for occupation a series of derelict huts fell to a group of artificers who were waiting to join the landing ships that were expected to arrive soon. Radio operators, destined to augment the amphibious forces, helped unload the Danish motor vessel *Aes* of stores addressed to NP89O1 (the RM garrison that had been captured in the Falklands).

The build-up in particular of ammunition was impressive and much was loaded into *Fort Austin*. After she sailed it became an urgent necessity to reduce any risks on the airfield by creating a dedicated ammunition depot. An ideal site was found in a remote valley but the only access was along a track liable to flash flooding. This led to one of many unusual demands for stores to be sent out from the UK: for a pipe or something similar, 20 feet long and 4 feet in diameter and able to withstand a 10 ton axle weight, capable of being used as a conduit under a makeshift road. This arrived within two days of the demand and ammunition was soon being trailered away from its unpleasant proximity to fuel, aircraft and vehicles and into some temporary shade.

A transport pool was formed by commandeering unit vehicles as they were unloaded from Hercules. A small unit of RM ran the pool and the most conspicuous volunteer drivers were a group of young medical officers waiting to join RMS *Canberra*. When the transport pool vehicles were depleted, night raiding parties removed the fuses from parked vehicles, thus forcing the would-be possessors to ask the transport officer for help, when he would promptly requisition the keys.

The PanAm accommodation was capable of taking about 200 men. A campsite at English Bay, which had been used by RAF signallers after the Second World War and by West Indian contract labour later, provided a roof for some 50 men more. Units pooled tents and rations and a field kitchen was established, manned by an RAF Field Catering Support Unit. Eventually three such field kitchens were set up, supervised by a RN catering officer, which fed over 1,000 men a day. For a while rations were one-man 24-hour type, donated by 42 Squadron RAF, requiring considerable wrist work to provide bulk meals. Very soon, however, the RN had moved in refrigerated containers and landed sufficient dry food to enable a varied and interesting diet.

It is claimed that the airfield at Wideawake became the busiest airfield in the world. It is true that on one day in April Wideawake logged more aircraft movements than Chicago O'Hare International Airport, a fact which was established by an anonymous telephone call to Chicago itself. It is also true that until at least early June helicopter movements outnumbered fixed-wing movements by a ratio of over 5 to 1. The helicopters came from visiting warships, of course, and from the newly resident Wessex Vs of D Flight 845 Naval Air Squadron. Particular credit is due to the youthful naval pilots who flew more hours in the early days of April than they might have expected in a year of peacetime activity. There was no choice on Ascension but to run the single airstrip and limited hardstanding like an aircraft carrier, with rotary and fixed-wing flying taking place simultaneously with the movement 'on deck' of men, stores and vehicles. The very low number of ground and air safety incidents (the author can remember none!) which resulted was not due to luck but to the training and professionalism of all who participated.

Though initially works activity on the island was carried out by C&W, augmented by naval ratings awaiting ships southbound, when it was recognised that the number of works tasks was multiplying geometrically with the flood of men and units, a Royal Engineers unit, consisting of an officer and some 40 men, arrived. They were a very impressive team. Their most obvious feat was laying a temporary pipeline over 3 miles from the fuel farm in Clarence Bay to the airfield, but many other vital jobs were also accomplished. They commissioned a desalination plant to supplement the island's meagre supplies of fresh water, renewed the sewage system at English Bay, erected portable buildings, organised enough portable power supplies for a small-sized village, and all the while continued the work of surveying and renovating derelict buildings. Nor did they allow themselves much rest, but as soon as any opportunity arose they took up community projects like repairing the old bridges and paths on Green Mountain.

Fuel, in particular aviation spirit, was a persistent problem. Fortunately the island's stocks for normal consumption were relatively large, but the frequent launch of large flights of aircraft necessary to support elderly Vulcans and Victors on operations far south soon depleted reserves. A continual train of oil tankers was necessary in Clarence Bay but the fuel pumped ashore from these ships required time to settle. A new tank farm of fabric pillows at Wideawake and a fleet of bowsers increased reserves, but fuel always required careful management.

Control over the flow of personnel onto Ascension eventually became a pressing and major task. Men and their equipment continued to arrive unannounced, and though sent with the best will in the world, there were never sufficient resources on the island to cater for and accommodate everyone. Their administration and the enforcement of discipline requires disparate skills which in the Army and RAF require distinct trades, but in the RN are carried out by Masters of Arms and their Regulators. So it was that when these tasks continued to grow a small team of one officer and six Regulators was sent for. They arrived complete with a patrol wagon and quickly made themselves familiar and well known, and discharged their varied duties with great tact and efficiency.

The two shops on Ascension were run by NAAFI under contract to the London Users Committee. The manager was seconded from NAAFI, the staff wore NAAFI coveralls, and the price labels and packaging was NAAFI. Only the prices did not follow this pattern but instead reflected the high cost of freighting goods to Ascension. The periodic supply ship did call in the middle of April, and generously the LUC allowed British forces to use the shops, there being no other source of nutty (chocolate), tobacco, soft drinks, etc., but when eventually these began to run out the shops were reluctantly closed to British forces. The price differential and the closing of the shops caused much resentment and misunderstanding by servicemen. Soon, however, the Expeditionary Force Institute or EFI, a uniformed branch of NAAFI previously unknown to most, arrived to establish a third shop, at prices more familiar to soldiers and airmen from British forces in Germany, in a disused bakery. It still left the problem that the forces had seriously depleted the islanders' stocks of even the humblest item which they might reasonably expect to find in their corner shop. Further, by drinking and eating in the private clubs which had been hospitably opened to them, British servicemen were continuing, albeit indirectly, to live off the land. This situation was in its turn relieved when, after some bureaucratic delay in London, space and free freight was approved for a weekly re-supply to the civilians on the island.

However, the supply ship RMS *St Helena* had also featured in every islanders' plan for shipping heavy luggage, receiving seamail and returning to the island of St Helena (which has no airport). The news that her owners had chartered her to the MoD was a great blow to civilian morale. Since CBFSU had not been warned in advance of this transaction, it was impossible to present in London any arguments against taking up from trade the *St Helena*. The contractor for shipping to from Ascension and St Helena eventually found two much smaller ships, though they were in many respects inadequate. Whether it was lack of sympathy or lack of awareness of the consequences of diverting *St Helena* from her normal trade, the charter only led to MV *Stena Inspector* and HMS *Dumbarton Castle* being diverted from operational tasks to carry civilian passengers between the islands of St Helena and Ascension. It also, of course, prejudiced the good community relations upon which the success of British operations was founded.

The distinctly odd geophysical properties of Ascension host many natural phenomena which were of interest even to Darwin, who visited in 1836 – also on his way to the Falklands. Most significant among the unique fauna were the green turtles and the sooty terns, also known as wideawakes. From the beginning concern for the environment, including the breeding grounds for these rare animals, loomed large in plans for using the island, whether as a logistics base, or for training. Accordingly, during the troop training phase on Ascension, care was taken to minimise damage. Helicopter flight paths over nesting areas were discouraged; Boatswain Bird Island, the home of thousands of seabirds, was not used for naval gunfire practice, and only one beach was used for amphibious landings. Fortunately, the most popular beaches for turtles were also the least suitable for boat traffic of any sort. The sooty terns nest and breed amongst the clinker, in 'fairs', their only enemy the feral cats once imported to exterminate the rats which man had accidentally introduced. Sadly the cats found the birds to be easier prey. But when ranges were needed to zero the weapons, one good effect in 1982 was that the presence of man and the sound of small arms and missile fire scared off the cats from the fairs but failed seemingly to disturb the birds very much.

Amongst many other tasks for which the BFSU planned and prepared were the reception of POW, the hospitalisation and evacuation of casualties, the handling of large numbers of transitees and the care of survivors. Many of these tasks eventually related to later phases, but the first and most significant was the reception of survivors from HMS *Sheffield*. The uniforms they wore at Lyneham were issued at Ascension, where they had been measured by a Chinese tailor landed from HMS *Exeter*, and they were also paid and fed. Thanks once more to the generosity of the civilian community, most were cared for in small parties in peoples' homes until their flight departures, which had obviously been timed to meet the deadlines of the evening news programmes in the UK. Eventually the arrangements for evacuees were so smooth that they were even given a chance to buy 'duty frees' from an EFI shop.

Everything was a learning process. The same principles and processes that had been developed for evacuation of survivors could be applied to repatriation of POW, except these were flown out in the dead of night. Every prisoner of war was photographed, and while prisoners were on the airfield lighting was arranged so they could gather no intelligence. Someone too had to read the Geneva conventions, in English and in Spanish, to make sure we knew what we were doing.

In Chapter 10 of this book, Colonel Ivar Hellberg has described how his own carefully structured organisation for the logistic support of the

RM was meticulously executed. There was no such structure on Ascension Island, where the arrangements grew pragmatically. They were, however, no less successful, as these few paragraphs dealing with some specific problems which emerged and how they were handled, have shown. Most were unique, requiring initiative and innovative skills to solve, all qualities which the various arms of British forces proved they possessed in full.

16

Invoking Munich, Expiating Suez: British Leadership, Historical Analogy and the Falklands Crisis

PAUL LATAWSKI

INTRODUCTION

Statesmen and soldiers have long looked to historical events to provide guidance during times of crisis. Historical analogy as an element in political or military decision-making seeks lessons from previous crises or brings forward the inherited legacies of previous mistakes into a contemporary situation. Historical analogy, however, has sometimes been a *faux ami* for crisis decision-makers. The application of 'lessons' of history can be inappropriate or irrelevant to the new circumstances confronting political and military leadership during a crisis or the lessons to be drawn from historical analogy can also be varied or contested and as a consequence difficult to apply. Often, the most powerful historical analogies are inherited legacies of failure or calamity that relate to the historical experience of a particular country. Speaking in Strasbourg in January 1990 to the Council of Europe, the then Polish Prime Minister Tadeusz Mazowiecki noted that Poles continued to 'feel reproachful because of Yalta . . . for having been left on the other side of the Iron Curtain'.[1] For Poland, Yalta is a historical analogy of the worst features of great power politics leading to an international order with deleterious consequences for its sovereignty and national interests. Some historical analogies provide 'universal' lessons as well as national ones. Václav Havel, the Czech President, in a speech in 1993 noted that Munich signified not only the dangers of democracies appeasing dictatorships but more particularly the lesson for the Czechs that their country needed the security certainties resulting from incorporation 'into a system of functioning collective defence [NATO]'.[2] National experience, however, does not yield clear lessons in all cases. For the United States, failure in Vietnam masks a highly contested debate over lessons to be applied from the traumatic national experience.[3] Although historical analogy may only be one of the myriad factors that drive crisis decision-making, it nevertheless often plays a powerful role. In the case of Britain during the 1982 Falklands crisis, two historical analogies influenced British political and military decision-makers – Munich and, in a more pronounced fashion, Suez.

HISTORICAL ANALOGY: LESSONS OF MUNICH AND SUEZ

During the Falklands crisis, the historical analogies of Munich and Suez were undoubtedly evident and played a powerful role on the thinking of British political and military leaders. These two historical analogies, however, could not have been more contrasting in terms of identifying their 'lessons'. The lessons of the Munich Conference of September 1938 are very well understood as a historical paradigm to guide political and military decision-makers. The agreement reached at Munich saw Britain and France agree to Nazi Germany's demand for the ethnically German-populated Sudetenland, roughly corresponding in geographical terms to the western mountainous rim of Czechoslovakia, to be ceded to Germany. The Czechoslovaks had no role in the negotiations over the fate of a substantial portion of their territory and the outcome of the conference was presented to them as a *diktat*. Moreover, faced with the united position of the great powers, it was a *diktat* they accepted without armed resistance.[4] This culmination of the British–French policy of appeasement, however, did not satiate Germany's territorial and political ambitions in Europe. The failure of appeasement and Munich could be seen a year later when the German aggression against Poland drew Britain and France into war with Germany. Munich thus became a shorthand for the folly of a democracy appeasing a dictator bent on aggression. The long-term price of appeasement was now seen as being invariably far more costly than the immediate cost of resisting the ambitions of aggressors, if necessary by engaging in armed conflict. As Jeffrey Record has argued: 'the great lesson the democracies...drew from Munich was simple and clear: appeasement of aggression only invites more aggression, and it is therefore imperative that early and effective force be used to stop it'.[5] With Britain having played such a leading part in the pursuit of appeasement in the 1930s, Munich as a historical analogy has had a profoundly powerful influence on the British political establishment. As a consequence across the British political spectrum the lessons of Munich have been scarcely contested.

If the historical analogy of Munich is well understood in political terms, then the same cannot be said of the lessons of Suez in 1956. The Suez crisis of October 1956 saw an Anglo-French military intervention to seize the Suez Canal (in secret collusion with Israel) in response to its nationalisation by the Egyptian leader Abdel Nasser. The operation lacked the legitimacy conferred by a UNSCR and, most importantly, the political support of Britain's (and France's) major ally the United States. In a speech given on 31 October 1956, President Dwight D. Eisenhower rebuked Britain and France, making clear that 'we do not accept the use of force as a wise or proper instrument for the settlement of international disputes'.[6] Ironically, the Eden Government's decision to mount the military intervention against Nasser was heavily influenced by the experience of Munich. 'As my colleagues and I surveyed the scene in these autumn months of 1956', wrote Eden in his memoirs, 'we were determined that the like should not come again'.[7] Eden's use of the Munich historical analogy proved mistaken. The Eisenhower Administration did not share Eden's view of the relevance of Munich. Soon after the onset of military operations American pressure, particularly economic pressure, was decisive in leading to Britain and France calling off the operation.[8]

The consequences of Suez were profound on Britain and its political classes even if its lessons proved less clear cut. The most often cited and least contested legacy of Suez was that it marked the end of Britain's role as a great power in world affairs that could exercise its power as an independent actor. As a leading article in *The Times* opined on the fortieth anniversary of the crisis, 'the illusion of global power was shattered'.[9] At the same anniversary, William Rees-Mogg commented that 'Eden did not recognise how far British power had already declined. Britain had been a world power in the Second World War, but was one no longer. The failure of his Suez policy only advertised that unpalatable fact.'[10] This 'unpalatable fact', however, had a profound impact on the confidence of Britain's political classes. Suez was a major political tremor that shook the confidence of the political establishment to its core. Although Britain no longer could aspire to a role as a power comparable to the United States, a presence in the world was not necessarily inconsistent with the influence of a medium power. But in the wake of Suez followed the acceleration of the retreat from Empire that was mirrored by a growing loss of will to employ military power beyond the confines of Cold

War Europe. As Britain divested itself of bases and air and naval assets designed to project power in the 1960s, it seemed as though Britain's rebirth as a medium power entailed a stark choice between 'Europe and the world'.[11] Written in the late 1960s, Max Beloff's *The Future of British Foreign Policy* captured the implications of this loss of will to exercise military power outside north-west Europe: 'there is the much more difficult question of whether it is possible to believe that a Britain which has once extricated herself from these [global] obligations is ever likely to persuade herself of the need to reassume them.'[12]

BRITISH POLITICAL PARTIES AND THE LESSONS OF SUEZ

Although the loss of great power status and shaken confidence of the British political establishment were discernible outcomes of the 1956 Suez crisis, the legacies of Suez were more complex and nuanced when taken from the perspective of individual political parties in Britain.

The Conservative Party (the party in power during the Suez crisis) drew a number of significant lessons from Suez as well as acquiring a few scars. Margaret Thatcher, recalling her political experiences at the time of the Suez crisis took four lessons from the Suez crisis:

- We should not get into a military operation unless we were determined and able to finish it.
- We should never again find ourselves on the opposite side to the United States in a major international crisis affecting Britain's interests.
- We should ensure that our actions were in accord with international law.
- He who hesitates is lost.[13]

While Thatcher drew lessons mostly associated with statecraft that also implicitly took into account the reality of Britain's decline to a medium power, not everyone in the Conservative Party carried forward such analysis of the lessons of the crisis. An important section of the party blamed the United States for the Suez failure. This element on the right of the Conservative Party in Thatcher's words 'never forgave the Americans'.[14] Indeed, Thatcher observed that 'for some in the Tory Party the memories of America's actions at the time of Suez remained for ever fresh'.[15] More broadly, the experience of Suez certainly left lingering doubts among many Conservatives about the reliability of Britain's American ally in a time of crisis.

During the Suez crisis, the initial supportive stance of the Labour Party gave way to staunch opposition to Eden's policy. Afterwards, opinion in the Labour Party viewed the Suez crisis as a major blunder. Sometimes this opinion could be expressed with considerable passion. Michael Foot (the leader of the Labour Party at the time of the Falklands crisis) was a staunch opponent of British action at Suez in 1956. Writing in *Tribune* in November 1956, Foot wrote: 'Eden's government must be destroyed. The crime done in our name must be expiated . . . not since Neville Chamberlain presented Hitler's terms to the Czechs in 1938 has a powerful Western nation treated a small nation with such brutal contempt.'[16] Denis Healey (on the Labour front benches during the Falklands crisis) was similarly blunt in his criticism of the Suez policy: 'Suez was a demonstration of moral and intellectual bankruptcy. In execution it was a political, diplomatic and operational disgrace.' Indeed, Healey went on to write that 'I have never been so angry for so long as I was during the Suez affair.'[17] David Owen, at the time of the Suez debacle a young Labour Party supporter at the beginning of his career, drew slightly different political lessons from the Suez debacle. He believed that it revealed that some circles of Labour Party leadership were 'afraid of exercising military power and have been for decades'.[18] Owen's critique believed that this ambivalence about military power could isolate the Labour Party during similar crises from its grass-roots supporters who took a more robust view. Moreover, Owen also believed that when members of the armed services were sent out on dangerous operations they deserved political unity and not political division back home.[19]

THE FALKLANDS CRISIS: THE LONG SHADOW OF MUNICH AND SUEZ

The Argentine invasion of the Falkland (Malvinas) Islands in April 1982 triggered a major crisis that ended only with its recapture by British forces two and a half months later. The operation to repossess the Falklands was one that entailed huge risks as well as practical problems for the British armed services. It is perhaps because of the enormous challenges faced by the Falklands operations that the decisions and actions of British political and military leadership during the crisis took place with reference to previous historical events. In particular, Munich and Suez cast long shadows in the corridors of power in the Palace of Westminster and Whitehall.

For Margaret Thatcher, the Falklands crisis was a defining moment of her premiership. It is also clear that in her approach to the Falkland's crisis she carried forward a set of 'historical' lessons she drew from the Suez crisis. She was also aware of the powerful effect Suez still had on thinking in the British political establishment. 'We developed what might be called the "Suez syndrome" ', she wrote in her memoirs; 'having previously exaggerated our power, we now exaggerated our impotence'. In her analysis of the Suez legacy, she argued that 'it entered the British soul and distorted our perspective on Britain's place in the world.'[20] The direction of the war was done by a small 'War Cabinet', OD(SA) chaired by Margaret Thatcher and including key political figures from the Cabinet and the CDS, Lord Lewin. As a group, it is clear that for the majority of them the legacy of Suez was ever present. As John Nott, the Secretary of State for Defence and key member of OD(SA) remarked, 'I know that Whitelaw, Lewin and I, in the early stages, thought "Suez, Suez, Suez" in many of our waking hours. Not least, we needed the support of the Americans.'[21] William Whitelaw, another OD(SA) member and a close political collaborator of Thatcher, initially supported the objectives of Suez in 1956 but was 'positively relieved' when the crisis ended because of its damage to relations with the United States and the hostility of 'world opinion'.[22] Whitelaw's view of Suez suggests that he carried forward more concerns than lessons when dealing with the Falklands crisis. Lord Lewin, the CDS, also had Suez very much on his mind. At the outbreak of crisis he was on an official visit to New Zealand. His biography recounts how determined he was that the Falklands crisis, either in its domestic management or its military conduct should not be a repeat of the Suez crisis. He was particularly determined that the armed services should receive a clear aim in any operation.[23] From the evidence available, it is clear that the legacy of Suez was enough of a factor among the political and military decision-makers to be mentioned in the memoirs of the principals. Although it is difficult to assess how influential it was in shaping decisions, it is clear that it formed a pervasive political backdrop for the war cabinet.

Another window on the impact of historical legacy on the British political establishment during the Falklands crisis was Parliament. In the debates devoted to the crisis, a more differentiated picture of the influence of historical legacy appears. During these debates the Prime Minister, Margaret Thatcher, made clear allusions to the principal legacy of Munich, to confront aggressors and not to appease them. Addressing Parliament on 8 April 1982, Thatcher stressed: 'Throughout the Western world and beyond there is a realisation that if this dictator [Argentina's General Galtieri] succeeds in unprovoked aggression, other dictators will succeed elsewhere.'[24] The echoes of Munich were also in the supportive statements by opposition party figures. The Labour Party leader,

Michael Foot, felt strongly about the lessons of Munich in his proffer-ing of cross-party support during the Falklands crisis. He said, 'there is the longer-term interest to ensure that foul and brutal aggression does not succeed in our world'.[25] Dr David Owen, the Social Democratic Party (SDP) leader, similarly alluded to Munich when he stressed in a speech that 'we have learnt lessons in this House from History. No one can draw too many parallels, but one thing that we do know is that weakness in the face of aggression only increases the appetite'.[26] Although the debate contained predictable, if rousing, advocacy of the lessons of Munich during the Falklands crisis debates, historical analogy also made its way into more critical contributions to House of Commons debates. On 3 April 1982, Edward du Cann simultaneously managed to allude to both Munich and Suez:

> If one tolerates a single act of aggression, one connives at them all. In the United Kingdom we must accept reality. For all our alliances and for all the social politenesses which the diplomats so often mistake for trust, in the end in life it is self-reliance and only self-reliance that counts. Suez, when I first came into the House 25 and more years ago, surely taught us that not every ally is staunch when the call comes. We have one duty only, which we owe ourselves – the duty to rescue our people and to uphold our rights.[27]

The speech by Edward du Cann illustrated the festering resentments and mistrust of the United States in some circles of the Conservative Party. Sniping was not only directed externally. For the Labour MP Douglas Jay the pernicious legacy of Munich was closer to home: 'The whole story will inevitably lead some people to think that the Foreign Office is a bit too much saturated with the spirit of appeasement.'[28] Although the criticism of the Foreign Office smacked of 'round up the usual suspects', more important were the undercurrents of suspicion about the support of the United States for Britain during the crisis. Not everyone serving President Ronald Reagan supported the British position. Although Britain could count on staunch support from the American Defence Secretary, Caspar Weinberger, the American Ambassador to the UN, Jeane J. Kirkpatrick, was at best torn between America's 'British and Latin American Allies'.[29]

The American dimension of the Falklands crisis was crucial to British efforts, both political and military, to repossess the Falkland Islands. In an article examining the parallels between Suez and the Falklands crisis, David Carlton observed: 'in 1982 no less than in 1956 there may be limits to what can be attempted in circumstances in which United States interests are, to say the least, not entirely identical with those of Great Britain.'[30] In the front line of British political efforts to ensure a convergence of the American and British view in the Falklands crisis was the British Ambassador in Washington, Sir Nicholas Henderson. He was widely credited for his effective diplomatic efforts to cultivate American support, particularly in the court of American public opinion. He also was remarkably candid about the impact of the Suez crisis and the way it undermined British confidence in the United States as an ally. In an interview on ABC News on 25 April 1982, Henderson said that the consequence of American policy over Suez had been to 'produce great bitterness in the UK because it's when you make a mistake or when you are in trouble that you need an ally'.[31] British jitters and concern over which way American policy would eventually favour, Britain or Latin America, surfaced in the British press. Two leading articles in *The Times*, 'An Ally not an Umpire' and 'Time to Take Sides', encapsulated these British worries in 1982.[32] Once the political (and indirect military) support was assured, there was almost a collective sigh of relief among the sceptical elements of the British political establishment regarding American intentions. A leader column of *The Times* entitled 'A Friend Indeed' captured the satisfaction with unambiguous American support.[33] These concerns over American policy, however, demonstrated the length of the long shadow cast by Suez on British–American relations.

CONCLUSION: THE LEGACY OF HISTORICAL ANALOGY

The conclusion that one may draw from the impact of the Munich and Suez historical analogies was that they did influence the thinking of British political and military elites in the course of the crisis. Regarding Munich, it reflected the depth of conviction born out of the Munich crisis that aggression must be challenged rather than appeased. As for the historical analogy of Suez, the Falklands crisis did not so much affirm it as a part of the canon of statesmanship but rather saw its most important role as serving as an exercise in political expiation. While Munich reflected enduring political truths, Suez was a historical burden to discard. This view of Suez can be seen in the memoirs of a number of Conservative politicians. The most prominent example was Margaret Thatcher. In her memoirs *The Downing Street Years* she wrote that:

> The significance of the Falklands was enormous, both for Britain's self-confidence and for our standing in the world. Since the Suez fiasco in 1956, British foreign policy had been one long retreat. The

tacit assumption made by British and foreign governments alike was that our world role was doomed steadily to diminish. We had come to be seen by both friends and enemies as a nation which lacked the will and capability to defend its interests in peace, let alone war. Victory in the Falklands changed that.[34]

Other Conservative political figures, such as Nigel Lawson, mirrored Thatcher's view of the importance of the Falklands War in overturning the Suez legacy. Lawson argued that 'the Falklands War exorcised the humiliation of Suez'.[35] So from the bitter legacy of Suez is born another historical analogy of the Falklands as the turning point that saw the British political establishment regain its self-confidence on the international stage. John Nott, the Defence Secretary during the crisis, bridged these analogies when he wrote that 'Suez was a disaster. The Falklands was a great victory and did much to restore the self-confidence of the nation.'[36] There are, however, dangers in relying on historical analogy and in creating new ones. As Tam Dalyell cautioned, 'it is not uncommon for political leaders to over-react to what they see as the mistakes of their predecessors in seemingly parallel situations, or to draw misleading conclusions'.[37]

NOTES

1. Speech by Tadeusz Mazowiecki, Prime Minister of Poland, to the Council of Europe, 30 January 1990, in Lawrence Freedman (ed.), *Europe Transformed: Documents on the End of the Cold War. Key Treaties, Statements and Speeches* (London: Tri-Service Press, 1990), p. 431.
2. Address by President Václav Havel to the Parliament of the Czech Republic, 12 October 1993, Ministry of Foreign Affairs Press Department, No. 15/93.
3. Jeffrey Record, *Making War, Thinking History: Munich, Vietnam, and Presidential Uses of Force from Korea to Kosovo* (Annapolis, MD: Naval Institute Press, 2002), pp. 18–26. See 'The Impact of Historical Analogy on American Foreign and Security Policy has been Extensively Studied', in Yuen Foong Khong, *Analogies at War: Korea, Munich, Dien Bien Phu, and the Vietnam Decisions of 1965* (Princeton: Princeton University Press, 1992) and Ernest R. May, *'Lessons' of the Past: The Use and Misuse of History in American Foreign Policy* (New York: Oxford University Press, 1973).
4. Igor Lukes, *Czechoslovakia between Stalin and Hitler: The Diplomacy of Edvard Beneš in the 1930s* (New York: Oxford University Press, 1996), pp. 253–6. The question of whether or not Beneš should have resisted Munich forms an important part of the Munich historical analogy from the Czech viewpoint. See: Neal Ascherson, 'In this Country, the Appeasers of Tyrants had their Moment of Triumph at Munich', *Guardian*,

18 October 1998: http://www.Guardian.co.UK/Columnists/Column/ 0%2C5673%2C 324992%2C00.html; and Karel Bartošek, 'Could We have Fought? – The "Munich Complex" in Czech Policies and Czech Thinking', in Norman Stone and Eduard Strouhal (eds), *Czechoslovakia: Crossroads and Crises, 1918–1988* (New York: St Martin's Press, 1989), pp. 101–19.

5. Record, *Making War, Thinking History*, p. 17.
6. Speech by President Dwight D. Eisenhower, 31 October 1956: http://www.US-Israel.Org/Jsource/US-Israel/Ike56.html.
7. Sir Anthony Eden, *Full Circle* (London: Cassell, 1960), p. 518.
8. Cole C. Kingseed, *Eisenhower and the Suez Crisis of 1956* (Baton Rouge: Louisiana State University Press, 1995), pp. 102–26.
9. 'Forty Years On: The Turning Point that Shocked Britain into the Modern World', *The Times*, 29 July 1996.
10. William Rees-Mogg, 'How Eden Erred at Suez', *The Times*, 25 July 1996.
11. Saki Dockrill, *Britain's Retreat from East of Suez: The Choice between Europe and the World?* (Basingstoke: Palgrave, 2002), p. 226.
12. Max Beloff, *The Future of British Foreign Policy* (London: Secker and Warburg, 1969), p. 74.
13. Margaret Thatcher, *The Path to Power* (London: HarperCollins, 1995), p. 88.
14. Ibid., p. 89. See also Denis Healey, *The Time of my Life* (London: Michael Joseph, 1989), p. 173.
15. Margaret Thatcher, *The Downing Street Years* (London: HarperCollins, 1995), p. 437.
16. As quoted in Mervyn Jones, *Michael Foot* (London: Victor Gollancz, 1994), p. 217.
17. Healey, *The Time of my Life*, p. 169.
18. David Owen, *Time to Declare* (London: Michael Joseph, 1991), p. 40.
19. David Owen, *Personally Speaking* (London: Pan Books, 1987), p. 183.
20. Thatcher, *The Downing Street Years*, p. 8.
21. John Nott, *Here Today Gone Tomorrow: Recollections of an Errant Politician* (London: Politico's, 2002), p. 247.
22. William Whitelaw, *The Whitelaw Memoirs* (London: Aurum Press, 1989), pp. 42–3.
23. Michael Charlton, *The Little Platoon: Diplomacy and the Falklands Dispute* (Oxford: Basil Blackwell, 1989), p. 193; Richard Hill, *Lewin of Greenwich: The Authorised Biography of Admiral of the Fleet Lord Lewin* (London: Cassell, 2000), p. 355.
24. *The Falklands Campaign: A Digest of Debates in the House of Commons, 2 April to 15 June 1982* (London: HMSO, 1982), p. 70.
25. Ibid., p. 10.
26. Ibid., p. 80.
27. Ibid., p. 10.
28. Ibid., p. 16.
29. Seymour Maxwell Finger, 'Jeane Kirkpatrick at the United Nations', *Foreign Affairs*, 62/2, (winter 1983/84), p. 452. See also Caspar Weinberger, *Fighting for Peace: Seven Critical Years at the Pentagon* (London: Michael Joseph, 1990), pp. 143–52; Jeane J. Kirkpatrick, 'My Falklands War and Theirs', *National Interest* (winter 1989/90), pp. 11–20.

30. David Carlton, 'The Suez Parallels that Could Swamp Mrs Thatcher', 15 May 1982.
31. As quoted in *American Foreign Policy Current Documents 1982* (Washington, DC: Department of State, 1985), p. 552.
32. 'An Ally not an Umpire', *The Times*, 12 April 1982; 'Time to Take Sides', *The Times*, 26 April 1982.
33. 'A Friend Indeed', *The Times*, 1 May 1982.
34. Thatcher, *The Downing Street Years*, p. 173.
35. Nigel Lawson, *The View from No. 11: Memoirs of a Tory Radical* (London: Bantam, 1992), p. 161.
36. Sir John Nott, 'Defence and the Suez Factor', *The Times*, 6 November 1986.
37. Tam Dalyell, *One Man's Falklands* (London: Cecil Woolf, 1982), p. 108.

PART 4
Lessons of the Falklands Conflict for Future Military Operations

17

The Impact of the Falklands Conflict on Defence Policy

SIR ROGER JACKLING

There is one reason I am very sorry to be making this contribution: it was originally intended that the late Sir Frank Cooper would do this, and it was after his death in early 2002 that I was invited to take his place. He would have contributed a unique perspective, the product of his period as Permanent Under Secretary from 1976 to the end of 1982, and as Under Secretary and Deputy Secretary for Policy during most of Denis Healey's term as Defence Secretary. I cannot provide that, but I was involved at the Whitehall end of Operation Corporate, and from 1989 until recently I was a corporate planner in the MoD. I was closely involved therefore in the defence reviews: 'Options for Change', the Defence Costs Studies (DCS) ('Front Line First'), the 1997/8 Strategic Defence Review, and the various exercises and planning rounds which have shaped Great Britain's response to changing strategic circumstance. That is my background and it conditions my conclusions about the impact of the Falklands Conflict on British Defence Policy. In tackling my brief I take defence policy to comprehend the higher-level appreciation of threats, risks, interests and what they imply for an appropriate defence posture. I try also to touch on the consequences of lessons from the conflict, both for organisation and for how we tackle certain dimensions of a major crisis, such as the press and media.

THE NOTT DEFENCE REVIEW

I should start with the UK's strategic appreciation before 2 April 1982. There was a very clear focus on the strategic threat from the Soviet Union and its Warsaw Pact allies. Membership of the North Atlantic

Alliance was the framework within which British defence policy and capabilities should respond to that threat. This was summarily but clearly set out in the 1981 White Paper 'The Defence Programme: The Way Forward' (Cmnd. 8288), which reported the conclusions of the Nott Defence Review. On taking office as Defence Secretary in the autumn of 1980 John Nott had found that the extant and planned force structure was a legacy from different times, grossly over-ambitious relative to available and anticipated resources, and unbalanced between platforms, on the one hand, and weapons systems and war stocks on the other. John Nott has subsequently written in his recently published and very readable autobiography:

> No-one in government when I joined MOD had suggested that the 3% annual growth target might last beyond 1983/84 yet public commitments to the equipment programme were being given on assumption that 3% volume growth would continue until 89/90. It was pretty clear that compound growth of 3% in volume terms given that defence costs invariably rose faster than inflation would have bankrupted the Exchequer long before the target had been realised.[1]

The review of the programme that John Nott set in hand was to bring the costs within a more realistic assessment of the money likely to be available and its purchasing power. And having reached his conclusions he set them out in Cmnd. 8288. This reaffirmed four roles for British Forces within the alliance:

A. an independent element of strategic and theatre nuclear forces committed to the North Atlantic Alliance;
B. the direct defence of the UK homeland;
C. a major land and air contribution on the European mainland;
D. a major maritime effort in the Eastern Atlantic and the English Channel.

In addition, we would commit home-based forces to the Alliance for specialist reinforcement contingencies, particularly on NATO's flanks (which was a key role for our amphibious capability). Beyond the European/North Atlantic theatre, we would 'Exploit the flexibility of our forces...so far as our resources permit to meet both specific British responsibilities and the growing importance to the West of supporting our friends and contributing to world stability more widely.'

The Nott Review made some important choices about the allocation of resources between those four roles. The contribution of the surface fleet to the major maritime effort in the Eastern Atlantic and English Channel was seen to lose out in order to preserve planned improvements to capabilities – first, for direct defence of the UK homeland: retention of two squadrons of Phantoms previously due to be phased out as the Tornado F3 entered service, the tanker force, a build-up of mine counter-measures force, and better use of reserves; and second, for the contribution on the European mainland: proceeding with Challenger, what became Warrior, the SP70 artillery piece, Multiple Launch Rocket System (MLRS), etc., and an increase in war stocks for Harrier GR3.

As to naval forces, it was concluded that the most effective maritime mix for the future would require the planned enhancement to maritime-air and submarines but a reduction in the planned size of our surface fleet, the scale and sophistication of new ship building, and a move away from the practice of costly mid-life modernisation. This translated into a plan to increase the Nimrod fleet; to increase SSNs from 12 to 17; to begin building of Conventional Submarine (SSK); to keep only two anti-submarine aircraft carrier (CVS). There was uncertainty over the replacement of the Sea King as an anti-submarine helicopter. The number of destroyers and frigates was to be reduced from 59 to 'about 50'. In addition three Royal Marine Commandos would be maintained, because the 'Government regards their special experience and versatility as of high value for tasks both in and beyond the NATO area'. However, it had already been decided that likely needs did not warrant replacement of the specialist amphibious ships HMS *Intrepid* and HMS *Fearless*, which were to be phased out earlier in 1982 and 1984 respectively. The RM were to be kept in the infantry role but without the specialist shipping which was necessary to an amphibious capability. But they were high-quality troops and at that time were better able to recruit than many Army infantry units, plus they also had a strong brand politically. I dwell on these decisions and perceptions because they are not those which prevail today. However, the Falklands campaign was not of itself enough to transform them.

Cmnd. 8288 also outlined our approach to interests and activity outside the NATO area. The reach and readiness of Soviet troops had extended the area of competition. Military forces had a part to play: military assistance, advice, training, loan of personnel and provision of equipment to friendly countries. The British Government wished to exploit more fully the characteristics of flexibility and mobility inherent in British forces, but there was not much hint of the requirement for permanent command arrangements or the prior identification of force elements to the OOA task; these developments came later. The RN would continue periodically to deploy a task group. There was a modest extra stockpile for the Army's OOA deployments – Stockpile Rex. Forces would continue as necessary to sustain specific British responsibilities overseas, for example in Gibraltar, Cyprus, Belize and the Falkland Islands. The last was, and would continue to be, discharged with a detachment of 30 marines and the availability in the South Atlantic for six months of the year of the ice Patrol Ship HMS *Endurance*, due to be phased out of service without replacement as decided by the previous Labour Government. That is where policy, priorities and the planned programme stood shortly before the Argentines invaded the Falkland Islands.

LESSONS LEARNED: COMMAND PAPER 8758

Against that background we can ask what would have changed if the Falklands campaign had had a profound impact on British defence policy? Perhaps the Government would have recoiled wholesale from the conclusions of Cmnd. 8288. Threats to British interests and territory outside the NATO area might have been given more recognition. It might have been suggested that protecting such interests and confronting such threats constituted an additional role of similar importance to the other four. It might have concluded that we should configure our forces and provide them with the equipment for national expeditionary campaigns similar to Operation Corporate. It might have decided that Defence deserved a much larger slice of public expenditure than currently planned, and, even if it did not, a grateful and impressed British people might have clamoured for such a charge. In the event the Falklands campaign did not cause any of these things to happen.

The Government in 1982 did, however, conduct an intensive internal review of the military lessons learned from the campaign, and it published its conclusions from the review in *The Falklands Campaign: The Lessons* (Cmnd. 8758). As to policy judgements at the strategic level, the internal review of the lessons from the campaign which the CDS forwarded to the Secretary of State for Defence in November 1982 asserts:

> Our major overall conclusion is that a substantial shift in defence policy is not justified. The experience of the South Atlantic should not be used as an excuse for ignoring the main threat or belittling the primary NATO and Home Defence tasks: but within that capability and without degrading it the middle and long term programme should be nudged towards greater strategic mobility and flexibility to meet the unexpected.

However, the conflict did have an impact on plans for the surface Fleet. It was decided not to proceed with the proposed sale of HMS *Invincible* to Australia, which meant with three CVS retained invariably two would be available for operations. The four destroyers and frigates lost in the campaign were replaced with four new Type 22 frigates in addition to the procurement of a further Type 22 which was not a replacement for a ship lost. Three of the ships were to be a new Batch III design with added point defence capability. The Batch III had the 4.5 inch gun restored to enable shore bombardment of which the Batch I and II had not been capable. It was significant also that four destroyers and frigates previously intended for a stand-by squadron were retained in the running Fleet. And the Search Water radar and associated avionics equipment for the Sea King helicopter would provide the Fleet with an organic AEW capability, which would be particularly valuable in future operations in the littoral areas.

A decision had already been taken in the late autumn of 1981 that the amphibious ships HMS *Fearless* and HMS *Intrepid* should not be retired prematurely. Although Cmnd. 8788 asserted that 'the success of the Falklands Campaign bore out our confidence and that of our allies in the ability of British amphibious forces to react swiftly and effectively to emergencies in and away from the NATO area', it was the 'Options for Change Review' in 1990 which confirmed that the amphibious ships should be replaced, and led to orders being placed in 1995. If Operation Corporate had transformed the perception of the amphibious capability I believe we would have initiated a replacement of the LPDs some years before that.

The lessons of Operation Corporate also underlined the ubiquity and utility of nuclear attack submarines (SSNs); some valuable pointers for warship design in future; the value and robustness of the Harrier – although 20 years later the bias of the Future Carrier Based Aircraft (FCBA) is towards Offensive Air Support rather than air defence – and the critical importance of support helicopters on the contemporary battlefield. All of these points were registered and pursued in programme and procurement action in the next 15 years.

THE FUTURE

As to the future, the Government acknowledged in Cmnd. 8788 that we had learned a great deal. Many of the lessons were not new but were no less important for that: the campaign had underlined the value of professional, well-maintained forces capable of responding quickly and imaginatively to the unexpected; the Armed Forces had demonstrated their capability to operate out of the NATO area on the other side of the world, in the most difficult circumstances, and they had gained direct experience of such an operation and the logistic effort necessary to support it.

The White Paper echoed the internal report by affirming 'this is not to say we now take a different view of the major threat to the security of the UK which comes from the Soviet Union'. The four roles of Cmnd. 8288 'remain the priority for our defence effort, and the enhancement and modernisation of the forces devoted to these tasks must still have the first call on our resources'. The approach beyond the NATO area was formulated in almost precisely the same terms as Cmnd. 8288, that is, military assistance, periodic deployments, and a 'capability to intervene unilaterally or with allies to protect national interests or in response to a request for help from our friends'. Such operations would be undertaken by Force elements whose primary role was in support of the NATO Alliance, but their ability to act would be enhanced by:

A. the designation of a 2-star HQ to command forces committed to such operations;
B. the establishment of a stockpile of material required for such expeditionary operations;
C. greater use of civilian assets to deploy and sustain an expeditionary force.

All of these measures had been envisaged and trailed before Operation Corporate. The clearest and most immediate consequence of the campaign for British defence policy was the decision to build a strategic airfield at Mount Pleasant on East Falkland, and to garrison the islands with a significantly more capable force. Initially this included Harriers, a larger naval element, and an infantry battalion group. Building airfield began in 1984 and after its completion in 1986 it was possible to reduce the permanent garrison. Today it consists of about 1,300 service men and women, and includes Tornado F3s, an infantry company and naval elements. The capital cost of the airfield and the associated garrison facilities was assessed at £450 million. By 1990 it was estimated that the total cost of the campaign, including replacement of equipment, stores, etc. had reached £1.8 billion. Up until then all of these costs and the costs of the Falkland Islands garrison had been financed from additions to the defence budget. At their peak in 1982/3 and 1984/5 these amounted to 4–5 per cent of the defence budget. Since 1990 costs have been met from the defence budget without a Falkland Islands specific uplift. The cost of the garrison today is around £70 million per annum, which represents 0.3 per cent of the budget. Clearly the Falklands campaign had significant consequences for the size of the defence budget in the years immediately after the campaign, and continues to have some consequences for the allocation of the budget even now. However, what it did not achieve was a transformation in political and public attitudes to defence expenditure such that the MoD was guaranteed a generous allocation in subsequent public expenditure rounds.

Thus Operation Corporate did *not* cause a rethink of our policy nor significantly overturn the conclusions and plans which emerged from the Nott Review. It did bring about some worthwhile enhancements. It reprieved – for a time – elements of the surface fleet. It contributed to developing ideas on organisation and command which matured later into important changes to which I return later. And it subsequently informed and conditioned other developments after the Cold War.

I should turn for a moment to an important issue of perceptions. I have argued that the Falklands campaign did not cause a fundamental change in British perceptions of the strategic context and the defence posture and capabilities appropriate to Great Britain. But what about its influence on the strategic calculus of others? Clearly the campaign, the subsequent construction of the airfield, and the fielding of a more capable garrison had a significant impact on the attitude of Argentina. Beyond that, Baroness Thatcher wrote in her autobiography:

> The war also had real importance in relations between East and West: years later I was told by a Russian general that the Soviets had been firmly convinced we would not fight for the Falklands, and that if we did fight we would lose. We proved them wrong on both counts and they did not forget the fact.[2]

I found some further collateral in a piece by a Soviet officer in a professional journal which appeared shortly after the Falklands campaign: 'The UK will and capacity to project force was probably underestimated and NATO solidarity was depressingly good from a Soviet point of view.' That said, I have been unable to lay my hands on any clear and unequivocal archival evidence of the impact of the campaign on Soviet perceptions. There is much anecdotal evidence, but neither the FCO nor the intelligence community has produced evidence to support the view that the campaign transformed the Soviet view of the West, and was therefore a significant catalyst in bringing to an end the Cold War and military competition between East and West. If that had been true we could conclude that the Falklands Conflict had a profound consequence for British defence policy – but that is not my conclusion.

Nevertheless, I do believe that the conflict and its outcome had a significant impact on British perceptions. For one reason or another I think it is fair to say that during the 1970s the confidence of the British Government in the Armed Forces had eroded somewhat. Perhaps the same is also true of the confidence of the Armed Forces in themselves. The Falklands Conflict changed that emphatically. Moreover the British people were hugely impressed by the professionalism and courage of the Task Force. I would date from this time a resurgence of the widespread view that the British Armed Forces are for their size as good as any in the world – or better. I would also date from this time a greatly increased willingness on the part of British governments to commit British Forces to the management of international crises. This inclination was well captured in Douglas Hurd's advocacy of the value of Britain 'punching above her weight'. And the current Government has been very ready to contribute British forces to help manage crises, confront wrongs and support peace initiatives and settlements. It is interesting that in the 1970s there was a prevailing view in the MoD that the trouble with all our contingency plans was that in the event ministers would not have the will to do what was necessary and would not be prepared to stand the risks and uncertainties inevitable in committing forces to operations. That is not a grumble that you hear these days.

COMMAND AND CONTROL

Notwithstanding many years of exercises in NATO's Wintex and Hilex series, Operation Corporate provided a demanding test of our arrangements for the direction and command of complex joint expeditionary operations. The operation succeeded; and so arguably those arrangements passed the test. However, the experience was a significant influence on the development of our organisation and processes over the next 15 years, even if the changes came incrementally. Most strikingly and immediately, Operation Corporate demonstrated and benefited from the developing role of the CDS. Admiral Lewin was emphatically the Government's principal military adviser from his return from New Zealand in the days immediately following the Argentinian invasion. The relationship between him and the designated joint commander Admiral Fieldhouse, at Northwood, was key. So was the relationship which he rapidly established with the Prime Minister. The former relationship ensured that Admiral Lewin was invariably and by some margin the best briefed member of the CoS Committee about the situation in the South Atlantic. His relationship with the Prime Minister ensured that he maintained the clearest view of the objectives and temper of the Government, and was able to secure political approval to the military means he judged most likely to secure those objectives. Within the MoD there is no doubt he was outstandingly the dominant figure throughout the crisis, and arguably the same was true of his position within Government as a whole – after the Prime Minister herself. He may, as John Nott recalled, have been reluctant to impose the views of the CoS during the 1981 Defence Review. Certainly he chaired meetings of CoS throughout Operation Corporate with a fastidious courtesy and consideration for his colleagues. But his clarity of purpose and will were dominant. In more than 30 years near the centre of the MoD I cannot recall a more dominant, professional and influential performance by a senior officer or official.

It was clear to most of us that in future significant operations it would be necessary for the CDS of the day to maintain the grip and exercise the influence which Admiral Lewin achieved during Operation Corporate. To achieve this he would need the support within MoD of operational planning and logistic staffs properly integrated on a tri-service basis; a HQ permanently established on a similarly joint basis, and commanders at every level educated, trained and accustomed to perform effectively in a joint environment. The internal 'lessons learned report' in November 1982 pointed to the problems of physically separated operations, logistics and movements staff, which was not finally overcome until the opening of the PINDAR complex in the early 1990s. It also called for 'examination of the need for a properly constituted Joint HQ in the UK to command OOA operations together with the creation and tasking of a 2-star joint HQ to command such operations overseas'. My recollection is that the authors would have cast their recommendation in less equivocal terms were they not inhibited by the well-known hostility to such an initiative from the CoS.

As we know, turning this aspiration into the PJHQ reality took some time. Organisational change came more quickly on other fronts. Michael Heseltine's review of defence organisation in 1984 (Cmnd. 9315) concluded:

> This country's experience of modern warfare – most recently the Falklands Campaign – has progressively demonstrated the need for the Services to be equipped and trained to fight together...At the heart of the present review therefore has been the recognition that future policy for each Service must be shaped increasingly with a common defence programme.

247

This represented a further significant step along the road to a fully integrated central staff with responsibility for policy, force structure definition, and allocation of resources, which was continued under the PROSPECT study in 1990, the DCS in 1993 and the Strategic Defence Review in 1997/98. The mechanisms for joint command of operations and for joint command and staff training were evolving more slowly. In 1994, in the context of the DCS it was decided to establish the PJHQ. Given the passage of time, this cannot be claimed as a consequence of the Falklands campaign; perhaps the success of Operation Corporate encouraged resistance. Certainly the individual services were inclined to argue that non-NATO operations could effectively be run by designating the most appropriate of the single-service operational commands (Fleet Command, Land Command or Strike Command), to provide the joint commander. Thus C-in-C Strike fulfilled this role in Operation Granby in 1991, and C-in-C Land exercised higher command of operations in the Balkans until 1997. Throughout this period the belief remained strong that it was important to the effectiveness and buzz of those single-service HQs to have responsibility for 'live operations', as well as for the day-to-day management and training of the units under their command. In the event it was not until the Cold War was over, and NATO's command arrangements were no longer exclusively the expected framework for demanding operations, that the PJHQ was established.

The MoD made some acknowledgement of lessons for its procurement processes form Corporate. The 'Lessons Learned' White Paper noted that urgent requirements were accommodated with shorter lead times, and with the acceptance of lower engineering and safety standards. These experiences were useful in the MoD's continuing quest for a more efficient and cost-effective procurement process. The report went on to say that there was a good case for considering whether some of the streamlined procedures introduced in the Falklands campaign could be introduced into the normal peacetime procurement processes. Procurement processes have continued to evolve over time culminating in our current Smart Acquisition initiative with the aim to provide equipment 'Faster, Better, Cheaper'.

THE PRESS AND THE MEDIA

There can be no doubt about the crucial importance of the media in the Falklands Campaign, and the Government made a considerable effort to influence the media's presentation of the causes and conduct of both the diplomatic and military campaign. It was important that international opinion, particularly in the United States, should perceive the British Government's cause, and response to the invasion, to be legitimate. It was vital that the world should see the UK to be making genuine and tireless efforts to co-operate with successive diplomatic attempts to resolve the dispute without conflict. If the United States Government had in the end adopted a different and less benign approach to the British cause, the outcome might have been different. Finally, it was crucial that British parliamentary and public opinion should support the campaign and have confidence in the eventual outcome. In the event, this dimension of the campaign was largely successful. But the House of Commons Defence Committee nevertheless heavily criticised the MoD's handling of the media during Operation Corporate.

There is no doubt that relations between MoD staff and the press were occasionally fraught. One of the civilian press officers who accompanied the Task Force south commented:

> The open warfare between the MoD and press which broke out during the Falklands campaign should not have come as a surprise. It could have been avoided, but we had ignored the lessons of history. Dislike of the press was endemic, the business of press relations was distasteful, and Public Relations had been under-resourced for too many years. The military in general and the Royal Navy in particular was conservative, arrogant, patronising, unnecessarily restrictive, and paranoically secretive. The press was anarchic, irresponsible, belligerent, rude, bloody-minded, suspicious (too often with good cause) of 'security', and determined to confront 'censorship'. Serious hostilities were inevitable.

Whatever else they caused, the frictions during the campaign and the post-mortem afterwards forced a sea-change in attitude. We now accept that handling the press is an unavoidable essential of operations in the modern world. Over the years since 1982, the Green Book on media arrangements during operations has been produced and gradually refined. Six junior-grade civilian information officers sailed with the Falklands Task Force in 1982. When the Gulf War broke out eight years later, a Brigadier and a team of senior officers and officials were dispatched to the region to prepare media handling plans which eventually involved over 60 military and civilian personnel headed by fistfuls of Colonels and Grade 7 civil servants. The press still whinged and complained, threw temper tantrums and considered it their duty to 'break the rules', but it worked.

Arguably it worked even better less than two years later during the early stages of the Balkan involvement, even to the irritation of coalition partners. In Bosnia and Croatia, the international media's preference for the experienced and more efficient British media-handling organisation led to complaints to home governments by national media contingents and was at least partially responsible for the greater coverage given by some foreign press to the British contingent than to their own.

During almost continuous operational deployments throughout the 1990s, we have continued to refine what we now call Media Operations, and practices up to and including the Falklands campaign now lie in the distant past. Within the MoD, procedures have been established to produce policy which is co-ordinated not only between ourselves and the Armed Forces but also the rest of Government, not least 10 Downing Street. A Joint Services Doctrine on media operations has been written and disseminated. The Services maintain rosters of identified and qualified personnel available for deployment. A start has been made on a dedicated training programme. When overseas operations involving British forces are initiated these days, PJHQ has an established and well-oiled procedure which, in consultation with Director General of Corporate Communication (DGCC) in the Ministry and the appropriate single-service Commands, rapidly puts together an appropriate organisation tailored for the particular emergency.

Today we tend to forget that the Falklands campaign in 1982 was the first time that Britain had been to war, in the full all-arms conventional and national sense, since Suez in 1956. In the intervening 27 years the modern media had developed in all its glory and we were not ready for what was our first modern media war. Our level of experience today is very different.

CONCLUSION

So what do I conclude were the consequences of the Falklands Conflict for the evolution of British defence policy, in its immediate aftermath and subsequently? First, it did not immediately transform our assessment of the threats and risks to British security, nor our perception of the role of British Armed Forces. The conventional wisdom at the time was that it was a 'one-off' crisis and operation. It was not thought by the MoD to have seriously challenged the conclusions of the Nott Review, which emphasised the NATO commitment in the European theatre, and reduced the surface Fleet and its priority relative to other roles and Armed Forces. We did not immediately conclude that we should make the necessary investment to renew the specialist shipping to sustain an amphibious capability. There were concessions to the view that the surface Fleet had much to offer as a flexible instrument of power projection, but we should not exaggerate them. Command Paper 8288 envisaged that the number of destroyers and frigates would decline from 59 to about 50. Over the next decade the figure became about 40 ships and today we plan on slightly more than 30 ships.

It was the end of the Cold War which catalysed a gradual redefinition of defence objectives and the means to sustain them. It was in the 1990s that we reformulated the three defence roles, and began to emphasise the expeditionary capability of the Armed Forces. The Statement on Defence Estimates 1993 was the first to publish the new approach to our analysis of defence policy, missions, and tasks, Force structures and the resources necessary to sustain them. In this analysis, we identified Defence Role Three as being 'to promote the UK's wider security interests through the maintenance of international peace and stability'. The subsequent attribution of force elements to the tasks implied by Defence Role Three was an explicit recognition of the possible demands of expeditionary operations and our ability to meet them. It was not until this Government's 1997/8 Strategic Defence Review that final decisions were taken on the next generation of aircraft carriers, and some of the more important enablers of expeditionary operations. And these decisions were taken against the assumption that such operations would invariably be conducted in coalition with allies – a very different context to Operation Corporate.

That said, the lessons learned from Operation Corporate certainly informed a number of important strands of defence policy, force definition, and organisational development. The development of joint staffs in the MoD to support the CDS's role in operations, and the Secretary of State's requirement for a joint approach to Force definition and development were certainly influenced by our experience of Operation Corporate. Our understanding of the importance of public and international opinion, and the requirements of managing the interface with press and media was another key lesson upon which we acted in the years following the Falklands Conflict. C2 outside the MoD developed more slowly, but we do now have the PJHQ, contingent arrangements for joint force command, and arrangements at the centre of government which are more flexible, robust and tested by real-life crises in a way that was simply not true in the 1970s. We also have joint doctrine and joint command and staff training in the way we used not to have. Our experience of procuring items of equipment, and modifications to aircraft, ships and other weapons systems during the Falklands Conflict has certainly informed our approach to peacetime procurement since then.

All of these things are important, and our experience of the Falklands Conflict was important to the way we tackled them. But I conclude by reaffirming that the most important influence of the Falklands Conflict on British defence policy was its effect on the confidence of British governments and the British people in the quality and effectiveness of their Armed Forces, And in the self-confidence of those Armed Forces themselves.

NOTES

1. John Nott, *Here Today Gone Tomorrow: Recollections of an Errant Politician* (London: Politico's, 2002), p. 208.
2. Margaret Thatcher, *The Downing Street Years* (London: HarperCollins, 1993; paperback edition, 1995), pp. 173–4.

18

Air Power: Strategic Lessons from an Idiosyncratic Operation

GROUP CAPTAIN PETER W. GRAY

Learning lessons from history – no matter how recent – is always a fraught exercise. It is, however, an essential one, not least because the sceptics, critics and other commentators will rarely be slow to offer criticism against those who shirk this task.[1] Nevertheless, General John Jumper, now Chief of the United States Air Force, advised in an article in the *Royal Air Force Air Power Review* that one should be very wary of drawing generic lessons from an idiosyncratic campaign.[2] General Jumper's comments were made in the context of Operation Allied Force (the air operations over Serbia and Kosovo in 1999), but arguably could be taken to apply to any conflict at any scale of activity.

It could very well be suggested that these sentiments were particularly applicable to the Falklands campaign. Military strategy at the time was predicated, almost exclusively, on NATO, the Warsaw Pact and the conduct of the Cold War.[3] An expeditionary operation to the far side of the world to regain sovereignty over a relic of Empire was neither envisaged, planned for, nor considered to be a precedent for the future. Air power advocates were content to note the campaign and then return to the apparent comfort zone of the Central Region and the North Atlantic. Strategic effect meant nuclear – or the projection of air power over long distances. The potential of having an *effect* – beyond obliteration – on the target regime was not an issue. By the same token, air defence involved peacetime policing of the United Kingdom Air Defence Region and of the German border. Harrier and helicopter support to the army in Germany (and elsewhere) was very much normal business. And the ground attack squadrons understood their targets, routes and airspace co-ordination details in minute detail. Logistics were predicated upon fortress stockpiles with massive reinforcement from the United States.

Exercises followed a well-trodden path of no-notice counter-surprise events or gradual build-up scenarios culminating in nuclear and/or chemical attack. Most were conducted from home bases with deployment exercises, again well scripted and rehearsed. Force development and equipment procurement were, likewise, predicated upon countering the Soviet threat. Expeditionary operations were viewed with considerable suspicion, as an anachronistic hankering for days of Empire; there was no scope for budgetary provision.

Yet, a mere 20 years on, and particularly after the al-Qaeda attacks on the United States on 11 September 2001, it is the Cold War that appears the more idiosyncratic. Iraq's invasion of Kuwait in 1990 and the dissolution of Yugoslavia shattered the symmetry and, at the same time, heralded an era of confusion, of peacekeeping and of the need to be seen to be doing something wherever the media highlighted the latest scenes of catastrophe. The strident clamour for peace dividends both complicated the issue and considerably retarded the transition to a reactive and mobile defence posture.

On the political stage, the Cold War was played as though it was an intricate, slow and ponderous game of chess. Deterrence required stalemate – not swift victories or militarily achievable end-states. The sophisticated cut and thrust that characterised the work of the United Kingdom Permanent Representative to the UN during the Falklands dispute was not only a step change, but was also a hugely important portent for the strategic post-Soviet era. The utility of the UN as a potent means for the resolution of international disputes is outside the scope of this chapter. What is directly relevant, however, is the inextricable linkage between political aspirations and the option of utilising military means as one of the strategic levers of power. The immediacy of the Falklands conflict left Prime Minister Thatcher with a compelling need to withdraw military assets from NATO commitments, either leaving gaps or prevailing upon Allies to backfill on our behalf. The demise of the Warsaw Pact resulted in more recent Prime Ministers having the greater luxury of contributing to coalitions of the willing with fewer strategic, political and resource restrictions.

This chapter does not purport to be a narrative history of the use of air power during the Falklands campaign of 1982.[4] Nor is it an exposition of the strengths and weaknesses of either side, or indeed of the inter-service aspects at play between the air elements of the RAF and RN. Rather, the chapter looks at the key, or core, capabilities of air power that were used during the conflict and seeks to analyse what high-level – or strategic – lessons could have been identified and may have relevance in today's openly expeditionary era.[5]

254

AIR POWER AND JOINT OPERATIONS

At the outset it is worth emphasising that air power is an inherent and essential element of any joint campaign. Arguably, this has been true for the vast majority of air power history. It is, however, not an unreasonable suggestion that joint, and/or combined, operations have suffered somewhat from inconsistency in the extent to which they have been joint merely in name. The Second World War saw 'jointery' fluctuate from true co-operation between commanders to examples of open animosity. To take but one example, Montgomery worked well with his airmen in the desert, but by Normandy, egos had taken over with disastrous consequences for co-operation. During the Cold War, potential operations were considerably more 'stove-piped' than they would need to be in the Falklands, and in more recent expeditionary operations. This may seem to be a glimpse of the blindingly obvious in the twenty-first century, but 'jointery' – as a formally recognised aspect of military art – was in relative abeyance in 1982. The CJO runs current operations in the PJHQ at Northwood. This organisation did not exist during the Falklands campaign and the Defence crisis management organisation had to cobble together the C2 aspects of the campaign as it went along. The road to 'purple' operations was given considerable impetus from the experiences of 1982.[6] As well as the PJHQ, purple initiatives have seen real power in the MoD going to truly joint Central Staffs; completely joint Command and Staff training; a joint Helicopter Command; and with particular resonance from the Falklands perspective, the formation of Joint Force Harrier.[7] Some may argue that the route to jointery was inevitable – not only doctrinally, but also in terms of economies of scale. Nevertheless, the strategic lessons from the Falklands campaign considerably accelerated the process.

COMBAT SUPPORT AIR OPERATIONS

Going back to the wise advice of General Jumper, the one lesson that he did invite us to learn from Allied Force was that we ignore Combat Support Air Operations at our peril. In this core capability we include such activities as AAR; strategic and tactical airlift (including support helicopters); air surveillance and reconnaissance; electronic warfare; suppression of enemy air defences (SEAD); and the elements of combat search and rescue and deployed search and rescue.[8] Again, it may seem empirically obvious that an operation spanning supply lines in excess of 8,000 miles would need considerable provision of strategic lift (air and sea). Yet traditionally the 'trash-hauling' element of air power has suffered from under-investment and overuse. The air bridge between the UK, Ascension Island and subsequently the airfield at Stanley was (and continues to be) vitally important.

The tactical element of the airlift equation can be broken into two parts. The use of support helicopters is the easier to deal with in that the considerably enhanced mobility that they provide on the battlefield is at once obvious. The loss of the container ship (*Atlantic Conveyor*) carrying a substantial proportion of the Chinook helicopter force had serious consequences at the tactical level and the operational level (where battle tempo was considerably slowed). This, combined with the losses following the attacks on the Fleet Auxiliaries *Sir Tristram* and *Sir Galahad*, came very close to having real strategic consequence. The second element of the tactical scene is more complex. It highlights the doctrinal differences in the use of 'tactical' and 'strategic'. Traditionally, the C130 Hercules has been considered to be a tactical asset – especially when used within a pre-determined theatre of operations. The complicating factor in 1982 was that the theatre dimensions were of strategic proportions. Probably of more utility would be to use the definitions prevalent today in which 'strategic', 'operational' and 'tactical' are used to refer to the level of war at which the military effect is intended to apply. This therefore takes the designation away from being platform-specific and allows us to focus on the importance of the activity. The use of the most appropriate platform for the insertion of special forces brings this distinction into close focus. C130 Hercules para-drops or support helicopters can be used in these operations with the full range of effects from local tactical engagements through to strategic reconnaissance.

At its simplest, AAR extends the range, time-on-task and flexibility of air power. Where take-off performance is critical AAR also provides the scope to utilise fully the weapons payload, on the basis that fuel can be topped up later. This can be particularly relevant with Carrier operations. During the Falklands, AAR made a range of operations feasible that could not otherwise have been contemplated. These vary from Nimrod maritime surveillance sorties, through C130 operations to the routine delivery of F4 Phantoms for the air defence of Ascension Island. Some of the most stunning AAR planning ever contemplated was ably put into practice with the 'Black Buck' sorties in which Vulcan bombers attacked the runway at Stanley and, subsequently, radar units in that vicinity.[9]

Military planners and strategists – whether of the armchair variety or otherwise – will be familiar with many of these concepts and their importance. Contemporary operations have demonstrated the vital importance of Combat Support Air Operations. The importance of heavy airlift capacity has been obvious during Allied Force operations with the movement of Task Force Hawk – Apache helicopters from Germany to Albania taking literally hundreds of C17 sorties to accomplish. In United States planning terminology, the airlift bill alone changed the whole campaign from small-scale contingency to the level of theatre war. Operation Enduring Freedom resulted in a similar scale of effort with movement of personnel and materiel to the Middle East and thence to Afghanistan. The need for movement within theatre – whether conventional or special forces – again highlights the need for lift. More specifically, the use of air power as an enabler for special forces who, in turn, enable direct offensive air power operations, highlights the precedent set in 1982.

Similarly, the widespread use of AAR is evident now in support of, *inter alia*, USAF B2 bomber sorties from mainland America to Serbia and back. While these sorts of mission are now commonplace, they were only envisaged during the Cold War in the deterrent mode.

CONTROL OF THE AIR

Control of the air has been a fundamental element of the use of air power since October 1914 when it was found to be of paramount importance to deny the enemy sight of what was on your side of the hill. The date chosen reflects the first confirmed air-to-air kill. From that date onwards, conflict consistently showed that control of the air had to be fought for, achieved and then maintained. Land, sea and air commanders have ruefully attested to the penalties of failing to achieve this mastery. The Cold War maintained the demand for control of the air with spiralling costs for aircraft and weapons systems. The legacy of programmes – some of which have yet to be delivered – is testimony both to the need and to the momentum that was generated. Ironically, these programmes and their vast costs, allied with recent experience, have served to bring the concept into some disrepute. To the cynics looking no further back than the Gulf in 1991 or Kosovo in 1999, control of the air no longer has to be fought for – it is automatically conceded in the face of overwhelming United States superiority.

The reality, however, is that the lessons of Dunkirk, Normandy and the Falklands are forgotten at the peril of those who have to suffer without such superiority. More subtly, and again taking the examples from Dunkirk and the Falklands, the reliance on total superiority is misleading. These two specific campaigns highlight what can be done – or undone – in situations of air parity. The perception is that, in the former operation,

257

the RAF was absent from the fray; this does no justice whatsoever to those who fought above the beaches at the peak times thereby ensuring that the Luftwaffe was limited in the damage that it could inflict. The reality, therefore, was that air parity prevented the Germans from carrying out uninhibited operations over the beaches – and, more importantly, over the harbour mole and surrounding area. That this air parity was limited in time and space is a reality of warfare.

During the Falklands campaign control of the air was evident in three discrete areas. The first of these was over Ascension Island where F4 Phantoms provided complete air defence should the Argentine air force have contemplated some form of asymmetric attack on the airhead. By the same token, the Argentine Junta felt obliged to provide their mainland and capital with the same level of protection following the Vulcan raids on Stanley. The final, and most contentious, area was over the Falkland Islands themselves where Sidewinder-equipped Harriers and Sea Harriers were able to prevent Argentine dominance. Having anticipated losses to Sea Dart, the Argentine Air Force soon learned that the air-to-air threat was the more potent, accounting for some 90 per cent of their losses.[10] These successes did not imply air superiority but, at the very least, air parity and again this was limited in time and space.

AIRPOWER FOR STRATEGIC EFFECT

The potential for the use of air power for strategic effect has been one of the most contentious issues in the history of flight. The various theories and counter-theories of the strategic use of air power have already filled innumerable pages. Authors have invariably felt that they are bound to cover the story of the birth of the RAF and its subsequent fight for survival. Some versions of the story have been the result of scholarly research while others have been rather superficial with selective analysis chosen to complement the theme of the host book.[11] The essence of the plot is that Trenchard inherited (from his rival, and fellow CAS, General Sir Frederick Sykes) a plan for a bombing strategy aimed at dislocating the enemy's key industries. Trenchard's position gradually switched from implacable opposition (based on the impracticalities of the scheme) to fulsome support. Trenchard heavily emphasised the damage that air attack could wreak on enemy morale. He believed wholeheartedly that air power must be used as an offensive weapon and that the defence of the UK could best be achieved by hitting the enemy so hard that he had to reallocate valuable offensive resources to the defence of the homeland. His emphasis on the importance of offensive action has remained a constant theme in the history of air power thinking.[12] The benefit of forcing the enemy to increase his investment in defence was also seen during the bomber offensives in both World Wars.[13]

The very survival of the fledgling Air Force was also understandably high on Trenchard's agenda. As post-First World War budgets were slashed, the RAF needed its own, distinct, role. If air power was primarily in support of land and naval forces, assets could be redistributed with an appropriate saving in organisation costs – and then the junior service would probably be allowed to wither on the vine. The strategic bombing role offered both a lifeline for the RAF and a cudgel with which to beat its sister services in the scrimmage for funding. As this was a continuing process, the concept of strategic bombing became embedded in the RAF psyche, particularly under the charismatic leadership of 'Boom' Trenchard. The vision of strategic bombing, in which fleets of invincible aircraft would strike terror into the hearts of the enemy populace causing their total collapse, was not, however, borne out by the technological realities of the inter-war years – or even until the advent of nuclear weapons.

In practical terms, however, the RAF needed a role in which air power could be utilised and developed in parallel with the mantra of strategic bombing. The use of aircraft for imperial policing provided this outlet.[14] Notwithstanding some of the more bellicose sentiments expressed over the strategic bombing concept, it was evident in the execution of the policing duties that causing widespread casualties was not the aim. In fact, Sir John Slessor makes it plain in his description of operations that efforts were made to avoid such an outcome.[15] Briefings to the RAF Staff College over the inter-war years highlight the pragmatic approach to real operations. Colonel Philip Meilinger quotes a presentation by Tedder in 1934 to describe the doctrine as being an air strategy for paralysis – not obliteration.[16] This description is particularly apposite in the light of the relevant chapter in the newly issued third edition of *AP 3000*.[17]

British Air Power Doctrine recognizes a single centre of gravity at the strategic and operational levels, but not in the tactical arena (unlike other forces that accept a number of centres at each of the higher levels). This effect could theoretically be created by independent and distinct use of air power alone, or, more likely, it will be part of joint or multi-national activity. Air operations for strategic effect are aimed at destroying or disrupting the defined strategic centre of gravity of an opponent.[18] It is worth emphasising at this point that the *effect* sought by the use of air power may not necessarily be the physical destruction of the chosen target set. Indeed, the centre of gravity may not be the enemy's army (which Clausewitz saw as being the natural choice), or a physical entity; it may be as ephemeral as a despot's ability to further his family's fortunes and influence. Warden has suggested that attacking the leadership of a foe could lead to strategic paralysis, thereby possibly obviating the need for attacks on fielded forces.[19] Air assets other than attack aircraft may, however, be involved in strategic air operations. Activities such as supervision of a no-fly zone or the provision of relief supplies may have strategic effect, depending on the circumstances prevailing at the time.

The objective of strategic air operations, consistent with the tenets of manoeuvre warfare, is to shatter the enemy's cohesion and will – not just to destroy men and materiel. Target sets will have been selected, as part of the estimate process, for their strategic relevance and may include the machinery of government, military forces, infrastructure and so on. Given the flexibility of air power, other targets at the operational and tactical levels may be attacked in parallel with, or subsequent to, strategic operations. The target sets at this high level of operations, and the weapons proposed, will inevitably excite considerable political, legal and humanitarian interest in the highest spheres of governmental machinery. Whilst the military preference is for the espousal of a clear political aim followed by centralised planning and then decentralised execution, it is entirely proper in a democratically accountable structure that political oversight is maintained. This is bound to be most appropriate, and most contentious, at the strategic level. The possible necessity of maintaining coalition solidarity may make this aspect of an operation or campaign particularly fraught.

A study of the historical uses of air power at the strategic level suggests a number of possible lessons that may influence coalition planning. The actual shock of aerial bombardment may be sufficient on its own to influence the target government – particularly if the intended victim has been sceptical as to the will of his foe. The psychology of this type of operation is at best hugely difficult and, more probably, such that each case is *sui generis*. The actual effect of the attack, rather than just the damage assessment, is extremely difficult to assess, particularly if it has been accompanied by information operations. The US operation against the Gaddafi regime in 1986 is held by some to have been successful in its shock effect; but it is by no means certain that Operation Eldorado Canyon did little more than force Libya to be more covert in its support for terrorism.[20]

A concerted bombing offensive can have a profound effect on a target population. In a democratic state, with open media, this may result in increased pressure on the ruling elite. In any event it may well force the target government to reallocate scarce assets to defence of the homeland.[21] The less accountable the leadership of the target state, however, or the more 'total' the war, the less likely they are to bow to public opinion. Furthermore, measuring 'public morale' is hardly a scientific art in any country let alone one that is subject to police control, censorship and propaganda.

The 'Black Buck' series of Vulcan raids on the Falkland Islands were ostensibly aimed at denying the Argentine Air Force the use of the runway at Stanley for C130 Hercules re-supply operations. Subsequent sorties were flown against radar sites on high ground on the islands. Critics have suggested that the damage wrought was minimal. At the simplest level, this betrays a lack of understanding of how runways (and airfields more generally) are targeted. Using a single bomber, the aim must be to put the 'stick' of bombs across the runway at a shallow angle – usually about 15 degrees. The centre of the 'stick' should cross the runway at about the two-thirds point with, in the ideal world, the remainder of the bombs striking support infrastructure. This is exactly what was achieved.

More important than the physical damage caused by the Black Buck raids was the stunning demonstration of the UK's determination and capability. It was immediately evident to the Argentine Junta that if the Vulcans could reach the Falkland Islands, they could also reach the mainland. This led directly to the redeployment of the Mirage 3 Squadron back to the north, where they could better protect the capital.[22] This was also the reality in 1944 where control of the air was not won – as Leigh-Mallory had thought – in a major battle of fighters over Normandy. Rather, the battles took place during a protracted period over the heartland of Germany. The need to defend the homeland is paramount. The Black Buck raids therefore had a profound and material *effect* on the Junta, far beyond the damage. This provides what should be regarded as a classic use of air power for strategic effect.

CONCLUSIONS: ENDURING LESSONS

For much of the decade that followed the Falklands conflict, air power theorists - like most other analysts – considered the campaign to be an aberration, a distraction from the routine conduct of the Cold War. Twenty years after the event, the realities of trying to conduct smaller-scale expeditionary operations over considerable distances have almost become the norm. The Cold War could be summarised as an era in which we procured to deter (or survive). If deterrence (and diplomacy) failed and conflict ensued, the lessons-learned process would almost certainly have been irrelevant. Logistics and stockpiles were, arguably, for 'window dressing' rather than use. The Falklands campaign showed that weapons had to be used, had to work and then had to be replaced. These were lessons that were relearned during the Gulf War and subsequently in Operation Allied Force. In short, we now have to procure to operate – for real.[23] This represents the first strategic lesson that could be drawn from events in 1982.

The second lesson is again a recurring one. Expeditionary operations require substantial investment in combat support air operations – AAR, support helicopters, air transport and the like. This may not be the glamorous end of air power, but it is nonetheless vital. That these operations have been an unloved, yet integral, part of the military use of aircraft since its inception emphasises the importance.

Control of the air has likewise been a critical facet of air operations – and indeed of all joint operations – since 1914. It is axiomatic that control of the air is not just the preserve of fighter aircraft. In virtually every operation there will be a need for a joint air defence 'matrix' involving all assets. Furthermore, all units must be aware of the tactics, procedures and technology in use to ensure air space is controlled and deconflicted; failure to do so will almost inevitably result in blue-on-blue incidents. The Falklands campaign provided a useful, albeit painful, lesson that control of the air must never be taken for granted; nor should it be assumed that control will be ceded. Notwithstanding the paucity of assets, and the range over which they were operating, the success achieved in hindering Mirage and Skyhawk activity provides eloquent testimony to the reality that air parity is still a very potent element in the spectrum of control of the air. A critical lesson that emerges from this is that if anything short of air supremacy is in prospect, the joint planning team must ensure that they are of one mind in determining when air parity should be sought.

Effects-based operations can mean differing things to different people. For example, if the desired effect is to put a power station out of operation, this can be done in two ways. The first would be to destroy the control room. Alternatively, the whole edifice could be razed to the ground. The effect is the same, but with the latter taking more aircraft and ordnance and putting more crews at risk. Furthermore, the rebuild in the ensuing peace is a more formidable challenge! Alternatively, effects-based operations can be iterated on the basis of the number of targets that an individual platform can attack (rather than the Second World War version where huge numbers of aircraft were required for each target).[24] UK doctrine prefers the emphasis to be on the effect that an attack has on the target decision-making system. This requires a real understanding of what the regime itself considers to be important (vice what our own centric vision thinks). It may also be difficult to measure, but this does not detract from what may actually be a war-winning approach. This was not the case with the use of the Black Buck sorties during the Falklands campaign, but the importance of the impact on the regime should not be underestimated. Furthermore, the withdrawal of the Mirage Squadrons highlights the air power reality that control of the air is not necessarily won directly over the battlefield. Trenchard would have been proud!

NOTES

1. For further discussion on the role of history, see the author's essay in P.W. Gray (ed.), *Military History into the 21st Century*, Strategic and Combat Studies Occasional Paper 43, December 2001.
2. General John Jumper, 'Kosovo Victory', *Royal Air Force Air Power Review*, 2/4 (Winter 1999). General Jumper was Commander of the United States Air Forces in Europe during Allied Force and therefore had a privileged, grandstand viewpoint.
3. See, for example, David Reynolds, *Britannia Overruled: British Policy and World Power in the 20th Century* (London: Longman, 1991), pp. 259 and 261.
4. For more detail see Max Hastings and Simon Jenkins, *The Battle for the Falklands* (London: Pan, 1983) and Admiral Sandy Woodward (with Patrick Robinson), *One Hundred Days: The Memoirs of the Falklands Battle Group Commander* (London: HarperCollins, 1992).
5. For a full description of the contemporary definitions of the core capabilities of air power see *AP 3000, British Air Power Doctrine*, 3rd edn (London: HMSO, 1999), Part 2.
6. Joint activity is labelled 'purple' from the mixing of Army red with the dark and light blue of the other two services.
7. At the time of the conference for which this paper was prepared, the author was Assistant Director for Joint Warfare in the MoD and had taught on the staff of the Higher Command and Staff Course.
8. *AP3000*, Chapter 8.
9. Dr Alfred Price, 'Black Buck to the Falklands', *Royal Air Force Air Power Review*, 5/2, (Summer 2002) for a useful description.
10. See the accompanying air power chapter in this book by a Mirage 5 pilot of the time – now Brigadier General Horacio Mir Gonzalez, 'An Argentine Airman in the South Atlantic' (Chapter 7 above).
11. For an example of the former see Air Vice Marshal Tony Mason, *Air Power: A Centennial Appraisal* (London: Brasseys, 1994), Chapters 1 and 2.
12. R.J. Overy, *The Air War 1939–1945* (New York: Stein and Day, 1980), p. 15.
13. Ibid., p. 121. See also Tami Davis Biddle, 'British and American Approaches to Strategic Bombing: Their Origins and Implementation in the World War II Combined Bomber Offensive', in John Gooch (ed.), *Air Power Theory and Practice* (London: Frank Cass, 1995), p. 98.
14. See David Omissi, *Air Power and Colonial Control: The Royal Air Force 1919–1939* (New York: St Martins).

15. John C. Slessor, *The Central Blue* (London: Cassell, 1956), p. 62.
16. Philip S. Meilinger, 'Trenchard and "Morale Bombing" The Evolution of Royal Air Force Doctrine before World War II', *Journal of Military History*, 60/2 (April 1996), p. 264.
17. *AP3000*, Chapter 6.
18. Ibid., p. 261.
19. John A. Warden III, *The Air Campaign* (New York: to Excel, 1998); the original version was first published in 1989 and was highly influential in the Gulf War air campaign.
20. See, for example, Joseph Lepgold, 'Hypotheses on Vulnerability: Are Terrorists and Drug Traffickers Coerceable?' in Lawrence Freedman (ed.), *Strategic Coercion, Concepts and Cases* (Oxford: OUP, 1998), pp. 144–7.
21. Overy, *The Air War 1939–1945*, p. 121.
22. This was confirmed by Brigadier-General Horacio Mir Gonzalez of the Argentine Air Force in the discussion period that followed the presentation of this paper. His recollections of the conflict also form part of this volume (Chapter 7).
23. The cynic would argue that the common theme in all this is that we continue to 'procure to employ'!
24. General David Deptula, 'Air Force Transformation, Past Present and Future', *Royal Air Force Air Power Review*, 5/1, (Spring 2002), p. 8.

19

Falklands Conflict 1982 – The Air War: A New Appraisal

PHILIP D. GROVE

INTRODUCTION

Britain's ability to retake the Falkland Islands in 1982 was centred on a series of strengths and capabilities. One such strength was its successful employment of air power. Outnumbered and thousands of miles from a British air base, Britain was able to support a vast Task Force of over 100 ships, provide air defence, anti-submarine operations, ground support, and a myriad of other duties in a war which many thought impossible. Without this great ability neither the Task Force nor the ground forces would have been successful in their ultimate aim.

But it was with aircraft that Argentina had its best chance of defeating British forces. Seemingly large, well trained and well equipped, the Argentine air forces posed the greatest threat to British success in the South Atlantic. Ultimately, it was whichever side handled and deployed their aerial assets best that would help create the conditions for their nation's overall victory in the conflict.

Yet readily noticeable by the military commanders on the warring sides was the fact that both nations' air forces were operating beyond their publicly and privately accepted capabilities.[1] The Argentine Air Force (Fuerza Aérea Argentina or FAA) had certainly not catered for over-water operations at ranges of over 400 miles. The Argentine Naval Air Arm's Comando Aviación Naval Argentina (CANA) power projection capabilities centred on modernising their only carrier and equipping it with new aircraft. Unfortunately, neither naval programme had been completed by the outbreak of war. Consequently, following its initial support role in the invasion of the Falkland Islands in April and its subsequent aborted strike against the RN Task Force at the start of May, the Argentine carrier spent most of the war in harbour.[2] Thus the CANA were forced to operate from land bases and suffer the same penalties as their land-based cousins. To extend their limited range and eyes both Argentine air forces could rely on only two Hercules air-to-air tankers and remarkably few, but often ingeniously used, over-water reconnaissance aircraft.

Britain surprisingly found itself in a worse situation, as its largest air service, the RAF, was neither mentally nor physically prepared for the operations in the South Atlantic.[3] The RN, which was to bear the brunt of the British air combat, was set to do so with its smallest number of operational aircraft carriers and carrier aircraft since the outbreak of the First World War. At the time of the conflict both of its two operational carriers, HMS *Hermes* and HMS *Invincible*, were cited for disposal as a result of the previous year's defence review.[4] Even more worrying for the Task Force was that on board its carriers were initially just 20 new, untested-in-battle, low payload Sea Harriers. This was an aircraft in which many commentators – service personnel included – did not hold much faith.[5]

The Falklands Conflict, which is increasingly overlooked by air power students and writers, is not simply an interesting occurrence in Britain's post-colonial era, nor the aberration which some commentators would have us believe, but a vital paradigm in the use and misuse of air assets.[6] We can primarily see this through the fact that neither side was judged at the time as being in possession of the correct equipment for successful prosecution of such a campaign as this. Moreover, the ranges within which both protagonists found themselves operating could well hold lessons for the modern world. Additionally, the deployment and use of a number of weapons systems that many thought either obsolete or unsuitable actually found very welcome homes amongst the warring nations. And finally, it should be remembered that it was the first occasion when air services from two Western forces would do battle since the Second World War, and do so in a multi-faceted battlespace.

The conflict is also notable for its employment of a large number of new and untried weapons systems, probably the most famous of which is the Sea Harrier. However, the naval 'jump jet' was only one such example. Both sides deployed a whole range of missiles, their use often resulting in devastating consequences, such as the employment of the Exocet for Argentina and Sea Skua and Sidewinder missiles for Britain. As usual, however, working hand in hand with the new technologies were a number of venerable systems, some operating in new and very testing conditions, whilst other platforms were noticeable by their very absence, such as AEW – an omission which was to have a very profound impact on operations.

Air power alone could not have won the war for Britain, although it might well have done for Argentina. Nonetheless, without the successful employment of air power assets Britain could not have retaken the Falkland Islands. The only truly practical air assets for the British Task Force were those employed and carried by the Task Force, and there were never sufficient numbers of these to have retaken the islands solely through air denial and air bombardment. The land-based machines at Ascension Island, although useful, proved to be too transitory in operation to have any major significance (except in the area of transportation of valuable equipment into the forward operating base area of Ascension and occasionally by air drop to the Task Force).[7] It was, in fact, the employment of the Task Force's air assets in four major areas that made the greatest contributions to victory from air power for Britain in the campaign. In the first place, the fleet was supported and defended throughout the conflict by the continual employment of air assets from the Task Force. Second, through the adoption of attritional tactics and the attempted denial of Argentina's use of the air and sea over and near the Falklands, the Sea Harriers provided bearable conditions for the fleet to prepare for invasion of East Falkland. Third, it was only through the support and defence of the amphibious operations in San Carlos waters against heavy Argentine air opposition – the Battle of San Carlos – that the land contingent could be placed ashore and maintained there. And finally, the continued air support, in many guises, was vital to the advance of British land forces across East Falkland until victory on 14 June.

However, none of this was guaranteed. The British Task Force that sailed on 5 April 1982 would be entering a war zone where the odds and the weather would be against them. In fact, Task Force personnel and commentators alike believed the air threat was going to be in the region of odds of at least 10–1 against the British.

THE AIR THREAT TO THE BRITISH TASK FORCE

Much has been written about the overwhelming preponderance of Argentine air power over the British Task Force. At the start of the campaign it seemed to the services and commentators involved that Argentina's air assets were fearsomely large. Yet in the 'true' light of battle their much vaunted strength now seems somewhat illusory.

Argentina's aircraft did indeed pose the greatest threat to British ambitions in the war. The numbers contained within the ranks of the Argentine air services dwarfed those in the Task Force, and the Argentine pilots were just as accomplished and well motivated as their British counterparts. However, less well known to the British were the problems the South American nation faced with its air services. Initially, much of the knowledge of the air threat to the RN came from shipboard sources, secondhand information and weapons suppliers.[8] Accurate intelligence was in fact woefully lacking in the Task Force, forcing the realisation amongst many that Britain's air strength faced a serious uphill struggle in all respects. At the outbreak of hostilities Argentina possessed the combat aircraft shown in Table 19.1,[9] but as can be seen, far from all would be operational.

Aircraft at the start of the campaign ranged from being in active squadron service to undergoing long-term maintenance or being used as a source of spares for other machines. Besides availability issues, Argentina had other problems. The Daggers of the FAA, for instance, had been only recently delivered from Israel and pilots were still 'working up' on the air-craft, resulting in the Dagger's potential not being fully realised or understood.[10] The same was true for the CANA with their Super Etendards and AM339s, both of which had been delivered only the year before. Impressive as the size of the force might be compared to Britain's seagoing combat strength, there were other important shortfalls. Argentina's true air defence capability rested with only a dozen or so Mirage 3 fighters. Aircraft that would be required not only to engage and defeat the Sea Harrier for air control but also defend Argentina's air space from possible British or

Table 19.1. Argentine combat aircraft during the war

FAA aircraft	On charge	Operational (at start of war)
FAA combat strength		
Mirage 3	15	12 (Grupo 8)
Dagger	37	25 (Grupo 6)
A-4B/C(P) Skyhawk	52	38 (Grupo 4 & 5)
Canberra	10	7–10 (Grupo 2)
Pucará	45	45? (Grupo 3)

CANA aircraft	On charge	Operational (at start of war)
CANA combat strength		
Super Etendard	5	4
A-4Q Skyhawk	10	8
AM339	10	10
S-2 Tracker	6	?
P-2 Neptune	3	2

even Chilean incursions.[11] Thus the RN with its initial 20 Sea Harriers actually had more dedicated fighters in theatre than Argentina, and this was a position which would not alter for the duration of the war.

In fact, the bulk of Argentine air power was concerned with the delivery of ordnance, although there were limitations here as well.[12] One happened to be the inexperience of attacking ships by the FAA pilots. CANA pilots were obviously well versed in anti-shipping strikes but their land-based counterparts were not. To compensate for this an intensive crash course run by CANA personnel was given to AA pilots at the start of the campaign and ultimately proved to be very successful.[13] Notwithstanding attack problems, range was perhaps the most important problem. Argentina's long-range bombing force consisted of some ten operational Canberras.[14] The majority of their aircraft were short-range machines and during the campaign these would be operating at the limit of their endurance. The range of quite a few aircraft types, but not all, could be extended by AAR using a pair of Hercules tankers, but in the end just two tankers would be of limited use. Consequently, the bulk of the Argentine aircraft had very little time on station over the Falkland Islands. This would force Argentina's pilots into using some very unfortunate tactics.

In the battle for air superiority the Mirage 3 was forced by lack of fuel to engage the Sea Harriers at high altitude, an altitude where the Sea Harriers were simply not going to roam. Without large-scale air-to-air engagements between the two main air defence assets the Argentinians effectively gave an element of air control directly to the British at the start of the campaign, without even a shot being fired. In the anti-shipping role, Argentine pilots were obliged to attack the first ships they encountered. They had very little choice as loiter time and slow selection of targets was not an option, owing to British air defences and lack of fuel, forcing them to attack British warships rather than the more valuable amphibious ships and STUFT. There were deficiencies in other areas as well, most notably in maritime reconnaissance and AEW. However, the FAA and CANA adopted ingenious solutions to these problems such as using transports, propeller and jetliner, to shadow the Task Force.[15]

But one area where the Argentine air services proved more than capable was the air-bridge between the contested islands and the mainland. Argentina quickly exploited the use of aircraft for transport in the early days of occupation. In April alone military and civilian aircraft carried into Stanley more than 5,000 tons of cargo and almost 11,000 personnel. This air-bridge was maintained, albeit at a much lower intensity, until the surrender of the Argentine garrison on 14 June.[16]

If the mainland air forces were experiencing a number of problems, what of the Argentine air garrison on the Falklands? Here too, Argentina's numerical strength was not going to pay dividends. The climate and conditions in the Falklands did not suit many of the aircraft and their serviceability began to suffer as the campaign drew on. Argentine aircraft were not used to operating in these conditions nor in fact from their southernmost bases for extended periods during winter months. They were normally based further north in milder conditions. Perhaps of more danger to the garrison's aircraft was British offensive activity, which took its toll on many of the aircraft. Special forces raids, such as the attack against Argentine aircraft at Pebble Island on the night of 14 May, naval gunfire against Goose Green and Stanley, and British air attacks on the capital's airfield all combined to reduce severely the number of available Argentine machines. Additionally, a number of garrison machines fell victim to air-to-air engagements, accidents, British surface-to-air missiles and Argentine friendly ground fire.

On the whole Argentina's Falklands air garrison did not pose a significant threat, although it certainly had the potential. Stocks of air weaponry were large, the pilots' training was generally high and at times the weather perfect and yet very few missions were launched against the ships in San Carlos and the land forces. Any major attacks would have augmented the mainland assault and split British defences, increasing Argentine success and damaging further British efforts.[17] The reasons for this must, for now, be left to speculation. On the other hand, the mobility afforded by a not insubstantial force of helicopters was put to good use in re-supply and general support, particularly towards the end of the campaign, with their remaining helicopters often flying in conditions for which neither their equipment nor training could have prepared them.

At the start of the occupation the Argentinians had considered basing more capable machines in the Falklands. However, following tests with a CANA Skyhawk at Stanley airfield, it was demonstrated that the existing runway was impractical and unsafe for heavily laden modern attack aircraft until adequately extended. This left the combat element of the Falklands garrison as 25 Pucarás of the FAA and ten AM339s and Mentors of the CANA (see Table 19.2).

THE BRITISH AIR WAR

The British did not have the same worries concerning the length of their runways. The pitching, heaving and almost continual sea spray covering them seemed of more importance. The overwhelming bulk of Britain's air

Table 19.2. Strength of the Argentine air
garrison in the Falklands

Type	Service	Number
Pucará[18]	FAA	25
AM339	CANA	6
Mentor	CANA	4
Chinook	Army	2
	FAA	2
Puma	Army	5
	Coastguard	1
Huey	Army	2
	FAA	2
A109	Army	3
Skyvan	CANA	1

missions were flown from the decks of the Task Force, and principally the two carriers, *Invincible* and *Hermes*. The conflict demonstrated the inherent characteristics of aircraft carriers and their vital role in supporting foreign policy beyond a nation's coastline. However, other flight decks would also be utilised on a variety of naval vessels, improvised merchantmen and also from a forward operating strip overlooking San Carlos, HMS *Sheathbill*, which was in operation towards the end of the campaign.

The centrepiece of the Task Force's defensive and offensive capability centred on the Sea Harrier. Harrier aviation was not new. Both the RAF and United States Marine Corps (USMC) had been successfully operating the Harrier for over a decade. What was new was the situation. No Harrier had ever gone to war before, certainly and not least gone to war on the back of ships, and certainly not in the role of fighter, ground attack and reconnaissance platform. Outnumbered, although perhaps not as greatly as many have believed, the Harrier was to be the key to retaking the Falklands. This novel British aircraft would lead the vanguard of Britain's air strength in the South Atlantic.

One of the major problems affecting the Sea Harrier, and all aspects of the British air war, was quantity. Only 20 examples would sail to begin with and, though they would be joined by further Sea Harriers during the campaign and an additional 14 Harrier GR3s of the RAF, lack of numbers continued to be a key aspect in the effort. Yet the RN Sea Harriers were to perform over 1,200 sorties and the RAF machines a further 150. Losses were remarkably few with only six Sea Harriers and four RAF Harriers being lost, of which two Sea Harriers and three

Harrier GR3s were victims of Argentine ground fire. The other machines were lost through accidents and weather-related incidents. None of the Harriers was lost in air-to-air engagements. Sea Harriers accounted for 23 enemy aircraft, 20 resulting from the use of Sidewinders. Contrary to popular belief, the majority of these were 'tailpipe' shots thus not exploiting the better engagement capabilities of the improved Sidewinders delivered from the Americans, and far superior to those of the Argentines or even existing British missiles.[19]

The Harriers also carried out anti-shipping strikes and combat air support (CAS). Initially the CAS role carried out by Sea Harriers but during the conflict the RAF Harrier GR3, specialised in ground attack, would replace the Sea Harriers in the 'mud-moving' capacity, freeing up valuable air defence aircraft for protection of the fleet. However, there were other problems. The lack of range of the Harriers would impact on transit and on-station times, as the British carrier group was forced to remain at a distance from potential air attack. This was made dramatically worse by the lack of a crucial element in any modern air war – AEW. This forced a higher number of Sea Harrier sorties for air defence of the fleet, gave less warning time and saw a number of ships hit by Argentinian aircraft which might otherwise have evaded damage.

Nonetheless, the Sea Harriers performed beyond the expectations of all bar those who really knew the aircraft, even in the area of availability. This was extremely high and amazingly only one sortie was cancelled through unavailability. This is all the more remarkable considering the conditions in which the aircraft were being operated and maintained. It can be seen that the combination of the Sea Harrier's presence and Argentina's own problems with providing air defence assets over the Falklands enabled the air umbrella to be much stronger than many expected.

However, the Sea Harrier and Harrier GR3s, although vital in the successful prosecution of the war, were only one part of the in-theatre aviation assets available to the Task Force. This can be seen from Table 19.3 where the Harriers formed part of a much bigger air fleet composed mostly of helicopters with over 150 from all services.

THE HELICOPTER AT WAR

The Navy deployed helicopters on all of their ships in the South Atlantic that possessed flight decks but perhaps more crucially they were also able to deploy from a large number of merchant ships that had been converted back in Britain as the Task Force mobilised. This enabled more helicopters to be carried in the fleet and provided a degree of redundancy, which was

Table 19.3. Aircraft in the Task Force during the conflict[20]

Type	Service	Number
Sea Harrier	RN	28
Harrier GR3	RAF	14
Sea King	RN	37 HAS2 & 5
		14 HC4
Wessex	RN	54 HU5
		2 HAS3
Lynx HAS2	RN	25?
Wasp HAS1	RN	10?
Gazelle AH1	RM	9 (3CBAS)
	AAC	6 (656 Sqn)
Scout AH1	RM	6 (3CBAS)
	AAC	6 (656 Sqn)
Chinook HC1	RAF	1 (18 Sqn)

especially true and important had an aircraft carrier been hit. Three ships in particular acted as auxiliary helicopter carriers and one, the *Atlantic Conveyor*, also acted as an aircraft transport by bringing Harriers into theatre.[21] The helicopters that flew from these vessels and their more normal platforms performed sterling service to the ships and men of the Task Force, and have often been overlooked since the war. Much has been written about the single RAF Chinook, 'Bravo November', and its use in the Falklands but much less concerning the helicopters of the RN, RM and Army Air Corps (AAC).

The Gazelles and Scouts of the Commando Brigade Air Squadron (CBAS) and 656 Squadron AAC provided crucial air transport, casualty evacuation, reconnaissance and limited fire support for the ground forces, without which the land forces would have sustained considerably higher losses and a war of longer duration. Their lift capacity, although minor compared to larger helicopters, still proved useful. Even the five-seat Scouts were regularly seen carrying seven passengers and two crew. Attempts at employing the Scouts and Gazelles as fire support platforms were, however, not hugely successful, although it did demonstrate what British forces might have achieved had the right equipment been available.[22]

In the end, however, the majority of British helicopters in the Falklands theatre belonged to the RN, with a mixture of Sea Kings, Wessex, Lynx and Wasp. These would give the Task Force a continuous anti-submarine screen (mostly Sea King HAS2 and HAS5), anti-surface

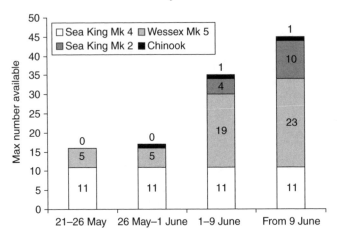

Figure 19.1. British transport helicopter availability.

capability (Lynx HAS2 and some Wasp HAS 1), and vital troop transport capacity. The Navy mobilised second-line units and converted a squadron of anti-submarine tasked Sea Kings into troop transports, whilst also employing all their available Wessex HU5s and Sea King Mk4s for troop and cargo transport (see Figure 19.1).[23] Although numbers were considerable, they were still not enough to give sufficient flexibility to planning or the movement of land forces that was really required or envisaged at the beginning of the campaign.[24]

A serious blow to the war effort was the loss of the MV *Atlantic Conveyor*. When lost following an Argentine Exocet hit she was carrying six Wessex HU5, three Chinook HC1 and one Lynx HAS2 helicopters. The loss of the transport machines was a major blow to the campaign, creating a number of unwanted consequences onto the land operations, forcing the land commanders to amend their plans to take into account the fact that they would have even fewer helicopters than they thought.[25] Another interesting role for some of the Task Force helicopters was the provision of Lynx on board the carriers to provide Electronic Counter Measure (ECM), decoy and jamming platforms for the defence of *Hermes* and *Invincible* against Exocet attacks.

ASCENSION AND RAF SUPPORT

The other aerial assets the British were able to deploy in support of the Task Force and ground forces were, of course, those of the RAF on

Wideawake airfield on Ascension Island. Their impact and roles were at times, like the dramatic Vulcan raids against in the Falklands, very newsworthy and high-profile but it was their lower-profile support services to the fleet and at Ascension Island that were of greater importance to the success in the war. In fact, the first ground crew and aircraft started arriving the day after the Argentine invasion. However, the same factor affected all their aircraft sorties into the operational theatre: their land-based aircraft were all transient machines. Although aircraft regularly spent 18 hours or more in the air for a single sortie, much of this was not 'on-station' time but time travelling to and from their mission zones. They were able to impact on the war only at very specific moments of the conflict owing to limitations of range and lack of air-to-air assets and at times were unable to do even this owing to a series of factors. Ultimately, their forward operating base at Ascension was some 4,000 miles away, making it a very distant forward base indeed.[26]

Nonetheless, the RAF provided transport and tanker forces, maritime patrol and reconnaissance assets, long-range bombers and land-based Phantom fighters for protection of Ascension Island and the American airstrip at Wideawake airfield.[27] The distance to and from Ascension was one of their greatest handicaps, yet they were able to mount a number of drops to the fleet from Hercules aircraft, with Hercules sorties often lasting over 24 hours. More importantly they provided some extra maritime patrol assets via their Nimrod and Victor aircraft, with the Nimrods even being fitted with Sidewinder missiles for self-defence, giving them the not too serious title of being the world's largest fighters.[28] The Victors should be noted for their provision to the naval forces retaking South Georgia in Operation Paraquat of accurate and timely information concerning the island and Argentine dispositions.

All these aircraft required extensive AAR, placing extra pressure and duties on an already stretched asset, and a large number had to be fitted with probes for refuelling for the first time, notably the Nimrod and Hercules fleets. The tankers were constantly required to provide fuel to aerial traffic departing from and arriving at Wideawake from the start of the campaign to a considerable time after its completion. The air-bridge to the island had to be maintained and during the war saw from Britain some 535 sorties from the start to the finish of the hostilities bringing in over 6,000 tons of supplies, 5,500 passengers, nearly 100 vehicles and more than 20 helicopters onto Ascension.[29]

From an offensive point of view the RAF Ascension-based force provided Vulcan bombers for long-range missions against Argentina's garrison in the Falklands. The Vulcan mission on 1 May – often cited as the start of the 'shooting war' – was the first of the 'Black Buck' Vulcan missions and was to have been followed by six others during the campaign.[30] Of the seven planned only six took to the air, a mixture of free fall bombing and Shrike missile anti-radar missions directed against targets on the Falklands. They were hailed at the time as the longest bombing missions in history – now eclipsed by US B-2 missions – for their massive and very complicated refuelling effort and for their impact on the conduct of the war. First, by hitting Port Stanley runway they put the facility out of action for fast jet operations. Second, the ability to target and hit Argentina's mainland was demonstrated, thus forcing the redeployment of a squadron of Mirage aircraft to defend Buenos Aires, denying them the chance to attack British air assets. In fact, neither impact was true.

Stanley runway was not put out of action and was in constant use until the last day of the conflict. More importantly Argentina had no intention of using fast combat aircraft from the runway following tests earlier in April, whilst the diversion of assets away from the air war consisted of just four Mirages for defence of the capital. In fact, of the seven Vulcan missions planned only one saw the target, a radar site, being hit successfully. The cost in terms of fuel, increased strain on air frames and one major diplomatic embarrassment, where a Vulcan landing at Rio de Janerio from lack of fuel, cannot today be seen as a satisfactory return for the effort.

Although in the capacity of power projection the effort was somewhat unsuccessful, the RAF forces at Ascension were ultimately much more important and useful in the air transport and maritime reconnaissance roles. The RAF in the transport role was augmented by two other elements, with aircraft from the US transport force and civilian transporters also providing lift: the aircraft being mostly civilian Boeing 707s and Shorts Belfasts – the latter ironically former RAF machines.[31]

CONCLUSION

It was with a more efficient and flexible use of air power that the British were able to help retake the Falklands in 1982. It would be untrue to argue that they managed to deploy and use their best possible force package. However, they were able to send south a fleet with a very capable fighter, eventually augmented by 'mud-movers', supported by a vast array of helicopters and at times a number of useful land-based sorties. There were deficiencies and problems but in the harsh light of battle it became obvious that these were fewer than Argentina's.

What also became obvious during battle were the problems the RN, Britain and a number of other 'maritime' powers could face whilst they continued to embark upon a new downward spiral of naval funding and government interest. By 1982, with very few exceptions, naval aviation was dying out. In fact, the future of balanced capability navies was also very bleak. Specialisation seemed to offer the best prospect for existence, but in the Falklands War and those that followed it specialisation could prove a folly. Neither specialised navies nor armed forces reliant on a land-based air force could have retaken the Falklands. Both sides in the conflict in the South Atlantic were operating at extreme ranges, and it was demonstrated that the most flexible force and the force capable of coping best with the distances and the force conditions involved would win the war.

It has been called a war of anachronisms by some commentators but in many ways it was a war of the future. The Falklands campaign was a watershed in British (and global) naval air power development. In Britain the domination of a land–air European mentality – which had certainly gripped Britain since the 1960s – had been shown to be inappropriate for a nation with global interests. If Britain only willed and wished to show influence and military power inside the borders of Europe, then the policies and reviews of the previous decades were essentially correct. If, however, Britain wanted to play a more substantial and serious role as it began to do in the 1980s and into the 1990s, then modern, ocean-going maritime air power was going to have to be retained and developed. This point was, and is still true for many nations, and not just Britain.

At the heart of this analysis of the air war during this conflict in the South Atlantic is the recognition that air power alone could not have won the war, but that it remains as one of the vital components for victory. Certainly without the Sea Harriers of the Fleet Air Arm and the other airborne assets of the Task Force, Britain would never have been able to recover the Falklands. Consequently, in the post-war period a series of developments took place to rectify a number of problems seen in the South Atlantic. The three carriers of the *Invincible* class were retained. The Royal Navy's Sea Harrier FRS1 fleet was evolved into the FA2, becoming Europe's most potent single-seat fighter with the weapons and radar fit surpassing all others in NATO outside of the US inventory.[32] The key albeit late creation was the acquisition of an all-important organic AEW platform with the Nimrod Searchwater radar being fitted into Sea Kings in the summer of 1982, a system that has been and continually updated since. And additionally, the RAF Harrier GR3's eventual successor was introduced along with the modernisation of Britain's transport and tanking fleet.[33]

Perhaps more importantly Defence Policy began to shift, albeit slowly. Britain's success in the Falklands demonstrated a strong resolve to the Soviet threat during the 1980s, in and out of Europe. And with the ending of the Cold War at the start of the 1990s Britain was able to start a real reassessment, moving away from what can be seen as the anachronistic and simultaneously 'aberrational' defence policy of the Cold War to a more traditional global maritime air posture. This shift was confirmed in the Strategic Defence Review (SDR) of 1997–8, which along with subsequent statements confirmed future carriers and aircraft to replace the *Invincibles* and Sea Harriers, thus demonstrating Britain's determination to wage war very much along the littoral lines of the Falklands conflict. As such the SDR and subsequent statements served to confirm the strength and relevance of the air lessons contained in the Falklands Conflict for operations in the twenty-first century.

NOTES

1. Both air forces were centred on regional air operations. Defence Statements in Britain's case saw the Soviet Union in Europe as the main threat and accordingly the bulk of aircraft catered for this scenario. See the various Statements on the Defence Estimates 1970 to 1981 (London: HMSO, 1970–81). Meanwhile Argentina saw its land neighbours as the main protagonists, particularly Chile.
2. The Argentine Navy was attempting to envelop Royal Naval ships in a pincer movement involving the *General Belgrano* from the south-west and the *Veinticinco de Mayo* from the north-west. Unfortunately, the carrier could not launch fully laden aircraft owing to her failing catapult.
3. Britain's strategic (if strategic can be seen in terms of range rather than effect here) airlift and attack capability had been run down since the mid-1970s. What was in effect Transport Command had been cut in half and Britain's Vulcan fleet was due for retirement. Their AAR probes had been removed prior to the war.
4. The Nott Review, '*The Way Forward*', in 1981 had earmarked the *Invincible* and *Hermes* for sale. Australia had agreed to buy the *Invincible* and Chile and India were both showing interest in *Hermes*.
5. The real story of the Sea Harriers' capabilities was somewhat different. See Peter E. Davies and Anthony M. Thornborough, *The Harrier Story* (London: Arms and Armour, 1996), John Godden (ed.), *Harrier: Ski Jump to Victory* (Oxford: Brassey's, 1983) and Nigel Ward, *Sea Harrier over the Falklands* (London: Leo Cooper, 1992).
6. Strangely the Falklands air conflict no longer seems to appeal to authors and commentators. For instance S. Cox and P. Gray (eds), *Air Power History: Turing Points from Kitty Hawk to Kosovo* (London: Frank Cass, 2002) fail to mention the Falklands War once, whereas the Gulf War of 1991 is treated to three complete chapters. Tony Mason in his chapter 'The Air Warfare Requirement', in Philip Jarrett, (ed.), *The Modern War Machine: Military Aviation since 1945* (London: Putnam, 2000) dismisses the air war in less than a paragraph, avoids mentioning naval aircraft and

then defines the war as 'an anachronism'. These omissions and sentiments are far from uncommon.

7. Ascension is almost 4,000 miles a way from the Falklands. More importantly, the RAF was orientated against European land threats, the Soviet armies and air forces, operations that required less range capability. Chile and South Africa could also have provided basing for British aircraft but both were politically and strategically unacceptable to the British Government at the time.

8. Initial information was very poor. If the ships and pilots of the Task Force were relying on Jane's publications then they soon realised that late 1970s, early 1980s editions would give them far from the true picture of the enemy threat. *Jane's Aircraft of the World* carried detailed information only about 'current' aircraft, and its air strength information in early years had been out of date, whilst *All the World's Fighting Ships* gave figures for CANA aircraft delivered but not necessarily in service. The International Institute for Strategic Studies' *Military Balance* for 1981–2 was the most accurate of the published and easily available sources but none would be present in the Task Force.

9. Compiled from various American, Argentine, British and Spanish published sources.

10. A Dagger was an Israeli Mirage 5. Not all on order had been delivered. Additionally there were problems with working up and supplies. See Mafe Huertas, S., *Dassault Mirage III/V* (Osprey: London, 1990), pp. 140–63, and Salvador Mafe Huertas, 'Mirage and Dagger in the Falklands', in *Wings of Fame*, vol. 6, (London: Aeropsace Publishing, 1997), pp. 4–27.

11. Even after the first British Vulcan raid on Port Stanley the FAA held back only four Mirage 3s for the air defence of Buenos Aires and surrounding area, but it would have taken a brave British politician to order the bombing of mainland Argentina, thus escalating the war.

12. The aerial power to carry out counter-insurgency operations against communist guerrillas and possible border disputes had established the FAA as a regional power projection force.

13. For ships lost and claims on victories see M. Middlebrook, *Battle for the Malvinas: The Argentine Forces in the Falklands War* (London: Penguin, 1990) and S. Mafe Huertas and D. Donald, 'A-4 Skyhawks in the Falklands', in *Wings of Fame*, vol. 12 (London: Aerospace Publishing, 1998), pp. 4–29.

14. It had been intended that FAA Canberras were to carry out the first Argentine airstrikes against the British. They actually did carry out the FAA's last airstrike. Ironically, prior to 1982 Argentina had shown interest in acquiring a dozen surplus Vulcan bombers from Britain. See J.C. Cicalesi *et al.*, 'Canberras of the Fuerza Aérea Argentina', in *Wings of Fame*, vol. 17 (London: Aerospace Publishing, 1999), pp. 136–47.

15. The FAA became rather adept at using civilian aircraft for reconnaissance; most notably Boeing 707s, Lockheed Electras, HS125s and Learjets.

16. Although there are differences in sources, these are minor and the total transported is seemingly impressive. For instance, by the end of April FAA C-130s and Fokker Fellowships, plus civil aircraft, had transported some 5,000 tonnes of cargo and over 9,000 personnel to the Falklands, while CANA Fellowships and Lockheed Electras brought a further 500 tonnes and another 1,500 personnel.

17. Amazingly, only one MB339 mission was launched against the ships – of one aircraft – and only a handful of Pucará missions were launched on to San Carlos against which the British logistical base certainly found itself ill-defended.

18. Not all the Pucarás were there at any one time, but in total 25 were deployed to the islands.

19. Peter E. Davies and Anthony M. Thornborough, *The Harrier Story* (Annapolis, Md.: US Naval Institute Press, 1996), pp. 91–2.

20. Amazingly even official sources differ on the number of aircraft in theatre. Table 19.3 refers to the total number of aircraft and helicopters deployed to the Falklands and does, represent the air capability at any one time.

21. Merchant ships MV *Astronomer*, MV *Atlantic Causeway* and MV *Atlantic Conveyor* were all converted to act as 'auxiliary' carriers. The *Astronomer* would be retained post-war to become RFA *Reliant*, employing the American containerised Arapaho helicopter handling system.

22. Scout helicopters were fitted to carry the AS12 missile whilst Gazelles had undergone SNEB rocket tests.

23. Julian Thompson, *The Lifeblood of War: Logistics in Armed Combat*, (London: Brasseys, 1991), pp. 373–74 n.21, and information from Major-General Thompson supplied via Mark Grove, who provided data for Figure 19.1. An idea of the requirements involved can be gauged from the fact that to lift a battery of six 105 mm light guns with 480 rounds of ammunition per gun, two half-ton vehicles and crews, took 82 Sea King sorties. Thompson, p. 373.

24. The land force was initially planned to fly to the enemy and battle, and of course be supported by air. This plan had to be altered to include 'yomping' and increased use of coastal shipping movements. That said, the helicopter fleets worked slavishly, the Sea King in particular. The Navy Sea Kings represented only a quarter the air assets in theatre, yet they accounted for half of the Royal Navy's flying time, with over some 12,000 hours out of a total of nearly 24,000 hours. Additionally, serviceability of these machines was consistently over 90 per cent in spite of the atrocious weather.

25. This is discussed elsewhere in the book, but it underlines the point that insufficient transport helicopters were provided to the Task Force. Only one frontline Chinook squadron was operational in Britain at the time of the Falklands. However, there were other assets such as RAF Puma, Wessex and Sea King SAR helicopters available back in Britain. Strangely, it was decided that British Pumas would find the weather conditions unsuitable. Argentina, however, deployed Pumas.

26. The war is often seen as one of great invention and innovation, such as in the area of flight refuelling, and the huge effort to fit probes. Yet some of this was actually refitting, whilst Argentina showed what could be done since some of their C-130s were already flight refuelling capable. The one area where the greatest impact could have been felt was in the area of AEW, but the ageing AEW2 Shackletons (younger than the V bombers) were felt to be too expensive and troublesome to be converted. This was a major failing in Britain's war effort.

27. One RAF Sea King HAR3 was also at Wideawake for SAR and transport duties.

28. Almost 150 Nimrod sorties were carried out with a total flying time of some 1,500 hours.

29. See J.D.R. Rawlings, *The History of the Royal Air Force* (London: Aerospace Publishing, 1984), pp. 306–7; and *AP3000: British Air Power Doctrine*, 3rd edn (London: HMSO, 1999), p. 2.10.9.
30. Of course, the shooting war had already begun in April when the Argentine submarine, *Sante Fe*, had been disabled by RN helicopters in Grytviken harbour during the retaking of South Georgia. Other potential 'shooting war' incidents were a nearly aborted Argentine Canberra bomber mission to South Georgia as it fell to British forces in April, and the launching of aircraft from the *Veinticinto de Mayo* against the Task Force prior to the *Belgrano* being sunk.
31. 'Civil air carriers supplemented the efforts of the RAF Air Transport Force and between April and June transported more than 350 tons of freight, including helicopters, to Ascension Island', *Lessons of the Falklands* (London: HMSO, September 1982).
32. Which it will remain until withdrawn from service in 2006 awaiting a replacement until 2012 and the JSF, leaving an air defence gap for naval operations.
33. The Harrier II from McDonnell Douglas and British Aerospace entered service with the RAF as the Harrier GR5, and has since been upgraded to the GR7 version and is currently undergoing a programme to see itself upgraded and last until 2015 as the Harrier GR9 and GR9A variants.

20

The Development of Joint Doctrine since the Falklands Conflict

MAJOR GENERAL JONATHAN BAILEY AND COLONEL DAVID BENEST

INTRODUCTION

Today we sometimes imagine that we live in times of unprecedented change, pace of change, and stress, both in society as a whole and in the military. We conduct military operations that seemed unthinkable a few years ago; and in the military doctrinal world there is much debate about RMAs, transformations, and keeping abreast of burgeoning new technologies. It is perhaps part of the culture of our day, which attributes unique and special importance to contemporary events. It is all too easy to forget the challenges of 1982. Some people are in danger of writing off the Cold War era as a sterile and predictable period of military affairs, in which doctrine and military thinking became fossilised; a view that is of course unwarranted. In many ways, the challenges for the Armed Forces that existed in the year of the Falklands Conflict were greater than those of today. In particular, in that era the British Army had to focus on Corps-level operations against the very real threat of a military superpower armed with nuclear weapons, and which had demonstrated its aggression in Afghanistan from 1979 onwards.

Far from being fossilised, the British Army of the 1980s like its allies and opponents had to take one particular form of warfare to a high art, driven by one overwhelming strategic imperative. Looking back now, and given the technology of the day, we should express some humility and acknowledge the extraordinarily high standards attained at that time – standards which in many respects we cannot approach today. Not only did the British Army field 1 British Corps on NATO's Central Front, a formation which (albeit with many flaws) was well trained for high-intensity armoured warfare, but we ran an entirely unrelated but very active Internal Security operation with a division of infantry in Northern Ireland, our own 'North West Frontier'. On top of that, and completely out of the blue, Great Britain found itself irrevocably swept up in the vortex of an entirely different expeditionary campaign in the South Atlantic that was as much about national honour as material interest, more maritime–land than air–land, on a vast scale and conducted at an immense distance from home. By comparison, today's challenges may look a little humdrum. In this chapter, we wish to look at the Armed Forces' development of Joint doctrine since 1982, considering 'what the Falklands did for us', and paying tribute to those who planned and led Operation Corporate in 1982.

JOINT DOCTRINE IN THE TWENTIETH CENTURY

As an island nation, all Britain's military operations have had a Joint dimension, meaning one involving more than one of the three Services. Without a robust Joint perspective, we will fail. But we must confess that our own experience of warfighting leaves us with a disproportionate knowledge of land warfare. This is not surprising: in the Falklands campaign Jonathan Bailey served as the Operations Officer for 4 Field Regiment Royal Artillery, which provided two gun batteries supporting both 3 Commando Brigade and 5 Infantry Brigade, and also Tac parties to all Army units; while David Benest served as Signals Officer for 2 Para. So inevitably our focus is on land warfare, with the hope that we have not got the air and maritime issues out of kilter, and also with gratitude for the advice provided by both the Air Warfare Centre (AWC) and the MWC in researching this chapter.

Over 300 years, the British have mounted numerous Joint Expeditionary Operations over much greater distances than Operation Corporate. In the twentieth century we were pioneers of Joint doctrine, but with mixed success. Deficiencies in Joint warfare are generally cited as a significant cause of misfortune at Gallipoli 1915–16; and a comparison of the Falklands and Gallipoli campaigns makes a fascinating study. At the Battle of Cambrai in November 1917, British forces demonstrated not merely innovative technology but a brilliant land–air concept; and every campaign since, including the Falklands, has to some extent been informed by these First World War experiences. In 1982, Great Britain had only fairly recently withdrawn from east of Suez, and there was a substantial legacy of equipment and experience well-suited to expeditionary operations. There was not actually much Joint doctrine about, and the very idea of doctrine was treated with deep suspicion in some quarters, yet despite that the Falklands campaign all seemed to go surprisingly well!

Today, our doctrine tries to capture, preserve and develop such capabilities, to record best practice and to give guidance for future operations. All our operations are seen in a three-dimensional context and topics such as Littoral Manoeuvre, Maritime Strike, and Air Manoeuvre are critical to all three Services, who now share a common intellectual understanding of the issues. The JDCC ensures that we have (or will have) a properly co-ordinated common view on issues such as Homeland Security, NBC Defence, Information Operations, and what is now termed Command, Control, Communications, Computers, Intelligence, Surveillance, and Reconnaissance (C4ISR) to cite just a few of the Centre's current projects.

THE DIRECTORATE GENERAL OF DEVELOPMENT AND DOCTRINE

It is fair to say that the renewed British appreciation of the importance of doctrine started in the Army, thanks to the late Field Marshal Sir Nigel Bagnall, who was determined to counter the apparent predictability and inflexibility of approach in the British Army of the Rhine (BAOR) during the Cold War years, or at least to introduce a more rigorous and systematic intellectual regime for its formulation. The structures of Army doctrine evolved through a series of organisations: from Armex, then Inspectorate General of Doctrine and Training (IGDT), then Directorate General of Land Warfare (DGLW), and ultimately to DG D&D, which was formed in 1997 and which now operates in a coherent Joint environment. The Joint Doctrine Concepts Centre (JDCC) was also established alongside the Joint Services Command and Staff College (JSCSC) at Shrivenham, clearly a great advance over the former Joint Services Defence College at Greenwich and the single Service Staff Colleges, but 34 years after the MoD itself became Joint, and six years after the creation of the PJHQ at Northwood. We now also have the Director Joint Warfare (DJW), whose job was created ten years ago. We have also become increasingly Joint in other areas, with the Defence Procurement Agency in 1999 and the Defence Logistics Organisation in 2000, a number of Joint units and training organizations, and probably with more to follow.

Why did it take so long to create the JDCC and the JSCSC? Was it that the three Services saw no need, or that there were sufficient exchanges of view between them anyway – or more simply, was it considered unaffordable? Even now, we have three entirely separate Warfare Centres to serve the needs of the RN, the RAF and the Army. That does not make us any the less mindful of the enduring relevance of the Joint dimensions. If anything, it points to the limits of Jointery, that the single-Service ethos is as enduring as it has been because in the reality of combat each does what it does best in the environments of land, sea and air. Perhaps we now have the right balance; it is certainly one envied by many other nations.

The main question for us all is not whether our doctrine was right for the war of 1982 (or for that matter for Afghanistan in 2002), but to remind ourselves of Professor Brian Holden Reid's remark:

> If there is one enduring feature of warfare in the twentieth century, it is this: we should never ask how right our doctrine is, or will be in future conflict. We should ask instead how wrong is it going to be? Another question should also lurk in the back of our minds, namely: can we hope that it is not too disastrously wrong that we can get it right before overwhelming defeat occurs? Usable, adaptable doctrine requires, above all, adaptable military structures and not those mesmerised by dogma and wedded to the slick marketing technique of arms salesmen. Trying to evolve doctrine from scratch in wartime, as the British Army tried to do in the Western Desert in 1941–2, does not recommend itself.[1]

It would be hard to argue with that, yet it was not the first time such a measure was required. In the First World War the British Army had had to re-invent its doctrine over the winter of 1914–15, virtually from scratch. At the same time, there is nothing worse for the Armed Forces than a 'doctrine commissar'!

Doctrine is nothing other than our thinking as to how we intend to fight and win, and unlike the old Soviet doctrine, compliance with which was enforced in their Armed Forces by law, ours serves to guide. The main difference between the state of our doctrine in 1982 and now is that we have formalised the process, both in the written word, and the structures that produce it. Whether that is a good or bad thing to do will only be known when we do fight our next war. What has been written will certainly be sitting on our bookshelves – or perhaps even in an unopened box on the floor of the training wing; the real test will be whether or not it exists in the minds of the troops. If Professor Holden Reid is correct, how quickly will those men and women adapt to the new circumstances? Our own view is one shared by many others, that we have achieved a broad and more educated consensus amongst our leadership at all levels of best practice and of where the advantage may lie in complex situations; and this is a valuable achievement. The Higher Command and Staff Course (HCSC) instituted under Bagnall has played a critical role in this, not merely for what it was founded to achieve, but for the fact that it is now genuinely Joint.

Although there is much talk of taking part in 'operations of choice', we must ensure that we do not merely think about and plan for the next war that we would *like* to fight, as opposed to the one we may have to. As Lord Kitchener put it when Secretary of State for War in 1915, 'We have to make war as we must – not as we should like to.'[2] If we may dare to elaborate on Kitchener's thought, doctrine is all about enabling us to fight as we should like to, in the style that suits our culture and means; but applied to situations which may not be of our choosing. Reconciling these elements will always create tensions.

THE FALKLANDS AND DOCTRINE FOR THE FUTURE

What has changed in the last 20 years, and what have we collectively learned from the whole experience of the Falklands Conflict? Inevitably the most obvious changes have been in equipment, and consequently in capability. The first area to address must be the air battle. It seems to be an enduring truth that if we cannot at least gain air parity or local dominance of the air, we have little hope of sustained success at sea or on land, something which was as true for 1982 as it is now. The best-known consequences of a lack of air dominance in the Falklands campaign were the loss of HMS *Sheffield* and, perhaps more shocking, the attack on RFA *Sir Tristram* and RFA *Sir Galahad* as they lay in Fitzroy harbour, both of which were sobering blows.

The issue today is how we are going to bridge the gap between the fact that the Royal Navy's Sea Harriers are to be withdrawn from service in 2006 and that the maritime version of the new Joint Strike Fighter is not due to come into service until 2012. Without air dominance, the prospect for air mobility today in an operation similar to the Falklands would seem to be poor, as the helicopters on which this depends are highly vulnerable to a capable air threat. That said, attack helicopters such as the Apache Longbow confer great advantages, and the availability in 1982 of any kind of attack helicopter would have been a potent asset for whichever side had deployed them, although it should be noted that the highly capable Argentine Pucará aircraft achieved little. On the other hand, Stinger or other later-generation shoulder-launched missiles, proven against the Soviet Union in Afghanistan in the same period, would have been even more important. The equations are not easy to construct given the huge improvements in capability since 1982, and that is really the point: in any operation today or in the future, the third dimension of war would be of much greater significance and we need to be masters in it. Not surprisingly, the air–land interface is today one of the most dynamic areas of doctrinal development.

Turning to the naval and amphibious operations, it is clear that in 1982 we were sailing pretty close to the wind: HMS *Intrepid* was to be scrapped; HMS *Invincible* was to be to be sold off. Admiral of the Fleet Sir Henry Leach and Sir John Nott have both written about the state of the RN and the impact of the 1981 Defence Review, including their contributions to this book. At present HMS *Ocean* seems to be fitting the bill rather well, and the MWC has taken major strides in developing Joint Maritime Doctrine. At the present time we certainly have a much reduced merchant fleet from which to take up ships from trade – 50 vessels were taken up in 1982 as STUFT. The requirement for Ro-Ro shipping and for an amphibious capability remains enduring, but at a recent Falklands Task Force reunion it was the opinion of the retired Merchant Navy officers, for whom the campaign had been a highlight of their careers, that we certainly could not do the same again now, at least with British crews, if only because they just do not exist in the same numbers.

Coming to the role of land forces, and the changes and lessons for the future since 1982, first a word is needed about the way we organise ourselves for operations. It is received military wisdom that you should organise yourself in peacetime as for war. On top of all the other frictions that occur, unnecessary task organising is one of the last things you would wish to inflict on yourself just prior to deployment. There will always be a degree of augmentation, bringing units and formations up to war establishment; but units and brigades which have trained together in peace, and who know each other, will have an advantage.

In the Falklands Conflict, 3 Commando Brigade had that advantage – up to a point. It was not broken up, but it was joined by two major units who had not trained with it: 2 Para and 3 Para from 5 Infantry Brigade. When 5 Infantry Brigade itself deployed to the Falklands, it included two units that had not previously been part of the brigade: 2 Scots Guards and 1 Welsh Guards. This order of battle was created for understandable reasons and all worked out reasonably well, but where possible it is best to avoid such frictions.

For the 1991 Gulf War, we were fortunate that 7 Armoured Brigade was fully trained as a brigade, but units of 4 Armoured Brigade had the disadvantage of not, for the most part, having trained together over the previous year. Today, a major unit deploying to the Balkans (for example) may well not be organic to the brigade whose HQ commands them in theatre. In PSO this is not much of a problem, but in recognition that it could be a major problem in war we now have the Force Readiness Cycle, which endeavours to have brigades and their units training and operating together. This is a lesson we have consciously tried to learn and do something about.

THE FALKLANDS AND THE FUNCTIONS IN COMBAT

Many even outside the Armed Forces will be familiar with the British doctrinal analytical tool called the 'functions in combat', a list of critical functions to consider in warfighting. It is obviously appropriate and also convenient to consider land operations in the Falklands and their lessons in these terms. Of these functions, Information and Intelligence remain fundamental to success. Despite the proliferation now and in the near future of such impressive Information, Surveillance, Target Acquisition (ISTAR) assets as Cobra, Phoenix, Watchkeeper, Astor, the Nimrod (R) and the Canberra PR9, the unit commander who might opt to leave his reconnaissance platoon out of the order of battle would be taking a major gamble. The use by 2 Para of their own reconnaissance platoon prior to the Battle of Goose Green is an example of their value: timely deployment of patrols from the reconnaissance platoon allowed the gathering of vital intelligence on the Argentinian dispositions on the isthmus. The same 'eyes-on' approach just prior to the battle for Wireless Ridge, on the final night of the war, also allowed the new CO of 2 Para, Lieutenant Colonel David Chaundler, to make a last-moment change to his plan.

It is interesting to note that after the Falklands Conflict, when examining the lessons learned, the absence of reconnaissance Drones[3] was highlighted as a major capability gap, and one which would have provided commanders with valuable information about the enemy's dispositions. In April 1982, Major 'Freddie' Clements, then commanding 22 Locating Battery RA, confident that he and his Drones would be needed, moved his battery without orders and parked on the roadside outside Southampton Docks, only to be told that he and his men would not be required; 22 Locating Battery drove back to their base at Larkhill as the Task Force sailed. This story of the Drones is significant, because 1982 was the beginning – albeit a missed opportunity – of a new world of capabilities. Along with the Command, Control, Communications, Computers, Intelligence (C4I) which gives it coherence, ISTAR is perhaps the area of greatest Joint doctrinal development since 1982, and will be in the coming decades.

Of the other functions in combat, *Firepower* has also moved on since 1982, although not as much as some would have liked. Apart from the replacement of the ageing SLR with the SA80 assault rifle and Light Support Weapon (LSW) in the late 1980s, not much has changed to affect dismounted close-combat directly. The new assault rifle was finally confirmed in 1998 as having a reliability of around 22 per cent, and the LSW a reliability of 0–5 per cent in the sort of extreme cold conditions that were experienced during the Falklands Conflict. At the time of writing both weapons are in the process of modification, raising SA80 reliability to around 97 per cent and making it one of the most reliable assault rifles in the world. Nor could the LSW have ever produced the degree of suppressive fire provided by the GPMG, which in 2 Para's case was scaled at two per section in the Falklands. It is worthy of note that the company of 1 Para adopted the same scaling in September 2000 during Operation Barras, the rescue of British Army hostages in Sierra Leone. The same weapon also showed its effectiveness in the Falklands in the sustained fire role, especially when co-ordinated with what was at the time the only night sight available, on the Combat Vehicle Reconnaissance Tracked (CVR(T)s) of the Blues and Royals, used together with their own main armament.

At a more basic level, the L2 grenade was known to be wanting in 1982, and it has taken 20 years to replace it with the enhanced-performance grenade. The 2-inch mortars had no HE rounds in 1982, and it has taken another 20 years to get an illuminating round for the 51 mm mortar. The need to project HE onto the enemy objective at close battle ranges was demonstrated in 1982, and the only way to do it at the time was with the M79 grenade launcher, or the 66 mm Light Anti-tank Weapon (LAW) rocket. This is still the case, although an under-slung grenade launcher is now being introduced.

A crucial innovation of 1982 was the use of the Milan anti-tank weapon, a precision guided munition, to attack bunkers, for example at Boca House during the Goose Green battle. This seems to have changed the rules regarding position warfare. The attacker could bring highly accurate and overwhelming precision fire to bear, with minimal self-exposure, and at a range of 2,000 m, outside the range of most of the defenders' direct firepower. This also meant that the previously assumed ratios of attack to defence were shown to be not valid, indeed, the attacker could be much smaller in numerical strength and actually had the advantage of mobility. We see the same phenomenon in Afghanistan today, with Global Positioning System (GPS) and lasers designating targets on a 24-hour, all-weather basis. There are proposals to buy a dive-attack anti-tank guided weapon system by 2005, which will further enhance the capability of light forces to take on 'heavy metal' when the odds are disproportionate. For indirect fire, the 81 mm mortar has stood the test of time well and remains every infantry COs personal artillery, although it still lacks a guided top-attack round to defeat armour.

Considering the artillery weapons, the 105 mm light gun performed superbly throughout the conflict, but it is the same weapon system that is deployed in Afghanistan today – the British Army's fourth Afghan War. There is still no smart 105 mm round, although a 105 mm top-attack round is available on the market for non-line of sight fire by tanks. Much longer ranges will be available for 105 mm light guns if they are upgraded as part of the new Light Mobile Artillery Weapon System (LMAWS) programme, which will probably include the new light 155 mm gun and Light Rocket System (LRS).

One must also remember that there were no vehicle-borne computers or meteorological data available in the Falklands in 1982. All command post calculations were done under a poncho, mathematically. Today, in a similar situation, a command post would use a pocket computer system. Allowing for the maximum meteorological variation, the error in fall of shot during the Falklands Conflict could amount to as much as a kilometre, which was tricky when firing in close support of troops at night, on featureless terrain, with often unknowable friendly force locations. That said, had the 155 mm FH-70 artillery piece been available, perhaps some battles could have been won without such costly infantry assaults. The effects of MLRS or some other LRS, if we had had them in 1982, would have been devastating; but then so too would they have been in Argentinian hands. The relative paucity of firepower on both sides was but one of the stranger aspects of the campaign.

Naval gunfire support deserves a strong mention here as an enduring requirement for littoral operations such as those in 1982. RN gunfire support was extremely effective especially in harassing fire, at least according to Argentinians. Incidentally, following the war, the Soviet Navy started to replace its 100 mm naval guns with 130 mm pieces. Today the RN has a long-range maritime strike capability with its Tomahawk missiles, and in future it may have 155 mm guns or a rocket system such as MLRS or Army Tactical Cruise Missile System (ATCMS). The difference that these would make in littoral operations can be imagined.

Turning now to *Manoeuvre* in the functions in combat, the need for dismounted infantry capable of carrying heavy loads over rough terrain, in all weather by day and night, remains crucial. Whilst we continue to count on support helicopters, their vulnerability to GBAD remains and, given the possible priority for movement of ammunition, casualties, heavy weapons and combat supplies, it would be rash to expect that all troop movement in the future will be by helicopter. The fundamentals have not gone away. Manoeuvre in the dark when the opposition has night vision confers few advantages, especially bearing in mind that even now not every British infantryman has a night vision capability, and will not until the arrival of Future Integrated Soldier Technology (FIST) in 2009, a full 16 years from the start of the programme. Similarly, tactical manoeuvre over low ground in the face of enemy-held high ground inevitably has tragic outcomes, as does the same over exposed open slopes covered by heavy rates of suppressive enemy fire. The only sensible option still appears to be to use all available means to suppress enemy positions by direct and indirect fire and from the air, and then – and only then – to consider manoeuvre. In this respect the example of 2 Para on Wireless Ridge springs particularly to mind. It is a battle that is hardly remarked upon in studies of the Falklands Conflict, but it remains one of the finest examples of the combined arms battle since the Second World War. This is reminiscent of an aphorism of Lieutenant General Sir Francis Tuker that the British never seem to study the battles in which our forces were successful and won with the fewest casualties, instead concentrating upon those which are glorious and heroic.

Of all functions in combat, *Protection* has probably improved most. The Blowpipe shoulder-launched AA missile was hardly an adequate answer even in 1982. The question really must be asked why we simply did not emulate the United States and our own Special Forces, and procure the Stinger missile. On the other hand, today our High Velocity Missile (HVM) is without rival against helicopters. In 1982, our Rapier AA missile system was at an early stage of development, and although highly effective (accounting for 14 confirmed aircraft kills and a further six probable kills), its use was hampered by problems with logistic support and the lack of cueing systems. Our C4I arrangements for ground-based air defence (GBAD) are essentially unchanged today and need improving. The next big investment in GBAD will be in a new C4I system, making the most of existing platforms, which are currently operating at less than their potential capacity. As for personal protection, there is no doubt that had combat body armour been available in 1982, it would have been worn and reduced our casualties considerably.

Combat Service Support, as a function in combat, remains crucial to any campaign. On the front line, the introduction of 5.56 mm ammunition along with the SA80 has been a major step forward, reducing the weight of small arms ammunition by 50 per cent. Casualty evacuation and medical support remain critical, and it may be wondered whether we could perform as well as we did in 1982 in this respect, given the ravages of the 1994 Defence Cost Study. It may also be wondered whether the *ad hoc* system of casualty evacuation, as seen at Goose Green, and at Mount Longdon and Mount Tumbledown, would not provoke public outcry if repeated today. One case that springs to mind is that of Captain John Young, who was injured by mortar fire and then lay on the battlefield for the next 14 hours before eventually being evacuated. This is no slur on the superb job done by Surgeon Commander Rick Jolly commanding the Medical Squadron of the Commando Logistic Regiment, and his 'Red and Green Life Machine' field hospital at Ajax Bay, to which so many both British and Argentinian owe their lives. The actions of Captain Sam Brennan of the Army Air Corps, a former Non-Commissioned Officer (NCO) in the Scots Guards, which led to his being awarded the Distinguished Flying Cross (DFC) for flying his Gazelle helicopter in to rescue wounded men of his former regiment on Tumbledown, speak more about regimental loyalty and personal courage than about any 'joined-up' system in the Falklands. Had the conflict been prolonged by tougher Argentinian resistance, perhaps air-delivery might have assumed greater significance, with an air-bridge from Ascension Island made possible by AAR en route.

A myth worthy of demolition is that the Royal Artillery (RA) in the Falklands was down to its last few rounds of 105 mm ammunition on the final day of the conflict. Not so! There were many thousands of rounds remaining with the guns, although one battery position was critically short. It was just as well that a costly infantry assault was not mounted on Port Stanley in the mistaken belief that artillery ammunition was in short supply. Had the Argentinians not surrendered when they did, it is quite possible that, in a hopeless situation, they could have been induced to give up by shellfire alone.

By no means least in the functions in combat, C2 remains as vital now as then. One only has to consider the friction imposed by the incompatibility of 3 Commando Brigade and 5 Infantry Brigade in terms of tactics, techniques and procedures, which could have had dire consequences. Communication Electronic Instructions had different formats, and new editions were often handwritten on soggy bits of paper, which usually could not be comprehensively distributed anyway. Often it was sensible to communicate in clear and to stay on the same frequency rather than disable our own operations. One would like to think that today it would be a very different story. Even so, the Clansman radio system is still in service, and until Bowman is introduced we shall continue to face the problem of how to distribute information securely and avoid being compromised at the tactical level.

Over the last 15 years or so, we have enshrined *Mission Command* in our doctrine, although some would maintain that it has always played a significant part in our military culture. On the other hand, on the North German Plain in Cold War Europe there was arguably not much scope for exercising it. One historian, Spencer Fitz-Gibbon, undertook in a PhD thesis to compare styles of command at Goose Green, a version of which was later published as a book – drawing much flak in the process![4] Much as the value of his study may be respected, it may be wondered if the change that has been brought about has been as dramatic as has been implied in this book. Rather, it seems that some commanders are 'naturally' mission-orientated, just as some feel a necessity for the most restrictive control of their subordinates. In comparing the performance of commanders in 1982, anyone may make their own judgements as to how styles differed at all levels, and whether we can actually bring about a change in what may be human nature rather than mannerisms.

CONCLUSIONS AND CONSEQUENCES

As an important additional aspect, the Falklands Conflict may prove to have been the last occasion in which the media were so tightly constrained, if only by geography and communications. Although a degree of control was exercised during the 1991 Gulf War, recent operations in the Balkans have demonstrated that the media have greater freedom of action than the Armed Forces really find comfortable. Indeed, during the Kosovo operation in 1999 there were 2,500 registered journalists among 30,000 troops. The profusion of camcorders makes the prospect of 'reality TV' a very real issue. This is a dilemma which will continue to try commanders but, as others have observed, expressions of irritation are really as futile as a sailor complaining about the weather. Also, as Sir Roger Jackling has himself pointed out, despite the increased numbers of the press and their product, relations between the military and the media are getting better, which suggests we are getting it right.

In conclusion, there are still many sensitivities about the Falklands Conflict. This book and the conference out of which it has grown have both touched on some of these sensitivities, yet others still seem to be taboo. Professor Lawrence Freedman's official history will undoubtedly be another case of publish and be damned – by some readers, at least – and we wish him luck! In a wider sense, the views expressed in this book by Sir John Nott and Sir Roger Jackling seem to be the correct ones. The most worthwhile and enduring legacy of the Falklands Conflict has nothing to do with technology or tactics, but rather with the moral component of our doctrine. The Falklands Conflict raised the self-image of the Armed Forces, and the nation's esteem for them.

Jonathan Bailey remembers standing to attention on deck as we sailed out of Southampton, surrounded by little boats with cheering people and horns sounding, swept off on a tide of immense goodwill, support, and a huge burden of national expectation. Failure really was unthinkable, and yet when one did think about it, it did not require much insight to appreciate all the things that could and were likely to go wrong. Fortunately, there was a heady cocktail of high morale and determination, tinged with realism, on board. At times this amounted to extraordinary, possibly misplaced self-confidence in the face of horrendous perils, yet events seemed to vindicate the prevailing assumption of inevitable victory – somehow or other. The British public were not let down, and other nations took note. We live with that self-confidence, and our Armed Forces have been great beneficiaries of its consequences. The British public still retain their high regard for the Armed Forces, and also their expectations of us, and it falls to us not to let them down.

NOTES

1. Brian Holden Reid, 'Enduring Patterns in Modern Warfare', in Brian Bond and Mungo Melvin (eds), *The Nature of Future Conflict: Implications for Force Development*, Occasional Paper 36 (Camberley: Strategic and Combat Studies Institute, 1998), p. 17.
2. This remark by Kitchener, quoted by various historians, was made at a meeting of the Dardanelles Committee on 20 August 1915, and is recorded in the minutes of the meeting held by the Public Record Office Kew, CAB 42/3/16.
3. Known at the time as RPVs (remotely piloted vehicles) and at present as UAVs (unmanned aerial vehicles).
4. Spencer Fitz-Gibbon, *Not Mentioned in Despatches...: The History and Mythology of the Battle of Goose Green* (Cambridge: Lutterworth, 1995).

Index

eBooks – at www.eBookstore.tandf.co.uk

A library at your fingertips!

eBooks are electronic versions of printed books. You can store them on your PC/laptop or browse them online.

They have advantages for anyone needing rapid access to a wide variety of published, copyright information.

eBooks can help your research by enabling you to bookmark chapters, annotate text and use instant searches to find specific words or phrases. Several eBook files would fit on even a small laptop or PDA.

NEW: Save money by eSubscribing: cheap, online access to any eBook for as long as you need it.

Annual subscription packages

We now offer special low-cost bulk subscriptions to packages of eBooks in certain subject areas. These are available to libraries or to individuals.

For more information please contact webmaster.ebooks@tandf.co.uk

We're continually developing the eBook concept, so keep up to date by visiting the website.

www.eBookstore.tandf.co.uk